T0311906

Avoided Deforestation

Deforestation and forest degradation accounts for up to a fifth of global greenhouse gas emissions, including carbon dioxide. It thus contributes substantially to global climate change, which is a threat to people, economies and the environment. Avoided deforestation can be characterized as the use of financial incentives to reduce rates of deforestation, with much of the focus on forests in tropical countries. The idea of 'reducing emissions from deforestation and degradation' (REDD) expands the concept of avoided deforestation to include reductions in forest degradation as well.

While avoided deforestation, as a policy issue, is not new, the current debate in academic and policy circles on including it as a future climate change mitigation strategy is gathering pace. This debate is only likely to intensify as negotiations continue over what should be included in the successor agreement to the Kyoto Protocol, which is set to expire in 2012. This book brings together, for the first time, a collection of new research findings in the area of avoided deforestation, along with their policy implications, as well as the latest developments in environmental and natural resource economics related to REDD.

Part I presents the cost effectiveness of avoided deforestation as a strategy to mitigate climate change. Part II looks at the policy and institutional barriers to including avoided deforestation as a climate strategy, while Part III looks at insights into how policy to reduce emissions by avoiding deforestation can be effectively and efficiently designed.

This edited collection is primarily aimed at postgraduate students, policymakers and researchers who are interested in tropical forest conservation and climate change. Environmental campaigners and lobbyists for NGOs will also find this book useful.

Charles Palmer is currently a Senior Researcher at the Institute for Environmental Decisions at the ETH Zurich in Switzerland, specializing in environmental and development economics.

Stefanie Engel is Professor of Environmental Policy and Economics at the Institute for Environmental Decisions at the ETH Zurich in Switzerland.

Routledge explorations in environmental economics
Edited by Nick Hanley
University of Stirling, UK

Avoided Deforestation

Prospects for mitigating climate change

Edited by
Charles Palmer and Stefanie Engel

LONDON AND NEW YORK

First published 2009
by Routledge
2 Park Square, Milton Park, Abingdon, Oxon, OX14 4RN

Simultaneously published in the USA and Canada
by Routledge
270 Madison Ave, New York NY 10016

*Routledge is an imprint of the Taylor & Francis Group,
an informa business*

First issued in paperback 2011

Typeset in Times New Roman by Swales & Willis Ltd, Exeter, Devon

British Library Cataloguing in Publication Data
A catalogue record for this book is available from the British Library

Library of Congress Cataloging in Publication Data
A catalog record for this book has been requested

ISBN 10: 0–415–44712–7 (hbk)
ISBN 10: 0–415–61980–7 (pbk)
ISBN 10: 0–203–88099–9 (ebk)

ISBN 13: 978–0–415–44712–6 (hbk)
ISBN 13: 978–0–415–61980–6 (pbk)
ISBN 13: 978–0–203–88099–9 (ebk)

Contents

List of contributors

Jennifer Alix-Garcia, Assistant Professor of Economics, University of San Francisco, USA.

Sandra Brown, Senior Program Officer, Ecosystem Services, Winrock International, USA.

Mariano C. Cenamo, Executive Director, Institute for Conservation and Sustainable Development of Amazonas (IDESAM), Brazil.

Alain de Janvry, Professor of Agricultural and Resource Economics, University of California at Berkeley, USA.

Michael Dutschke, Senior Consultant Climate Change, Land Use and Bioenergy, BioCarbon Consult, Germany.

Stefanie Engel, Professor of Environmental Policy and Economics, ETH Zurich, Switzerland.

Maryanne Grieg-Gran, Programme Director, Environmental Economics Programme, International Institute for Environment and Development (IIED), UK.

Nancy L. Harris, Senior Program Associate, Ecosystem Services, Winrock International, USA.

Tracy Johns, Policy Advisor and Research Associate, Woods Hole Research Center (WHRC), USA.

Georg Kindermann, Research Fellow, International Institute for Applied Systems Analysis (IIASA), Austria.

Axel Michaelowa, Senior Founding Partner, Perspectives GmbH, Switzerland.

Paula F. Moreira, Research Associate, Amazon Institute for Environmental Research (IPAM), Brazil.

Paulo Moutinho, Research Coordinator and Senior Scientist, Amazon Institute for Environmental Research (IPAM), Brazil.

Brian C. Murray, Director for Economic Analysis, Nicholas Institute for Environmental Policy Solutions, and Research Professor at the Nicholas School of the Environment and Earth Science, Duke University, USA.

Michael Obersteiner, Research Fellow, International Institute for Applied Systems Analysis (IIASA), and Research Economist, Department of Economics and Finance at the Institute for Advanced Studies (IHS), Austria.

Krystof Obidzinski, Scientist, Forests and Governance Programme, Center for International Forestry Research (CIFOR), Indonesia.

Charles Palmer, Senior Researcher and Lecturer of Environmental Policy and Economics, ETH Zurich, Switzerland.

Silvia Petrova, Program Associate, Ecosystem Services, Winrock International, USA.

Alexander Pfaff, Associate Professor of Public Policy Studies, Duke University, USA.

Ewald Rametsteiner, Research Fellow, International Institute for Applied Systems Analysis (IIASA), and Head of the European Forest Institute (EFI), Austria.

Juan Robalino, Research Fellow, Environment for Development (EfD), Tropical Agricultural Research and Higher Education Center (CATIE), Costa Rica.

Elisabeth Sadoulet, Professor of Agricultural and Resource Economics, University of California at Berkeley, USA.

Bernhard Schlamadinger, Senior Scientist, Institute of Energy Research, Joanneum Research, Austria.

Brent Sohngen, Professor of Agricultural, Environmental and Development Economics, Ohio State University, USA.

Sven Wunder, Principal Scientist, Forests and Livelihoods Programme, Center for International Forestry Research (CIFOR), Brazil.

Tobias Wünscher, Senior Researcher, Department of Economics and Technological Change, Center for Development Research (ZEF), Germany.

Acknowledgements

We wish to thank all the authors whose work appears in this volume. They have worked hard to put their contributions together under quite tight deadlines. We are grateful to Florian Habermacher for formatting the chapters contained in this volume in addition to offering useful editorial assistance throughout. We are also thankful to Stefan Rieder for additional formatting assistance. Comments on Chapter 1, introducing the volume, were provided by Ulrike Joras, while additional, useful comments on Chapter 7 on Indonesia were provided by Luca Tacconi. The final chapter (14) benefited from comments and corrections from Ken Chomitz, Michael Dutschke, Brian Murray and Sven Wunder: many thanks for these inputs.

We would like to dedicate this book to the life and work of Dr. Bernhard Schlamadinger, whose passion and innovative thinking in the field of forests and climate has had a great impact on the UNFCCC process, and on the lives of many around the world. Bernhard's pioneering spirit inspires us to continue to recognize and optimize the vital role of forests in efforts to address global climate change both now and in the future.

Charles Palmer
Stefanie Engel
Zurich, Switzerland

List of abbreviations

AIJ	activities implemented jointly
AR	afforestation/reforestation
C	carbon*
CAIT	climate analysis indicators tool (of the World Resources Institute; also WRI CAIT)
CCS	Registry of Social Environmental Responsibility (*Cadastro de Compromisso Socioambiental*)
CDM	clean development mechanism
CER	certified emission reduction
CfRN	Coalition for Rainforest Nations
CO_2	carbon dioxide*
CO_2e	CO_2 equivalent*
COP	Conference of the Parties (of the UNFCCC)
CR	compensated reduction (of deforestation)
DFID	Department for International Development (of the United Kingdom)
DRC	Democratic Republic of the Congo
EEA	European Environment Agency
ERU	emission reduction unit
ES	environmental service
ETS	Emission Trading Scheme (of the European Union)
EU-15	EU member countries Austria, Belgium, Denmark, Finland, France, Germany, Greece, Ireland, Italy, Luxembourg, the Netherlands, Portugal, Spain, Sweden, and the United Kingdom
EU-28	all current EU member states (as of 2008)
FAC	forest area change
FAO	Food and Agriculture Organization (of the United Nations)
FCPF	forest carbon partnership facility
FDI	foreign direct investment
FONAFIFO	*Fondo Nacional de Financiamiento Forestal*
G8	Group of Eight
GDP	gross domestic product
GEF	global environment facility

GEOMOD	geographical modelling
GHG	greenhouse gas
GtC	gigaton carbon (10^9 tonnes carbon)*
GtCO$_2$	gigaton carbon dioxide (10^9 tonnes carbon dioxide)*
IFCA	Indonesian Forest Climate Alliance
INPE	Brazilian Space Agency
JI	joint implementation
LUCS	land-use carbon sequestration
LULUCF	land use, land-use change and forestry
MT	Mato Grosso (state of Brazil)
MtC	megaton carbon (10^6 tonnes carbon)*
MtCO$_2$	megaton carbon dioxide (10^6 tonnes carbon dioxide)*
MtCO$_2$e	megaton carbon dioxide equivalent
NBDC	National Biofuel Development Committee (of Indonesia)
NCCC	National Commission on Climate Change (of Indonesia)
NGO	non-governmental organization
NPV	net present value
OA	official aid
ODA	official development assistance
OECD	Organization for Economic Cooperation and Development
PES	payments for environmental services
PLUC	potential land-use change
PNG	Papua New Guinea
PSA	*Pagos por Servicios Ambientales*
RED	reducing emissions from deforestation
REDD	reducing emissions from deforestation and degradation
SBSTA	subsidiary body for scientific and technological advice
SFC	suitability for change
tC	tonnes carbon*
US$	US dollar
UNFCCC	United Nations Framework Convention on Climate Change

Note: * One mass unit of carbon corresponds to 3.664 mass units of carbon dioxide

1   Introduction

Reducing CO_2 emissions through avoided deforestation?

Charles Palmer and Stefanie Engel

Evidence for anthropogenic warming of the climate system as a consequence of greenhouse gas (GHG) emissions, including CO_2 (carbon dioxide), into the earth's atmosphere is unequivocal (IPCC, 2007). Annual CO_2 emissions from deforestation in tropical and sub-tropical countries accounts for up to one-fifth of global emissions (Baumert *et al.*, 2005). Conserving carbon stored in biomass could be a cost-effective strategy to mitigate future climate change impacts (see Chomitz *et al.*, 2006; Stern, 2007). Reducing emissions from deforestation was, however, excluded from the climate change regime that resulted from the Kyoto Protocol negotiations, held during the 1990s. The first commitment period of Kyoto is due to end in 2012. At the Bali Conference of the Parties (COP-13) in December 2007, countries agreed to reconsider emissions reductions through reducing deforestation as a potential component of a post-2012 climate change regime (UNFCCC, 2007).

Following COP-14 held in Poznan in December 2008, more precise rules and modalities are still to be developed by COP-15, which is due to take place in Copenhagen in December 2009. Many open questions remain on how reducing deforestation could be credibly incorporated into a climate regime. There is, therefore, a need to take stock and consider the merits of such a mitigation strategy and how it might be implemented on the ground. This is the motivation for the present volume, which aims to assess the potential of so-called 'reducing emissions from deforestation and degradation' (REDD)[1] mechanisms from the perspective of economics and policymaking.

Forests and climate change

According to widely cited data published by the World Resources Institute (see Baumert *et al.*, 2005), global anthropogenic GHG emissions, dominated by CO_2 (carbon dioxide), are mainly given off via the burning of fossil fuels and from agriculture and land-use changes. Emissions from deforestation and forest degradation occur as carbon stock is depleted and released to the atmosphere through changes in forest and other woody biomass stock, forest and grass land conversion, the abandonment of managed land and forest fires. A 20 per cent decrease in forest area since 1850 has contributed to 90 per cent of emissions from land-use changes (IPCC, 2001). Throughout the 1990s around 1.5 billion tons of carbon (GtC) was released annually through deforestation (Gullison *et al.*, 2007). Two countries, Indonesia and Brazil, dominate CO_2 emissions released through deforestation and as a result are, respectively, the third and fourth largest GHG emitters in the world, behind the United States and China (Houghton, 2003; cited in Baumert *et al.*, 2005).

Impacts of climate change

Anthropogenic interference in the climate system is a real and growing threat to people, economies and the environment (Chomitz *et al.*, 2006). On current trends, the average global temperature could rise by 2–3°C within the next 50 years. This rise is likely to change the earth's climate rapidly, for example, leading to rising sea levels and a higher frequency of heatwaves and heavy precipitation (IPCC, 2007). Business-as-usual or 'baseline' climate change implies increasingly severe economic impacts if action is not taken to mitigate the worse effects.

Climate change can perhaps be characterized as the world's largest 'market failure' (Stern, 2007). The earth's atmosphere, into which anthropogenic GHG are emitted, is a global public good, i.e. it is non-rival and non-excludable. These emissions are an externality in that those who produce them impose social costs on the world and future generations but do not face the full consequences of their actions. The actual source of emissions, whether producer or consumer, rich or poor, is irrelevant to the overall growth in global GHG stocks and the corresponding, future changes in the climate. Nevertheless, the worst impacts of climate change are expected to fall disproportionately on people living in some of the poorest regions of the world. People living in these regions are the most vulnerable to adverse changes in, for example, food production and water resources.

Climate change policy

The global causes and consequences of climate change imply the need for international collective action for an efficient, effective and equitable policy response. The first global attempt to put a price on the social costs of emissions by stabilizing the amount of GHG in the atmosphere was seen in the formation of the United Nations Framework Convention on Climate Change (UNFCCC). Ratified by 182 parties as of May 2008 (UNFCCC, 2008), the Kyoto Protocol of the UNFCCC originally entered into force in 2005. It committed Annex I, mainly industrialized countries to reducing their collective GHG emissions by about 5 per cent below their 1990 levels by 2008–2012. In fulfilling these commitments, countries are able to achieve reductions in their emissions through several mechanisms including the clean development mechanism (CDM). The CDM allows entities in non-Annex I countries to develop 'offset' projects leading to verified reductions in GHG emissions emitted from Annex I countries. So-called certified emissions reductions (CERs) are then transferred to Annex I countries at a price set by the carbon markets.

Reducing GHG emissions in order to stabilize the climate requires the deployment of a portfolio of GHG emissions-reducing technologies along with the application of appropriate and effective incentives (IPCC, 2007). These include adaptation and mitigation measures such as carbon storage and capture and reducing deforestation, all with varying, generally uncertain, costs. None of these measures on its own, for example, the halting of all deforestation, would achieve the UNFCCC's goal (Pacala and Socolow, 2004). But conserving forest carbon could likely be an important part of the climate change solution, particularly if it proves to be cost effective compared to other mitigation options (see Chomitz *et al.*, 2006; Stern, 2007). Negotiations on the types of admissible project in Kyoto included a range of options for increasing forest stock and removing carbon from the atmosphere. Reducing emissions from deforestation was discussed, but was finally excluded from the CDM (see later).

Forests as carbon sources and sinks

The Forest Resources Assessment (FAO, 2006) estimated that one-third of the earth's land surface, up to 4 billion hectares, is covered by forest. Of this, around half is located in the tropics and subtropics. The largest intact tropical forests are found in the Amazon Basin (Brazil), the Congo Basin (Democratic Republic of the Congo) and in the Indo-Malayan region (Indonesia, Malaysia and Papua New Guinea). These forests provide important traded and non-traded environmental goods and services, including carbon. Tropical forests have particularly high carbon stocks, perhaps holding as much as 50 per cent more carbon per hectare than forests in other regions (Houghton, 2005). In terms of economic value, even relatively low traded carbon values have been found to comfortably dominate the non-market values of other tropical forest environmental services (see Pearce *et al.*, 2002). These include direct use values, although perhaps excluding the returns from unsustainable timber extraction.

Over the past century, tropical deforestation and forest degradation have increased dramatically. The former occurred at an average rate of 13 million hectares per year, between 1990 and 2005 (FAO, 2001, 2006). Brazil and Indonesia accounted for, on average, around 40 per cent of annual deforestation by area over this period. The causes of the continuing loss and degradation of tropical forests are many, varied and complex (Chomitz *et al.*, 2006; Geist and Lambin, 2002; Kaimowitz and Angelsen, 1998). However, understanding these is important for the design and implementation of policy to reverse their effects, whether related to policy to reduce CO₂ emissions or not. This requires identifying the underlying market and policy failures and understanding how these relate to activities both inside and outside the forest sector. The latter include those related to agriculture, migration and infrastructural development. Recent government and non-government efforts to slow down or reverse overall deforestation and degradation trends, either through forest policy or policy made in other sectors have been relatively unsuccessful for various reasons (see Bulte and Engel, 2006). Given the many interlinked pressures on forests, the challenge now for climate policy is to design a strategy for capturing the carbon value of natural forest stock that is not only effective but also efficient and equitable.

Avoided deforestation and climate change policy

Without effective policies to slow deforestation, business-as-usual tropical defor-estation could release up to 130 GtC by 2100 (Houghton, 2005). 'Avoided defor-estation' is a concept where countries are compensated for preventing deforestation that would otherwise occur (Chomitz *et al.*, 2006). Reducing emissions by slowing deforestation could be a substantial and important component of climate mitigation policy, and has been discussed as such by researchers and policymakers for a number of years (see, for example, Brown *et al.*, 1996; Schneider, 1998). The avail-able evidence shows that potential carbon savings from slowing tropical deforesta-tion could contribute substantially to overall emissions reductions. Moreover, forests protected from deforestation could persist in the coming decades despite 'unavoidable' climate change (Gullison *et al.*, 2007). Possible side benefits from the realization of natural forest carbon values include other forest environmental values such as biodiversity.

Avoided deforestation projects were excluded from the 2008–2012 first commitment period of the Kyoto Protocol's CDM due to a number of concerns revolving around sovereignty and methodological issues (Fearnside, 2001; Laurance, 2007). The former arose as a consequence of forests per se not being con-sidered as a global public good despite the public good nature of some forest serv-ices. Since exclusion, discussions have been ongoing to try to resolve these concerns through, for example, the UNFCCC's recent 2-year initiative (Subsidiary Body on Scientific and Technical Advice or SBSTA). This has acted as a useful forum for assessing new policy approaches and incentives for REDD in developing countries. Meanwhile, tropical forest nations such as Brazil, Costa Rica and Papua New Guinea have been floating various initiatives to protect forests through utiliz-ing their value as carbon sinks.[2] Forest carbon finance has also been endorsed by the United Nations, the World Bank, and the majority of nation states, with the Bank's forest carbon partnership facility (FCPF) aiming to attract US$300 million in donor funding for pilot REDD schemes (World Bank Carbon Finance Unit, 2008). With support from Australia, Indonesia is hoping to be the first country to develop and host a REDD project, beginning in late 2008 (Jakarta Post, 2008).

Avoided deforestation: prospects for mitigating climate change?

The Bali and Poznan COPs are part of an ongoing process that will carry on through 2008 and 2009. It is hoped that a post-2012 international climate regime will be agreed by the end of 2009 at COP-15 in Copenhagen. Whether or not avoided deforestation or REDD will be included in a final framework agreement and what this arrangement might look like is beyond the scope of this volume.[3] Instead, and for the most part, it looks at what might be gained from including REDD as a feasi-ble option in a post-Kyoto agreement and at how some of the challenges of such inclusion could be tackled from the perspective of economics and policymaking.

Part I, consisting of three chapters, looks at the costs and benefits of avoided deforestation as a climate change mitigation strategy utilizing different approaches and sets of assumptions. Building on background research carried out for the Stern Review (2007), *Maryanne Grieg-Gran* examines the cost effectiveness of avoided deforestation in Chapter 2, using data collected in eight tropical forest countries. In Chapter 3, *Michael Obersteiner, Georg Kindermann, Ewald Rametsteiner* and *Brent Sohngen* summarize the results from a scenario-modelling analysis of the potential effects of financial mechanisms to avoid deforestation. *Brent Sohngen* utilizes a global timber market model to examine the potential for avoided deforestation to provide credits due to reductions in carbon emissions in Chapter 4. Overall, these three chapters make an important case for including avoided deforestation as a climate change strategy in any future international climate regime. However, certain barriers would need to be overcome for ensuring cost effectiveness, among other things.

Part II examines some of these barriers to including avoided deforestation in any climate regime. In Chapter 5, *Tracy Johns* and *Bernhard Schlamadinger* revisit the international policy barriers and institutional barriers that prevented the inclusion of avoided deforestation in the Kyoto Protocol. In particular, they examine the findings of the SBSTA. The following two chapters look at the initiatives and barriers in Brazil and Indonesia, two of the would-be key players in any avoided deforestation policy adopted at the international level. In Chapter 6, *Paulo Moutinho, Mariano Cenamo* and *Paula Moreira* discuss the various national and sub-national initiatives to realize forest carbon values in Brazil and some of the problems in policy implementation. In Chapter 7, *Charles Palmer* and *Krystof Obidzinski* study current plans by Indonesia to expand timber and biofuel plantations, and assess the problems and opportunities these create for avoided deforestation policy, particularly with respect to the estimation of deforestation baselines. The final chapter in Part II, Chapter 8, by *Axel Michaelowa* and *Michael Dutschke*, examines the fears of many researchers and practitioners that a potentially large supply of credits from avoided deforestation could upset the balance of the carbon market. They emphasize the institutional design of an international agreement to cut overall emissions and the ability of supplier countries to enact the governance reforms necessary for avoided deforestation to be effective in mitigating climate change.

There are a number of technical and methodological issues that may hinder the effectiveness and efficiency of any kind of payment or compensation scheme that transfers financial resources from carbon buyers to sellers. While touched on in previous chapters, Part III focuses on the practical issues involved in establishing such payment schemes. In Chapter 9, *Brian Murray* examines the importance of recognizing, estimating and, where possible, ameliorating the risks of leakage from avoided deforestation policies. The difficulty in determining the baseline projection for forest conservation necessary for generating credible emissions reductions and approaches to overcome this is the focus of Chapter 10 by *Nancy Harris, Silvia Petrova* and *Sandra Brown*. In Chapter 11, *Alexander Pfaff* and *Juan Robalino* look at the importance of being able to evaluate the impacts of policy for avoided deforestation both ex ante and ex post, and the role of evaluation for correctly estimating deforestation baselines.

While compensation payment schemes are not a panacea for dealing with environmental problems, carbon benefits from forest conservation could be improved through better targeting. The following two chapters assess efficiency gains from payments targeting using existing payments schemes and lessons that could be learned for potential avoided deforestation payments programmes. First, *Stefanie Engel, Tobias Wünscher* and *Sven Wunder* examine empirical evidence from the Costa Rican national payments for environmental services (PES) scheme, in Chapter 12. Second, *Jennifer Alix-Garcia, Alain de Janvry* and *Elisabeth Sadoulet* discuss efficiency gains from including deforestation risk as a targeting criterion in the Mexican national PES scheme, in Chapter 13. Finally, Chapter 14, by *Stefanie Engel* and *Charles Palmer*, attempts to pull together the findings from all three parts of the volume and highlights some ways forward and avenues for further research if avoided deforestation is to be an effective and efficient strategy for mitigating global warming.

Notes

1 'Avoided deforestation' is otherwise known as reducing emissions from deforestation (RED). Inclusion of forest degradation extends this definition to REDD. The contributions to this volume generally distinguish between either RED/avoided deforestation or REDD depending on the topic under discussion.
2 For example, at the COP-11 in Montreal in 2005, a coalition of 15 rainforest nations led by Papua New Guinea and Costa Rica floated a proposal to allow CDM-type credits, bought by industrialized nations, in exchange for reducing deforestation. See: http://www.rainforestcoalition.org/eng/.
3 The importance of international collaboration in solving the global collective action in climate change policy is reviewed in Gupta *et al.* (2007). The relative merits of Kyoto and alternative arrangements for international cooperation can be seen in Forner *et al.* (2006).

References

Baumert, K., Herzog, T. and Pershing, J. (2005) *Navigating the Numbers: Greenhouse Gas Data and International Climate Policy*, Washington: World Resources Institute (WRI).

Brown, S., Sathaye, J., Cannell, M. and Kauppi, P. (1996) 'Management of forests for mitigation of greenhouse gas emissions', in R.T. Watson, M.C. Zinyowera and R.H. Moss (eds) *Climate Change 1995. Impacts, Adaptations and Mitigation of Climate Change: Scientific-Technical Analyses. Contribution of Working Group II to the Second Assessment Report of the Intergovernmental Panel on Climate Change*, Cambridge: Cambridge University Press.

Bulte, E. and Engel, S. (2006) 'Conservation of tropical forests: addressing market failure', in R. López and M. Toman (eds) *Economic Development and Environmental Sustainability*, Oxford: Oxford University Press.

Chomitz, K.M., Buys, P., De Luca, G., Thomas, T.S. and Wertz-Kanounnikoff, S. (2006) *At Loggerheads? Agricultural Expansion, Poverty Reduction and Environment in the Tropical Forests*, World Bank Policy Research Report, Development Research Group, Washington: World Bank.

FAO (Food and Agriculture Organization of the United Nations) (2001) *Global Forest Resources Assessment 2000*, Rome: FAO.

FAO (Food and Agriculture Organization of the United Nations) (2006) *Global Forest Resources Assessment 2005*, Rome: FAO.

Fearnside, P. (2001) 'Saving tropical forests as a global warming countermeasure: an issue that divides the environment movement', *Ecological Economics*, 39(2): 167–184.

Forner, C., Blaser, J., Jotzo, F. and Robledo, C. (2006) 'Keeping the forest for the climate's sake: avoiding deforestation in developing countries under the UNFCCC', *Climate Policy*, 6(3): 275–294.

Geist, H. and Lambin, E. (2002) 'Proximate causes and underlying driving forces of tropical deforestation', *BioScience*, 52(2): 143–150.

Gullison, R.E., Frumhoff, P.C., Canadell, J.G., Field, C.B., Nepstad, D.C., Hayhoe, K. *et al.* (2007) 'Tropical forests and climate policy', *Science*, 316(5827): 985–986.

Gupta, S., Tirpak, D.A., Burger, N., Gupta, J., Hoehne, N., Boncheva, A.I. *et al.* (2007) 'Policies, instruments and co-operative arrangements', in B. Metz, O.R. Davidson, P.R. Bosch, R. Dave and L.A. Meyer (eds) *Climate Change 2007: Mitigation. Contribution of Working Group III to the Fourth Assessment Report of the Intergovernmental Panel on Climate Change*, Cambridge and New York: Cambridge University Press.

Houghton, R.A. (2005) 'Tropical deforestation as a source of greenhouse gas emissions', in P. Moutinho and S. Schwartzman (eds) *Tropical Deforestation and Climate Change*, Belém, Brazil: Amazon Institute for Environmental Research (IPAM), and Washington: Environmental Defense.

IPCC (Intergovernmental Panel on Climate Change) (2001) *Climate Change 2001: Synthesis Report. A Contribution of Working Groups I, II, and III to the Third Assessment Report of the Intergovernmental Panel on Climate Change*, Cambridge and New York: Cambridge University Press.

IPCC (Intergovernmental Panel on Climate Change) (2007) *Climate Change 2007: Synthesis Report. Contribution of Working Groups I, II and III to the Fourth Assessment Report of the Intergovernmental Panel on Climate Change*, Geneva: IPCC.

Jakarta Post (2008) 'RI to begin forest carbon projects', 4 August 2008 [online]. Available at: http://www.thejakartapost.com/news/2008/06/17/ri-begin-forest-carbon-projects.html [accessed 4 August 2008].

Kaimowitz, D. and Angelsen, A. (1998) *Economic Models of Tropical Deforestation: A Review*, Bogor: Center for International Forestry Research (CIFOR).

Laurance, W.F. (2007) 'A new initiative to use carbon trading for tropical forest conservation', *Biotropica*, 39(1): 20–24.

Pacala, S. and Socolow, R. (2004) 'Stabilization wedges: solving the climate problem for the next 50 years with current technologies', *Science*, 305(5686): 968–972.

Pearce, D.W., Putz, F. and Vanclay J.K. (2002) 'Is sustainable forestry economically possible?', in D.W. Pearce, C. Pearce and C. Palmer (eds) *Valuing the Environment in Developing Countries: Case Studies*, Cheltenham: Edward Elgar.

Schneider, S. (1998) 'Kyoto Protocol: the unfinished agenda. An editorial essay', *Climatic Change*, 39(1): 1–21.

Stern, N. (2007) *The Economics of Climate Change: The Stern Review*, Cambridge: Cambridge University Press.

UNFCCC (United Nations Framework Convention on Climate Change) (2007) *Decision-/CP.13 Bali Action Plan* [online]. Available at: http://unfccc.int/files/meetings/cop_13/application/pdf/cp_bali_action.pdf [accessed 15 June 2008].

UNFCCC (United Nations Framework Convention on Climate Change) (2008) *Kyoto Protocol Status of Ratification* [online]. Available at: http://unfccc.int/files/kyoto_protocol/status_of_ratification/application/pdf/kp_ratification.pdf [accessed 1 August 2008].

World Bank Carbon Finance Unit (2008) *About Forest Carbon Partnership Facility (FCPF)*, Washington: World Bank [online]. Available at: http://carbonfinance.org/Router.cfm?Page=FCPF&ft=About [accessed 20 July 2008].

Part I

Cost effectiveness of avoided deforestation

2 Costs of avoided deforestation as a climate change mitigation option

Maryanne Grieg-Gran

Introduction

The IPCC Fourth Assessment report estimates that land-use change and forestry contributed 17 per cent of greenhouse gas emissions in 2004, but acknowledges that considerable uncertainty remains (Nabuurs *et al.*, 2007). Deforestation in the tropics is considered to be the major factor responsible for emissions in land-use change and forestry although there is disagreement about the extent to which it is offset by expanding forest areas. Tropical forests have particularly high carbon stocks, holding on average 50 per cent more carbon per hectare than forests in temperate and boreal areas (Houghton, 2005). They are also experiencing the highest rates of deforestation. The Food and Agriculture Organization (FAO) estimates deforestation to equal 13 million hectares per year, most of it in tropical countries (FAO, 2005).

Despite this large contribution to greenhouse gas emissions, deforestation in tropical countries has been given little space in the flexibility mechanisms of the Kyoto Protocol. The clean development mechanism (CDM) notably allows credits for afforestation and reforestation but not for *avoided deforestation*. But there has been increasing attention to deforestation recently and several calls from governments of countries with tropical forest, notably Papua New Guinea, for financial mechanisms to provide positive incentives for developing countries to reduce their emissions from deforestation (Moutinho *et al.*, 2005). The Coalition for Rainforest Nations[1] has organized a party grouping under the UNFCCC to address the role of carbon emissions from deforestation and is calling for a review of the international regulations on carbon emissions trading to include assets based on forest carbon sequestration and/or emissions caused by deforestation. Brazil also submitted a proposal to the 12th Conference of the Parties to the United Nations Framework Convention on Climate Change in Nairobi in 2006, proposing that developed countries provide positive financial incentives to developing countries that voluntarily reduce their emissions from deforestation in relation to a reference emission rate (see Moutinho *et al.*, Chapter 6 in this volume).

By the time of the 13th Conference of the Parties in Bali, December 2007, there was a considerable groundswell of support for addressing emissions from deforestation and forest degradation. The Bali Action Plan, which initiated the process of negotiating international action on climate change beyond 2012, notably included among the mitigation actions to be considered 'policy approaches and positive incentives on issues relating to reducing emissions from deforestation and forest degradation in developing countries' (UNFCCC, 2007). It is increasingly likely that the post-2012 climate change architecture will incorporate avoided deforestation as a mitigation option in the flexibility mechanisms.

This raises questions about the scale of finance needed and the cost of reducing deforestation compared with other mitigation options such as improved energy efficiency. The aim of this chapter is to examine the cost effectiveness of avoided deforestation as a mitigation option. It builds on background research on the cost of avoiding deforestation carried out for the Stern Review of the Economics of Climate Change (Stern, 2007). In this work, estimates were made for eight countries (Bolivia, Brazil, Cameroon, Democratic Republic of the Congo [DRC], Ghana, Indonesia, Malaysia and Papua New Guinea), which together report annual net forest loss of 6.2 million ha or about 46 per cent of FAO's estimate of annual global deforestation (FAO, 2005).

The chapter first looks at what avoided deforestation as a mitigation option means in practice as this is key to making estimates of cost. It then examines some of the issues involved in making cost estimates and sets out the approach used in the background research for the Stern Review. The cost estimates made for the Stern Review are then presented in terms of cost per hectare of avoided deforestation. The next section of the chapter explores how these costs translate into costs per tonne of CO_2 equivalent and how this compares to other mitigation options. The final section presents conclusions and highlights some areas of caution in interpreting the results.

Avoided deforestation as a mitigating option in practice

Economic drivers of deforestation

In order to estimate the cost of avoiding deforestation, it is necessary to think through what this would mean in practice. This requires analysis of the main drivers of deforestation. In line with much of the economic literature on the drivers of deforestation and forest environmental services (e.g. Angelsen, 1995; Chomitz *et al.*, 2006), this chapter takes the view that the financial incentives facing holders of forest land are the key. Landholders clear forests because given the skills, finance and technology available to them, they can get a higher return from converting the forest to agriculture or ranching than they can from sustainable forest management or forest conservation. Forest clearing may be illegal but if the probability of being caught is low or the sanctions involved are minimal then the expected returns from deforestation can still be high. Measures are needed that alter the financial incentives facing landholders so that it is more profitable for them to keep their land as forest than to clear it for other land uses.

Payments to avoid deforestation

One way of changing the incentives is by paying landowners enough to compensate them for what they would have earned from the land over time had they deforested it. The returns from alternative land uses to forest are therefore a good indicator of the minimum funding required to tackle deforestation. Chomitz *et al.* (2006) made the point that much deforestation takes place to convert land to relatively low return uses. This suggests that the financial incentives may not need to be very high to reduce deforestation.

The payments for environmental services schemes in Costa Rica and Mexico provide an idea of a possible approach to tackling deforestation (see Engel *et al.* and Alix-Garcia *et al.*, Chapters 12 and 13 in this volume, respectively). In Costa Rica, landowners enrolled in the national payments for environmental services scheme are currently paid US$64 per hectare per year[2] for conserving their forest (MINAE, 2008). In Mexico, communities that protect their forest are receiving US$27 per ha per year or US$36 if they have cloud forest (Muñoz-Piña *et al.*, 2008). Both schemes can claim some success in that landowners receiving payments have conserved their forests. However, in both schemes there is little evidence that this behaviour on the part of landowners is the result of the payments and is not due to other factors (see chapters in Part III for further discussion on additionality and leakage issues).

Paying landowners is, of course, not the only way of reducing deforestation. The conventional way is to place legal restrictions on deforestation but this has proved ineffective in practice. Chomitz *et al.* (2006) identify a range of other interventions that governments can use to tackle deforestation such as fire prevention programmes, improvement of tenure security, taxation of large-scale land clearance, promotion of off-farm employment and intensification. He also argues that measurement, monitoring and transaction costs are prohibitively high at the property level, especially for small properties, raising doubts about the practicality of relying solely on payments to conserve forest at the individual forest owner level. In practice, a payment scheme is likely to be most effective if introduced in conjunction with these other measures. The costs of a payment scheme are, therefore, a minimum indicator of the costs of avoiding deforestation. If the payment scheme is to operate effectively and make an impact on rates of deforestation, there will have to be investment also in the necessary accompanying measures.

Achieving long-term emissions reduction

While an energy-focused mitigation option, such as replacing a fossil fuel power plant with a renewable energy-based one, results in a permanent emission reduction, the impact of avoiding deforestation is temporary. The emission reduction lasts only as long as forest cover is maintained. If a few years later the forest is cleared, sequestered CO_2 will be released into the atmosphere assuming that a large part of the forest biomass is burnt or goes into short-life forest products. As greenhouse gases once released stay in the atmosphere at least 50 years but with some decay over time, deforestation of a given area of land should be avoided over up to 50 years to have an impact equivalent to a permanent emissions reduction.

In order for payments for avoiding deforestation to be comparable with energy-focused mitigation options, i.e. in terms of providing equivalent emission reductions, they need to be maintained over a lengthy period spanning several decades.

Approach to estimating the cost of avoided deforestation

Types of cost

Two main types of cost are involved: the payment to the landholder, compensating for opportunity cost of foregone land use along with the costs of any actions necessary for conservation such as fencing or employment of guards; and the transaction costs of designing, setting up and operating the payment scheme, including contract management, fund management, transfer of funds and monitoring. Landholders could also incur transaction costs in applying to the payment scheme and meeting procedural requirements relating to land title and other land characteristics but much depends on the design of the scheme.

The opportunity costs and the recurrent costs of administering the payment scheme are discussed here. There will also be some initial fixed costs for elements that need to be in place for a payments system to function such as the measurement of existing forest areas and carbon stocks. These are not included due to a lack of information.

Estimating opportunity cost

Land-use returns

The estimates draw from existing estimates in the literature on returns to different land uses in the eight countries under study. In some cases, these studies are at the local level, often in small communities; in others they involve more generic estimates based on average production costs and revenues per tonne of product. Both types of estimate have their disadvantages. Local-level studies while sound for the location concerned may not be suitable for extrapolation to a larger area. As commonly pointed out (e.g., Chomitz *et al.*, 2006) the returns to land vary considerably by location as a result of the soil and climatic conditions, the scale of operation, the inputs and technology used and the distance from market and quality of transport infrastructure.

More generic estimates, by way of contrast, may not capture local variation in yields or differences between scales of operation. This means that they may not predict accurately the response to payments set at given levels. Both types of estimate are affected by price swings in agricultural commodities. Ideally, estimates should be more than snapshots of prices and costs in a single year and take some account of future trends. But projecting prices and costs for agricultural commodities over a period as long as 30 years with any degree of accuracy is fraught with difficulty. The estimates in this chapter are based on a combination of local level studies and more generic estimates depending on data availability.

Annual returns per hectare were converted to net present value per hectare in most cases with a 10 per cent discount rate and a time horizon of 30 years. This represents the total cost over 30 years of paying a landholder every year to retain forest cover over this period. The time horizon and discount rate were selected so as to be in line with the majority of the estimates in the literature.[3]

The estimated returns to each land use in each of the eight countries can be found in the Appendix (Table 2A.1) at the end of this chapter together with details about the assumptions made and the sources of information.

It can be seen that one factor which significantly affects the estimates of land-use returns is the extent to which there is commercial logging as part of the forest conversion process. In some parts of the world, revenue from timber harvesting may help to finance subsequent forest clearing, for example, in Indonesia (see Palmer and Obidzinski, Chapter 7 in this volume). In other places, because of distance to markets and practical and legal restrictions on harvesting, forests are burnt to clear them for agriculture and little logging takes place. Returns to timber harvesting also vary considerably depending on location and proximity to market as well as density of commercial species. For example, the country report for Cameroon of the alternatives to the slash and burn programme (Kotto-Same *et al.*, 2000) did not incorporate timber revenues in its estimates of returns to land use. It was argued that deforestation is driven primarily by smallholder agriculture and that smallholders are prohibited from harvesting timber except for their own use.

Land price information, although in theory an indicator of discounted returns to land, was not used for these estimates. This was because the problem of deforestation often reflects lack of clear ownership and land markets. Where land markets do exist, they are often not well developed with relatively few transactions so prices are not representative. Moreover, studies reporting land prices rarely make clear the essential characteristics of the land such as tenure security, soil fertility and location that may affect its price.

Determining the area to which cost estimates apply

A significant challenge is to estimate the area over which different land uses would apply as this will indicate how much avoided deforestation would be achieved for different incentive levels. Most of the cost estimates in the literature do not go beyond estimating a return per hectare to different land uses. To estimate the cost of avoiding deforestation at a national level it is necessary to apply these estimates to a geographical area. The starting point for determining this is the annual area deforested. FAO figures on net forest loss[4] were used for this purpose as shown in Table 2.1.

Table 2.1 Rates of deforestation

Country	Deforestation rate[a] 2000–2005 ('000 ha/yr)
Bolivia	270
Brazil	3103
Cameroon	220
DRC[b]	319
Ghana	115
Indonesia	1871
Malaysia	140
PNG[c]	139
Total	**6177**

Source: FAO (2005)

Notes
a Figures refer to net forest loss.
b Democratic Republic of the Congo.
c Papua New Guinea.

The next step is to predict how much of the area deforested each year will end up as different land uses, whether pasture, soybeans, food crops etc. In other words, how many hectares would be cleared for low return use and how many for high return crops? As land-use patterns depend on a number of local factors such as soils, climate, access to markets, as well as relative prices that can change due to external factors, it is challenging to make robust predictions. Where estimates of returns differ according to scale it is also necessary to determine how much of the area deforested is likely to involve farms of different scales.

To make such predictions for Brazil, data were used from Chomitz and Thomas (2001) on proportions of cleared land in forest margin area that are dedicated to different types of land use. These authors show that 77 per cent of cleared land in forest margins in Brazil is under pasture with 8 per cent under annual crops. It might be reasonable therefore to assume that 77 per cent of further land deforested in Brazil in the next few years will end up as pasture (see also Moutinho *et al.*, Chapter 6 in this volume). Chomitz and Thomas (2001) also show that almost half of the agricultural land in these areas corresponds to large-scale farms and only 1.5 per cent to farms of fewer than 20 ha. Unfortunately, similar studies with such quantification of land-use patterns do not appear to be available for the other significant deforestation countries.

The percentage breakdown of land uses in most cases is, therefore, based on a more subjective assessment, drawing from qualitative statements in the literature about the importance of different land uses in deforested areas and land-use patterns at national level.

These assumptions are cross-checked where possible by recent trends in the number of hectares dedicated to different land uses. For example, for Indonesia, oil palm is considered to be a significant driver of deforestation (see Palmer and Obidzinski, Chapter 7 in this volume). Between 1990 and 2003, the area dedicated to oil palm increased by roughly 12 per cent per year (Zen *et al.*, 2005). Expansion in 2004 and 2005 has been at a similar rate. If it is assumed that all of this increase is associated with deforestation, then the current annual increase of oil palm area corresponds to 32 per cent of the annual rate of deforestation. This provides some justification for assuming that 32 per cent of the area deforested each year will be used for oil palm. This, of course, assumes that past trends are a good guide to future trends, which may not be the case, particularly when prices change.

Table 2A.2 in the Appendix shows the breakdown of land uses in areas likely to be deforested for each of the eight countries together with details on the underlying assumptions.

Additionality and leakage

Implicit in the estimates just examined are assumptions that the operators of a payment scheme can identify the areas of forest most at risk of deforestation and can put in place measures to prevent leakage, that is, prevent a transfer of deforestation from areas in the payment scheme to areas outside the payment scheme (for more on leakage, see Murray, Chapter 9 in this volume). If some of the payments are made for land that would have been kept as forest without the payments, implying that some land at high risk of deforestation will not be covered, then the overall target for deforestation reduction will not be met. This is illustrated by the experience of Mexico's payments scheme. A model of deforestation risk was developed and a comparison was made with areas at risk and areas in the payment scheme (Muñoz-Piña *et al.*, 2008). The results showed that there was a lack of additionality. In 2003, only 11 per cent of the participating hectares were classified as having high or very high deforestation risk. This increased to 28 per cent in 2004 but later fell again to 20 per cent in 2005 (Karousakis, 2007). There are similar concerns about the payment for environmental services scheme in Costa Rica where forestlands in some isolated areas in the Osa Peninsula are included in the payment scheme but are at little risk of deforestation (Sierra and Russman, 2006). Payments targeting is addressed in more detail in Engel *et al.* (for Costa Rica) and Alix-Garcia *et al.* (for Mexico) (Chapters 12 and 13 in this volume, respectively).

Targeting has implications for both opportunity costs and transaction costs. If, as seems likely, it is not possible to target the land at risk from deforestation with 100 per cent accuracy, payments would have to be directed to an area larger than the desired reduction in deforestation at least in the initial years. It would have to be accepted that some of the payments would not change landowner behaviour. The other implication is that achieving higher levels of additionality and preventing leakage would require considerable outlay by the administering authority. There is a tradeoff between outlay on compensation payments and administration costs.

Transaction costs

The operational costs to the administrators of the scheme and to the participants can be estimated by examining the experience of payments for environmental services schemes in Latin America where such schemes have been operating for some years.

FONAFIFO (*Fondo Nacional de Financiamiento Forestal*), the organization that administers the payments scheme in Costa Rica, is required by law to spend no more than 7 per cent of its budget on administering the scheme and the rest on the payments. According to Rodriguez (2005), FONAFIFO's total budget over 10 years has been 40 billion colones (US$110 million) giving an average annual administration expenditure of US$770,000, assuming that the whole 7 per cent is used up. By October 2005, the programme had approximately 250,000 ha under contract (GEF, 2005), implying an average annual administration cost of US$3 per hectare over the whole contracted area.[5]

Mexico's payment scheme, initiated in 2003, also has a ceiling for costs of operation, evaluation and monitoring stipulated in the legislation, in this case 4 per cent (Muñoz-Piña *et al.*, 2008). The annual budget for the scheme was US$18 million in 2003, increasing to US$26 million in 2004. This implies expenditure on administration of up to US$700,000 and US$1,040,000 in 2003 and 2004, respectively. This does not include fixed costs of computers, satellite access, land registry update, etc., which were paid for by Mexico's forestry agency (ibid.). Over the first 3 years of the programme some 480,000 ha were incorporated into the scheme, implying an operational cost (excluding fixed costs) of US$2.2 per ha per year if the cumulative total is considered or US$6.0 per ha per year if new applications only are considered.

The national schemes in Costa Rica and Mexico have been introduced in contexts where there were already institutions in place and a history of subsidies to forestry, and so may underestimate administration costs in less favourable contexts. They are also not oriented specifically to GHG emission reductions but additionally or exclusively to other environmental services such as watershed protection. Monitoring has been mainly of changes in forest cover rather than delivery of carbon emission reductions. This information needs to be considered as a lower bound for administrative costs and to be supplemented by cost figures more representative of less favourable contexts where there is little existing institutional capacity.

Another issue is that PES recipients also incur costs in the application process and this will affect their decisions. The payment therefore needs to cover both the opportunity costs of the land-use restriction (plus any direct costs of conservation) as well as the transaction cost for applicants of entering the scheme. An indication of the magnitude of transaction costs assumed by applicants is given by the charges made by local intermediaries in Costa Rica to assist applicants with the process including technical assistance and monitoring. These range from 12 per cent to 18 per cent of the total amount of the contract over 5 years (Miranda *et al.*, 2003). Not all PES recipients need to make use of intermediaries. Assuming that 50 per cent of PES recipients have to contract intermediaries to help them with their applications, including these costs in the calculation would almost double the administration costs bringing them to US$6 per ha at least for the first 5 years of a payment contract.[6] For renewal of the payment contract it is likely that administration costs for applicants would be lower.

To some extent the division of transaction costs between the administering agency and the applicants reflects the design of the scheme, as well as the strength of local institutions and the capacity of applicants. In contexts where there is less institutional capacity, it may be necessary for the administering agency to take on more of these costs. For this reason, we take the lower bound of administration costs to be US$4 per ha per year (one-third higher than the average annual cost in the Costa Rican scheme and double the average annual cost in Mexico to cover the transaction costs incurred by landowners).

At the other extreme, small local PES schemes have relatively high transaction costs reflecting the large fixed-cost element. For the scheme in Pimampiro, Ecuador, which has contracts with 19 landholders covering 550 ha of forest and native Andean grassland, the costs of monitoring and management are US$867 per year (Wunder and Albán, 2008). To this the costs of the start-up phase at US$38,000 (ibid.) needs to be added. Spreading this cost over 30 years at an interest rate of 10 per cent and adding the annual monitoring and management costs gives an annual administration cost of US$9 per ha per year.[7]

From these schemes, a lower bound figure for annual administration costs of US$4 per ha and an upper bound of US$9 per ha can be derived. These represent the likely range of operational costs of a compensation scheme employing a system of payments. This range includes the cost for the administering authority and the transaction costs likely to be incurred by landholders to apply to the scheme. These annual administration costs need to be discounted over 30 years in the same way as the opportunity costs. This is the amount of money that will be necessary to implement and maintain a payment scheme over the period required for avoided deforestation to constitute mitigation.

Cost estimates

Cost scenarios

In view of the high returns to commercial logging, the three main scenarios of cost were formulated around the extent to which there is timber harvesting as part of the conversion process. One scenario looked at costs on the assumption that there was no commercial logging as part of the conversion process. The high cost scenario assumes that commercial logging takes place in 100 per cent of the annual deforestation area. While more realistic than the low cost scenario it is likely to be an overestimate for the reasons discussed earlier that some deforestation takes place without any commercial logging. An intermediate scenario was therefore formulated (see Table 2.2), which takes account of practical, market and legal constraints on commercial timber harvesting in the countries concerned, in particular the involvement of smallholders.

Other factors that could affect the costs are the discount rate used to calculate net present value (NPV), the time horizon over which returns are calculated and the assumptions on commodity prices, whether a single year estimate at a low or a high point of the cycle or an average of several years. A major influence on the results,

Table 2.2 The medium timber harvesting scenario

Country	Extent of commercial timber harvesting (% of annual deforestation area)	Rationale
Bolivia	30	No commercial timber harvesting in the cattle ranching area because too remote
Brazil	70	No commercial timber harvesting in areas of small-scale cattle ranching and food crops and perennials
Cameroon	0	Deforestation is smallholder driven and logging is prohibited
DRC[a]	0	Deforestation is smallholder driven
Indonesia	66	No commercial timber harvesting in smallholder rice and manioc areas
Malaysia	80	No commercial timber harvesting in rice fallow area
PNG[b]	100	All forests are community owned

Source: Author

Notes
a Democratic Republic of the Congo.
b Papua New Guinea.

however, is the assumption about the proportion of deforested area that will be in high or low value agricultural (alternative) use. A fourth scenario therefore examines the cost if it is assumed for each country that the highest return land use[8] in that country applies over the whole deforestation area.

Opportunity costs in each scenario

The estimates of the costs of foregone land use if deforestation in the eight countries is to be completely halted, range between US$3 billion (no commercial logging before forest clearing) and US$6.5 billion (all areas logged before clearing) with a central estimate of US$5 billion in a realistic scenario that takes account of practical, legal and market constraints to timber harvesting. For the high return land-use scenario, total costs exceed US$11 billion (excluding returns from one-off timber harvesting) and exceed US$14 billion if returns from one-off timber harvesting are included. Table 2.3 shows the breakdown of these costs by country for each scenario.

Administration costs

Annual administration costs per ha discounted over 30 years at 10 per cent gives a range of net present cost from US$38 to US$85 per ha with total costs for the eight countries ranging from US$233 million to US$0.5 billion, for the range of US$4 to 9 per ha per year as shown in Table 2.4. This is the cost of administering a payment scheme covering 6.2 million hectares over a 30 year period.

Table 2.3 Estimates of opportunity cost for eliminating deforestation

Country	Cost (million US$)[a]				
	Main scenarios			*High return land-use scenarios*	
	No commercial logging	*Medium commercial logging*	*100% commercial logging*	*Excluding commercial logging*	*100% commercial logging*
Bolivia	227	247	291	513	576
Brazil	1165	1678	1898	5891	6624
Cameroon	191	191	379	300	488
DRC[b]	276	276	549	435	708
Ghana	23	121	121	23	121
Indonesia	859	2059	2795	3125	5061
Malaysia	67	183	212	234	379
PNG[c]	137	281	281	232	376
Total	**2945**	**5036**	**6526**	**10,752**	**14,334**

Source: Author

Notes
a Net present value of opportunity costs over 30 years discounted at 10%.
b Democratic Republic of the Congo.
c Papua New Guinea.

Table 2.4 Costs of administering a payment scheme

Country	Costs for administering authority (net present value in million US$)	
	Lower	*Upper*
Bolivia	10	23
Brazil	117	263
Cameroon	8	19
DRC[a]	12	27
Ghana	4	10
Indonesia	71	159
Malaysia	5	12
PNG[b]	5	12
Total	**233**	**524**

Source: Author

Notes
Note: Based on an annual lower bound of US$4/ha and upper bound of US$9/ha.
a Democratic Republic of the Congo.
b Papua New Guinea.

Comparison with other mitigating options

Estimation of CO_2 emissions from deforestation

In order to compare these costs with other mitigation options, it is necessary to estimate the greenhouse gas emissions associated with deforestation. This is not straightforward as carbon stocks are heavily dependent on the type of forest (tropical moist or tropical dry forest) and the region where forests are located (Houghton, 2005). The official estimates of emissions provided by country governments to the UNFCC are not helpful for this purpose as for some countries, for example, Malaysia and Papua New Guinea, they record land-use change and forestry as a sink rather than a source of emissions (UNFCCC, 2005).

Estimates of emissions from land-use change at a national level made by Houghton (2003) are available on the World Resources Institute's Climate Analysis Indicators Tool (WRI CAIT) database. These estimates, however, appear to include emissions from selective timber harvesting and use of fuelwood as well as from forest conversion.[9] As selective timber harvesting is not always followed immediately by forest conversion, leading rather to forest degradation, this will be an overestimate of the emissions from deforestation. Total annual emissions from the land-use change and forestry sector for the eight countries averaged over 1991–2000 amount to 2.2 billion tonnes of carbon (5.4 billion tonnes of CO_2) or nearly 70 per cent of the total world land-use emissions according to CAIT.[10]

The upper bound estimates in this chapter are based on generic figures for carbon content in vegetation (different forest types) by region given in Houghton (1999) (see Table 2.5). It is assumed that deforestation in these countries is entirely in tropical moist forest and that 90 per cent of carbon in vegetation is released when forests are cleared (based on FAO, 2005). This gives total emissions from deforestation for the eight countries of 1.2 billion tonnes of carbon (4.3 billion tonnes CO_2). This is somewhat lower than the total for the eight countries in CAIT.

An alternative and considerably lower estimate for the eight countries in total (albeit not for DRC) is given by the national estimates of carbon stocks in the Forest Resources Assessment (FAO, 2005) (see Table 2.6). Dividing these by the

Table 2.5 Upper bound estimates of CO_2 emissions from deforestation

Country	Carbon in vegetation (tC/ha)	Carbon released from deforestation (tC/ha)	Annual deforestation ('000 ha)	Annual emissions of carbon (MtC/yr)	Annual emissions of CO_2 (MtCO_2/yr)
Bolivia	200	180	270	49	178
Brazil	200	180	3103	559	2046
Cameroon	136	122	220	27	99
DRC[a]	136	122	319	39	143
Ghana	200	122	115	14	52
Indonesia	250	225	1871	421	1542
Malaysia	250	225	140	32	115
PNG[b]	250	225	139	31	115
Total			**6177**	**1171**	**4290**

Source: Author's estimates based on generic regional figures for carbon in tropical moist forest from Houghton (1999)

Notes
a Democratic Republic of the Congo.
b Papua New Guinea.

Table 2.6 Lower bound estimate of CO_2 emissions from deforestation

Country	Carbon in vegetation[a] (tC/ha)	Carbon released from deforestation (tC/ha)	Annual deforestation ('000 ha/yr)	Annual emissions of carbon (MtC/yr)	Annual emissions of CO_2 (MtCO₂/yr)
Bolivia	100	90	270	24	89
Brazil	110	99	3103	306	1122
Cameroon	99	89	220	20	72
DRC[b]	183	164	319	52	192
Ghana	103	92	115	11	39
Indonesia	74	67	1871	125	456
Malaysia	193	174	140	24	89
PNG[c]	193[d]	174	139	24	88
Total			**6177**	**586**	**2147**

Source: Author

Notes
a Calculated from official national level estimates of carbon in above ground and below ground biomass and deadwood in forests in FAO (2005).
b Democratic Republic of the Congo.
c Papua New Guinea.
d Not reported in FAO (2005) so assumed same as for Malaysia.

area of forest in each country gives an estimate of carbon stock per ha. This takes account of differences in the type of forest and the extent to which it is degraded. It can be seen that the figure for Indonesia is particularly low. The FAO (2005) notes that Indonesia recorded a significantly lower level of carbon per hectare in 2005 than in 2000, which indicated that not only the forest area but also the biomass and carbon stock per hectare had decreased. For other countries reporting reduction in total carbon stocks this was primarily due to loss of forest area.

Cost of compensation payments

This provides an upper and lower estimate of carbon emissions per ha for each of the eight countries and for the eight countries in total. Upper and lower estimates of costs per tonne of CO_2 are then calculated for the main scenarios. In the medium timber harvesting scenario, the cost per tonne of CO_2 avoided averaged over the eight countries ranges from US$1.2 to US$2.3, depending on the assumptions about carbon stocks per ha of forest. Summarized results are shown in Table 2.7 and presented for each land use in Table 2A.6 in the Appendix. Marginal costs as represented by the different land uses in each country range from less than US$0.1 for small-scale beef cattle in Brazil and cassava monoculture in Indonesia to US$11.1 for large-scale oil palm in Indonesia.

For the high cost land-use scenario, the average cost per tonne of CO_2 avoided for the eight countries in total is US$3.3 for the higher estimate of carbon stocks per ha of forest and US$6.7 for the lower estimate.[11]

Table 2.7 Costs per tonne of CO_2 avoided in the medium timber scenario

Country	Costs (US$/tCO$_2$)	
	Lower bound emissions	Upper bound emissions
Bolivia	2.8	1.4
Brazil	1.5	0.8
Cameroon	2.7	1.9
DRC[a]	1.4	1.9
Ghana	3.1	2.3
Indonesia	4.5	1.3
Malaysia	2.0	1.6
PNG[b]	3.2	2.5
Average over eight countries	**2.3**	**1.2**

Source: Author

Notes
a Democratic Republic of the Congo.
b Papua New Guinea.

Cost of administering a payment scheme

The estimates just given represent the price that would have to be paid to land-holders to compensate for the foregone land-use returns. The price that the administering agency would have to charge buyers of emission reductions to cover all costs including administration would be higher. Table 2.8 shows the range of additional administration costs for each country. On average the inclusion of administration costs raises the price per tonne of CO_2 avoided by between US$0.1 and US$0.2 but this range is wider for some of the eight countries, in particular Indonesia.

Table 2.8 Administration costs per tonne of CO_2 avoided

Country	Lower bound cost (US$/ha)		Upper bound cost (US$/ha)	
	Upper CO$_2$	Lower CO$_2$	Upper CO$_2$	Lower CO$_2$
Bolivia	0.06	0.11	0.13	0.26
Brazil	0.06	0.10	0.13	0.23
Cameroon	0.08	0.12	0.19	0.26
DRC[a]	0.08	0.06	0.19	0.14
Ghana	0.08	0.11	0.19	0.25
Indonesia	0.05	0.15	0.10	0.35
Malaysia	0.05	0.06	0.10	0.13
PNG[b]	0.05	0.06	0.10	0.13
Average over eight countries	**0.05**	**0.11**	**0.12**	**0.24**

Source: Author

Notes
a Democratic Republic of the Congo.
b Papua New Guinea.

Comparison with costs of other mitigation options

The cost of paying to avoid deforestation including the cost of administering a payment scheme ranges from less than US$0.1 per tonne CO_2 for small-scale cattle ranching in Brazil (at the lower bound of average per ha administration costs) to US$11.4 per ha for large-scale oil palm in Indonesia. This compares with the average price of emission reductions in the CDM. In 2006, this was US$10.90 per tonne of CO_2 with most emission reductions being in the range of US$8–14 (Capoor and Ambrosi, 2007). While avoided deforestation may not be able to compete with the large hydrofluorocarbon (HFC) destruction projects that have dominated the CDM, it is generally lower cost than most of the energy efficiency and renewable projects in the CDM. It is only where the main alternative land use is large-scale and high yield oil palm in Indonesia, that paying to avoid deforestation would be more expensive than other mitigation options. The cost of paying to avoid deforestation also compares quite well with the cost of afforestation and reforestation. Nabuurs *et al.* (2007) cite costs in the range of US$0.5 to US$7 per tonne of CO_2 for forestry projects in developing countries and US$1.4 to US$22 per tonne of CO_2 for similar projects in industrialized countries.

The inclusion of administration costs does increase the cost but does not change the overall conclusion that paying to avoid deforestation seems cost effective compared to other mitigation options.

Conclusions

Our estimates suggest that in many countries with tropical forest, paying landholders to conserve forest may be more cost effective than some of the other mitigation options commonly available. There are, of course, areas in which the returns from alternative land uses are so high that it would not make sense from a mitigation point of view to attempt to pay to hold back deforestation. This applies particularly to areas suitable for high value crops such as oil palm and soy.

There are other caveats that need to be acknowledged. Since these estimates were prepared, there have been substantial increases in agricultural commodity prices, including timber, the result of a number of factors such as increasing demand in China, bad weather leading to poor harvests and the biofuels boom. Estimates based on today's prices would be somewhat higher. However, commodity prices are notoriously cyclical and it is likely that they will fall again in the future. These estimates also do not take account of dynamic effects. They are based on the assumption that the restrictions on land use in each country will not be large enough to affect the availability of timber and agricultural commodities and increase prices. This may not be realistic if deforestation is to be completely halted in some countries. But this may not be problematic in the case of small reductions in deforestation spread over a number of countries. Much depends also on the measures that accompany a payment scheme to avoid deforestation. Promotion of increased productivity in existing agricultural land or in forest plantations may offset the impact of reduced forest conversion.

There are also the practicalities of implementing a payment scheme in contexts of poor governance and limited institutional capacity. The upper bound for the estimates of administration costs aims to take differences between countries into account. In some countries, however, some of the fundamental building blocks for a scheme such as a functioning justice system to uphold land rights and enforce contracts may not be present. The cost of implementing a payment scheme in such circumstances would be orders of magnitude higher and it is questionable whether a scheme could be introduced at all.

It also needs to be considered whether paying to avoid deforestation could be cost effective in terms of meeting other objectives such as the sustainable development objective of the CDM or providing co-benefits such as conservation of biodiversity. Such a scheme has potential to benefit rural livelihoods as it could provide a stable income to forest landowners at least as great as their current options and open up new income generating possibilities such as ecotourism but there are significant risks involved. As with most payments for environmental services initiatives, the extent of local livelihood benefits depends on the detail of the scheme: who is eligible for payment, the level of payment and the accompanying measures to build capacity. The payment scheme would have to be implemented as part of a package of measures aimed at improving rural livelihoods. Even with such measures, there are likely to be some tradeoffs between achieving livelihood improvements and securing least cost emission reductions, particularly in terms of transaction cost.

APPENDIX (facing page)

Table 2A.1 Derivation of land-use return

Country	Land uses	Returns 2005 (US$/ha)	Source/rationale
Bolivia	Beef cattle	390	Assume Brazil figures apply
	Soya	1999	Assume Brazil figures apply – assume US$100/ha for clearing costs
	One-off timber harvesting	236	Assume same as for Brazil
Brazil	Beef cattle medium/large scale	390	Margulis (2003) – average of 5 representative farms in Para, Rondonia and Mato Grosso
	Beef cattle small scale	2	Lewis et al. (2002) (ASB Brazil)
	Dairy	154	Arima and Uhl (1996) Costs of clearing assumed at US$100/ha
	Soybeans	1899	Diaz (2005) – return to farmers in Mato Grosso. Assume US$100/ha clearing cost
	Manioc/rice	2	Assume same as for pasture. Negative in ASB report
	Perennials bananas	2	Assume that perennials, fallow and degraded land have same return as manioc/rice
	Tree plantations	2378	Assume same as for coffee – bandarra system in Lewis et al. (2002) (ASB Brazil)
	One-off timber harvesting	236	Average stumpage fee in Paragominas in Barreto et al. (1998)
Cameroon	Annual food crops short fallow	774	Kotto-Same et al. (2000) Table 16 page 35. Social returns to take account of trade restrictions
	Annual food crops long fallow	346	Kotto-Same et al. (2000) Table 16 page 35. Social returns to take account of trade restrictions
	Cocoa with marketed fruit	1365	Kotto-Same et al. (2000) Table 16 page 35. Social returns to take account of trade restrictions
	Cocoa without marketed fruit	740	Kotto-Same et al. (2000) Table 16 page 35. Social returns to take account of trade restrictions
	Oil palm and rubber	1180	Kotto-Same et al. (2000) Table 16 page 35. Social returns – assume same return for rubber
	One-off timber harvesting	n.a.	Assume same as for Ghana
DRC[a]	Annual food crops short fallow	774	Assume same as for Cameroon
	Annual food crops long fallow	346	Assume same as for Cameroon
	Cocoa with marketed fruit	1365	Assume same as for Cameroon
	Cocoa without marketed fruit	740	Assume same as for Cameroon

Table 2A.1 Derivation of land-use return (cont.):

Country	Land uses	Returns 2005 (US$/ha)	Source/rationale
	Oil palm and rubber	1180	Assume same as for Cameroon
	One-off timber harvesting	n.a.	Assume same as for Cameroon
Ghana	Small-scale maize and cassava	197	Revenue per ha from Osafo, 2005. Assume 15% return
	One-off timber harvesting	830	Osafo, 2005 – community's share of stumpage fees = US$498/ha. Total stumpage fees used
Indonesia	Large scale oil palm	1,670	Vermeulen and Goad (2006) drawing from Zen et al. (2005)
	Supported growers – oil palm	1,050	Vermeulen and Goad (2006) drawing from Zen et al. (2005)
	High yield independent – oil palm	1,170	Vermeulen and Goad (2006) drawing from Zen et al. (2005)
	Low yield independent – oil palm	480	Vermeulen and Goad (2006) drawing from Zen et al. (2005)
	Smallholder rubber	36	Tomich et al. (1998) (ASB Indonesia). Social prices 20% discount rate
	Rice fallow	26	Tomich et al. (1998) (ASB Indonesia). Social prices (upper bound) 20% discount rate
	Cassava monoculture	18	Tomich et al. (1998) (ASB Indonesia). Social prices 20% discount rate
	One-off timber harvesting	1,035	Tomich et al. (2002)
Malaysia	Oil palm Large scale/government	1,670	Assume same as for Indonesia
	Oil palm supported growers	1,050	Assume same as for Indonesia
	Oil palm Independent grower	1,170	Assume same as for high yield independent growers, Indonesia
	Smallholder rubber	36	Assume same as for Indonesia
	Rice fallow	26	Assume same as for Indonesia
	Cassava monoculture	18	Assume same as for Indonesia
	One-off timber harvesting	1035	Assume same as for Indonesia
PNG[b]	Oil palm estates	1670	Assume same as for Indonesia
	Smallholder oil palm	480	Assume same as for Indonesia
	Smallholder subsistence crops	702	Gross returns from Anderson (2006) assume 15% return
	One-off timber harvesting	1035	Tomich et al. (2002). Assume that Indonesia estimates apply to PNG

Note

Returns are net present values in 2005 US$ at discount rate of 10% over 30 years except where otherwise stated.

[a] Democratic Republic of the Congo.

[b] Papua New Guinea.

n.a. denotes 'not applicable'.

Table 2A.2 Derivation of land uses

Country	Land uses	% of deforested area	Rationale
Bolivia	Beef cattle	70	According to Merry et al. (2002) important beyond peri-urban areas. Increase in cattle since 2001
	Soya	30	Over 40% increase in area planted 1999–2004. Implies 70,000 ha/yr, 26% of deforestation
Brazil	Beef cattle medium/large scale >200ha	63	Chomitz and Thomas (2001): 77% of forest margin land was pasture. 3% of agricultural land in farms of 20–200 ha = 14% of pasture. Assume that divided equally between beef cattle and dairy
	Beef cattle small scale (<200ha)	7	
	Dairy	7	
	Soybeans	5	Chomitz and Thomas (2001): 8% of forest margin land was used for annual crops. Assume that most but not all is for soybeans and rest for manioc/rice
	Manioc/rice	3	
	Perennials bananas	1	Chomitz and Thomas (2001): less than 2% of agricultural land in perennials or planted forest
	Tree plantations	1	
	Fallow	3	Chomitz and Thomas (2001) – assume return to manioc/rice applies
	Abandoned/degraded land	10	
Cameroon	Annual food crops short fallow	39	Kotto-Same et al. (2000) ASB Cameroon pages 6–7 and 52–53
	Annual food crops long fallow	20	Kotto-Same et al. (2000) ASB Cameroon pages 6–7 and 52–53
	Cocoa with marketed fruit	30	Dominant land use but production not increasing because of low price
	Cocoa without marketed fruit	10	Assume 25% of cocoa-driven deforestation is in area too remote for sale of fruit
	Coffee	0	Dominant land use but production area decreasing because of low price
	Oil palm and rubber	1	Not considered a threat to deforestation by Kotto-Same et al. (2000) ASB but increasing prices may change this. Oil palm area has increased by roughly 1000 ha/yr since 2000
DRC[a]	Annual food crops short fallow	39	Same as for Cameroon
	Annual food crops long fallow	20	Same as for Cameroon
	Cocoa with marketed fruit	30	Same as for Cameroon
	Cocoa without marketed fruit	10	Same as for Cameroon
	Coffee	0	Same as for Cameroon
	Oil palm and rubber	1	Same as for Cameroon

Table 2A.2 Derivation of land uses (*cont.*):

Country	Land uses	% of deforested area	Rationale
Ghana	Small-scale maize and cassava	100	Osafo (2005)
Indonesia	Large-scale oil palm	20	12% annual average rate of expansion in area planted 1990–2003 and 2003–
	Supported growers – oil palm	6	2005. 12% of area in 2005, which equals 32% of annual deforestation area
	High yield independent – oil palm	2	(Vermeulen and Goad, 2006). Assume percentages at national level apply in
	Low yield independent – oil palm	4	deforestation area
	Smallholder rubber	30	Assumption based on land-use systems in Tomich *et al.* (1998) (ASB Indonesia)
	Rice fallow	19	Assumption based on land-use systems in Tomich *et al.* (1998) (ASB Indonesia)
	Cassava monoculture	19	Assumption based on land-use systems in Tomich *et al.* (1998) (ASB Indonesia)
Malaysia	Oil palm – large scale/government	18	Assume percentages at national level from Ismail *et al.* (2003) apply in deforested areas
	Oil palm – supported growers	9	Assume percentages at national level from Ismail *et al.* (2003) apply in deforested areas
	Oil palm – independent grower	3	Assume percentages at national level from Ismail *et al.* (2003) apply in deforested areas
	Smallholder rubber	30	Based on Malaysian Rubber Board Statistics – area increasing in Sabah and Sarawak since 1998
	Rice fallow	20	Assumption based on land-use systems in Tomich *et al.* (1998) (ASB Indonesia)
	Cassava monoculture	20	Assumption based on land-use systems in Tomich *et al.* (1998) (ASB Indonesia)
PNG[b]	Oil palm estates	33	Oil palm fastest growing agricultural export so assume 50% of deforestation area
	Smallholder oil palm	17	Split between estates and smallholders based on their share of production
	Smallholder subsistence crops	50	Assumption based on importance of subsistence agriculture

Notes
a Democratic Republic of the Congo.
b Papua New Guinea.

Table 2A.3 Global and national costs of foregone land uses (excluding one-off timber harvesting)

Country	Land uses	Cost (US$/ha)	Area ('000 ha)	Cost (US$ '000)
Bolivia	Beef cattle	390	189	73,645
	Soya	1899	81	153,779
	Sub-total		**270**	**227,424**
Brazil	Beef cattle medium/large scale	390	1955	761,735
	Beef cattle small scale	2	217	528
	Dairy	154	217	33,353
	Soybeans	1899	155	294,553
	Manioc/rice	2	496	1208
	Perennials	2	31	75
	Tree plantations	2378	31	73,779
	Sub-total		**3103**	**1,165,232**
Cameroon	Annual food crops short fallow	774	85.8	66,373
	Annual food crops long fallow	346	44	15,222
	Cocoa with marketed fruit	1365	66	90,062
	Cocoa without marketed fruit	740	22	16,279
	Oil palm and rubber	1180	2.2	2595
	Sub-total		**220**	**190,530**
DRC[a]	Annual food crops short fallow	774	124.41	96,241
	Annual food crops long fallow	346	63.8	22,071
	Cocoa with marketed fruit	1365	95.7	130,589
	Cocoa without marketed fruit	740	31.9	23,604
	Oil palm and rubber	1180	3.19	3763
	Sub-total		**319**	**276,269**
Ghana	Small-scale maize and cassava	197	115	22,667
	Sub-total		**115**	**22,667**
Indonesia	Large-scale oil palm	1670	380	634,148
	Supported growers – oil palm	1050	109	114,778
	High yield independent – oil palm	1170	30	35,645
	Low yield independent – oil palm	480	79	38,022
	Smallholder rubber	36	561	20,174
	Rice fallow	26	355	9276
	Cassava monoculture	18	355	6476
	Sub-total		**1871**	**858,519**
Malaysia	Oil palm – large scale/government	1670	25	42,323
	Oil palm – supported growers	1050	13	13,341
	Oil palm – independent grower	1170	4	4623
	Smallholder rubber	36	42	1510
	Rice fallow	26	28	731
	Cassava monoculture	18	28	510
	Sub-total		**140**	**63,037**
PNG[b]	Oil palm estates	1670	46	77,377
	Smallholder oil palm	480	23	11,120
	Smallholder subsistence crops	702	70	48,777
	Sub-total		**139**	**137,273**
	TOTAL		**6177**	**2,940,951**

Note
a Democratic Republic of the Congo.
b Papua New Guinea.

Table 2A.4 Global and national costs of foregone land uses (including one-off timber harvesting)

Country	Land uses	Cost (US$/ha)	Area ('000 ha)	Cost (US$ '000)
Bolivia	Beef cattle	626	189	118,249
	Soya	2135	81	172,895
	Sub-total		**270**	**291,144**
Brazil	Beef cattle medium/large scale	626	1955	1,223,523
	Beef cattle small scale	239	217	51,838
	Dairy	390	217	84,663
	Soybeans	2135	155	331,203
	Manioc/rice	239	496	118,487
	Perennials	239	31	7405
	Tree plantations	2614	31	81,109
	Sub-total		**3103**	**1,898,229**
Cameroon	Annual food crops short fallow	1629	86	139,732
	Annual food crops long fallow	1201	44	52,842
	Cocoa with marketed fruit	2220	66	146,492
	Cocoa without marketed fruit	1595	22	35,089
	Oil palm and rubber	2035	2	4476
	Sub-total		**220**	**378,630**
DRC[a]	Annual food crops short fallow	1629	124	202,611
	Annual food crops long fallow	1201	64	76,620
	Cocoa with marketed fruit	2220	96	212,413
	Cocoa without marketed fruit	1595	32	50,879
	Oil palm and rubber	2035	3	6490
	Sub-total		**319**	**549,014**
Ghana	Small-scale maize and cassava	1052	115	121,008
	Sub-total		**115**	**121,008**
Indonesia	Large-scale oil palm	2705	380	1027
	Supported growers	2085	109	228
	High yield independent	2205	30	67
	Low yield independent	1515	79	120
	Smallholder rubber	1071	561	601
	Rice fallow	1061	355	377
	Cassava monoculture	1053	355	374
	Sub-total		**1871**	**2795**
Malaysia	Oil palm – large scale/government	2705	25	68,556
	Oil palm – supported growers	2085	13	26,492
	Oil palm – independent grower	2205	4	8713
	Smallholder rubber	1071	42	44,984
	Rice fallow	1061	28	29,713
	Cassava monoculture	1053	28	29,493
	Sub-total		**140**	**207,951**
PNG[b]	Oil palm estates	2705	46	125,336
	Smallholder oil palm	1515	23	35,100
	Smallholder subsistence crops	1737	70	120,716
	Sub-total		**139**	**281,152**
	TOTAL		**6177**	**6,522,312**

Notes
a Democratic Republic of the Congo.
b Papua New Guinea.

Table 2A.5 Global and national costs of foregone land uses (medium scenario of one-off timber harvesting)

Country	Land uses	Cost (US$/ha)	Area ('000 ha)	Cost (US$ '000)
Bolivia	Beef cattle	390	189	73,645
	Soya	2135	81	172,895
	Sub-total		**270**	**246,540**
Brazil	Beef cattle medium/large scale	626	1955	1,223,523
	Beef cattle small scale	2	217	528
	Dairy	154	217	33,353
	Soybeans	2135	155	331,203
	Manioc/rice	2	496	1208
	Perennials	239	31	7405
	Tree plantations	2614	31	81,109
	Sub-total		**3103**	**1,678,330**
Cameroon	Annual food crops short fallow	774	86	66,373
	Annual food crops long fallow	346	44	15,222
	Cocoa with marketed fruit	1365	66	90,062
	Cocoa without marketed fruit	740	22	16,279
	Oil palm and rubber	1180	2	2595
	Sub-total		**220**	**190,530**
DRC[a]	Annual food crops short fallow	774	124	96,241
	Annual food crops long fallow	346	64	22,071
	Cocoa with marketed fruit	1365	96	130,589
	Cocoa without marketed fruit	740	32	23,604
	Oil palm and rubber	1180	3	3763
	Sub-total		**319**	**276,269**
Ghana	Small-scale maize and cassava	1052	115	121,008
	Sub-total		**115**	**121,008**
Indonesia	Large-scale oil palm	2705	380	1,027,205
	Supported growers	2085	109	227,927
	High yield independent	2205	30	67,181
	Low yield independent	1515	79	120,014
	Smallholder rubber	1071	561	601,173
	Rice fallow	26	355	9276
	Cassava monoculture	18	355	6476
	Sub-total		**1871**	**2,059,252**
Malaysia	Oil palm – large scale/government	2705	25	68,556
	Oil palm – supported growers	2085	13	26,492
	Oil palm – independent grower	2205	4	8713
	Smallholder rubber	1071	42	44,984
	Rice fallow	26	28	731
	Cassava monoculture	1053	28	29,493
	Sub-total		**140**	**178,968**
PNG[b]	Oil palm estates	2705	46	125,336
	Smallholder oil palm	1515	23	35,100
	Smallholder subsistence crops	1737	70	120,716
	Sub-total		**139**	**281,152**
	TOTAL		**6177**	**5,032,048**

Note
a Democratic Republic of the Congo.
b Papua New Guinea.

Table 2A.6 Costs per tonne of CO_2 avoided in the medium timber scenario

Country	Land uses	Cost (US$/tCO$_2$) (Lower bound emissions)	(Upper bound emissions)
Bolivia	Beef cattle	1.2	0.6
	Soya	6.5	3.2
	Sub-total	**2.8**	**1.4**
Brazil	Beef cattle medium/large scale	1.7	0.9
	Beef cattle small scale	0.01	0.004
	Dairy	0.4	0.2
	Soybeans	5.9	3.2
	Manioc/rice	0.0	0.0
	Perennials (bananas, sugarcane pineapples)	0.7	0.4
	Tree plantations	7.2	4.0
	Sub-total	**1.5**	**0.8**
Cameroon	Annual food crops short fallow	2.4	1.7
	Annual food crops long fallow	1.1	0.8
	Cocoa with marketed fruit	4.2	3.0
	Cocoa without marketed fruit	2.3	1.6
	Oil palm and rubber	3.6	2.6
	Sub-total	**2.7**	**1.9**
DRC[a]	Annual food crops short fallow	1.3	1.7
	Annual food crops long fallow	0.6	0.8
	Cocoa with marketed fruit	2.3	3.0
	Cocoa without marketed fruit	1.2	1.6
	Oil palm and rubber	2.0	2.6
	Sub-total	**1.4**	**1.9**
Ghana	Small-scale maize and cassava	3.1	2.3
	Sub-total	**3.1**	**2.3**
Indonesia	Large-scale oil palm	11.1	3.3
	Supported growers	8.5	2.5
	High yield independent	9.0	2.7
	Low yield independent	6.2	1.8
	Smallholder rubber	4.4	1.3
	Rice fallow	0.1	0.0
	Cassava monoculture	0.1	0.0
	Sub-total	**4.5**	**1.3**
Malaysia	Oil palm – large scale/government	4.2	3.3
	Oil palm – supported growers	3.3	2.5
	Oil palm – independent grower	3.5	2.7
	Smallholder rubber	1.7	1.3
	Rice fallow	0.0	0.0
	Cassava monoculture	1.7	1.3
	Sub-total	**2.0**	**1.6**
PNG[b]	Oil palm estates	4.3	3.3
	Smallholder oil palm	2.4	1.8
	Smallholder subsistence crops	2.7	2.1
	Sub-total	**3.2**	**2.5**
	TOTAL	**2.3**	**1.2**

Notes
a Democratic Republic of the Congo.
b Papua New Guinea.

Notes

1 See www.rainforestcoalition.org.
2 US$320 per hectare to be disbursed over a period of 5 years with the option to renew for a further 5 years.
3 Ideally, the time horizon should be longer to be comparable with permanent emission reductions from energy-focused mitigation options. However, when discounting at 10 per cent or more, extending the time horizon beyond 30 years has a minimal effect on cost.
4 The FAO's Forest Resources Assessment (2005) does not give deforestation figures at a national level. Net forest loss includes afforestation, reforestation, natural expansion and deforestation and is, therefore, likely to underestimate deforestation.
5 Engel *et al.*, Chapter 12 in this volume, estimate higher administration costs if targeting within the Costa Rican scheme could be improved to consider spatial variation in deforestation risk, environmental services provided and the costs of provision.
6 If 50 per cent of PES recipients pay 15 per cent of their contracted amount to an intermediary, this implies an expenditure of roughly US$800,000 per year (50 per cent of annual budget for payments net of administration costs = US$5.1 million times 15 per cent = US$0.77 million). Including these costs in the calculation would almost double administration costs.
7 Payments made equal to US$4,200 per year, US$6–12 per ha per year depending on whether primary or secondary forest or grassland.
8 In the case of Brazil, the returns to soya were used for this estimate rather than the highest return land use (tree plantations) as this was considered to be a more likely threat at a larger scale.
9 Houghton (undated) states that the regional fluxes of carbon calculated include clearing of natural ecosystems for permanent croplands and permanent pastures, shifting cultivation and wood harvest (including fuelwood).
10 WRI/CAIT based on Houghton (2003) estimates total emissions from land-use change and forestry at 7619 $MtCO_2$ equivalent in 2000. The IPCC's 4th Assessment Report gives a somewhat lower figure of 5800 $MtCO_2$ per year for the 1990s (Nabuurs *et al.*, 2007).
11 The totals for the eight countries for high cost land-use scenario in Table 2.3 are divided by the totals for upper and lower bound estimates of CO_2 emissions in Tables 2.5 and 2.6.

References

Alix-Garcia, J., de Janvry, A. and Sadoulet, E. (2009) 'The role of risk in targeting payments for environmental services', in C. Palmer and S. Engel (eds) *Avoided Deforestation: Prospects for Mitigating Climate Change*, London: Routledge.

Anderson, T. (2006) *Oil Palm and Small Farmers in Papua New Guinea*, Report for the Centre for Environmental Law and Community Rights on the Economic Prospects for Small Farmers in PNG's Oil Palm Industry, Port Moresby, Papua New Guinea: Centre for Environmental Law and Community Rights (CELCOR).

Angelsen, A. (1995) 'Shifting cultivation and "deforestation": a study from Indonesia', *World Development*, 23(10): 1713–1729.

Arima, E. and Uhl, C. (1996) '*Pecuária na amazônia oriental: desempenho atual e perspectivas futuras*', *Série Amazônia*, 1, Belém: Amazon Institute of People and the Environment (IMAZON).

Barreto, P., Amaral, P., Vidal, E. and Uhl, C. (1998) '*Custos e benefícios do manejo florestal para produçao de madeira na Amazônia Oriental*', *Série Amazônia*, 10, Belém: Amazon Institute of People and the Environment (IMAZON).

Capoor, K. and Ambrosi, P. (2007) *State and Trends of the Carbon Market 2007*, Washington, DC: World Bank and International Emissions Trading Association.

Chomitz, K.M., Buys, P., De Luca, G., Thomas, T.S. and Wertz-Kanounnikoff, S. (2006) *At Loggerheads? Agricultural Expansion, Poverty Reduction and Environment in the Tropical Forests*, World Bank Policy Research Report, Development Research Group, Washington, DC: World Bank.

Chomitz, K.M. and Thomas, T.S. (2001) *Geographic Patterns of Land Use and Land Intensity in the Brazilian Amazon*, Development Research Group, World Bank with contributions by IBGE (*Instituto Brasileiro de Geografia e Estatística*, Brazilian Institute of Geography and Statistics), the University of Washington's CAMREX Project, and IMAZON (Amazon Institute of People and the Environment, Belém), Washington, DC: World Bank.

Diaz, M. del C.V. and Schwartzman, S. (2005) 'Carbon offsets and land use in the Brazilian Amazonas', in P. Moutinho and S. Schwartzman (eds) *Tropical Deforestation and Climate Change*, Belém: Amazon Institute for Environmental Research and Washington: Environmental Defense.

Engel, S., Wünscher, T., and Wunder, S. (2009) 'Increasing the efficiency of forest conservation: the case of payments for environmental services in Costa Rica', in C. Palmer and S. Engel (eds) *Avoided Deforestation: Prospects for Mitigating Climate Change*, London: Routledge.

FAO (Food and Agriculture Organization of the United Nations) (2005) *Global Forest Resources Assessment Progress towards Sustainable Forest Management*, Rome: FAO.

GEF (Global Environment Facility) (2005) *Project Executive Summary GEF Council Submission* [online]. Available at: http://www.gefweb.org/Documents/Work_Programs/documents/Costa_Rica_Mainstreaming_Instruments_ExecSumm.pdf [accessed 5 August 2008].

Houghton, R.A. (1999) 'The annual net flux of carbon to the atmosphere from changes in land use 1850–1990', *Tellus*, 51B(2): 298–313.

Houghton, R.A. (2003) 'Revised estimates of the annual net flux of carbon to the atmosphere from changes in land use and land management 1850–2000', *Tellus*, 55B(2): 378–390.

Houghton, R.A. (2005) 'Tropical deforestation as a source of greenhouse gas', in P. Moutinho and S. Schwartzman (eds) *Tropical Deforestation and Climate Change*, Belém: Amazon Institute for Environmental Research and Washington: Environmental Defense.

Houghton, R.A. (undated) 'Emissions (and sinks) of carbon from land-use change data', *Note for Climate Analysis Indicators Tool (CAIT)*, World Resources Institute [online]. Available at: http://cait.wri.org [accessed 5 August 2008].

Ismail A., Simeh, M.A. and Mohd Noor M. (2003) *The Production Cost of Oil Palm Fresh Fruit Bunches: The Case of Independent Smallholders in Johor*, Selangor, Malaysia: Malaysian Palm Oil Board.

Karousakis, K. (2007) *Incentives to Reduce GHG Emissions from Deforestation: Lessons Learned from Costa Rica and Mexico*, Organization for Economic Cooperation and Development (OECD) Papers 7(1): 50.

Kotto-Same, J., Moukam, R., Njomgang, R., Tiki-Manga, T., Tonye, J., Diaw, C. *et al.* (2000) *Alternatives to Slash-and-Burn in Cameroon: Summary Report and Synthesis of Phase II*, Nairobi: World Agroforestry Centre (ICRAF).

Lewis, J., Vosti, S., Witcover, J., Erickson, P.J., Guevara, R. and Tomich, T. (2002) *Alternatives to Slash and Burn in Brazil: Summary Report and Synthesis of Phase II*, Nairobi: World Agroforestry Centre (ICRAF).

Margulis, S. (2003) *Causas do Desmatamento de Amazônia Brasileira*, Brasília: World Bank.

Merry, F.D., Hildebrand, P.E., Pattie, P. and Carter, D.R. (2002) 'An analysis of land conversion from sustainable forestry to pasture: a case study in the Bolivian Lowlands', *Land Use Policy*, 19(3): 207–215.

MINAE (*Ministro del Ambiente y Energía*) (2008) *Decree No. 34371*, Costa Rica: *El Presidente de la República y el Ministro del Ambiente y Energía* [online]. Available at: http://www.fonafifo.com/text_files/servicios_ambientales/Decretos/Dec34371.pdf [accessed 6 August 2008].

Miranda, M., Porras, I.T. and Moreno, M.L. (2003) *The Social Impacts of Payments for Environmental Services in Costa Rica. A Quantitative Field Survey and Analysis of the Virilla Watershed*, London: International Institute for Environment and Development (IIED).

Moutinho, P., Cenamo, M., and Moreira, P. (2009) 'Reducing carbon emissions by slowing deforestation: REDD initiatives in Brazil', in C. Palmer and S. Engel (eds) *Avoided Deforestation: Prospects for Mitigating Climate Change*, London: Routledge.

Moutinho, P., Schwartzman, S. and Santilli, M. (2005) 'Introduction', in P. Moutinho and S. Schwartzman (eds) *Tropical Deforestation and Climate Change*, Belém: Amazon Institute for Environmental Research and Washington: Environmental Defense.

Muñoz-Piña, C., Guevara, A., Torres, J.M. and Braña, J. (2008) 'Paying for the hydrological services of Mexico's forests: analysis, negotiations and results', *Ecological Economics*, 65(4): 725–736.

Murray, B. (2009) 'Leakage from an avoided deforestation compensation policy: concepts, empirical evidence and corrective policy options', in C. Palmer and S. Engel (eds) *Avoided Deforestation: Prospects for Mitigating Climate Change*, London: Routledge.

Nabuurs, G.J., Masera, O., Andrasko, K., Benizez-Ponce, P., Boer, R., Dutsckhke, M. *et al.* (2007) 'Forestry', in B. Metz, O.R. Davidson, P.R. Bosch, R. Dave and L.A. Meyer (eds) *Climate Change 2007: Mitigation. Contribution of Working Group III to the Fourth Assessment Report of the Intergovernmental Panel on Climate Change*, Cambridge and New York: Cambridge University Press.

Osafo, Y.B. (2005) 'Reducing emissions from tropical deforestation: applying compensated reduction in Ghana', in P. Moutinho and S. Schwartzman (eds) *Tropical Deforestation and Climate Change*, Belém: Amazon Institute for Environmental Research and Washington: Environmental Defense.

Palmer, C. and Obidzinski, K. (2009) 'Choosing avoided deforestation baselines in the context of government failure: the case of Indonesia's plantations policy', in C. Palmer and S. Engel (eds) *Avoided Deforestation: Prospects for Mitigating Climate Change*, London: Routledge.

Rodriguez, J.M. (ed.) (2005) 'The environmental services program: a success story of sustainable development implementation in Costa Rica', *FONAFIFO, Over a Decade of Action*, San José: Costa Rica National Forestry Fund (FONAFIFO).

Sierra, R., and Russman, E. (2006) 'On the efficiency of environmental service payments: a forest conservation assessment in the Osa Peninsula, Costa Rica', *Ecological Economics* 59(1): 131–141.

Stern, N. (2007) *The Economics of Climate Change: The Stern Review*, Cambridge: Cambridge University Press.

Tomich, T.P., De Foresta, H., Dennis, R., Ketterings, Q., Murdiyarso, D., Palm, C. *et al.* (2002) 'Carbon offsets for conservation and development in Indonesia?', *American Journal of Alternative Agriculture*, 17(3): 38–50.

Tomich, T.P., van Noordwijk, M., Budidarsono, S., Gillison, A., Kusumanto, T. and Murdiyarso, D. (1998) *Alternatives to Slash and Burn in Indonesia: Summary Report and Synthesis of Phase II*, Nairobi: World Agroforestry Centre (ICRAF).

UNFCCC (United Nations Framework Convention on Climate Chance) (2005) 'Sixth compilation and synthesis of initial national communications from parties not included in Annex 1 to the convention', *Inventories of Anthropogenic Emissions by Sources and Removals by Sinks of Greenhouse Gases*, FCCC/SBI/2005/18/Add.2.

UNFCCC (United Nations Framework Convention on Climate Change) (2007) *Bali Action Plan Decision 1/CP.13* [online]. Available at: http://unfccc.int/files/meetings/cop_13/application/pdf/cp_bali_action.pdf [accessed 20 June 2008].

Vermeulen, S. and Goad, N. (2006) *Towards Better Practice in Smallholder Palm Oil Production*, London: International Institute for Environment and Development (IIED).

Wunder, S. and Albán, M. (2008) 'Decentralized payment for environmental services: the cases of Pimampiro and PROFAFOR in Ecuador, *Ecological Economics*, 65(4): 685–698.

Zen, Z., Barlow, C. and Gondowarsito, R. (2005) *Oil Palm in Indonesian Socio-economic Improvement: A Review of Options*, Working Paper in Trade and Economics, 11. Economics, Research School of Pacific and Asian Studies, Canberra: Australian National University.

3 Economics of avoiding deforestation

Ewald Rametsteiner, Michael Obersteiner,
Georg Kindermann and Brent Sohngen

Introduction

Deforestation is considered the second largest source of greenhouse gas emissions (IPCC, 2007) and is expected to remain a major emission source. The deforestation issue has been at the centre of the international environmental debate for two decades. Yet, despite a large number of studies, commitments, initiatives and strategy papers on the issue, deforestation continues at a rate of about 13 million ha per year (FAO, 2006). Apart from the loss of carbon, deforestation typically is associated with inter alia loss of biodiversity, disturbed water regulation and the destruction of livelihoods for many of the world's poorest people (Williams, 2003).

Governmental and non-governmental attempts to slow down, or even reverse, current trends of disappearing forests have not been successful as the result of many pressures, both local and international. While the more direct causes are rather well established as being agricultural expansion, infrastructure extension and wood extraction (Angelsen and Kaimowitz, 1999; Geist and Lambin, 2002; Schaeffer *et al.*, 2005), indirect drivers of deforestation are made up of a complex web of inter-linked and location-specific factors, as described in the introduction of this volume.

Some see a glimmer of hope for more effective policies with the rise of innovative financial mechanisms under a global climate policy regime (Fearnside, 2006; Gullison *et al.*, 2007; Moutinho *et al.*, 2006; Persson and Azar, 2006; Schulze *et al.*, 2003). Indeed, in 2005, Papua New Guinea proposed to the United Nations Framework Convention on Climate Change (UNFCCC) that carbon credits be provided to protect existing native forests.[1] The proposal triggered a flurry of discussion on the topic. The potential for synergies between forest and carbon policies is quite substantial. For instance, Soares-Filho *et al.* (2006) suggest that protecting around 130 million hectares of land from deforestation in the tropical Amazon could reduce global carbon emissions by 17 gigatonnes carbon (GtC) over the next 50 years.

Official international discussions were initiated at the UNFCCC 11th Conference of Parties (COP-11) on the issue of reducing emissions from defor-estation and degradation (REDD) in developing countries (UNFCCC, 2005). At COP-11 the UNFCCC launched a process for investigating the technical issues surrounding the feasibility of reducing greenhouse gas (GHG) emissions from deforestation. At the Bali UNFCCC meetings in December 2007, two processes were agreed upon in the negotiations to continue work on deforestation-related issues, including undertaking 'a programme of work on methodological issues related to a range of policy approaches and positive incentives that aim to reduce emissions from deforestation and degradation in developing countries' and consideration of 'policy approaches and positive incentives on issues relating to reducing emissions from deforestation and degradation (REDD) in developing countries' (UNFCCC, 2007).

What is unclear, however, is how much it would cost to achieve a substantial reduction of deforestation and which types of policy could be most effective. There are two basic options available to influence behaviour towards avoiding deforestation through financial mechanisms. One is to enhance the value of the existing forest through financial support for keeping the forest carbon stock, to be paid at certain time intervals. The other is to reduce the value of deforestation by increasing costs through taxing land conversion and thereby emissions from deforestation, for example, through a land clearance tax and wood sales taxes.

In this chapter, we use scenario-modelling approaches to assess the costs of reducing global deforestation and examine the two different financial mechanisms to combat deforestation. In the first, the incentives-based mechanism, forest owners are benefiting from retaining forest biomass through periodically receiving a carbon price for the carbon stored in the standing forest biomass, for example, through a 'compensation' contract that is issued to known deforestation agents ex ante. In the second, the tax-based mechanism, a carbon price has to be paid for releasing the stored carbon to the atmosphere, through a 'tax'-type payment which is assumed to be enforceable by an impartial agency ex post.

Methods

We use a spatially explicit biophysical and socioeconomic land-use model (Kindermann *et al.*, 2006, 2008), mainly based on the global afforestation model of Benítez and Obersteiner (2006). Land-use changes are simulated in the model as a decision based on a difference between net present value (NPV) of income from production on agricultural land versus NPV of income from forest products. The impact of economic incentives to reduce deforestation is then calculated by comparing shifts in NPVs of competing forms of land use to existing forest land. Assuming fixed technology, the model calculates for each 0.5° longitude–latitude grid cell the net present value difference between agricultural and forest land uses in 1-year time steps. Key model parameters, such as agricultural land use and production, population growth, deforestation and forest product consumption rates were calibrated against historical rates. The model results are annual, spatially explicit estimates of the forest area and biomass development from 2000 to 2100, with particular focus on the period 2006 to 2025.

The NPV of forestry is mainly driven by planting costs, income from carbon sequestration, growing stock of wood, rotation period length, discount rates, wood prices (fuelwood and timber) and, to some extent, ancillary benefits from forests.

Main drivers for the net present value of agriculture on current forest land are population density, agricultural suitability and risk-adjusted discount rates. These two values are compared against each other and, assuming profit-maximizing behaviour by the owners, deforestation is subsequently predicted to occur in the base scenario when the agricultural value exceeds the forest value by a certain margin. The speed of deforestation itself is, in turn, constrained by a range of factors, in particular, regional forest share, agricultural suitability, population density and economic wealth of the country. In order to more realistically mirror deforestation processes in our scenarios, the maximum possible deforestation in a given year is restricted by setting it to 5 per cent of the total land area per year in a certain location (grid cell). That means an area of about 50 × 50 km covered totally with forests cannot be deforested in a shorter time period than 20 years.

As mentioned earlier, we calculate the differences in net present value of different land uses to estimate the impact of financial incentives to reduce deforestation. When carbon market prices, transferred through a financial mechanism, balance out differences between the net present value of agricultural land and forest-related income, it is assumed, given profit-maximizing behaviour, that deforestation is avoided. We examine how the net present value difference of forest versus other land uses can be balanced out through two mechanisms. One is to reduce the difference by adding costs to conversion through taxing emissions from deforestation, for example, through a land clearance tax and wood sales taxes. The other is to enhance the value of the existing forest by financial support when keeping the forest carbon stock, to be paid at certain time intervals. In principle, such payments to avoid emissions from deforestation can be transferred to cover all of the globe's forests, they can target to large 'deforestation regions' or small areas. The approach taken here is to focus money transfers to those regions where a change in biomass takes place or is foreseen to take place. Money transfers would go to those entities executing wood-harvesting rights. While the model explicitly considers transaction costs of this transfer, it assumes clear and enforced property rights on wood harvesting.

The value of forest carbon stock is assumed to be pegged to carbon market prices and the incentives examined are within the range of recently observed carbon prices such as for certified emission reduction (CER) units within the clean development mechanism (CDM), i.e. 0–50US$/tC. The modelling results for different hypothetical tax or subsidy levels show the potential magnitude of avoided deforestation through financial incentive or disincentive mechanisms. The carbon price represents the effective benefit which will directly go to the forest owner. Different levels of transaction cost are considered based on the governance indicators on 'political stability', 'government effectiveness' and 'control of corruption' provided by the World Bank (World Bank, 2007).

Costs of reducing deforestation by half

Based on what we have seen already, the model estimates baseline deforestation without economic incentives at close to 212 million ha or around 5 per cent of today's forest area between 2006 and 2025, resulting in a release of some 17.5 GtC.

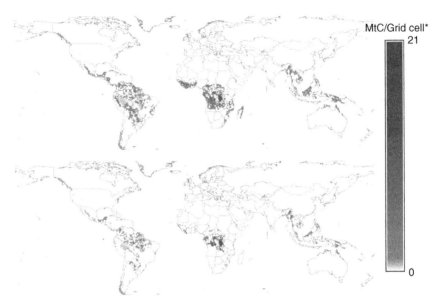

Figure 3.1   Forest carbon loss (upper section, no carbon policy) and avoided forest carbon
loss (lower section, with carbon policy) until 2025

Note: Grid cells are defined with 0.5 degree longitude–latitude.

In comparison, the global timber or GTM model predicts an amount of 25.5 GtC and
the generalized comprehensive mitigation assessment process or GCOMAP model
18.1 GtC for the same period (Kindermann *et al.*, 2008). The baseline deforestation
rates per grid cell that the model calculates were estimated statistically using forest
share, agricultural suitability, population density and economic wealth as independent variables. Sub-Saharan Africa is predicted to be responsible for about 50 per cent
of global deforestation emissions over the next 20 years, while Latin America and
Asia contribute 35 and 12 per cent, respectively (see Figure 3.1 and Table 3.1).

When aiming to reduce the deforestation rate by say 50 per cent until 2025, an
arbitrarily chosen reduction rate and year, the model results show that some
US$0.16 billion in 2006 to US$2.9 billion in 2025 is required to balance out NPV
differences on exactly those forests that would otherwise be converted, i.e. in the
case of perfect information on areas where deforestation would take place in the
absence of incentives. The increase from 2006 to 2025 is due to increasing geographic coverage of the carbon incentive scheme, as deforestation pressure occurs
on increasingly large areas and payments have to continue on previously 'saved'
forest areas. The lack of precise information on areas that are about to be cut and a
range of monitoring and administrative difficulties between parties involved make
it impossible to design a perfectly targeted instrument. In the contrarian case of
complete absence of information on deforestation pressure, a global forest carbon
conservation program aiming at avoiding half of baseline deforestation would

Table 3.1 Scenarios of forest biomass saved according to financial mechanism

Region	Deforestation baseline (GtC)	Incentive payment of US$6/tC/5yr	Carbon tax		
			US$9/tC (slashburn)	US$25/tC (timber sales)	US$12/tC (sale/ burn)
			Carbon savings (GtC/20yr)		
Asia	2.19	1.49	1.50	1.41	1.32
Australia	0.22	0.06	0.03	0.12	0.17
Caribbean	0.02	0.02	0.01	0.02	0.01
Europe	0.02	0.00	0.00	0.00	0.02
Latin America	6.22	2.75	2.55	2.65	3.02
North Africa	0.00	0.00	0.00	0.00	0.00
North America	0.04	0.00	0.00	0.00	0.00
Pacific	0.00	0.00	0.00	0.00	0.00
Sub-Saharan Africa	8.82	4.90	4.77	4.67	4.08
Sum	**17.54**	**9.22**	**8.86**	**8.85**	**8.63**

Source: Authors

require financial resources in the much higher order of US$197 billion in 2006 and US$188 billion in 2025 (i.e. on average US$6/tC/5yrs; see Table 3.1). In reality, costs would lie somewhere between these two extremes of perfect information and total absence of information on deforestation locations. Using the more realistic assumption of targeted payments to (legally entitled) deforestation agents in areas (grid cells) of high deforestation pressure, average annual costs were calculated at an estimated US$33.5 billion per year.[2]

Carbon tax schemes do not suffer as much from an information problem, as global earth observation systems can already detect deforestation with some degree of reliability. In tax scenarios, e.g. simulated introduction of a forest clearance tax, an average carbon tax of US$9/tC would reduce emissions from deforestation by half if we assume deforestation by slash and burn. If the carbon from the harvested wood is assumed to be temporarily sequestered in a timber products pool, a timber sales tax of US$25/tC would have a similar effect. In practice, these two taxes would be additional, i.e. a timber sales tax on top of a land clearance tax. Revenues from such carbon taxes on deforestation would result in annual revenues in the magnitude of US$5.9 billion in 2006, declining to US$4.2 billion in 2025 (Table 3.1 and Figure 3.1). Results from the scenario analysis show that almost independent of the financial mechanism (incentive payments or tax), more than half (53 per cent) of all forest carbon that would be saved via the mechanisms would be located in sub-Saharan Africa, 30 per cent in Latin America and 16 per cent in Asia.

The 'deforestation baseline' in Table 3.1 shows the amount of forest biomass (in GtC) lost through deforestation over the coming 20 years. The columns headed 'Incentive payment' and 'Carbon tax' give the amount of avoided deforestation in GtC per 20 years at the price and tax levels indicated. Slashburn and timber sales assume that 100 per cent of the biomass will either be burned on the spot or stored in a harvested wood products pool respectively. Sale/burn is a more realistic and geographically differentiated combination of slashburn and the wood products pool. The share is region specific, based on empirical evidence of region-specific deforestation drivers (FAO, 2006; Geist and Lambin, 2002).

The upper section of Figure 3.1 shows the geography of baseline deforestation up to 2025 assuming no carbon policy (no incentive payments, no tax) and the lower figure illustrates the carbon saved assuming a carbon tax of US$12/tC on deforestation. The lower section shows that large areas could be saved from deforestation if a carbon price of US$12/tC is introduced, which would, in effect, reduce deforestation by half.

Funding sources and tailoring funding mechanisms

As stated earlier, the model calculates that incentive payments needed to cut deforestation in half would require annual payments of at least US$33.5 billion. This would require funds that are more than double the total annual global investment in forestry, currently estimated at around US$18 billion (Tomaselli, 2006). Only a small fraction of the current investment in forestry is non-domestic, i.e. private foreign direct investment or official development assistance (ODA) or official aid (OA). According to the United Nations Conference on Trade and Development, worldwide foreign direct investment (FDI) in agriculture, forestry, hunting and fishing activities combined reached US$1.8 billion in the period 2001–2003, i.e. US$600 million per year, most of which is dedicated to agriculture (UNCTAD, 2005). Recent data from the Organization for Economic Cooperation and Development (OECD, 2005) on total ODA/OA commitments to forestry by OECD countries and multilateral agencies show an annual average commitment to forestry of US$564 million between 1996 and 2004. Even if all current FDI and ODA funding for forestry combined could be redirected to reduce emissions from deforestation, this would reach only around 3.5 per cent of the funding required to reduce emissions from deforestation by half. Around 40 per cent of all ODA, i.e. not just including forestry, would be needed to achieve the same goal.

Financing avoided deforestation through the CDM or other climate policy-related financing mechanisms seem unlikely to be sufficient to convince deforestation agents and their respective governments to curb deforestation. In fact, given current realpolitik, international financial flows are likely to remain below 10 per cent of the US$33.5 billion needed to cut deforestation in half in the foreseeable future. For instance, in 2007 the overall value of the global aggregated carbon markets was estimated at over US$64 billion (Capoor and Ambrosi, 2008), up from US$10 billion in 2005 (Capoor and Ambrosi, 2006). Around 847 MtCO$_2$e (corresponding to 231 MtC; some 87 per cent CDM projects) were transacted at a value of US$13.6 billion[3] (Capoor and Ambrosi, 2008). Thus, even if half of the funds generated through project-based transactions had been earmarked to avoid deforestation it would have covered only some 40 per cent required to cut deforestation by the arbitrary figure of 50 per cent. In fact, some two-thirds of CDM projects in volume terms are related to energy efficiency and renewable energy and only 0.1 per cent are agroforestry projects.

Table 3.2 Domestic and international financial policy instruments targeting deforestation

Funding	Incentives type	Tax type
International	ODA funding support to national 'avoided deforestation' policies Carbon credits trading	International agreements: payment above negotiated 'accepted' deforestation rates
Domestic	'Avoided deforestation' policies financed through subsidies Redistributive budget schemes Environmental services payment	Land clearance tax Timber sales tax Non-renewable energy tax Emission tax

Source: Authors

It becomes apparent that existing international sources and mechanisms, including carbon trading, can only contribute to a limited extent to fund avoided deforestation. Thus, contrary to the expectations of many in the policy debate, climate policy will not be the silver bullet that solves the deforestation problem. A wide range of existing and new instruments is needed, both international and domestic (Table 3.2). Given the magnitude of funding required compared to existing funding it is unlikely that the financial resources needed could be mobilized through the current international ODA system or that alternative international funding sources could be quickly identified and mechanisms established. Given that domestic investments are a magnitude higher than international investment flows in forestry, it seems that 'bailout' hopes should not be pinned on international financial mechanisms – or at least not on the international mechanisms alone. Possibly the most important share of financial resources will have to be generated first and foremost from domestic sources. Obviously, developing countries cannot be expected to generate sufficient funding alone, particularly in Africa and parts of Asia. International funding will be needed, particularly to develop and support national mechanisms.

Incentive-type instruments as designed here provide GHG-related revenues to holders of rights for deforestation, while tax-type instruments would create costs to potential deforestation agents. Domestic financial incentives need to be based on programmes that target and are adjusted to diverse and often small-scale local and regional deforestation and forest degradation contexts. Such incentives need to address and reach people that drive forest cover changes because of subsistence needs such as food, energy or living space, be it legal or unauthorized. Decentralized and smaller scale redistributive financial mechanisms that work on a national and sub-national scale and are supported through international funds pose many problems, including transaction costs and leakage of funds. However, a large pool of experience is available on how to address small-scale diversity and needs, such as through micro-finance infrastructures and payments for environmental services of forests (Maynard and Paquin, 2004; Pagiola *et al.*, 2005; see also Part III of this volume).

Existing international incentive channels, including bilateral and multilateral

ODA and specific funds, such as the global environment facility (GEF), can be used to fund baskets of national measures aimed to address local and regional drivers of deforestation. If the annual amount of total ODA spent on forestry were tripled from 2004 levels to US$1.6 billion, i.e. from 0.7 per cent to 2.1 per cent of total annual ODA, the model calculates that this would result in 1.7GtC of saved carbon corresponding to an area avoided from deforestation of 26.5 million ha. In addition, existing and emerging carbon credit-based transfer schemes with appropriate rules to channel funds from larger scale (e.g. CDM-type) projects towards avoided deforestation could emerge, given appropriate policy signals (Victor *et al.*, 2005).

Tax-type payments based on international agreements seem to be difficult to negotiate now and in the future. On the domestic (national) level, redistributive financial mechanisms, such as taxing land clearance and timber sales in combination with earmarked rerouting of revenues to promote financing of forest conservation and sustainable forest management programmes, might turn out to be the most effective policy instrument to address deforestation. Given that in practice the by far largest proportion of forests is government owned (FAO, 2006), domestic taxes such as for land clearance or timber sales by local levels of government or forest management concession holders could be established. In addition, tax income from private land clearance and timber sales could be channelled back to keeping other forests standing. However, tax collection and redistribution systems are notoriously difficult to operate effectively in situations with low levels of government enforcement capacity and weak private property rights. This, however, is a common situation in exactly those areas where deforestation pressure is the highest.

Conclusion

Reducing emissions from deforestation, a major source of CO_2, could potentially be a highly cost-effective option for climate policy. Comparatively low amounts of financial flows could save millions of hectares from deforestation. Equally important is that, if appropriately spent, such financial flows would be a highly welcome tool to help reduce poverty by improving livelihoods of some of the hundreds of millions forest-dependent people in the developing world and secure many forest ecosystem services. However, it appears that only a fraction of the funding needed, the latter estimated in the magnitude of US$33 billion per year, can be realized in the context of climate policies. A basket of financial mechanisms will be needed to properly address the deforestation challenge.

Notes

1   FCCC/CD/2005?misc.1 11 November 2005.
2   For more on targeted payments, see Engel *et al.*, and Alix Garcia *et al.*, Chapters 12 and 13, respectively, in this volume.
3   European Union allowances (EUAs) worth US$50 billion were traded in 2007, up from US$8.2 billion in 2005 (Capoor and Ambrosi, 2008 and 2006, respectively).

References

Alix-Garcia, J., de Janvry, A., and Sadoulet, E. (2009) 'The role of risk in targeting payments for environmental services', in C. Palmer and S. Engel (eds) *Avoided Deforestation: Prospects for Mitigating Climate Change*, London: Routledge.

Angelsen, A. and Kaimowitz, D. (1999) 'Rethinking the causes of deforestation: lessons from economic models', *World Bank Research Observer*, 14(1): 73–98.

Benítez, P.C. and Obersteiner, M. (2006) 'Site identification for carbon sequestration in Latin America: a grid-based economic approach', *Forest Policy and Economics*, (8)6: 636–651.

Capoor, K. and Ambrosi, P. (2006) *State and Trends of the Carbon Market 2006*, Washington, DC: World Bank and International Emissions Trading Association.

Capoor, K. and Ambrosi, P. (2008) *State and Trends of the Carbon Market 2008*, Washington, DC: World Bank and International Emissions Trading Association.

Engel, S., Wünscher, T. and Wunder, S. (2009) 'Increasing the efficiency of forest conservation: the case of payments for environmental services in Costa Rica', in C. Palmer and S. Engel (eds) *Avoided Deforestation: Prospects for Mitigating Climate Change*, London: Routledge.

FAO (Food and Agriculture Organization of the United Nations) (2006) *Global Forest Resources Assessment 2005. Progress Towards Sustainable Forest Management*, FAO Forestry Paper 147, Rome: FAO.

Fearnside, P.M. (2006) 'Mitigation of climatic change in the Amazon', in W. F. Laurance and C.A. Peres (eds) *Emerging Threats to Tropical Forests*, Chicago: University of Chicago Press.

Geist, H.J. and Lambin, E.F. (2002) 'Proximate causes and underlying driving forces of tropical deforestation', *BioScience*, 52(2): 143–150.

Gullison, R.E, Frumhoff, P.C., Canadell, J.G., Field, C.B., Nepstad, D.C., Hayhoe, K. *et al.* (2007) 'Tropical forests and climate policy', *Science*, 316(5825): 985–986.

IPCC (Intergovernmental Panel on Climate Change) (2007) *Climate Change: Synthesis Report*, New York: Cambridge University Press.

Kindermann, G., Obersteiner, M., Rametsteiner, E. and McCallum, I. (2006) 'Predicting the deforestation-trend under different carbon-prices', *Carbon Balance and Management*, 1(15): 17.

Kindermann, G., Obersteiner, M., Sohngen, B., Sathaye, J., Andrasko, K., Rametsteiner, E. *et al.* (2008) 'Global cost estimates of reducing carbon emissions through avoided deforestation', *Proceedings of the National Academy of Sciences of the United States of America*.

Maynard, K. and Paquin, M. (2004) *Payments for Environmental Services: A Survey and Assessment of Current Schemes*, Montreal: Unisféra International Centre for the Commission for Environmental Cooperation of North America.

Moutinho, P., Santilli, M., Schwartzman, S. and Rodrigues, L. (2006) 'Why ignore tropical deforestation? A proposal for including forest conservation in the Kyoto Protocol', *Unasylva*, 222(56): 27–30.

OECD (Organization for Economic Cooperation and Development) (2005) 'Efforts and policies of the members of the development assistance committee', *Journal on Development*, 7(1), Paris: Organization for Economic Cooperation and Development (OECD).

Pagiola, S., Arcenas, A. and Platais, G. (2005) 'Can payments for environmental services help reduce poverty? An exploration of the issues and the evidence to date from Latin America', *World Development*, 33(2): 237–253.

Persson, U.M. and Azar, C. (2006) 'Tropical deforestation in a future international climate policy regime – lessons from the Brazilian Amazon', *Environmental Conservation*, 12(7): 1277–1304.

Schaeffer, R., Rodrigues, R.L.V., Laurance, W.F., Albernaz, A.K.M., Fearnside, P.M., Vasconcelos, H.L. *et al.* (2005) 'Underlying causes of deforestation', *Science*, 307(5712): 1046–1047.

Schulze, E.D., Mollicone, D., Achard, F., Matteucci, G., Federici, S., Hugh, D.E. *et al.* (2003) 'Climate change: making deforestation pay under the Kyoto protocol?', *Science Policy Forum*, 299(5613): 1669–1683.

Soares-Filho, B.S., Nepstad, D.C., Curran, L.M., Cerqueira, G.C., Garcia, R.A., Ramos, C.A. *et al.* (2006) 'Modelling conservation in the Amazon Basin', *Nature*, 440: 520–523.

Tomaselli, I. (2006) *Brief Study on Funding and Finance for Forestry and Forest-based Sector*, report to the United Nations Forum on Forests Secretariat, New York: United Nations.

UNCTAD (United Nations Conference on Trade and Development) (2005) *World Investment Report 2005*, New York and Geneva: United Nations Conference on Trade and Development.

UNFCCC (United Nations Framework Convention on Climate Change) (2005) *Reducing Emissions from Deforestation in Developing Countries: Approaches to Stimulate Action*, submissions from parties [online]. Available at: http://unfccc.int/resource/docs/2005/cop11/eng/misc01.pdf [accessed 15 June 2008]; draft conclusions proposed by the president [online]. Available at: http://unfccc.int/resource/docs/2005/cop11/eng/l02.pdf [accessed 15 June 2008].

UNFCCC (United Nations Framework Convention on Climate Change) (2007) *Decision-/CP.13 Bali Action Plan* [online]. Available at: http://unfccc.int/files/meetings/cop_13/application/pdf/cp_bali_action.pdf [accessed 15 June 2008].

Victor, D.G., House, J.C. and Joy, S. (2005) 'A Madisonian approach to climate policy', *Science*, 309(5742): 1820–1821.

Williams, M. (2003) *Deforesting the Earth – From Prehistory to Global Crisis*, Chicago: University of Chicago Press.

World Bank (2007) 'Worldwide governance indicators: 1996–2006', *Governance Matters 2007*, Washington, DC: World Bank.

4 Assessing the economic potential for reducing deforestation in developing countries

Brent Sohngen

Introduction

Forestry has widely been considered by policymakers as a low cost option for reducing net greenhouse gas emissions into the atmosphere. The basic idea, as described elsewhere in this volume, is that an increase in the stock of forests or forest products (either absolutely or in comparison to a baseline) constitutes a reduction in carbon in the atmosphere. The current, global stock of carbon in forests is estimated to be around 860 GtC (1 Gt = 1 Pg = $1 \cdot 10^{15}$ grams) and current rates of deforestation suggest that it could be declining by 0.7–1.2 GtC per year over the coming decades (Metz *et al.*, 2007). Most of these losses are projected to occur in developing countries located in Africa, South America and Southeast Asia. While it is widely recognized that reductions in the rate of deforestation would increase the stock of carbon in forests, and reduce emissions to the atmosphere (Soares-Filho *et al.*, 2006), there is relatively little information available on what the costs of avoiding this deforestation may be.

This chapter examines the potential cost of achieving reductions in deforestation and consequently reductions in carbon emissions to the atmosphere. It focuses on actions undertaken in developing countries, using an economic model of global timber markets and land use to assess the potential costs (for a description of the model, see Sohngen and Mendelsohn, 2003; Sohngen and Sedjo, 2006). Large-scale, global economic models are useful for examining the costs of carbon sequestration for a number of reasons. First, they account for market adjustments and interactions that occur when policy actions are undertaken. For example, if carbon policy increases the stock of forests (and carbon), then the supply of timber will increase in the future, the price of timber will decline and these changes in price will affect the costs of avoiding deforestation. Second, they account for the opportunity costs of shifting land out of agricultural production and into forests. Most of the deforestation currently occurring, and expected to occur in the next 20–50 years, will result from the conversion of forestland to agricultural land (either crops or grazing land). It is important to account for the opportunity costs associated with reducing the amount of agricultural land. Further, it is important to account for the idea that these costs will increase as more and more land is utilized for forests rather than agriculture. Third, they account for regional differences in the quantity of carbon and the opportunity costs of maintaining land in forests. Differences in both the carbon content of forests and the value of forestland across regions may have important implications for when and particularly where carbon sequestration can be undertaken efficiently.

In addition to reducing deforestation, there are many other actions in forestry that can be undertaken to increase the stock of carbon in forests or products. These include afforestation (which has been much more widely considered in the context of the Kyoto Protocol), changes in forest management and storage of carbon in forest products. The model utilized in this chapter accounts for some of these other actions. Their associated costs will be examined to provide an assessment of the relative costs of avoided emissions from reduced deforestation versus the costs of carbon sequestration via more traditional methods of afforestation and enhanced forest management.

This chapter focuses on presenting results from a single global model of forestry and land use. The model assumes that forestry actions can be undertaken efficiently (e.g., with few transaction costs), that baselines can be established, that carbon gains can be measured, monitored, and paid for, and, finally, that leakage can be controlled. Of course, setting actual policies is more complicated than simply providing results from a model. Thus, the chapter also discusses these implementation issues in light of the results.

The chapter is organized as follows. It begins with a general discussion about deforestation in the tropics. Within this section, the global forestry and land-use model utilized in the chapter is described briefly. Next, the results of an analysis of carbon sequestration options are presented. The options focus on different price scenarios for carbon. The chapter then concludes by discussing limitations of the analysis, focusing on the issues raised in the chapter – baselines, measuring and monitoring and leakage.

Potential deforestation in tropical countries

Deforestation is an ongoing process dependent largely on demographic and economic forces. In the developing regions of South and Central America, Africa, and Southeast Asia, deforestation mostly results from expansion of the agricultural frontier, driven by the demand for land and changes in productivity in the agricultural sector. Over time, most economists expect that productivity in agricultural sectors will continue to increase (Ludena *et al.*, 2007), but that it will not rise quickly enough to offset the demand for additional land used in the crop and livestock sectors.

The economic model used for this analysis is the one utilized by Sohngen and Sedjo (2006) and Sohngen and Mendelsohn (2007). The model maximizes the present value of the economic gains to consumers and producers in the forestry sector. Forestry has to compete with the agricultural sector for land within the model. The model represents agricultural demand for land in all regions through a series of upward sloping land rental functions. In the initial period, the elasticity of these land rental functions is assumed to be 0.25, such that a 1 per cent increase in forestry land rental rates will increase the area of forestland by 0.25 per cent. In developed countries, these land supply functions are assumed to be constant over time, while in developing countries, they are assumed to shift inward over time. These assumptions have important implications for the future path of land-use change projected by the model. The inward shift in the land supply functions in developing countries is due to the assumption that the demand for land in agriculture in those countries is increasing over time, for example, the opportunity costs associated with holding land in forests rather than converting them to agriculture increase. For developed countries, the demand for agricultural land is assumed to be stable over time. As a consequence, additional land will be converted to agriculture in tropical countries unless forestland rental values increase enough to offset these rising opportunity costs. In developed countries, land-use change will depend entirely on changes in forestland rental rates. If they are increasing, the land area in forests will increase and if they are decreasing the land area in forests will decrease.

When carbon becomes a valued commodity, the value of standing and newly planted forests will increase. Thus, in the scenarios analyzed in this chapter, different carbon prices are postulated and the model projects a different pathway for deforestation. In the baseline, carbon prices are assumed to be US\$0/tC. When the carbon price is positive and markets can use forestry credits as offsets, the area of land deforested each year declines. It is important to recognize that the model does not account for measuring, monitoring and verification costs. In addition, we assume that all forests are effectively enrolled in the programme and paid appropriately so that leakage does not occur. All of these issues are, of course, important and it will be important to develop methods to account for the entire costs of developing programmes to reduce deforestation.

Baseline deforestation in the tropical regions modelled in this research is projected to be 13.1 million hectares per year over the period 2005 to 2015 (Figure 4.1).[1] Rates of deforestation are projected to decline over time, as demand for land by the agricultural sector is assumed to slow down due to slower population expansion and continuing improvements in technology (Nin *et al.*, 2003). For example, rising crop yields could reduce the demand for new land to be used in agriculture. While a large area of land is lost to deforestation each year, the net loss of forests is smaller in total due to afforestation of old agriculture or pasture lands. The model projects a net loss of around 11.8 million hectares per year in tropical forest regions over the next 10 years. Deforestation is consequently projected to add around 1.5 GtC to the atmosphere each year over the next 10 years and, when reforestation is considered, to lead to net losses of 1.4 GtC per year. Over the next 50 years, the trend in deforestation shown in Figure 4.1 leads to a cumulative loss of 56 GtC of carbon from forests in the tropical regions modelled. Of this total, 19 GtC result from deforestation in Africa, 17 GtC from South America, 16 GtC from Southeast Asia and 4 GtC from Central America.

These estimates are roughly consistent with many other estimates of tropical deforestation from the recent past. Dixon *et al.* (1994), for example, suggest that the net effects of deforestation may lead to emissions of up to 0.9 GtC per year for the entire world. DeFries *et al.* (2006) and Potter *et al.* (2003) also estimate a net global

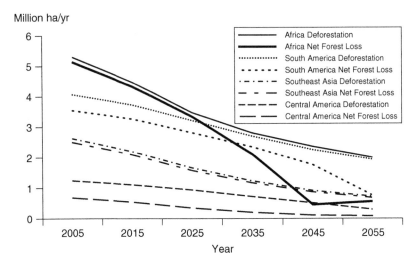

Figure 4.1 Baseline change in land use in tropical regions projected by the global forestry and agricultural model

Source: Sohngen *et al.* (2008)

emission of around 0.9 GtC per year, while Achard *et al.* (2002) suggest that 1.1 GtC per year are emitted from deforestation. A study by Houghton (2003) indicates potentially far larger net emissions from deforestation of 2.2 GtC per year during the 1990s. The results of these studies are based on forest inventory data and changes in land uses observed through satellites or by other means. Gurney *et al.* (2002) use different methods (a so-called inversion model), but they find consistent numbers for deforestation in the tropics (1.2 GtC per year of emissions).

Costs of reducing emissions by avoiding deforestation

To assess the potential for reducing emissions by avoiding deforestation, we implement a carbon-pricing policy within the economic model. There are two important issues related to this. First, it is important to clearly identify what and who will be credited, and, second, it is important to clearly identify how the carbon will be paid. For the first issue, we assume that additional carbon gained above the baseline is credited and we use as our baseline the deforestation trajectories (and resulting carbon trajectories) shown in Figure 4.1. From the perspective of policymakers, different schemes for setting baselines could be established. For example, policymakers might assume that current deforestation rates continue indefinitely so that all future reductions in deforestation measured relative to current rates of deforestation are credited. While an alternative baseline would have important implications for the total costs of the carbon sequestration policy, it does not change the marginal cost estimates produced in this chapter (e.g., the cost of the last ton sequestered as a result of the deforestation policy). This point is discussed later in the chapter when considering the effects of different crediting schemes on the overall costs of the programme.

Identifying *who* is credited is important as well. For this analysis, a global policy that credits all deviations from the baseline is assumed. Thus, at the same time we are crediting reductions in deforestation in tropical countries, we are also crediting afforestation, changes in rotation ages, enhanced management and storage in forest product pools that occur in tropical regions, as well as other regions of the world. The results thus are inclusive (or net) of leakage by ensuring that all actions that enhance carbon in forests or products are credited and those that reduce carbon are debited. While we do account for the effects of carbon policies implemented globally, most of the results in the chapter focus only on the regions where deforestation is a dominant issue, namely South America, Central America, Africa and Southeast Asia.

The second issue just raised relates to pricing for carbon. In the context of this study, it is assumed that carbon prices are given by the market and for the first set of scenarios, it is assumed that they are fixed for the entire time period of analysis. The constant carbon prices range from US$5/tC to US$100/tC (US$1.36/tCO$_2$ to US$27.25/tCO$_2$). While a rather strong assumption, constant prices simplify the analysis. Within the analysis, we assume that new and additional carbon is rented during the period it is held in the forest. The annual rental rate, when carbon prices are constant, is given as:

$$R_C = r \cdot P_C$$

where R_C is the rental rate for carbon (the annual value paid per tC for holding carbon in the ecosystem), r is the interest rate and P_C is the price of carbon. In addition to the rental of carbon stored in forests, carbon stored permanently in forest products is paid the carbon price, P_C, at the time the forest is harvested.

One could, of course, choose alternative payment schemes, such as the optimal subsidy and tax recommended by van Kooten *et al.* (1995). This proposal would pay the carbon price, P_C, for each annual increment in carbon (as opposed to renting the stock) and would tax each ton emitted at harvest time at the same rate. The marginal incentives in the rental scheme and the subsidy/tax scheme are exactly the same in the model (e.g., see Sohngen and Sedjo, 2006). In addition to considering the fixed price scenarios, a set of scenarios is considered with rising prices. For the rising price scenarios, we utilize the subsidy and tax programme.

Results

The first set of results presented here examines the relative efficiency (in terms of carbon sequestration) of reductions in deforestation versus afforestation versus improvements or adjustments in the management of existing timber stocks. Results from the model utilized in this study suggest that reductions in deforestation have substantially lower marginal costs for reducing carbon emissions than other options in forestry (Figure 4.2). For example, for US$100/tC, the US, Canada, Europe, and Russia each can potentially sequester 0.07–0.12 GtC per year over the next 50 years by changing the management of forests. For the same price, tropical regions can potentially sequester 0.17 GtC per year with similar activities. The value in the tropics looks larger, but readers should recognize that *all* tropical regions are aggregated for the purposes of the figure. Tropical regions in the figure constitute a larger total area of forests than the individual countries, so it makes sense that the marginal cost function for the tropics lies to the right of the other regions. It is, however, surprising that the tropics cannot sequester substantially more carbon at any particular carbon price, given the additional area in tropical forests. The result in Figure 4.2(A) indicates that there are relatively few opportunities for increasing carbon through management in tropical forests in comparison to the temperature zones.

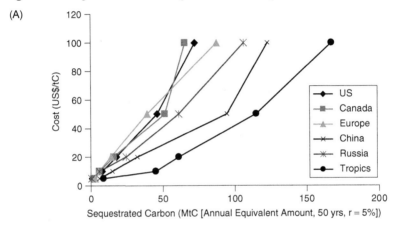

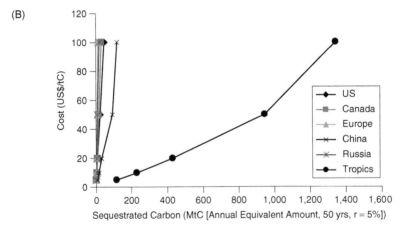

Figure 4.2 Comparison of the marginal costs of carbon sequestration through management and land-use change options regionally
(A) Marginal cost of carbon sequestration from aging forests, enhancing management, and setting forests aside from timber production and land-use change
(B) Marginal cost of carbon sequestration from afforestation or reduced deforestation

Source: Sohngen *et al.* (2008)

Reducing deforestation can potentially lead to carbon benefits of 1.4 GtC per year in tropical forests for the same US$100/tC carbon price. This is over eight times as much as is possible through management actions in the same set of tropical countries. By contrast, conducting afforestation projects in developed countries, which has been widely accepted in policy regimes, provides relatively high cost carbon. For US$100/tC, only 0.12–0.48 GtC per year can be sequestered through afforestation in the regions shown in Figure 4.2(B). This relatively low number for afforestation reflects the fairly high cost of land in those regions, combined with slower growing forests. Reduced deforestation has a relatively immediate impact on the atmosphere and land values are generally lower in tropical regions.

Costs will vary by region according to a number of factors, including opportunity costs of land (the value of agricultural and forestry land), the carbon density in forests and other locally specific factors. The costs of agricultural land are influenced by the types of crop grown, the markets they serve, the technologies used in production and other factors. Within the context of the model used for this chapter, the lowest cost opportunities for reducing deforestation are found in Africa, followed by South America, Southeast Asia, and Central America (Figure 4.3). One important reason for this is that land rental values are assumed to be lowest in Africa. For US$100/tC, deforestation could be reduced by up to 3.2 million hectares per year in Africa, 3.0 million hectares per year in South America, 1.5 million hectares per year in Southeast Asia and 0.6 million hectares per year in Central America (see Figure 4.3).

When the marginal cost curves of Figure 4.3(A) are translated so that 'area' becomes 'carbon' on the horizontal axis, the results change because the quantity of carbon obtained from reductions in deforestation in different regions differs (see Figure 4.3(B)). Forests in Southeast Asia have relatively high carbon intensities, so the marginal cost of avoided carbon emissions there is low compared to the other regions. In the model, it is assumed that the average tropical forest hectare in Southeast Asia has 130 tC, while the average hectare in South America has 119 tC, Africa has 100 tC and Central America has 83 tC (for a discussion about the carbon calculations used in the model, see Sohngen and Sedjo, 2006; Sohngen and Mendelsohn, 2007). At carbon prices of US$100/tC, the annual carbon rental value will be US$5/tC per year if interest rates are 5 per cent. This means that on average, landowners in Southeast Asia could receive up to US$650/hectare/year for carbon storage to maintain their forests rather than harvest them (US$5/tC/yr multiplied by 130 tC). Landowners in South America could receive US$595/hectare/year, while those in Africa and Central America could receive US$500/hectare/year and US$415/hectare/year, respectively. These relatively large values would provide substantial incentives to avoid deforestation.

To put these numbers in context, consider recent empirical work by Seo and Mendelsohn (2007). They surveyed farmers in Latin America and found that the average value of land in a selection of countries there ranges from US$3/hectare to US$2600/hectare, with the higher values occurring in Brazil and Argentina. These land values roughly translate into annual rental values of < US$1/hectare/year to

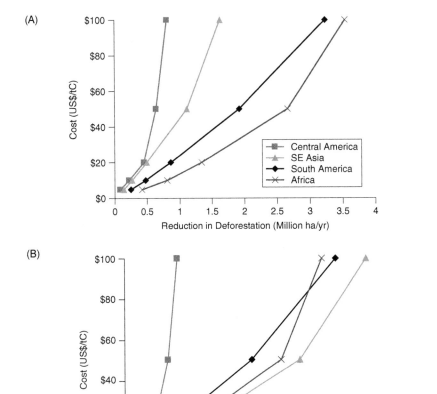

Figure 4.3 Marginal cost curves for reducing deforestation in four tropical regions
(A) Marginal cost of reducing hectares of deforestation in four tropical regions
(B) Marginal cost of reduced emissions from avoided deforestation in four trop-
ical regions

Source: Sohngen *et al.* (2008)

US$130/hectare/year at interest rates of 5 per cent. Average net revenues for the
farms sampled in that study were US$449/hectare/year. For Africa, Kurukulasuriya
and Mendelsohn (2007) found that average net revenues per hectare averaged
US$462/hectare/year, ranging from an average of US$119/hectare/year in Niger
with dryland agricultural practices to US$1660/hectare/year in Egypt with irrigated
agricultural practices. While it is difficult to translate an estimate of net revenue
directly into the value of land, these results suggest that there are many low cost
options for carbon mitigation in both Latin America and Africa.

One of the limiting assumptions in the analysis so far is that carbon prices are assumed to remain constant over time. Many economic studies, however, suggest that carbon prices are likely to rise as carbon policy becomes more stringent (see, for example, Weyant *et al.*, 2006). What happens to the potential for avoiding deforestation if carbon prices are rising over time? Four additional scenarios were considered to show carbon sequestration potential under the rising carbon price scenarios. The initial prices in these scenarios are similar to the constant price scenarios, with initial carbon prices ranging from US$3.67–110/tC. In each of these scenarios, carbon prices were assumed to rise at 5 per cent per year and capped at US$916.67/tC. These price paths are consistent with stabilization-type policies with backstop technologies providing carbon abatement at US$917/tC. From the perspective of policy focused on reducing deforestation, these alternative policies simply tell us something about how the carbon market potentially behaves under different carbon price sets.

Rising carbon prices change the time path of avoided emissions. Compared to the constant price scenarios, emission reductions are initially delayed because individuals will put off some projects in anticipation of higher future prices. Compare, for example, the US$20/tC constant price scenario and the US$18/tC rising price scenario (Figure 4.4). Under the rising price scenario, carbon prices rise to US$210/tC by 2055. If carbon prices initially are US$18/tC, but rise at 5 per cent per year, emission reductions are calculated initially to be around 200 MtC per year (where 1000 Mt = 1 Gt), but rising to around 800 MtC per year over the next 20 years. In contrast, if carbon prices initially are US$20/tC, and remain constant, emission reductions are estimated to be around 650 MtC per year and they fall over time (Figure 4.4). Under the rising carbon price scenario, deforestation has been

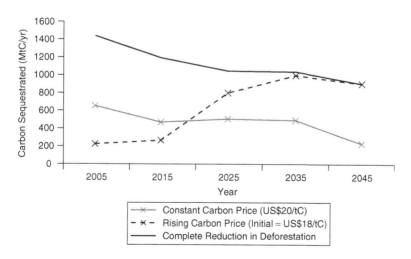

Figure 4.4 Comparison of carbon sequestration pathways under constant and rising carbon prices

Source: Author's calculations based on results originally presented in Sohngen *et al.* (2008); Sohngen and Sedjo (2006)

eliminated by 2035, while under the US$20/tC constant price scenario it takes far longer to eliminate. The rising carbon price policy achieves a larger cumulative reduction in emissions by 2055, 32 GtC versus 24 GtC, but a smaller annual equivalent (discounted) reduction in emissions, 443 MtC per year versus 542 MtC per year. These results suggest that scenarios that assume constant carbon prices overstate the potential reduction in emissions that is available initially, at least if carbon prices are rising.

It is not obvious or clear what will happen to carbon prices in the future. These results only tell us that if carbon prices are increasing, results from models assuming constant carbon prices likely overstate the quantity of carbon available at a given price (or they understate the actual marginal costs). They also tell us, not surprisingly, that higher prices in the future lead to more carbon sequestration. In general, carbon prices should rise if society decides to put more stringent controls on climate change and they should rise more strongly if society attempts to stabilize future carbon stocks in the atmosphere. Of course, these price increases are predicated on current assumptions about future technologies, which are in themselves uncertain.

These results focus largely on assessing the overall potential of reductions in deforestation and they compare reductions in deforestation to other forestry options. It is perhaps useful to provide a broader comparison with climate mitigation strategies, including reducing energy emissions, improving energy efficiency, renewable energy resources and carbon capture and storage. To compare these many options, it is necessary to include carbon sinks and reduced deforestation in the types of energy models that are widely used to analyze policy options available to the entire economy. Only a few studies to date have done this. Sohngen and Mendelsohn (2003) linked the forestry model utilized thus far in this chapter with the DICE model of Nordhaus and Boyer (2000). That research indicated that along an efficient climate abatement path, forestry could accomplish around 30 per cent of the global mitigation effort. A large proportion of this mitigation by forestry resulted from reductions in deforestation. The price of carbon they examined, however, ranged only from US$6–20/tC in 2000, to US$60–187/tC in 2100, suggesting that the efficient policy is not very stringent.

A more stringent policy was examined by Tavoni *et al.* (2007), who also utilized the forestry model in this study, but linked it with a different energy model, the WITCH model (Bosetti *et al.*, 2006). Tavoni *et al.* considered the cost-effective policies that would be necessary to stabilize carbon concentrations at 550 parts per million. They included forestry as an option. These authors also found that forestry could have substantial consequences for global climate change mitigation policy. In their model, annual reductions in deforestation provided around 0.7 GtC of mitigation efforts per year in the next 20 years, compared to around 0.1 GtC of mitigation efforts over the same time period through afforestation and forest management in the temperate and boreal zones. The cumulative reduction in emissions by forestry by 2050 was calculated to be 65 billion tons C, compared to around 130 billion tons C abated by the energy sector. A comparison of stabilization scenarios with and without the inclusion of forest carbon sinks was made. Global carbon prices were reduced by around 40 per cent with forest carbon sinks compared to a stabilization policy that utilized energy options alone. One of the more widely considered options for mitigation is carbon capture and storage – the idea that carbon gases can be captured from flue gases and then stored in deep wells for long periods of time. By 2050 carbon capture and storage amounts to around 1 GtC per year in Tavoni *et al.* (2007). While this is a large amount of carbon, it is worth noting that reductions in deforestation achieve similar levels of annual sequestration (0.7 GtC per year), albeit earlier, and at lower carbon prices.

Policy considerations

The results from the modelling exercise just examined tell us that reductions in deforestation are competitive with other carbon abatement options and they are the most competitive forestry or land-use option. It is often assumed in models that forestry options can be easily and cheaply measured, that individual actors will have no incentive to cheat and that leakage can be controlled. All of these assumptions will be difficult to achieve in reality and, thus, the carbon programme may be more expensive than suggested earlier. Carbon is difficult to measure. Individuals will have incentives to cheat by providing less carbon that they claim if they are not carefully audited and subjected to fines when they are caught cheating. Leakage will occur and it will be difficult to control. It is useful, therefore, to consider how some of these policy issues potentially affect the results described earlier.

Setting the baseline and additionality

An issue often raised in policy debates relates to establishing the baseline (see also Harris *et al.*, Chapter 10 in this volume). The baseline is the agreed on amount of carbon that would be released from a given area that is likely to be deforested in the absence of climate policy. Baselines are important because they set the basis for future measurement and crediting. The baseline establishes how much the landowner, or a country, can receive. Baselines are difficult to create because the discussion about a baseline is a discussion about property rights, for example, the quantity of carbon credits a country can claim from reducing deforestation and a discussion about what will happen in the future. Ultimately, the decision over the baseline affects the value embodied in the carbon maintained on the land.

From the perspective of the modelling exercise conducted earlier, the baseline for deforestation is affected by assumptions made about the agricultural and forestry sectors. If one assumes that agricultural rents rise more rapidly over time, so that more deforestation occurs in the baseline, then the estimates of the costs of avoiding deforestation would increase (see Sohngen and Sedjo, 2006). The baseline in a model assumes that policymakers can 'see' the correct baseline and set policy based on this 'true' baseline. The baseline used in the modelling effort reflects a different issue than the one that policymakers face when they are trying to choose how to set the baseline for a particular project or country. When choosing a baseline for the purposes of an actual programme, policymakers are deciding what will be considered 'additional' carbon. Unlike the modeller, they are faced with the problem of not knowing what the future will actually bring. Whatever decision is made, it does not necessarily reflect the actual gain in carbon relative to the actual baseline that would have emerged without the project or programme.[2] The policy choice over the baseline affects the total amount paid out to the country or to landowners. A more generous baseline, obviously, will increase the total payments that landowners receive.

One way to choose a baseline is to utilize a projection based on an economic model, such as the baselines shown in Figure 4.1 for various regions. Many countries are likely to want to develop their own baselines with more specific local data and knowledge of markets and the drivers of deforestation. For the purposes of this discussion, however, assume that the projections in Figure 4.1 are the generally accepted baselines for policy purposes. The figure suggests that deforestation declines over time in all regions of the world.[3] If the countries in these regions obtain credits for reductions in deforestation, this baseline implies that the new credits they receive will decline over time simply because fewer and fewer hectares are being deforested each year. Thus, if carbon prices are a constant US$20/tC, then South American countries would obtain US$2.9 billion per year during the following decade for reducing deforestation from 4.04 to 2.85 million hectares per year. Carbon emissions with this reduction in deforestation would decline in the first decade from 428 to 283 MtC per year (the 283 MtC per year is derived from the 428 MtC per year initial emission minus the 145 MtC per year emission reduction resulting from the policy; see Table 4.1, Panel A). Because of the baseline emissions decline, countries in South America would only obtain US$2.0 billion per year by 2024, and US$1.7 billion per year by 2044 (see Table 4.1, Panel A). The question of how one would measure and monitor progress towards meeting this baseline is discussed later in this chapter.

As an alternative, policymakers could make a simpler assumption and assume that deforestation will remain constant over time at some given rate. An example of a constant baseline is the concept of a *baseline year*, where a single year is chosen for the baseline. A constant baseline means that regions or countries where deforestation rates are likely to decline over time, for example, South America, will get larger credits in the future for reductions in deforestation as compared to the case of a decreasing baseline. That is, if deforestation declines anyway, because of the choice of a single baseline year for future crediting, they will get credited for reductions that would have happened anyway. Table 4.1 (Panel B) shows baseline year deforestation rates and carbon emissions in columns 1 and 2, followed by the change in annual deforestation rates and carbon emissions with the US$20/tC payment compared to the baseline year in columns 3 and 4. Since deforestation rates would have been increasing over time, a policy that uses a baseline year looks like it provides increasing reductions in deforestation each decade because the reductions are measured relative to the baseline year.

In this example, countries in South America will get credit not only for reductions that they actually try to obtain through policy, but also for reductions that would have occurred anyway. That is by choosing this alternative baseline,

Table 4.1 Comparison of carbon credits, reduction in deforestation and costs for the modelled baseline approach (Panel A) and the baseline year approach (Panel B), for South America only, 2005–2055

Column	1	2	3	4	5	6
			Panel A			
Time period	*Actual baseline*		*Scenario with US$20/tC*			
	Deforestation (million ha/yr)	*Carbon emission (MtC/yr)*	*Change in deforestation (million ha/yr)*	*Change in carbon emission (MtC/yr)*	*Total payments (billion US$/yr)*	*Actual carbon gain (MtC/yr)*
2005–2014	4.0	428.1	1.2	145.3	2.91	145.3
2015–2024	3.7	401.3	1.0	121.2	2.42	121.2
2025–2034	3.2	350.0	0.8	100.0	2.00	100.0
2035–2044	2.7	297.6	0.7	87.1	1.74	87.1
2045–2054	2.2	252.7	0.7	82.5	1.65	82.5
Annual equivalent costs (billion US$)					2.45	

			Panel B			
Time period	*Baseline year*		*Scenario with US$20/tC*			
	Deforestation (million ha/yr)	*Carbon emission (MtC/yr)*	*Change in deforestation (million ha/yr)*	*Change in carbon emission (MtC/yr)*	*Total payments (billion US$/yr)*	*Actual carbon gain (MtC/yr)*
2005–2014	4.0	428.1	1.2	145.3	2.91	145.3
2015–2024	4.0	428.1	1.3	148.0	2.96	121.2
2025–2034	4.0	428.1	1.6	178.1	3.56	100.0
2035–2044	4.0	428.1	2.1	217.6	4.35	87.1
2045–2054	4.0	428.1	2.5	258.0	5.16	82.5
Annual equivalent costs (billion US$)					3.30	

Source: Author's calculations based on original results in Sohngen *et al.* (2007)

Note
Panel A represents estimates assuming that the baseline is the model projection for the model used in the chapter. Panel B represents estimates assuming a baseline year.

policymakers would have allowed crediting for carbon that is not actually additional. This is seen by column 5, which shows the actual gain in carbon. The actual gain in carbon in this case is the difference between the true baseline (assuming that the modelled baseline is the true baseline) and the carbon emissions with the policy. The actual gain in carbon in the case of using a baseline year, or a constant baseline, is the same as if the true baseline had been known and used (e.g., the case in Panel A of Table 4.1). From the perspective of the policy, one appears to be gaining 178 MtC per year in 2025, but because baseline rates would have declined anyway, society would actually only be gaining 100 MtC per year.

In general, if deforestation rates are declining, using a constant baseline or a baseline year overstates gains and increases payments to the country. This can be seen with the higher level of overall payments in Panel B of Table 4.1 compared to Panel A. The opposite would be true if one used a baseline year and deforestation rates were growing in the baseline. Obviously, it is unlikely that policymakers would fix a specific baseline deforestation rate and use it for a 50-year period, but the example is used to illustrate the point that a discussion about baselines is mainly a discussion about property rights.[4] A discussion about property rights in turn is mainly a discussion about how much a country will gain (or lose) out of a specific policy.

Another alternative is to project deforestation rates forward based on rates from some historical past. This is just a different projection than that provided by the model used in this chapter and shown in Panel A of Table 4.1. It may be simpler, but similarly to using a baseline year, all it influences are the total carbon payments a country can get from the policy. It is not possible to say whether this method is better or worse than using a model. It only reflects a different set of assumptions about how deforestation will unfold in the future.

This comparison of several baselines raises an interesting point about baselines and additionality. Negotiating a baseline is a step that ultimately determines what individual actors, which include countries, carbon project developers, or others who stand to benefit from projects, will obtain. This means that all these parties will have incentives to advocate for using the method that will benefit them the most. Policymakers must carefully choose the methodologies used to determine baselines in order to limit the adverse incentives that this decision may cause.

While it is always possible to project deforestation rates into the future (see Harris *et al.*, Chapter 10 in this volume), knowing the actual rate in advance is obviously impossible. For actual policy setting, it is implausible to rely on projections that go too far into the future, say more than 10–20 years. The long-term projections of deforestation rates provided in the model presented here are developed only to assess potential marginal costs, not for the purposes of crediting over a long time horizon (e.g., 50 years). A more practical method would be to set deforestation baselines every 10 years (or at some regular interval), and to base crediting on deviations from each newly established baseline. The decadal baselines would best rely on economic modelling of land-use change conducted by global models with regional detail. Resetting baselines every few years eliminates the problem of using long-term projections. It also likely allows us to readjust incentives so they are better in line with emerging new economic conditions that are likely to occur over time.

Measuring, monitoring and leakage

To address the measuring and monitoring question, it is perhaps easiest to consider the context of a proposed deforestation reduction programme. For this example, it is assumed that there is a carbon rental programme, where a country is paid the equivalent of US$20/tC to reduce carbon emissions by avoiding deforestation. Consider the case of Brazil, which constitutes about 75 per cent of total deforestation in South America (FAO, 2005). In this case, initial deforestation rates for the decade 2005–2014 for Brazil would be 3.0 million hectares per year. The average carbon density for Brazil is assumed to be 122 tC/hectare. For the US$20/tC carbon price, rental payments are US$1/tC per year given a 5 per cent interest rate. At this price, each hectare where deforestation is avoided will fetch US$122 per year to remain in forest. Payments will commence the year the land would have been converted to some other use and are continued indefinitely.

The model projects that for the first decade deforestation will decline by 0.9 million hectares per year at US$20/tC. This means that the government of Brazil could agree to preserve 0.9 million new hectares each year for the price of US$20/tC. If they pay rent on the hectares that are preserved they would have to pay the rental equivalent of preserving the carbon on those hectares or US$122/hectare/year (122 tC multiplied by US$1/tC). By the end of the decade, Brazil should be able to prove that they preserved 9.0 million hectares from deforestation.

The question is how Brazil could prove this reduction? First, at the most basic level, policymakers need to ensure adequate record keeping among countries and among the developers of individual projects. Adequate records include measured levels of initial forest area and carbon stored, measured levels of forest area and carbon stored at regular intervals (perhaps every 5 years) and realistic methods used to project the baseline for individual land units or for the country. Second, adequate and verifiable protocols to measure carbon located on the projects themselves will need to be developed. Third, forest inventories, using both ground-based and satellite data should be employed to measure the change in forest cover for the entire country over each 5–10 year period to some measure of statistical confidence (with the exact levels to be determined by policymakers). The most important aspect of the measurement system will be the component that measures forest inventories and determines the change in forest area over time. For deforestation efforts, this will allow for measurement of the net gains in land area in forests. Forest cover inventories will be necessary both to be sure that the projects sum up to some national level savings and to guard against leakage, an issue that will be discussed later.

Under the rental programme described earlier, Brazil would be paid by some other country or a set of energy companies US$122/hectare/year for reducing deforestation by 0.9 million hectares per year from 2005–2014. Its total payments will rise from US$109 million in the first year to US$1.1 billion in 2014 (because the total area rented would have risen from 0.9 million to 9.0 million hectares in 2014). If Brazil started with 478 million hectares of forest, then according to the baseline, this would have declined by 30 million hectares over the 10 year period to 448 million hectares. Under the crediting scheme, however, it should instead have 457 million hectares by 2014, i.e. a net reduction of only 21 million hectares.

The important verifiable numbers here are 448 million hectares in 2014 and the level they actually achieve in 2014 – the baseline quantity and the quantity achieved as a result of the policy. An agreement clearly needs to be in place between Brazil and other countries about their baseline deforestation rates. In this case, it has been assumed that Brazil agrees to provide 9.0 million hectares of reduced deforestation for US$20/tC, so this would be its target. Note, however, that once an agreement is in place on the baseline, Brazil can negotiate with buyers on the price and quantity of reductions it will achieve (or they can allow individual companies or organizations to make these negotiations directly with local non-governmental agencies, timber concessionaires, farmers, indigenous tribes or others who actually hold the land rights).

If Brazil agrees to be paid US$122/hectare/year[5] to reduce the area deforested over the 10-year period by 0.9 million hectares per year or 9.0 million hectares over the decade, then one would expect to see 457 million hectares of forest in 2014. What happens if there are fewer hectares than this in 2014? There are three plausible reasons for this: (a) the baseline was calculated incorrectly so that more deforestation was occurring than believed in the baseline; (b) the country was less effective than it thought it would be (including the possibility that the costs are higher than it thought, there were some additional disturbances, such as forest fires, or it actually cheated); or (c) there was leakage within Brazil. The purchasers of the credits, the country, and other observers would like to know which of these explanations is correct, but it is unlikely that a clear answer will emerge. It is more likely that a combination of the three reasons is the cause. From the perspective of the atmosphere, however, it does not really matter which explanation is correct.

If the credits were used to offset fossil fuel emissions and less carbon is obtained than was offset, then adjustments should be made. Adjustments could include requiring Brazil to purchase credits on the open market to make up for the losses.[6] Alternatively, the people who purchased the credits could be held responsible. There are also all kinds of correction factors being proposed to try to account for what amounts to non-compliance. Using 'fudge' factors will just simply raise the costs of doing business, but without providing more certainty about the outcomes.

The key issue is that the implementation of scientifically valid measuring and monitoring protocols, conducted at the country level, are likely to be necessary for any emergent carbon market that allows credits for reductions in deforestation. All fungible, widely traded and valuable commodities also have good monitoring – or, in other words, ways to measure the output. Because carbon is a newly emerging commodity, these monitoring protocols have yet to be fully developed or established. One reason for this is that policymakers, particularly those involved in international negotiations like the United Nations Framework Convention on Climate Change (UNFCCC) and Kyoto processes have consistently devalued forestry in their negotiations. It should thus be expected that there has been little emphasis to date on developing adequate monitoring protocols. If society wants to achieve the low cost possibilities provided by reductions in deforestation, society will have to get more serious about developing protocols for country-wide monitoring of deforestation in tropical countries.[7]

The chapter thus far has largely focused on discussing actions related to reductions in deforestation and has avoided discussion of degradation of forest resources. The author recognizes this as an important issue to developing countries with large areas of tropical forests. One difficulty with handling degradation issues at the current time is the need for reliable, accurate and cost-effective measuring and monitoring protocols despite recent advances. The ability to measure forest cover change with satellite technology is more realistic than the ability to broadly measure carbon stock levels and adjustment in stock levels. Until good methodologies are developed to handle the measurement of carbon gains from reducing forest degradation, it would be unwise to develop policies that provide credits for such reductions.

Project-based approaches

Most of the discussion so far has focused on measuring and monitoring programmes at the country level. Little attention has been paid to how individual projects could be credited. Most carbon sequestration to date has been accomplished via specific projects, so it is reasonable to consider what these results mean for individual projects. With the exception of leakage, the issues discussed already are similar for individual projects. With respect to the baseline, a project must develop a reasonable one that can be agreed upon. This can be based on historical averages for the region where the project is located, a model projection or some other method. Measuring and monitoring protocols must be in place to ensure that the carbon is present during the time the project is undertaken. Both of these should be subjected to third-party audits.

The key difference in the project world is leakage. It will be difficult, from the perspective of each individual project, to measure leakage. Modelling or empirical studies, of course, can be applied to assess potential leakage and they can be used to adjust the credits of a project (see, for example, Sohngen and Brown, 2004; see also Murray, Chapter 9 in this volume). But these methods do not prove that leakage has or has not occurred, instead merely providing an assessment that it is likely to occur and suggesting the potential scale of leakage thus providing adjustment factors. While adjusting credits assigned to a particular project is a reasonable first step, any adjustment factors should be changed over time to reflect results of measuring and monitoring conducted at the country scale.

Permanence is also an important issue in the policy world. In the context of a market for carbon credits, however, permanence should mainly be considered a financial issue. For example, if carbon credits are currently selling for US$20/tC on the global market, then one might expect that the credits derived from a well-designed project in a country with good measuring and monitoring protocols in place to sell for close to US$20/tC. Credits derived from a project that is haphazardly put together and in a country that does not have good measuring and monitoring systems will sell for less than that. Alternatively, if the carbon is only rented and the buyers recognize that land use is not permanent at the outset, then they will only pay the rental value for the time the credits are maintained in a project. If the credits disappear in the future, then obviously the credits should no longer be used as offsets. The value of short-term storage is by definition less than the US$20/tC price.

Conclusion

This chapter has examined the potential for avoided deforestation to provide credits due to reductions in carbon emissions. A global timber market model is utilized to show the potential costs of these emissions reductions. The results of the modelling effort suggest that carbon credits for reductions in deforestation appear to be at relatively low cost in comparison to other options both in forestry and in the energy market. For US$20/tC, the model projects that emission reductions of around 542 MtC per year could be obtained in the regions of Southeast Asia (187 MtC per year), Africa (164 MtC per year), South America (122 MtC per year) and Central America (69 MtC per year). Baseline deforestation rates average around 13.1 million hectares per year in the initial decade and these are projected to decline by around 3.2 million hectares per year at US$20/tC.

In addition to considering constant carbon price scenarios, the analysis considers rising carbon prices. Rising carbon prices alter the time path of carbon sequestration. Because future prices are higher, some projects would be delayed to take advantage of these future higher prices. This makes sequestration in earlier periods more expensive to attain (or, in other words, for any price, fewer emission reductions will be accomplished). With the rising price scenarios, of course, future prices become very high, so the reductions in deforestation are only put off to the future. While it is not clear what will happen to future carbon prices, if carbon policy continually gets more stringent over time, it is likely that these prices will rise.

Several important issues related to setting baselines, measuring and monitoring and leakage are discussed in the context of the results from the model. The discussion of these issues illustrates that it is vitally important to develop baseline estimates that can be generally agreed on for policy purposes and that it is important to develop valid measuring and monitoring programmes in developing countries where reductions in deforestation may be accomplished. The importance of leakage was also identified. Leakage cannot be controlled at the level of individual projects and is indeed one of the most important problems faced by project developers. However, national level measuring and monitoring programmes will help determine the scale of leakage and whether or not it has been reducing the net benefits of the programmes being undertaken.

Acknowledgements

The author appreciates financial support for this research from the US Environmental Protection Agency, Office of Atmospheric Programs, through RTI International under Contract GS-10F-0283K, TO# 14, and managed by Kenneth Andrasko. The views and opinions of the authors herein do not necessarily state or reflect those of the United States government or the US Environmental Protection Agency.

Notes

1 The baseline and many of the results from the global forestry and land-use model presented in the chapter have been obtained largely from Sohngen *et al.* (2008).
2 This actual gain is easy to show from the perspective of the modeller, but of course, quite difficult to show in reality as Pfaff and Robalino discuss in Chapter 11 in this volume.
3 This is based on the assumption that the derived demand for land as an input into agricultural production stabilizes over time. Consequently, the demand for additional land slows.

4 If baselines are substantially different than reality, the level of credits generated by reducing deforestation can ultimately influence carbon prices. If baselines are too generous, as in column 4 of Table 4.1 Panel B, then large quantities of 'baseline' carbon entering carbon markets can potentially depress prices (see Michaelowa and Dutschke in Chapter 8 in this volume). Thus, it is clearly in the policymakers' interest to try to set realistic baselines.

5 While Brazil could incur significant transactions costs for establishing a payment scheme they may or may not be reflected directly in the value of commodities or land, e.g. if they are subsidized in the same way as infrastructure that benefits the agricultural sector. Note also that this payment reflects the value of the carbon and the marginal cost of the last ton saved on the landscape. Brazil would probably be able to reduce much of this carbon for less than US$122 per hectare per year.

6 It may also be possible for a country to develop new assessments that show the reason for the difference. If the difference is caused by economic conditions that are different from the projections, e.g., from a baseline that was different than the projection, the country may be able to show this and thus avoid purchasing credits on the open market. If the difference is due to leakage or not making the target, then, of course, the country should be held responsible.

7 Of course, the ability to monitor and verify carbon is only one condition. Countries also need to be able to enforce contracts to make carbon trading work.

References

Achard, F., Eva, H.D., Stibig, H.J., Mayaux, P., Gallego, J., Richards, T. *et al.* (2002) 'Determination of deforestation rates of the world's humid tropical forests', *Science*, 297(5583): 999–1002.

Bosetti V., Carraro, C., Galeotti, M., Massetti, E. and Tavoni, M. (2006) 'WITCH: a world induced technical change hybrid model', *The Energy Journal*, 27(1): 13–38.

DeFries, R.S., Achard, F., Brown, S., Herold, M., Murdiyarso, D., Schlamadinger, B. *et al.* (2006) *Reducing Greenhouse Gas Emissions from Deforestation in Developing Countries: Considerations for Monitoring and Measuring*, Report of the Global Terrestrial Observing System (GTOS) number 46, Rome: GTOS, and Global Observation of Forest and Land Cover Dynamics (GOFC-GOLD) report 26, Alberta, Canada: GOFC-GOLD.

Dixon, R.K., Brown, S., Houghton, R.A., Solomon, A.M., Trexler, M.C. and Wisniewski, J. (1994) 'Carbon pools and flux of global forest ecosystems', *Science*, 263(5144): 185–190.

FAO (Food and Agriculture Organization of the United Nations) (2005) *Global Forest Resources Assessment 2005: Progress towards Sustainable Forest Management*, FAO Forestry Paper 147, Rome: FAO.

Gurney, K.R., Law, R.M., Denning, A.S., Rayner, P.J., Baker, D., Bousquet, P. *et al.* (2002) 'Towards robust regional estimates of CO_2 sources and sinks using atmospheric transport models', *Nature*, 415: 626–629.

Harris, N.L., Petrova, S. and Brown, S. (2009) 'A scalable approach for setting avoided deforestation baselines', in C. Palmer and S. Engel (eds) *Avoided Deforestation: Prospects for Mitigating Climate Change*, London: Routledge.

Houghton, R.A. (2003) 'Revised estimates of the annual net flux of carbon to the atmosphere from changes in land use and land management 1850–2000', *Tellus*, 55b: 378–390.

Kurukulasuriya, P. and Mendelsohn, R. (2007) *A Ricardian Analysis of the Impact of Climate Change on African Cropland*, Policy Research Working Paper 4305, Washington, DC: World Bank.

Ludena, C.E., Hertel, T.W., Preckel, P.V., Foster, K. and Nin, A. (2007) *Productivity Growth and Convergence in Crop, Ruminant and Non-Ruminant Production: Measurement and Forecasts*, West Lafayette, IN: Department of Agricultural Economics, Purdue University.

Metz, B., Davidson, O., Bosch, P., Dave, R. and Meyer, L. (2007) *Climate Change 2007: Mitigation. Contribution of Working Group III to the Intergovernmental Panel on Climate Change Fourth Assessment Report*, New York: Cambridge University Press.

Michaelowa, A. and Dutschke, M. (2009) 'Will credits from avoided deforestation in developing countries jeopardize the balance of the carbon market?' in C. Palmer and S. Engel (eds) *Avoided Deforestation: Prospects for Mitigating Climate Change*, London: Routledge.

Murray, B. (2009) 'Leakage from an avoided deforestation compensation policy: concepts, empirical evidence and corrective policy options', in C. Palmer and S. Engel (eds) *Avoided Deforestation: Prospects for Mitigating Climate Change*, London: Routledge.

Nin, A., Arndt, T.C., Hertel, T.W. and Preckel, P.V. (2003) 'Bridging the gap between partial and total factor productivity measures using directional distance functions', *American Journal of Agricultural Economics*, 85(4): 928–942.

Nordhaus, W. and Boyer, J. (2000) *Warming the World: Economic Models of Global Warming*, Cambridge: MIT Press.

Pfaff, A. and Robalino, J. (2009) 'Human choices and policies' impacts on ecosystem services: improving evaluations of payment and park effects on conservation and carbon', in C. Palmer and S. Engel (eds) *Avoided Deforestation: Prospects for Mitigating Climate Change*, London: Routledge.

Potter, C., Klooster, S., Myneni, R., Genovese, V., Tan, P.N. and Kumar, V. (2003) 'Continental-scale comparisons of terrestrial carbon sinks estimated from satellite data and ecosystem modeling 1982–1998', *Global and Planetary Change*, 39(3–4): 201–213.

Seo, N. and Mendelsohn, R. (2007) *A Ricardian Analysis of the Impact of Climate Change on Latin American Farms*, Policy Research Working Paper 4163, Washington, DC: World Bank.

Soares-Filho, B.S., Nepstad, D.C., Curran, L.M., Cerqueira, G.C., Garcia, R.A., Ramos, C.A. *et al.* (2006) 'Modelling conservation in the Amazon Basin', *Nature*, 440: 520–523.

Sohngen, B., Beach, R. and Andrasko, K. (2008) 'Avoided deforestation as a greenhouse gas mitigation tool: economic issues', *Journal of Environmental Quality*, 37(4): 1368–1375.

Sohngen, B. and Brown, S. (2004) 'Measuring leakage from carbon projects in open economies: a stop timber harvesting project as a case study', *Canadian Journal of Forest Research*, 34: 829–839.

Sohngen, B. and Mendelsohn, R. (2003) 'An optimal control model of forest carbon sequestration', *American Journal of Agricultural Economics*, 85(2): 448–457.

Sohngen, B. and Mendelsohn, R. (2007) 'A sensitivity analysis of carbon sequestration', in M. Schlesinger (ed.) *Human-Induced Climate Change: An Interdisciplinary Assessment*, Cambridge: Cambridge University Press.

Sohngen, B. and Sedjo, R. (2006) 'Carbon sequestration in global forests under different carbon price regimes', *The Energy Journal*, 27(1): 109–126.

Tavoni, M., Sohngen, B. and Bosetti, V. (2007) 'Forestry and the carbon market response to stabilize climate', *Energy Policy*, 35(11): 5346–5353.

van Kooten, G.C., Binkley, C.S. and Delcourt, G. (1995) 'Effect of carbon taxes and subsidies on optimal forest rotation age and supply of carbon services', *American Journal of Agricultural Economics*, 77(2): 365–374.

Weyant, J., de la Chesnaye, F. and Blanford, G. (2006) 'Overview of EMF-21: multigas mitigation and climate policy', *Energy Journal*, 27(1): 1–32.

Part II

Policy and institutional barriers to avoided deforestation

5 International policy and institutional barriers to reducing emissions from deforestation and degradation in developing countries

Tracy Johns and Bernhard Schlamadinger

Introduction

In the 1990s tropical deforestation and other uses of land accounted, on average, for around 20 per cent of anthropogenic greenhouse gas (GHG) emissions. For the period from 2000–2006, the 'residual terrestrial sink' approximated to about 30 per cent of total anthropogenic emissions (Canadell *et al.*, 2007). Representing, therefore, both a source of emissions and an important mechanism for reducing atmospheric GHG concentrations, forests in this dual climate role have been a constant source of debate and misunderstanding. In many ways, emissions from forest destruction can be treated like any other emission – from transportation or energy production, for example. All release CO_2 into the atmosphere and, when it comes to the impact on global climate, unit for unit, the atmosphere does not distinguish among emission sources. However, there are important differences in measuring, monitoring and accounting for the carbon dynamics of a forest that require special treatment and that have, in the past, caused disagreement among policymakers over how to incorporate forests into global efforts to reduce GHG emissions.

When limits were set on GHG emissions in the Kyoto Protocol, the initial focus was on emissions from industry in the developed world. While negotiators did agree to include emissions and sequestration from land use, land-use change and forestry (LULUCF), the subject aroused intense disagreement. When negotiations turned to the role of forests in developing countries, only reforestation or afforestation activities qualified for credit in the clean development mechanism (CDM). The issue of emissions from deforestation in developing countries was an especially divisive one, splitting not only the parties, but also the non-governmental organization (NGO) community. In the end, negotiators decided against allowing developing countries to earn credits by reducing deforestation.

Now, just over a decade later, the issue of deforestation in developing countries has returned to the spotlight in United Nations climate negotiations, not least because scientific evidence has been mounting concerning the vital role of forests, especially tropical forests, in mitigating climate change, and of their vulnerability to it (Houghton, 2005; Nabuurs *et al.*, 2007; Nepstad *et al.*, 1999).

In 2005 a group of developing countries breathed new life into the forest debate at the United Nations Framework Convention on Climate Change (UNFCCC) annual meeting of the parties to the convention and protocol. Led by Costa Rica and Papua New Guinea, they successfully petitioned the UNFCCC's Subsidiary Body for Scientific and Technological Advice (SBSTA) to begin a new track of negotiations on 'reducing emissions from deforestation' (RED) in developing countries. Subsequent SBSTA investigations into the topic revealed a renewed energy and commitment among both developed and developing countries to revisit the issues that kept the reduction of emissions from tropical deforestation out of the Kyoto Protocol. Those issues included, among others, a general scepticism about the ability to accurately account for reduced emissions from deforestation, as well as a claim among many NGOs that this would allow developed countries the option to pay for emissions reductions abroad instead of reducing emissions domestically.

The Conference of the Parties (COP 13) meeting in Bali, in December 2007, marked the end of a 2-year SBSTA investigation and negotiation process dedicated to RED. Negotiations concluded with a decision that includes RED as a legitimate and key piece of a broader UNFCCC mitigation strategy. Continuing discussions and negotiations on RED were also placed on the same timeframe as the negotiations for the post-2012 climate agreement, which are set to end in 2009 in Copenhagen. Moreover, parties agreed to expand the official investigation of RED to include not only deforestation, but also forest degradation. Degradation refers to a process whereby significant forest carbon is unsustainably removed without a complete transition to non-forest. It could include such activities as selective logging of forests or fuelwood gathering. With degradation included, the common acronym has been expanded to REDD (reducing emissions from deforestation and degradation). The Bali decision on REDD includes a mandate to investigate the role of conservation, sustainable management of forests, and enhancement of forest carbon stocks in developing countries (UNFCCC, 2007a).

Fresh ideas and renewed international attention have given the topic increasing momentum. Both developed and developing countries have stated their commitment to negotiating a strong outcome in Copenhagen that will establish a plan for including REDD in efforts to meet international climate goals. However, even under the assumption of a decision in 2009 that establishes a framework for REDD, there remain significant challenges to successful implementation of an effective, equitable and sustainable mechanism. Challenges related to international policy negotiations as well as national institutional challenges will require political will, new and sustainable financial resources and enough flexibility to insure maximum participation, while still guaranteeing credible results. Many of the policy-related challenges have already surfaced in the SBSTA negotiation process and are thus part of the ongoing debate. Others, especially institutional challenges, will become more central as negotiations progress to the details relating to mechanism structure and implementation.

This chapter examines the barriers to bringing REDD into the international climate regime and discusses what it might take to overcome these barriers. The chapter focuses on the international policy barriers, but also includes a limited discussion of institutional barriers. International policy barriers include, but are not limited to: the drivers of deforestation; the ability to measure deforestation and its resulting emissions; how to address emissions from unsustainable forest harvesting that falls short of full-scale deforestation; and deciding on a metric to measure success of REDD programmes. Institutional barriers, while they have not been the centre of negotiations (which have focused more on policy issues thus far), are now an increasing focus of attention and discussion, as countries, NGOs, and financing institutions grapple with the 'readiness process', i.e. what it will take for a country to be ready to participate in an international REDD mechanism. Briefly, these barriers include, but are not limited to: land tenure and forest protection law enforcement; effective engagement of civil society, including forest-dependent and indigenous communities; and the ability of countries to maintain forests as long-term stores of carbon.

International policy barriers

The UNFCCC process on REDD offers an opportunity to develop a global agreement and the support needed to reduce emissions from deforestation and degradation. Certainly, the work of making REDD a success does not end with a successful negotiation. But if countries can agree on a REDD framework then this may provide a positive signal and direction for the many national and sub-national actors and processes that will transform REDD from a concept into an effective emissions-reducing tool. First, however, countries must agree on a framework.

As SBSTA negotiations have advanced since 2005, certain issues have surfaced as key factors affecting the feasibility of a future UNFCCC agreement on REDD. While this chapter is by no means an exhaustive catalogue of these issues, we have selected several as representative of the ongoing debates and discussions within the SBSTA process. These include: the design of a REDD mechanism that can address the drivers of deforestation; deforestation and degradation monitoring capability; agreement on the scale and scope of the REDD accounting framework; measures of success; and agreement on a financing approach.

Drivers of deforestation

As noted in a recent World Bank report on deforestation: 'People clear and log forests because they gain from doing so' (Chomitz *et al.*, 2006). This could be via raising cattle or growing crops, acquiring valuable timber, building roads or simply finding a place in which to live. Any policy that does not address this basic fact or does not provide the support and flexibility for individual nations to address it is doomed to fail in the long run.

Significant progress has been made on identifying and analyzing drivers of deforestation at varying spatial levels from individual households in Central Africa, cattle ranches in Brazil, to oil palm plantations in Indonesia. In most cases, multiple factors explain deforestation patterns, including agricultural expansion, wood extraction and infrastructure expansion, with agricultural expansion dominating land-use change, associated with 96 per cent of all deforestation cases (Geist and Lambin, 2001).

In Africa, degradation and deforestation come mostly from domestic uses such as fuelwood gathering. In mainland and insular Asia commercial timber extraction followed by clearing for agriculture is a more common driver. Land clearing for cattle ranching is by far the largest cause of deforestation in mainland South America (Brown *et al.*, 2006a). As the causes and underlying factors behind deforestation can differ so markedly among regions, policies to address deforestation should be built on an understanding of these factors and a tailored approach to them. As the production of biofuels surges in many tropical forest countries, policymakers will need to consider interactions of international REDD policies with biofuel incentives and efforts to increase biofuels production to reduce fossil fuels use. The challenge for international policymakers is to provide flexible support for national efforts to respond to local and regional drivers and to assist the agents of deforestation in becoming stewards of forest resources.

Monitoring capability

During previous negotiations on deforestation in developing countries, sceptics have questioned whether scientific tools and methods are adequate to monitor deforestation and calculate emission reductions. While more of a technical issue, insufficient monitoring capacity is a barrier to successful policy implementation.

However, advances in the field of remote sensing have changed the nature of this debate. It is no longer necessary to rely solely on relatively expensive ground-based forest inventories. Expert groups such as the GOFC-GOLD network,[1] the Woods Hole Research Center,[2] the European Union's Joint Research Center and others have been actively engaged in developing, improving and adapting specialized satellite-based forest monitoring tools and methodologies that work hand in hand with ground-based verification. The UNFCCC SBSTA process on REDD has actively engaged the scientific community in providing technical support to the policy process. As a result, remote sensing experts have provided presentations in SBSTA REDD workshops (UNFCCC-SBSTA, 2006), made submissions at the request of the SBSTA and focused their own efforts on understanding and responding to the technical needs of the political process (see DeFries *et al.*, 2006; Herold and Johns, 2007; Kellndorfer *et al.*, 2007). Inadequate technical feasibility to monitor deforestation is now far less of a barrier than in the past.

Submissions by party and observer organizations to the SBSTA have reflected an increased awareness of the relevance of these developments to the policy process. The importance of space-based observations for REDD has been highlighted by many. Several parties specifically expressed their support for consideration and/or use under a future REDD mechanism, as well as providing support through the hosting of pilot activities (see for example India, Bolivia, Vanuatu, EU submissions in UNFCCC-SBSTA, 2007a). Developing countries consistently call for support to acquire the technology and sufficient training to monitor their forests. The more relevant barrier now is that technical feasibility does not immediately translate into the ability of a country to actually use the technology to develop own programmes and expertise.

The GOFC-GOLD report states that: 'There is limited capacity in many developing countries to acquire and analyze the data needed for a national system of GHG reporting for deforestation and degradation' (DeFries *et al.*, 2006). This report identifies cost and access to high resolution data as two constraints to national implementation. Developing country parties have expressed the need for support to build capacity within their own countries to create and maintain the institutional infrastructure necessary to guarantee the long-term viability of REDD policies (for example see Submission of Views of Australia, Congo Basin Countries, Malaysia in UNFCCC-SBSTA, 2007a). So, while great strides have been made in turning technical feasibility into a reality, challenges related to full implementation of new tools and methods must be met through improving access to data and training in new technologies.

Scale of emissions reductions

One issue currently under debate in the SBSTA process is the scale at which a REDD mechanism should operate. Should it employ a CDM-type approach in which individual projects are credited under separate baselines? Or should it be a national approach in which credits are earned based on performance throughout the whole country? There are advantages and disadvantages to both approaches.

The concept of 'leakage' is often linked with a sub-national approach. Under the CDM project-by-project approach, if a project is initiated that protects a certain area of forest from being cut down, deforesters could simply move their deforestation activities to an area outside the project boundary, thus, in the end, providing no real reduction in emissions. This relocation of emissions outside of project boundaries is known as 'leakage' of emissions (see Murray, Chapter 9 in this volume). While even under a national approach international leakage could still occur in some situations, it is generally considered more of a problem at the sub-national project scale.

Since the CDM debate, many forest protection projects have been initiated outside the climate convention and some have developed and tested methodologies to estimate and address leakage. Notable among these is the Noel Kempff Climate Action Project, the world's largest forest conservation project designed to generate carbon offsets by avoiding deforestation. This project, through a combination of methodologies, estimated potential leakage from its 642,458 ha project in the Velasco and Itenez provinces of Bolivia. The results were used to discount the amount of offsets the project could sell in the voluntary market (Brown, 2002). Discounting of credits to reflect the possibility of deforestation relocation is one of several methods proposed for addressing potential leakage in REDD projects.

The CDM rules for forestry projects do not bind SBSTA in its deliberations on REDD and SBSTA negotiations have moved the REDD concept into new territory since the CDM debates. Several countries, such as Bolivia, Costa Rica and Papua New Guinea have proposed that developing countries agree to a national emissions target for deforestation, similar to that of Annex I emissions targets, instead of working and accounting on a project-by-project level. Unlike Annex I targets, these countries are proposing voluntary targets, entailing rewards for meeting the targets but no penalties for *not* meeting them. Additionally, rather than an economy-wide target, these targets would only cover deforestation emissions. By moving to a national level, problems with leakage inside national boundaries are greatly reduced or eliminated. Operating at the national scale also means that national governments are more directly engaged in emission reduction activities, and since institutions must be developed and strengthened to administer programmes, more in-country capacity must be built and maintained.

However, support among countries for a national approach is not universal and there are concerns about how it would operate. Many developing countries do not have sufficient infrastructure to manage and monitor their forests or estimate carbon losses. Developing this capacity relies on strong and continuous in-country government support as well as significant outside financing. Unstable and/or corrupt governments and institutions make this a serious challenge for some countries. Some developing countries do not have sufficient control over their forest reserves, due to problems such as conflict and political unrest. Additionally, in situations like that in Indonesia, which is spread over thousands of islands, local governments may have more direct control over the management of their resources than national governments, which challenges the concept of a national approach.

Another challenge with use of a national approach is that it may discourage private investors, who may be vital to the success of such a mechanism. If a government takes on a national target for deforestation emissions, then, under most proposed schemes, it must meet the agreed national target in order to receive any credits. Therefore, if a private entity undertakes a project within the country in order to earn credits to sell and this project succeeds but projects in other parts of the country fail and cause the country to miss its target, a project developer may have no guarantee that even a successful project would be eligible for compensation. Depending on the design within the country, the success of any one project may therefore be dependent on the success of all or most projects in the country.

One often misunderstood, but important distinction is the difference between national- or project-level *accounting* and national- or project-level *implementation*. Project-level accounting means that projects are credited individually, while national-level accounting generally refers to a national target, with credit being earned based on the combined results of all projects in the country. No matter what level of accounting is decided on, actual implementation (except perhaps in the case of very small countries or countries with small areas of forest) will take place at the project scale. Individual projects, tailored to local or regional forest type, geography, historical land-use patterns and deforestation drivers will form the basis for whatever level of accounting system is developed.

In light of the reality of project-level action, some parties and participating organizations have considered and proposed flexibility regarding the scale of activity and accounting, to encourage maximum participation.

A 'basket of approaches' is a common term used to describe the concept of giving countries the flexibility to choose a level of participation that they can realistically accomplish. For example, countries with limited or no inventories of forest land could participate through a mechanism that builds capacity for the development of an inventory, including the necessary institutions and monitoring programmes to maintain such an inventory. Those countries with some capacity for assessing deforestation could begin with project-level emissions reduction programmes, aimed at addressing deforestation/degradation hotspots. The highest level could be a national or sub-national quantifiable emissions limitation programme, for example, including historical emissions, trends or projections and the earning of market-based credits for emission reductions below an established amount (Johns, 2006).

Another option would be to use a hybrid policy mechanism that incorporates features of both national and sub-national scales. One such mechanism has recently been proposed by several Latin American countries including Honduras, Mexico, Panama, Paraguay and Peru (UNFCCC-SBSTA, 2007b). This mechanism includes a national target or reference level but also calls for authorization for private or public entities to implement REDD activities. Credits for successful implementation of these sub-national emission-reducing activities would be guaranteed, before a national deforestation emissions target is agreed or met, taking leakage into account. This nested approach could be used with a time limit that requires a country to adopt a national approach within a certain time period or could be used along with the requirement that once a specific percentage of the forested area is included in project-scale activities that the country must move to a national approach. The advantage of such an approach is that it might enable and encourage early and broad participation by countries with limited capacity to act on a national scale or that have limited political will to commit to a national deforestation target in the first stage of REDD implementation. However, there are significant challenges with such an approach, including dealing with leakage, the specifics of how to credit individual projects that exist under a national baseline or target and liability for credits granted through individual projects.

This issue of scaling a REDD programme is one of the more complex design issues to be resolved by parties negotiating a REDD framework.

Scope of a REDD mechanism: degradation, sequestration, regrowth

While the original mandate of SBSTA specified only emissions from deforestation, questions over how inclusive the mechanism should be have been a significant part of the debate since the beginning. Two main activities for possible inclusion have been under discussion: forest degradation and regrowth/sequestration.

The question of whether to include forest degradation is an important one. The role of forest degradation relies heavily on how the term is defined and the IPCC special report on this topic discusses several definitions that may be applied (IPCC, 2003). Forest degradation in the REDD context is generally agreed to refer to an unsustainable decrease in the carbon content of a forest without actually causing a full land classification change from forest to non-forest. Its importance stems from several key points. First, there are several countries, such as the Congo Basin countries, in which complete deforestation is not yet a serious problem, but where forest degradation still contributes significant emissions through activities such as selective logging and fuelwood harvesting (Brown *et al.*, 2006b). If the focus of the mechanism is on deforestation alone, these countries may be largely excluded from participation. Several parties, as well as participating organizations, have advocated for the inclusion of degradation (Skutsch *et al.*, 2007) (see SBSTA submissions of Colombia, Japan, Nepal, Slovenia in UNFCCC-SBSTA, 2008). Second, recent research has shown that forest degradation, even in countries with deforestation, contributes significantly to emissions, and can in some cases leave forests more vulnerable to fire and future deforestation (Asner *et al.*, 2005). Additionally, excluding countries such as the Congo Basin countries may, in some cases, leave these countries more vulnerable to increased pressure for forest products if REDD succeeds in other countries where similar forest products are currently produced. Research has shown that in the case of the Congo Basin countries, much of the currently forested land is suitable for crops such as oil palm (Stickler *et al.*, 2007) and vast areas of forested land are already under concession agreements that have not yet been exercised.

One of the main challenges of including degradation is the increased cost and difficulty in accurately monitoring it and estimating the resultant emissions. The 2006 GOFC-GOLD report states that monitoring degradation is technically more challenging than monitoring deforestation and requires the use of high resolution data. New methods such as radar or the visual interpretation of spatial patterns show potential for increasing future application (Asner *et al.*, 2005; Kellndorfer *et al.*, 2007; Pearson *et al.*, 2006; Souza *et al.*, 2005). At the present time, however, the inclusion of degradation significantly increases the complexity and costs of monitoring programmes.

The second issue concerns the inclusion of compensation for the maintenance and growth in carbon stocks, in addition to emissions reductions from avoiding deforestation. India has been one of the main proponents of this more inclusive approach, one that would not only reward countries that decrease currently high deforestation rates, but also reward those, such as Chile, China and India that have successfully slowed and reversed deforestation trends and whose forests are now either stable or growing. The Indian proposal claims that these countries should be compensated for the increase in forest carbon that results from their ongoing efforts to protect their forests (see submission of India, UNFCCC-SBSTA, 2007a). In Bali, India successfully negotiated the inclusion of language requiring the consideration of conservation of carbon stocks and sustainable forest management in future deliberations on REDD (UNFCCC, 2007a).

Monitoring and measuring capability is a major complication with this approach. Monitoring changes in carbon stocks rather than forest cover loss is much more technically challenging and currently requires extensive ground-based inventories to calculate. While India has a very strong forest-monitoring programme, most other developing countries do not and the capacity for remote sensing tools to measure forest biomass is still being developed and tested (Pearson *et al.*, 2006).

India and other countries have raised important issues. Is it equitable for a policy mechanism to offer a potentially higher 'reward' to countries that have high current deforestation rates, while reducing the potential reward to countries that are already taking steps to protect their forests? Does it make sense to wait until a country begins to significantly deplete its forest stores before offering incentives to avoid deforestation? Potential answers to these questions are complicated by the need for additionality in any REDD mechanism that establishes a success-based, competitive framework for crediting (countries receiving payments only on demonstration of success). This is especially pertinent if REDD efforts are linked to the Annex I commitments of developed countries. If developed countries are able to purchase REDD credits in order to meet their commitments, then issues of additionality may arise in the case of countries with already steady or increasing forest carbon stocks, i.e. developed countries may be purchasing credits that do not represent a truly additional emission reduction, while emitting more domestically as a result of the purchase. Moreover, since the CDM afforestation/reforestation (AR) mechanism already credits increasing carbon stocks in developing country forests, possibilities for double counting or overlap with CDM projects are high in the case of a subnational approach.

For both degradation and the conservation of stocks, the issue of how a reference level is established is also a key factor, since it is possible through the use of projections to create incentives for a range of deforestation rates and for the conservation of stocks.

Measure of success: setting reference levels

REDD activities, under whatever scale, level of inclusiveness, and finance structure, will need to be assessed for effectiveness. The most commonly discussed method for this is the use of some sort of national historical reference or baseline period of emissions from deforestation, although other options such as a global average (Achard *et al.*, 2002) and a carbon stock approach, for example, by the Centre for International Sustainable Development Law (CISDL, 2007), have also been proposed. A 5- to 10-year reference period is most often advocated, as a way to address the year-to-year variability in rates of deforestation. The GOFC-GOLD report states that high resolution remote sensing data are available from the 1990s onward at low or no cost (DeFries *et al.*, 2006). Since 'sufficient' baseline deforestation data exists for countries from 1990 to 2005, Mollicone *et al.* (2007) recommend using this time period for the reference level.

Bolivia, Brazil, Gabon and Malaysia, in their 2006 submissions to the SBSTA, all recommended either a 5- or 10-year base period as the reference level against which to measure future deforestation levels in a REDD mechanism (UNFCCC-SBSTA, 2007b). Whether this emissions amount would be used as the actual target or only as a basis for negotiating a target (such as Annex I countries' negotiated percentages of 1990 emissions as an emissions target) has not yet been discussed in detail. Many developing countries have endorsed the concept of a 'development adjustment factor', a negotiated percentage that could be applied to a historical emissions rate to account for national circumstances of countries that are less developed than others.

Since deforestation patterns and trends differ markedly among developing countries, discussion of the level of flexibility that should be granted in establishing a reference period has produced a range of positions. Brazil recommended in their submission (referenced earlier) that each country select a minimum of four dates within a set time period for the historical reference and that the recalculation of future emissions should update the reference period every 3 years. The approach recommended by Santilli *et al.* (2005) is to recalculate the reference level every 20 years so that the reference level can reflect ongoing changes in deforestation rates.

In this context, it is important to keep in mind that emissions from deforestation can be subject to great year-to-year changes or even changes over longer periods. Thus, with a single reference level, there is a risk that countries may significantly 'overshoot' their reference level and lose any incentive to generate carbon credits or that countries may be significantly below the reference level, for example, because commodity prices may fall on world markets. Ways of addressing this have been proposed, such as the corridor approach whereby two reference levels would be set, between which there would be an increasing degree of crediting, the closer the emissions of a country are to the lower reference level (Schlamadinger *et al.*, 2005).

There has also been discussion of applying projections to a historical reference period in order to reflect current trends and expected changes in land-use policy. While attractive as a means to avoid the production of 'hot air' credits for the reduction of deforestation resulting from fluctuations in forest-based commodities or shifts in land management priorities, the use of projections is challenging. It would involve different calculations and considerations for each country. Thus, such an approach would be difficult to negotiate internationally.

As previously discussed, some parties have raised concerns over the concept of a historical reference period because they claim it makes it easier for countries with high historical rates of deforestation to gain rewards while providing far less incentive for countries with lower deforestation rates to reduce them further still. One major challenge in establishing a robust equitable measure of REDD success is in agreeing on a method that could effectively incentivize emissions reductions in countries that contribute most to deforestation emissions worldwide, while still supporting the maintenance of forests that may be under more threat of deforestation or degradation in the future.

Financing approaches

One of the more heavily debated topics around REDD is how to finance these activities. Developing countries are justifiably firm in stating that any future financial assistance for REDD should be new, and not drawn from existing, development funding streams. Many ideas have been proposed to fund REDD, but most fall into one of two main categories: those based on carbon market access to sell REDD credits and those with an approach that does not include the creation and sale of fungible credits for REDD. A third category, *indirect market approaches*, proposes drawing proceeds from the market without a direct link to market credits.

Two issues make up the core of the arguments on financing approach. The first relates to the level of funding different approaches can contribute and the second to the role that REDD may play in helping developed countries set and meet stiffer emissions reductions targets in a post-2012 climate treaty. Both relate strongly to the appropriateness of a market, non-market, indirect market or mixed funding approach. Estimates and opinions on the amount of funding needed for REDD vary widely, with the Stern Review's US$5 billion per year to address 70 per cent of deforestation offering a basis for further deliberation (Stern, 2006). Part I of this volume provides a discussion of the various cost estimates for REDD. Non-market approaches typically involve the creation of a new fund, supplied by developed countries and accessed by developing countries for capacity building and as a reward for reducing emissions below an agreed reference level. But most countries and observer organizations have expressed doubt as to the potential of such a fund to deliver sufficient and sustainable financing on the scale needed to implement REDD globally. The second issue is whether or not potential credits earned from REDD should be included as a means of compliance for developed countries to meet future emissions targets agreed as a part of the post-2012 climate treaty currently under negotiations.

Non-market approaches

Non-market approaches refer to approaches that are not tied to the carbon market. Examples include the creation of an international deforestation fund, debt-for-nature swaps or other types of development assistance targeting deforestation. Under a non-market approach, developing countries could access funds for a variety of uses, including an initial carbon inventory, monitoring and enforcement needs, as well as compensation for foregoing revenue from deforestation. The main challenge to a fully non-market approach is guaranteeing enough funding to curtail deforestation and support long-term management and protection of forests. While at times successful on smaller scales, these kinds of programmes have so far not demonstrated that they can provide long-term funding on the scale needed for REDD to succeed.

Indirect market approaches

Indirect market approaches refer to mechanisms such as applying surcharges on emission credit-trading schemes that are used for REDD or earmarking proceeds from emissions permit auctions to a REDD fund. Unlike purely non-market approaches, these approaches may have the potential to provide significant income streams if allocated to REDD activities. For example, in the EU European Trading Scheme (ETS) approximately two billion emission permit allowances are currently allocated for free (European Commission, 2006). If, for example, 50 per cent of these allowances were to be auctioned instead of allocated free of charge, at current market prices, and if only a small percentage of these auction proceeds were dedicated to REDD, these proceeds could potentially range in the billions of dollars to support REDD activities. While indirect market approaches may not alone raise sufficient REDD financing, they offer significantly higher financing opportunities than non-market approaches.

Market approaches

The market approach is based on the creation of credits for successful REDD activities that could be sold to developed countries to contribute to their emissions reductions commitments.

There are concerns regarding the impact of a new source of credits on the carbon market. Would a market-based REDD mechanism flood the carbon market with a large and cheap source of credits, thus driving down the overall cost of carbon worldwide (see Michaelowa and Dutschke, Chapter 8 in this volume)? One way to address concerns over cheap credits flooding the market is by significantly tightening Kyoto targets in order to reflect the extent of emissions reductions needed to realistically address climate change. In this way, market-based REDD credits would allow the world to set a more ambitious goal of emissions reduction (Chomitz *et al.*, 2006).

Furthermore, it is highly unlikely that a sudden flood of REDD credits (focusing only on emissions reductions and not on conservation of stocks) could hit the market at once and drive the price down for a number of other reasons. These include the amount of capacity building that would be necessary in most developing countries before emissions can be significantly reduced and the time required to change land-use practices and account for these changes in terms of CO_2. So long as reference levels limit the amount of 'hot air' credits into the system, REDD credits are more likely to enter the market slowly and steadily increase as countries gain experience in the programmes and accounting systems that will underpin REDD activities.

Another concern is whether the availability of a new credit stream would leave developed countries 'off the hook' regarding tougher domestic energy policies. This concern only arises if the targets for Annex I countries are set first, without considering additional mitigation opportunities arising from REDD. Most groups in favour of a market-based approach insist that a new source of credits must be met by increased demand in the form of much tighter emissions targets for Annex I, that would theoretically ensure a steady price for credits and encourage increasing global commitment to address emissions in both developed and developing countries (CAN, 2007; see Bolivia submission in UNFCCC-SBSTA, 2007a).

Combined approaches

Proponents of market-based mechanisms for REDD typically acknowledge the need for inclusion of non-market funding as well, especially to build in-country capacity or fund pilot projects (see UNFCCC, 2007b). The World Bank's Forest Carbon Partnership Facility (FCPF) is an example of such a multifaceted approach.[3] The FCPF is designed as a combination of funds for capacity building with the later initiation of a market-preparatory mechanism that will allow countries to compete for the sale of emission reduction credits. This experience with the sale of REDD credits will help participating countries that elect to participate in a future REDD market, should one be set up by the UNFCCC.

There are differing views over how market and non-market approaches could be combined. One option is to grant full market access only to countries that take on a national target, thereby avoiding issues such as leakage, and rewarding governments for an elevated level of commitment. Another is to allow a country to produce and sell credits from sub-national activities through the carbon market as long as appropriate guidelines on issues such as leakage are established and compliance is demonstrated. A compromise option could be to allow countries carbon market access for sale of REDD credits at the sub-national scale for a limited time period (e.g. 10 years), as suggested in the nested approach put forward by several Latin American countries (UNFCCC-SBSTA, 2007b). When that time period has elapsed, the country should either adopt a national level target and accounting approach or be denied market access.

The decisions over how to finance REDD activities have a significant impact on almost every other policy issue concerning REDD. The agreed solution should provide adequate, consistent, long-term funding of REDD activities, while also providing real and additional climate benefit. Ideally, it should also promote synergies with biodiversity protection, social equity and other UN environmental protection agreements.

Institutional barriers

The previous discussion has focused on issues involving international policy challenges to the creation and implementation of a REDD mechanism. A strong international REDD agreement is an important first step toward successfully reducing emissions from deforestation. However, real implementation happens at the individual country level and at scales of state/province and local communities. For this implementation to succeed, the right national and sub-national frameworks must be in place and must be financially and politically supported. Several challenges exist at this level as well and while most of these cannot or should not be directly decided by an international agreement, they are vital to the success of any international agreement on REDD and therefore must be considered from the early stages of mechanism design. Some of these institutional barriers include land tenure issues, stakeholder involvement, compensation structure and governance.

Land tenure

A recent World Bank report identifies weak land tenure as a key factor in deforestation, stating that: 'Where governance is weak and tenure poorly defined, powerful interests can seize forest resources, and smallholders can engage in conflict-ridden races for property rights.' And going on to add that even in cases of secure tenure, landholders may still choose to deforest for high returns (Chomitz *et al.*, 2006). In many parts of the world, degrading or destroying forests is an effective way to establish land tenure, leading to extensive land clearing in Asia and South America, for example (FAO, 2005).

Without secure land tenure it is difficult to imagine a landholder choosing to protect forest resources for an uncertain future return rather than exploiting those resources as quickly and extensively as possible for a guaranteed and more immediate return. Because land tenure structures vary so widely among and even within countries, land tenure issues pose a serious challenge to success in REDD implementation. Targeted support to developing clear and long-term land tenure protocols should be a priority in national capacity-building activities. In order to turn landholders and local forest users into providers of forest carbon, they need to have security over their claim to the land. Nevertheless, as Engel and Palmer (2008) have shown, paying for REDD may also help to induce more secure property rights.

Stakeholder involvement

A companion issue to that of land tenure is the importance of including relevant stakeholders at the local and regional levels in the design and implementation plans for REDD. Of course, those with traditional rights to land use make up a key stakeholder group for inclusion in REDD design. But other stakeholders such as NGOs with expertise in the specific region, local civil society organizations and communities whose livelihoods and culture are bound in some way to the forest may all be important potential participants in REDD. In the past, similar efforts designed and managed only by central governments and financial institutions have failed, and critics of these past efforts cite lack of stakeholder involvement as the main cause (Winterbottom, 1995). Non-governmental interest in and concern over the REDD process is high. REDD offers a unique opportunity to bring together governments, indigenous and traditional communities and civil society organizations to participate meaningfully in REDD design. Without this level of cooperation, agreement among nations on a REDD framework will not produce national, regional and local solutions to forest destruction.

The issue of stakeholder involvement is a significant challenge to REDD and should be a focus of REDD readiness efforts by supporters of REDD, including NGOs, developed countries and financing institutions. Together, these groups can help to build capacity, strengthen the voice of civil society and ensure that the relevant local groups have a voice in the design of REDD and an equitable share in future REDD benefits.

Compensation structure

Ensuring that communities dependent on forest resources and those most able to protect forest carbon receive benefits from reducing deforestation is a significant challenge in designing a national REDD implementation plan. Regardless of the scale of crediting, without careful design, forest-dependent communities may find their access to forest resources threatened, without comparable access to the flow of funding from an international REDD mechanism. The goal in designing a compensation structure should be to ensure that such communities are included in the benefits, thereby recruiting them in REDD efforts and providing them with an income source that is both economically and environmentally sustainable.

Governance

Strong national and sub-national governance of REDD programmes is key to success. In many developing countries, forest governance is one of the largest barriers to successful implementation of REDD. Governance covers a broad range of issues. Governance barriers may include weak governing states, lack of transparency and accountability, lack of involvement of important stakeholders, corruption and lack of respect for indigenous rights. All these barriers are relevant to REDD implementation.

For developing countries participating in the REDD debate, there is variation in whether their deforestation is primarily driven by legal or illegal activities. Increased clarity and security of land tenure may help to curb some illegal deforestation and degradation, but some countries will still have to face extensive large-scale illegal forest destruction. In these countries, one of the primary targets of capacity-building support should be the strengthening of regional and local institutions to police forests and enforce new or existing forest protection laws.

As an example of the financial impact of illegal activities on developing country governments, a recent World Bank report found that: 'Illegal logging in public lands alone causes estimated losses in assets and revenue in excess of US$10 billion annually, more than six times the total official development assistance dedicated to the sustainable management of forests' (World Bank, 2006). Additional costs noted by this report include those resulting from the erosion of institutions, the spread of corruption across the economy and negative environmental, economic and social consequences at the national and global levels.

An FAO report on forest governance identifies low cost priorities to improve governance in the forestry sector in developing countries. These include prioritizing law enforcement efforts towards specific illegal actions or actors, increasing the capacity of forest administration to detect and suppress forest crimes and engaging in bilateral agreements to limit the illegal timber trade, among others (FAO, 2005).

The institutional barriers described here are key issues that must be addressed in order for any international policy to be successfully applied and consistently maintained. These institutional barriers will need time, sustained political will, international cooperation and financial support in many cases, to overcome.

Conclusions

Making REDD work will be difficult. But the alternative – trying to tackle the climate change crisis while ignoring approximately 20 per cent of worldwide emissions – is unrealistic. The UNFCCC SBSTA process has successfully engaged the scientific, financial and environmental communities to provide technical support and a range of new ideas and tools that, given political commitment, can stimulate and support a new and much needed approach to protect the world's rich stores of carbon and biodiversity.

The political will to meaningfully address REDD has never been greater. The Kyoto Protocol relegated developing country forests to a supporting role. REDD offers the opportunity to correct that handicap and turn forests into a powerful tool in the effort to curb disruptive climate change.

Acknowledgements

This work was supported through the European Commission EuropeAid project RE-Impact[4] and by the Goldman Sachs Center for Environmental Markets.[5]

Notes

1 See: http://www.gofc-gold.uni-jena.de/.
2 See: http://www.whrc.org/programs/landcover.htm.
3 See: http://carbonfinance.org/Router.cfm?Page=FCPF&ft=About.
4 See: http://www.ceg.ncl.ac.uk/reimpact/index.htm.
5 See: http://www2.goldmansachs.com/citizenship/environment/center-for-environmental-markets/index.html.

References

Achard, F., Eva, H., Stibig, H., Mayaux, P., Gallego, J., Richards, T. *et al.* (2002) 'Determination of deforestation rates of the world's humid tropical forests', *Science*, 297(5583): 999–1002.

Asner, G.P., Knapp, D.E., Broadbent, E., Oliviera, P., Keller, M. and Silva, J. (2005) 'Selective logging in the Brazilian Amazon', *Science*, 310(5747): 480–482.

Brown, S. (2002) *Land Use and Forests, Carbon Monitoring, and Global Change*, Cooperative Agreement between Winrock International and the EPA. Report of leakage analysis for the Noel Kempff averted deforestation component ID# CR 827293–01–0 Winrock International, Ecosecurities Ltd [online]. Available at: http://www.winrock.org/ecosystems/files/Summary%20of%20project—Brown%202002.pdf [accessed 22 August 2007].

Brown, S., Harris, N., Pearson, T. and Walker, S. (2006a) *Background Paper for the Workshop on Reducing Emissions from Deforestation in Developing Countries. Part I: Scientific, Socio-economic, Technical and Methodological Issues Related to Deforestation in Developing Countries* [online]. Available at: http://unfccc.int/files/methods_and_science/lulucf/application/pdf/part_i_scientific_issues.pdf [accessed 10 April 2008].

Brown, S., Pearson, T., Moore, N. *et al.* (2006b). *Use of Aerial Digital Imagery to Measure the Impact of Selective Logging on Carbon Stocks of Tropical Forests in the Republic of Congo: Deliverable 9: Aerial Imagery Analysis of Logging Damage*, report submitted to US Agency for International Development (USAID). Cooperative Agreement No. EEM-A-00–03–00006–00, Arlington, VA: Winrock International.

CAN (Climate Action Network) (2007) *Submission on Reducing Emissions from Deforestation in Developing Countries: Approaches to Stimulate Action* [online].

Available at: http://unfccc.int/resource/docs/2007/smsn/ngo/013.pdf [accessed 22 August 2007].

Canadell, J.G., Le Quéré, C., Raupach, M.R., Field, C.B., Buitenhuis, E.T., Ciais, P. *et al.* (2007) 'Contributions to accelerating atmospheric CO_2 growth from economic activity, carbon intensity, and efficiency of natural sinks', *Proceedings of the National Academy of Sciences of the United States of America*, 104: 18866–70.

Chomitz, K. M., Buys, P., De Luca, G., Thomas, T.S., and Wertz-Kanounnikoff, S. (2006) *At Loggerheads? Agricultural Expansion, Poverty Reduction and Environment in the Tropical Forests*, World Bank Policy Research Report, Development Research Group, Washington, DC: World Bank.

CISDL (Centre for International Sustainable Development Law) (2007) *A Carbon Stock Approach to Creating a Positive Incentive to Reduce Emissions from Deforestation and Forest Degradation* [online]. Available at: http://unfccc.int/resource/docs/2007/smsn/ngo/001.pdf [accessed 22 August 2007].

DeFries, R.S., Achard, F., Brown, S., Herold, M., Murdiyarso, D., Schlamadinger, B. *et al.* (2006) *Reducing Greenhouse Gas Emissions from Deforestation in Developing Countries: Considerations for Monitoring and Measuring*, Report of the Global Terrestrial Observing System (GTOS) number 46, Rome: GTOS, and Global Observation of Forest and Land Cover Dynamics (GOFC-GOLD) report 26, Alberta, Canada: GOFC-GOLD.

Engel, S. and Palmer, C. (2008) 'Payments for environmental services as an alternative to logging under weak property rights: the case of Indonesia', *Ecological Economics*, 65(4): 799–809.

European Commission (2006) *Communication from the Commission to the Council and to the European Parliament on the Assessment of National Allocation Plans for the Allocation of Greenhouse Gas Emission Allowances in the Second Period of the EU Emissions Trading Scheme, COM(2006) 725 Final* [online]. Available at: http://eur-lex.europa.eu/LexUriServ/site/en/com/2006/com2006_0725en01.doc [accessed 23 August 2007].

FAO (Food and Agriculture Organization of the United Nations) (2005) *Best Practices for Improving Law Compliance in the Forest Sector* [online]. Available at: http://www.fao.org/docrep/008/a0146e/a0146e00.htm [accessed 20 August 2007].

Geist, H.J. and Lambin, E.F. (2001) *What Drives Tropical Deforestation? A Meta-analysis of Proximate and Underlying Causes of Deforestation Based on Subnational Case Study Evidence*, LUCC Report Series 4, Louvain-la-Neuve: LUCC International Project Office.

Herold, M. and Johns, T. (2007) 'Linking requirements with capabilities for deforestation monitoring in the context of the UNFCCC-REDD process', *Environmental Research Letters*, 2(4): 045025.

Houghton, R.A. (2005) 'Tropical deforestation as a source of greenhouse gas emissions', in P. Moutinho and S. Schwartzman (eds) *Tropical Deforestation and Climate Change*, Belém, Brazil: Amazon Institute for Environmental Research (IPAM), and Washington, DC: Environmental Defense.

IPCC (Intergovernmental Panel on Climate Change) (2003) *Report on Definitions and Methodological Options to Inventory Emissions from Direct Human-induced Degradation of Forests and Devegetation of Other Vegetation Types*, Kanagawa, Japan: Institute for Global Environmental Strategies (IGES).

Johns, T. (2006) *Ecosystem Marketplace* [online]. Available at: http://ecosystemmarketplace.com/pages/article.opinion.php?component_id=4472&component_version_id=6744&language_id=12 [accessed 20 August 2007].

Kellndorfer, J., Masanobu, S., Rosenqvist, A., Walker, W., Kirsch, K., Nepstad, D. *et al.* (2007) *New Eyes in the Sky: Cloud-Free Tropical Forest Monitoring for REDD with the Japanese Advanced Land Observing Satellite*, The Woods Hole Research Center [online]. Available at: http://www.whrc.org/policy/BaliReports/assets/Bali_ALOS.pdf_ [accessed 20 August 2007].

Michaelowa, A. and Dutschke, M. (2009) 'Will credits from avoided deforestation in developing countries jeopardize the balance of the carbon market?', in C. Palmer and S. Engel (eds) *Avoided Deforestation: Prospects for Mitigating Climate Change*, London: Routledge.

Mollicone, D., Achard, F., Federici, S., Eva, H.D., Grassi, G., Belward, A. *et al.* (2007) 'An incentive mechanism for reducing emissions from conversion of intact and non-intact forests', *Climatic Change*, 83(4): 477–493.

Murray, B. (2009) 'Leakage from an avoided deforestation compensation policy: concepts, empirical evidence and corrective policy options', in C. Palmer and S. Engel (eds) *Avoided Deforestation: Prospects for Mitigating Climate Change*, London: Routledge.

Nabuurs, G.J., Masera, O., Andrasko, K., Benitez-Ponce, P., Boer, R., Dutschke, M. *et al.* (2007) 'Forestry', in B. Metz, O.R. Davidson, P.R. Bosch, R. Dave and L.A. Meyer (eds) *Climate Change 2007: Mitigation. Contribution of Working Group III to the Fourth Assessment Report of the Intergovernmental Panel on Climate Change*, Cambridge and New York: Cambridge University Press.

Nepstad, D.C., Verssimo, A., Alencar, A., Nobre, C., Lima, E., Lefebvre, P. *et al.* (1999) 'Large-scale impoverishment of Amazonian forests by logging and fire', *Nature*, 398: 505–508.

Pearson, T., Walker, S., Grimland, S. and Brown, S. (2006) *Carbon and Co-Benefits from Sustainable Land Use Management. Deliverable 17: Impact of Logging on Carbon Stocks of Forests: The Brazilian Amazon as a Case Study*, Report for the US Agency for International Development (USAID). Arlington, VA: Winrock International.

Santilli, M., Moutinho, P., Schwartzman, S., Nepstad, D., Curran, L. and Nobre, C. (2005) 'Tropical deforestation and the Kyoto Protocol', *Climatic Change*, 71(3): 267–276.

Schlamadinger, B., Ciccarese, L., Dutschke, M., Fearnside, P.M., Brown, S. and Murdiyarso, D. (2005) 'Should we include avoidance of deforestation in the international response to climate change?' in P. Moutinho and S. Schwartzman (eds) *Tropical Deforestation and Climate Change*, Belém, Brazil: Amazon Institute for Environmental Research (IPAM), and Washington, DC: Environmental Defense.

Skutsch, M., Bird, N., Trines, E., Dutschke, M., Frumhoff, P., de Jong, B.H.J. *et al.* (2007) 'Clearing the way for reducing emissions from tropical deforestation', *Environmental Science and Policy*, 10(4): 322–334.

Souza Jr., C. M., Roberts, D. and Cochrane, M.A. (2005) 'Combining spectral and spatial information to map canopy damages from selective logging and forest fires', *Remote Sensing of Environment*, 98(2–3): 329–343.

Stern, N. (2006) *Stern Review: the Economics of Climate Change*, Cambridge: Cambridge University Press. Available at: http://www.hm-treasury.gov.uk/independent_reviews/stern_review_economics_climate_change/stern_review_report.cfm [accessed 21 August 2007].

Stickler, C.M., Coe, M.T., Nepstad, D.C., Fiske, G. and Lefevbre, P. (2007) *Readiness for REDD: A Preliminary Global Assessment of Tropical Forested Land Suitability for Agriculture*, The Woods Hole Research Center [online]. Available at: http://www.whrc.org/policy/BaliReports/REDDReady/index.htm [accessed 19 August 2007].

UNFCCC (United Nations Framework Convention on Climate Change) (2007a) *Bali Action Plan Decision 1/CP.13* [online]. Available at: http://unfccc.int/files/meetings/cop_13/application/pdf/cp_bali_action.pdf [accessed 26 April 2008].

UNFCCC (United Nations Framework Convention on Climate Change) (2007b) *Investment and Financial Flows to Address Climate Change* [online]. Available at: http://www.un.org/ga/president/62/ThematicDebates/gpicc/iffacc.pdf [accessed 26 April 2008].

UNFCCC-SBSTA (United Nations Framework Convention on Climate Change – Subsidiary Body for Scientific and Technological Advice) (2006) *Report on a Workshop on Reducing Emissions from Deforestation in Developing Countries, FCCC/SBSTA/2006/10* [online]. Available at: http://maindb.unfccc.int/library/view_pdf.pl?url=http://unfccc.int/resource/docs/2006/sbsta/eng/10.pdf [accessed 21 August 2007].

UNFCCC-SBSTA (United Nations Framework Convention on Climate Change – Subsidiary Body for Scientific and Technological Advice) (2007a) *Views on the Range of Topics and Other Relevant Information Relating to Reducing Emissions from Deforestation in Developing Countries*, Submissions from Parties FCCC/SBSTA/2007/MISC.2 [online]. Available at: http://unfccc.int/resource/docs/2007/sbsta/eng/misc02.pdf [accessed 21 August 2007].

UNFCCC-SBSTA (United Nations Framework Convention on Climate Change – Subsidiary Body for Scientific and Technological Advice) (2007b) *Views on Issues Related to Further Steps under the Convention Related to Reducing Emissions from Deforestation in Developing Countries: Approaches to Stimulate Action, FCCC/SBSTA/2007/MISC.14* [online]. Available at: http://unfccc.int/resource/docs/2007/sbsta/eng/misc14.pdf [accessed 21 August 2007].

UNFCCC-SBSTA (United Nations Framework Convention on Climate Change – Subsidiary Body for Scientific and Technological Advice) (2008) *Views on Outstanding Methodological Issues Related to Policy Approaches and Positive Incentives to Reduce Emissions from Deforestation and Forest Degradation in Developing Countries, FCCC/SBSTA/2008/MISC.4* [online]. Available at: http://unfccc.int/resource/docs/2008/sbsta/eng/misc4.pdf [accessed 20 April 2008].

Winterbottom, R. (1995) 'The tropical forestry action plan: is it working?', *National Association for the Practice of Anthropology Bulletin*, 15(1): 60–70.

World Bank (2006) *Strengthening Forest Law Enforcement and Governance Addressing a Systematic Constraint to Sustainable Development*, Report No. 36638, Environment and Agriculture and Rural Development Departments, Sustainable Development Network, Washington, DC: World Bank.

6 Reducing carbon emissions by slowing deforestation

REDD initiatives in Brazil

Paulo Moutinho, Mariano C. Cenamo and Paula F. Moreira

Introduction

Brazil could make a substantial contribution to climate change mitigation should the UNFCCC include a 'reduction of emissions from deforestation and degradation' (REDD) mechanism in its post-2012 framework. About 75 per cent of Brazil's CO_2 emissions do not result from the burning of fossil fuels, as is the case in the industrialized countries and in countries such as China and India, but rather from land-use changes, specifically deforestation and fires in its tropical forests. This emission profile is similar to that of Indonesia. Thus, Brazil's most effective potential contribution to climate change mitigation is to reduce deforestation.

Brazil's position regarding the reduction of tropical deforestation as a valid action against climate change has historically been conservative and based on the premise that actions for the purpose of forest conservation or avoided deforestation represented no real benefits to the atmosphere (Fearnside, 2001; Moutinho *et al.*, 2005). Since the UNFCCC Ninth Conference of Parties (COP-9) in Milan in 2003, when a group of Brazilian and American scientists (Moutinho and Schwartzman, 2005; Santilli *et al.*, 2005) launched the concept of 'compensated reduction' (CR) of deforestation, the Brazilian position has gradually changed. According to CR, developing countries that succeeded in reducing their national deforestation rates against a reference scenario would receive compensation from the international community or through trading in international carbon markets (carbon credits). This and other proposals triggered a discussion about the real impact of deforestation on global climate change and possible policy solutions, as reflected in the Stern Review, launched in 2006, and the most recent IPCC report (IPCC, 2007).

In November 2006, at the COP-12 in Nairobi, the Brazilian government submitted a proposal 'to provide positive financial incentives for developing countries that voluntarily reduce their greenhouse gas emissions from deforestation'.[1] This proposal (identified in the text as the 'Brazilian Proposal' hereafter) was based on the CR concept and represented a significant shift in the Brazilian position regarding GHG emissions from deforestation. It represented the beginning of a real engagement of the government and society in actions – deforestation reduction – that might trigger a real contribution to climate change mitigation with potential added benefits to biodiversity conservation and the sustainable development of the region. The Brazilian Proposal was the first submitted proposal that addressed the REDD issue. It helped instigate the establishment of the Bali Road Map, at COP-13, which determined a 2-year period to discuss and establish a REDD and forest conservation mechanism under the UNFCCC that is acceptable to all tropical countries.

The international and Brazilian communities are therefore open to a discussion on the possible mechanisms to address carbon emissions from deforestation. In this chapter, we present a brief analysis of Brazil's current position on avoided deforestation, in both the national and international (UNFCCC) arenas and the potential funding mechanisms (including CR) currently under discussion. We will focus our discussion in this chapter on the development of alternatives for Brazil to reduce deforestation that could be funded by REDD mechanisms. To begin, we present Brazil's carbon emissions profile with emphasis on the role of the Brazilian Amazon. We briefly analyze the proposals currently under debate in Brazil to reduce deforestation in the Amazon. We also discuss some barriers to these proposals, for example, the lack of consensus on the role of the carbon market to sustain REDD and differences in methods or approaches related to baseline and carbon accounting. Lastly, we propose solutions to overcome the barriers to implementing a REDD policy proposal.

Carbon emissions from deforestation and forest impoverishment in Brazilian Amazonia

The tree trunks, branches and roots of tropical forest ecosystems store about 50 years' worth of current global carbon emissions (~ 430 billion tons). This carbon is being released into the atmosphere at the rate of approximately 0.8 to 2.4 billion tons per year through deforestation and forest thinning (Houghton, 2005). Deforestation in the Brazilian Amazon during the last decade released 200 million tons of carbon per year (3 per cent of global CO_2 emissions) (Houghton, 2005), representing 70 per cent of total Brazilian CO_2 emissions (Santilli *et al.*, 2005).

The rate of Amazon deforestation was 1.8 million hectares (18,165 km²) annually during the 1990s with a peak in 1995 (2.9 million hectares). However, recently the rate dropped to 1.1 million hectares, mainly as a consequence of governmental actions (higher enforcement and protected area expansion) and low prices for some commodities in the international market (Nepstad *et al.*, 2008). An area equivalent in size to France (ca. 64.5 million hectares) has already been deforested and converted, mainly to pasture (see Figure 6.1).

This figure does not include the emissions resulting from Amazon forest fires, which are frequent in El Niño years, when severe drought is common in the region. For example, in 1998, when a strong El Niño episode triggered severe droughts in the Amazon and Southeast Asia, Amazon fires burned 2.6 million hectares of forest in the south of Pará and north of Mato Grosso. Resultant annual emissions varied from 36 (during years without El Niño influence) to 472 million tons of carbon (years under strong El Niño influence) (Alencar *et al.*, 2006; Mendonça *et al.*, 2004).[2]

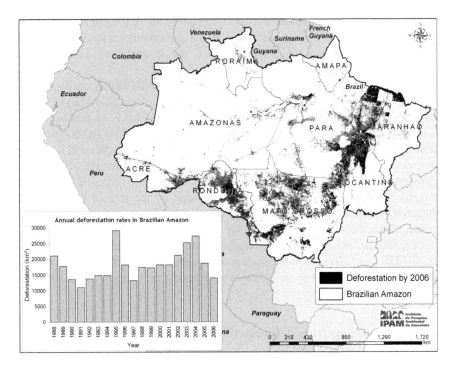

Figure 6.1 Arc of deforestation in the Brazilian Amazon

Source: PRODES/INPE (http://www.obt.inpe.br/prodes/index.html)

Deforestation causes and future projections

The rate of tropical deforestation is projected to increase in the coming decades because of three interrelated trends. First, agro-industrial expansion has shifted to the tropics in recent years, partly because there is relatively little available land for agricultural expansion in the temperate zone (Nepstad *et al.*, 2006b). Second, the demand for grains (for animal feed) and grazing lands is increasing rapidly through the growing level of meat consumption in the world's emerging economies (ibid.). Finally, higher oil prices have triggered an enormous flow of investment into bio-fuels, increasing the competition for available agricultural land and driving up pressure to clear rainforests on land that is suitable for agriculture (Stickler *et al.*, 2007).

Around 40 per cent of land covered by global tropical forest that is susceptible to conversion to soy, palm, pasture or sugar cane plantation is found in the Amazon Basin (Kellndorfer *et al.*, 2007). This trend has already begun in the Amazon, where deforestation rates oscillate depending on the prices of soy and beef and the strength of the Brazilian real against the US dollar (Nepstad *et al.*, 2006b). In recent years, the weakness of the real coincided with growing demand for soy in Europe as well as China and soaring prices for beef. Deforestation rates climbed to 2.7 million hectares in 2004, almost 50 per cent above the average of 2.0 million hectares recorded between 1989 and 2000. With the decline of soy and beef prices in 2005 and 2006, in association with the strengthening of the real against the dollar, deforestation rates slowed to 1.88 million hectares and 1.31 million hectares, respectively (INPE, 2006). But this decline was also at least partially caused by the Brazilian government's actions to govern the agricultural frontier (see later). Currently, soy prices are climbing again as the demand for corn to make ethanol grows in the US, as sugar cane production for ethanol expands in southern Brazil (displacing soy production), and as the demand for soy oil as a diesel substitute increases.

Total Brazilian CO_2 emissions have the potential to increase further in the future if current road construction and paving plans, particularly in the Amazon, remain on the agenda through the 'National Plan for Development Acceleration'.[3] Road building in the Amazon is *demonstrably* and *directly* linked to deforestation. More than 70 per cent of deforestation in the region is concentrated within a 50-km band on either side of paved roads (Alves, 2002).

A recent study indicated that should current rates of agricultural expansion and road building continue, two-thirds of forest that cover the five major Brazilian watersheds and 10 ecoregions[4] will disappear (Soares-Filho *et al.*, 2006). This could potentially release approximately 32 billions tons of carbon into the atmosphere by the year of 2050, a carbon volume equivalent to 4 years of current annual global emissions.

The historical debate on climate change in Brazil: CDM and avoided deforestation

Currently, the only way in which a developing country such as Brazil can participate in international efforts to reduce GHG emissions is through the clean development mechanism (CDM) of the Kyoto Protocol. By this mechanism, Annex I countries can support sustainable development projects in developing countries that reduce emissions, while generating emissions offsets to meet their targets. As described elsewhere in this volume, the CDM only allows plantation projects in the forestry sector (reforestation and afforestation), with the purpose of sequestering carbon from the atmosphere.

Historically, Brazil's position on the reduction of tropical deforestation as a strategy for mitigating climate change has been very conservative and based on the argument that forest conservation or avoided deforestation would represent actions without real benefits to the atmosphere (Fearnside, 2001; Moutinho *et al.*, 2005). The strong Brazilian opposition against including avoided deforestation in the CDM was also related to technical arguments, for example, permanence, leakage, additionality, difficulties of measuring deforestation and so on (see Johns and Schlamadinger, Chapter 5 in this volume). While these may be resolved, a number of political problems and governance issues remain in Brazil and in other tropical nations, for example, sovereignty threats, uncertainties about the capacity to control deforestation, right to 'development' among others (see Lamy *et al.*, 2007).

Brazil's position, however, has changed substantially over the last few years due to three factors. First, a submission by Papua New Guinea was made to the UNFCCC Secretariat, supported by Costa Rica and other tropical countries.[5] It was a call to put back on the official agenda the issue of reducing emissions from tropical deforestation and created an immediate demand for Brazil to have a positive position on it. Second, the Stern Review (2007) broadcast to the world the real economic impacts of GHG emissions from deforestation. Lastly, there has been an intensification of the debate in Brazil involving government and civil society about Amazon deforestation, climate change and mechanisms of compensation for deforestation reduction. Since Brazil is the major emitter of GHG related to deforestation, the UNFCCC's decision to reconsider emissions from deforestation pressured Brazil to take a more proactive position on the issue. In addition, the national debate on climate change became more qualified with the publication of several scientific studies relating the role of Amazon forest to the regional hydrological balance and global carbon cycle. There is growing awareness of the negative effects of climate change and deforestation on the Amazon.[6] At the same time, the discussion relating to the compensated reduction of deforestation (CR) concept has intensified and involved the Brazilian government, particularly the Environment Ministry.

In September 2006, during a UNFCCC workshop on deforestation in developing countries in Rome, Brazil presented a proposal 'to provide positive financial incentives for developing countries that voluntarily reduce their greenhouse gas emissions from deforestation'.[7] Part of this proposal was based on the CR proposal. The Brazilian Proposal opened an official way to definitively engage Brazilian government and society in deforestation reduction with real potential to contribute to climate change mitigation. Since the COP-12 in Nairobi in 2006, the debate in Brazil on establishing mechanisms to compensate deforestation reduction efforts has intensified, especially after the COP-13 held in Bali in December 2007. In Bali, REDD was finally included in negotiations for the potential post-2012 agreement on climate change and has been discussed in the light of the CR concept. The 'Bali Road Map' determined a 2-year long (2008 until end of 2009) process to design a new international framework agreement.[8] In this, participating nations are committed to reaching a consensus on a framework to implement REDD regimes under the UNFCCC.

For Brazil, particularly, there are many opportunities to establish pilot projects for REDD in the country. The states of Brazilian Amazonia and the Brazilian government are now elaborating and proposing REDD plans for reducing deforestation, especially through payments for environmental services (PES) mechanisms, which may also involve the active participation of forest-dependent communities residing in the Amazon.[9]

Compensating for deforestation reduction in Brazil: the current debate and proposals on REDD

There is a growing consensus in the Brazilian government and society that developed countries should provide financial support (i.e. compensation) for efforts to reduce deforestation rates. There are at least three basic reasons that could explain this potential for a national consensus. First, there is now the perception of Brazilian society that the cost involved with conservation of Amazonia and the reduction of deforestation must be shared by both national and international societies. Second, reducing deforestation offers a viable cost-effective means to reduce GHG that could be used to bring benefits to developing countries and effectively engage them in global efforts against climate change. Finally, decreasing deforestation can contribute effectively to a robust, inclusive international emissions reduction regime after 2012, while possibly contributing to the preservation of global biodiversity.

However, Brazil has assumed that any compensation for deforestation reduction should only be accepted considering the fundamental principle of UNFCCC, the 'common but differentiated responsibilities' of countries and that the REDD mechanism should be voluntary. Also, given industrialized countries' difficulties in reaching their emissions reduction goals any commitment will only be assumed by developing countries after emission reductions targets have been reached by developed countries. Therefore, the likelihood of significant emissions reductions in developing countries will depend on the incentives available to them. Since COP-12, Brazil has been arguing that the historically greatest emitters should compensate developing countries, directly or indirectly, for reductions in emissions from avoiding deforestation.

There are several important initiatives in Brazil with the potential to involve REDD mechanisms and generate significant results, particularly in the Amazon region. These initiatives are described in the following subsections. The challenge involved in all these initiatives, however, is related to which mechanism would be more successful to sustain compensations worldwide: positive voluntary incentives, carbon credits or a hybrid mechanism. Another challenge is how to integrate the regional state initiatives into a federal framework proposal that will be taken into consideration under the UNFCCC by the Brazilian delegates.

Compensated reductions of deforestation (CR)

As mentioned already, CR was originally launched during the COP-9 in 2003. This credit-based mechanism proposes that developing countries voluntarily elect to effect, and achieve, reductions in their emissions from deforestation (Santilli *et al.*, 2005). The proposed baseline for the 5 years of the first commitment period (say 2008–2012) is the average of annual deforestation in the 1980–1990s. In exchange, these countries would receive financial compensation for the emissions avoided, based on the average market value of carbon in 2012. Thus, it is *deforestation rates*, verified trough uniform and consistent technical criteria, that would form the basis for compensation. Conversely, if these countries were to increase their deforestation rates during the first commitment period, they would take the increment as an obligatory limit during the second commitment period without compensation. After achieving this target, they would again be eligible for financial compensation for additional reductions. As a control, the IPCC or a new UNFCCC body could establish common criteria for baselines. It is hoped that this proposal would more effectively engage developing countries in international efforts to combat climate change. This would not, like the CDM, be a market mechanism limited to specific projects, but a commitment among countries.

Compensation would be due ex post once emissions reductions have been verified and regardless of how they were achieved. It is important to note that, by allowing tropical forest holders in developing countries to participate, the proposal attempts to establish the basis for effectively addressing deforestation. On a most general level, for any private actor in tropical forest areas, economic incentives tend towards activities leading to deforestation. For governments, which in the Amazon are responsible for the overwhelming majority of forestlands, forest protection implies high costs and little economic return. The CR principle creates the means by which positive economic forest values can be created for private actors, forest-dependent people and governments in order to induce forest preservation. In this sense, its intergovernmental, national-based and global character, as opposed to the project-based approach, is a key characteristic.

This instrument would be appropriate for dealing specifically with deforestation, with national strategies focusing on the measures required to sustain consistent reductions in deforestation rates. For CR to work, the drivers underlying deforestation would need to be identified, particularly those associated with random or seasonal factors such as emissions from burning pastures or forest fires. As noted earlier, forest fires, a significant source of emissions of greenhouse gases, are closely and positively linked to deforestation (Alencar *et al.*, 2006; Soares-Filho *et al.*, 2006); actual reductions in deforestation rates could potentially lead to reductions in the area affected by fire.

A REDD mechanism based on a credit-based proposal like CR could be implemented immediately if an early crediting mechanism linking REDD actions could be realized now (i.e. during the first commitment period of the Kyoto Protocol) with rewards made during the second commitment period. The country that manages to reduce its deforestation emissions in a measurable, reportable and verifiable manner would then be qualified to issue carbon certificates, with the support of the relevant multilateral bodies. These would be equivalent to the volume of reductions and eligible for sale on the international carbon market (Soares-Filho *et al.*, 2006).

In order to avoid 'flooding' the carbon market with REDD credits, only some proportion of these certificates would be certified as offsets during the first commitment period, with another valid for subsequent periods. Countries could transact sales at any point, but buyers could only use the certificates in their respective periods of validity. In contrast to the CDM, which allows offsets for past emissions, this mechanism would guarantee reductions first, with gradual offsets afterwards. Resources received by developing countries that actually reduced deforestation would be invested as they see fit, in national programmes and actions that combat deforestation and generate sustainable development. The choice of programme or action should be a sovereign choice of the country that receives the compensation. In Brazil, for example, a national pact for deforestation reduction (see next section) has been discussed as a mechanism of benefits distribution that might be politically and technically feasible.

Reducing deforestation will depend on the implementation of policies that combine legal enforcement and the promotion of sustainable activities with the necessary involvement of local level government on the agricultural frontiers and in areas where new infrastructural projects are being developed (see following sections). There are already GIS-based systems that allow effective monitoring of deforestation on large landholdings and settlement projects.

The Brazilian Proposal for positive incentives

After the Rome workshop in 2006, the Brazilian government formally submitted its proposal of positive incentives during the COP-12 in Nairobi (November 2006). Under this proposal, Brazil reaffirmed its position against 'any mechanism using avoided deforestation that could be used by Annex I countries to meet their quantified greenhouse gas emission limitation and reduction commitments under the Kyoto Protocol'.[10] Brazil proposed 'positive incentives' to developing countries that achieve – voluntarily – a net reduction in their GHG emissions from deforestation below a national reference point of historical emissions (established from the average of the deforestation rate during a certain (5–10 year) time period in the recent past). This reference period would be periodically updated. The incentives would be calculated by the difference between the annual rate of emissions from deforestation and the historical emission rate. The proposal established that financial incentives would be provided by developed countries through an international fund created for this purpose. Brazil strongly recommended that its proposal and other ones involving deforestation reduction should be considered under the UNFCCC.

The main difference between the Brazil Proposal and the CR proposal is that the former is not based on a market mechanism (carbon credits) to compensate developing countries for deforestation reduction in their territories. In fact, Brazil is proposing an international 'positive incentive fund', fed by donations from developed nations as a source of funds for payments. A preliminary version of this fund is the Amazon Fund, which was launched by the Brazilian government in July 2008 with an initial donation of US$ 100 million by the Norwegian government (Economist, 2008).

Under the 'positive incentive fund' proposal, the amount of emissions reduced could not be used by developed countries to reach their targets of emissions reduction established through the Kyoto Protocol. The Brazilian Proposal did not suggest a secure source of funding for these reduction efforts. Instead, it assumes that Annex I countries would provide financial resources for this fund in addition to those already provided through the global environment facility (GEF) or international cooperation programmes. These funds would also be in addition to the cost of efforts they must put forward to reduce their own emissions. A funding mechanism based on donations may be less attractive for developed countries, if they are unable to use any portion of emissions reductions achieved with deforestation reductions to help them reach their own emissions reduction targets established by a post-2012 agreement. Then again, this may not be the case if the tradeoff for developed countries is between agreeing to stricter emissions targets or contributing to a fund instead.

The utilization of a funding mechanism based on donations alone may also be risky in terms of the long-term sustainability of payments. This is due to the ephemeral characteristics of possible donations. Moreover, international organizations are classifying Brazil as a country with income high enough to elect it as a donor.

The Brazilian Proposal is different from that submitted by the Coalition of Rainforest Nations led by Papua New Guinea and Costa Rica in that the Coalition is open to market mechanisms, similar to the CR proposal.

In summary, there are a number of proposals presented under the aegis of the UNFCCC: a voluntary mechanism (Brazil), a market mechanism (Rainforest Nations Coalition) and a Forest Carbon Partnership Facility launched by the World Bank in Bali to promote pilot REDD projects. The last comprises donations from countries, NGOs and other banks. Given that the Bali Action Plan commits to the consideration of 'various approaches, including opportunities for using markets, to enhance the cost-effectiveness of, and to promote, mitigation actions[11] to enhance actions on mitigation of climate change', a hybrid REDD framework uniting the market mechanism and donations may be the most feasible of all.

Other initiatives to compensate for deforestation reduction in Brazil

The Amazonas Initiative

The state of Amazonas is the largest state in Brazil, at 157 million hectares, and with 98 per cent forest cover. In 2003 the state government assumed an official commitment, locally known as the 'Green Free Trade Zone' to convey sustainable development options for local rural people, while maintaining the options of keeping forests standing and environmental services flowing. Since 2003 this commitment has been demonstrated via an increase of 133 per cent (from 7.4 to 17.4 million ha) in the state area protected by law while the state economy grew at a rate of 11.8 per cent a year (Viana, 2006). In the same period, the rate of deforestation declined by 53 per cent, partly due to the creation of new state protected areas and the fall in international prices for some commodities (soy and beef).

To maintain these achievements in the long run and to control the growing pressure from agricultural frontier expansion coming from surrounding states in southern Amazonia, the state government launched the Amazonas Initiative. This is an independent proposal for creating a voluntary mechanism for compensation for environmental services to complement the Brazilian Proposal, which could be implemented in parallel with international negotiations. The proposal was first presented during the COP-11 as an alternative mechanism for action in reducing emissions from deforestation through payments for environmental or ecosystem services (PES) (Viana *et al.*, 2005). In November 2006 the Amazonas Initiative was officially presented at COP-12 (Viana, 2006).

The initiative seeks to establish a new mechanism that would enable interested parties to become partners in the implementation of programmes to reduce deforestation through PES and compensation for reduced emissions from deforestation. The goal is to establish a fund which can be accessed to purchase ecosystem services provided by standing forests in the state, to develop activities that help prevent deforestation and to contribute to sustainable development in the following major programmes:

- support to monitoring and law enforcement
- income generation through sustainable businesses
- community development, scientific research and education
- PES to 'forest guardians'.

While only 2 per cent of Amazonas state is currently deforested, the rapidly advancing deforestation frontier coming from the state's borders suggests that its rate of deforestation may increase in the near future. In addition to past rates, the initiative is also considering future scenarios, in which a projected baseline for deforestation is calculated by using recognized deforestation models (Soares-Filho *et al.*, 2006). For example, the business-as-usual (BAU) scenario (low governance and no incentives for reducing deforestation) suggests that the level of carbon emissions for Amazonas state could be as high as 50 million hectares (30 per cent of state forest cover) or 162 million tons of CO_2 by 2050.

In June 2007 the government of Amazonas created the 'Amazonas State Policy for Climate Change', which provides the legal framework and basis for voluntary partnerships for the mechanism proposed (Amazonas, 2007). Serving as an early action and practical example for international negotiations within the UNFCCC, the Amazonas Initiative will thus complement Brazil's federal government proposal towards a new UNFCCC mechanism as well as other initiatives towards forest conservation and the maintenance of ecosystem services provided by forests. The funding that the Amazonas Initiative has obtained comes mostly through donations from private firms, such as the Bradesco Bank Foundation and the Marriott Hotel group.[12]

The Mato Grosso State Initiative

In contrast to Amazonas state, Mato Grosso (MT) state (90.3 million hectares (903,358 km²), 50 per cent covered by Amazon forest and 40 per cent by savannas) has been intensively deforested over the previous decade. About 30 per cent of its forest area and 40 per cent of its savannas are devastated already. MT is the most important national producer of soy (30 per cent of national production) and beef in the Amazon region with production currently under expansion (Nepstad *et al.*, 2006b). The state, with the support of local and national NGOs, is elaborating its plan to control deforestation through several initiatives:

1   strengthening of monitoring and controlling capacity of deforestation
2   PES to landowners in priority areas (under deforestation threat)

3   increase the total area under state protection (i.e. protected areas)
4   incentives for intensive cattle ranching and sustainable forest management.

The implementation of this plan is currently being discussed by the government and society.

Zero Deforestation Pact

Another initiative in Brazil based on compensation for deforestation reduction has been elaborated by Brazilian NGOs and supported by social movements (rubber tappers, indigenous people, small producers and the private sector), national congress and Amazon state governors (of Mato Grosso, Amapa, Acre and Amazonas). The 'Zero Deforestation Pact'[13] established an Amazon agreement within the legal territory of the Brazilian Amazon forest (Amazônia Legal). Launched on October 2007, it represented a tremendous advance for the political engagement of governors and society to control deforestation in Brazilian Amazonia. For the first time, targets for deforestation reduction were publically assumed by the states' governors. The goal proposed by the pact is to reduce deforestation over the next 7 years through the establishment of incremental deforestation reduction targets. The funding mechanism for deforestation reduction of the pact is based on the CR proposal and a national fund, and could be fundamental in providing political support to the Brazilian Amazon Fund.

   The pact shows a way of implementing a deal to reduce deforestation. It may be a plausible mechanism to regulate the national distribution of benefits coming from international compensation for deforestation reduction. These are to be accompanied by measures to strengthen forest governance and implement economic incentives for the government and local stakeholders. It is hoped that strategies of development that sustain the elimination of deforestation in the region could be supported via these measures. The main instrument supporting this pact would be the CR proposal. The pact represents a clear indicator on how a tropical country could implement a deal to reduce deforestation and distribute the benefits from compensation at the national level.

Reducing deforestation and associated carbon emissions in Brazilian Amazonia: what is the appropriate approach?

Considering the initiatives presented earlier, in order to implement any compensation mechanism for deforestation reduction it will be necessary to develop credible programmes that stand up to the scrutiny of early action investors, including transparent and efficient frameworks for receiving and managing these investments. In this section, we will emphasize some key issues – some of them already addressed by the initiatives reported earlier – that we judge fundamental to achieve significant reductions in GHG emissions from deforestation and forest degradation.

   Successful national programmes of deforestation reduction should be based on the following key features:

1 *Deforestation monitoring system*: it is necessary to implement a system to monitor deforestation at the national level.
2 *Effective multiple stakeholders' engagement*: any programme needs to be supported by local society (governments, industry and social movements) living in the deforestation frontiers.
3 *Opportunity cost*: it should cover the opportunity costs involved with the decision to maintain standing forest rather than convert it to pasture or agriculture through, for example, payments for reducing deforestation or the implementation of subsidies for forest products such as rubber or Amazon nuts.
4 *Establishment of regional plans for deforestation reduction*: these plans should integrate a number of factors including multi-stakeholder processes and information about the spatial variation of the most promising economic activities in forested landscapes.

The plans in 4 should be based on the results of 1, 2 and 3. Moreover, unsustainable land uses inducing deforestation and forest degradation need to be identified. For example, pasture established in unproductive soils that are typically abandoned after 5 years and used for land price speculation must be curtailed. Sound economic planning needs to be incorporated into regional development plans. Overall, these plans need to reconcile forest conservation with economic development and livelihood goals. It could do this through the maximization of the returns from opportunities for reducing GHG emissions, while bringing the greatest benefits for biodiversity conservation and improvements in rural livelihoods. Note that due to possible tradeoffs, however, it may not be possible to achieve all these goals at the same time.

In Brazil, the four key features just described are achievable. As described in the following subsections, technology is enabling better monitoring while governance is improving all the time. For instance, the National Plan for Control of Amazon Deforestation launched by the federal government in 2004 represented an important step for improving governance in the region. In the following subsections, we discuss the economics of the Amazon forest and how potential payments for REDD compare with the returns of other land uses. Carbon pricing in international carbon markets along with the pricing of other forest environmental services may also assist in reducing deforestation rates in Brazil.

Monitoring technology

Doubts have frequently been raised about the practicality and reliability of a deforestation monitoring system with the capacity to serve the UNFCCC REDD proposal. Uncertainties regarding the amount of forest land and the rate at which it is being deforested are compounded by those relating to the corresponding volume of carbon emitted into the atmosphere. Advances in the field of remote sensing and technological transfer agreements among countries could, however, address the numerous barriers to more precise measurements of tropical deforestation for the purposes of agreements such as the UNFCCC.

Brazil has demonstrated that it is possible to implement an efficient deforestation monitoring system through the one developed by the Brazilian Space Agency (INPE). INPE has begun to build the capacity of neighbouring South American countries to monitor their forest cover using approaches similar to Brazil's own system. A historical data set of high resolution optical remote sensing imagery has now been complemented with radar imagery from European, Canadian and Japanese satellite missions. All these nations plus the United States have plans to increase remote sensing capacities with radar sensors in the near future. Radar is particularly well suited to tropical forest observation due to its ability to penetrate the cloud cover that is so common over dense humid forests. The Advanced Land Observing Satellite (ALOS),[14] which carries a novel radar sensor (PALSAR), was launched in 2006 by the Japanese Space Agency, JAXA. As part of this mission, a dedicated observation plan was designed, which provides pan-tropical, high resolution imagery on an annual basis, thus having great potential to monitor tropical deforestation within very narrow timeframes. In addition, space-borne light detection and ranging (LIDAR) systems (e.g., geoscience laser altimeter system – GLAS sensor aboard the 'Ice, Cloud, and land Elevation Satellite' – IceSAT) have shown significant potential when used with radar and optical imagery to support the estimation of carbon from biomass in secondary forests mostly growing on abandoned pasture (Lefsky *et al.*, 2005).

Protected area policy

Although rates of deforestation in the Amazon declined in 2005 and 2006 in part because of falling soy and beef prices, there is now evidence that effective 'frontier governance' promoted by the Brazilian government and actions taken within civil society resulted in deforestation reduction in several areas in the region (MMA, 2007). In 2004 and 2005, for example, the Brazilian government created 24 million hectares of new protected areas in the Amazon, mostly in the forest frontier, i.e. the area of active deforestation. More than half of this newly protected area will, however, eventually be open to commercial sustainable forest management under Brazil's new logging concession policy. Despite reducing the amount of land available for agricultural production, the creation of these areas met with surprisingly mild opposition and was supported by organizations of smallholder farmers along the Transamazon highway (Campos and Nepstad, 2006). It was also supported by the regional planning process that had been underway for 3 years in anticipation of the paving of a major highway (the BR163, from Santarém to Cuiaba). This process was initiated by civil society and engaged hundreds of organizations of smallholder farmers, rubber tappers, indigenous groups and some logging and ranching firms. The plan has been endorsed by the Brazilian government.

Brazil's previous commitment to expand its network of protected areas through the Amazon region protected areas (ARPA) program and to expand its network of national forests (through the *Politica Nacional da Floresta*) also helped to create a legal framework for the establishment of these protected areas. In recent years and in an unprecedented display of political will to control the illegal exploitation of natural resources, the Brazilian government has sent army troops into regions of illegal deforestation and logging and jailed illegal loggers, illegal ranchers and corrupt government personnel. In the long run, to maintain the protected areas, the challenge is to combine this demonstration of the government's capacity for law enforcement with a sustainable development programme (ecotourism, payments for forest conservation, economic incentives for forest products). Effective protected areas created in regions of active agricultural expansion have the potential to reduce deforestation and associated carbon emissions by restricting the amount of land available for clearing. The displacement of deforestation to other regions can be reduced by the absence of infrastructure (paved roads) that allows access to remote forest, but this 'passive' protection can be discontinued if new roads (official and non-official – for example, roads opened by loggers) are built in remote areas of Amazonia. The protected areas created since 2004 in the Brazilian Amazon could potentially reduce carbon emissions from the region by approximately 1 billion tons by the year 2015 (Soares-Filho *et al.*, 2006). However, the Brazilian government has no intention of requesting compensation for emission reductions produced in these new protected areas.

Protected areas, indigenous parks, extractive reserves and national forests exert a strong inhibitory effect on deforestation and fire in Brazilian Amazonia (Nepstad *et al.*, 2006a). Indigenous lands are the most important type of protected area today in slowing Amazon deforestation because they include 21 per cent of all the forests of the Brazilian Amazon and are often located in the active agricultural frontier. Parks and nature reserves are often created in remote places where the risk of invasion and opposition from local landholders is low. It is in this context that Brazil's recent accomplishments in creating new protected areas are remarkable. The protected areas that are located in regions of active agricultural expansion are the most important ones in curbing deforestation and preventing the emissions of GHG to the atmosphere, damages to biodiversity and threats to regional rainfall systems that are associated with forest destruction. But these protected areas can also be the most expensive to create from the perspective of regional economies.

Cost of reducing deforestation

In preventing the expansion of profitable agriculture, ranching or logging, protected areas can reduce significantly the revenues of these economies with negative consequences for the local and national tax bases, employment opportunities and investments in roads and human services. For example, the prohibition of logging in current and proposed protected areas in the Brazilian Amazon will cut profits to the Amazon timber sector by approximately US$0.4 billion annually in the next 15 to 20 years, once timber stocks are depleted outside these protected areas (Merry *et al.*, 2008).

The economic cost of setting aside land in protected areas can exceed US$200 per hectare annually in regions of high potential rents to agriculture. Calculations of the breakeven carbon price (i.e. the price of carbon at which forest conservation becomes financially attractive for loggers and ranchers) indicated that US$0.30–4 per ton of CO_2 would be enough to cover the opportunity cost of pasture (US\$28/ha/yr) or soy plantation (US\$212/ha/yr) (Diaz and Schwartzman, 2005). By comparison, the average carbon price in the European Union Emissions Trading Scheme (ETS) from January 2004 until April 2005 was US\$5.63/ton of CO_2 (see Lecocq and Capoor, 2005). A recent study launched during the COP-13, indicated that to reduce deforestation to zero in the Brazilian Amazon over a period of 10 years will cost less than 0.7US\$/ton of CO_2 to cover the opportunity cost of pasture (Nepstad el al, 2007).

Fragile lands that are of marginal suitability for crops or livestock are logical targets for the creation of protected areas for nations that are trying to reduce their GHG emissions from deforestation at the lowest possible opportunity cost. Much of the clearing of tropical rainforests does not provide high enough returns to landholders in the long term, although low returns do not prevent deforestation. For example, pastures can be used for 5–8 years, but new areas need to be incorporated into the productive system to maintain productivity. Despite the low returns to landholder investments in agriculture or livestock, low land prices ensure the continuation of deforestation. Also, deforestation has been used as a way to demonstrate land possession by landowners. Consequently, the demand for new land continues.[15]

Market forces could assist in lowering carbon emissions from deforestation. Embedded in the growing worldwide demand for agricultural commodities is an increasingly rigorous set of environmental and social standards, even in Brazil where the demand for eco-products is increasing rapidly. Finance institutions, commodity traders, consumer groups, environmental NGOs and human rights organizations are pushing to raise the bar on the socioenvironmental 'quality' of the agricultural commodity production chain. Financial institutions that are striving to adopt the 'equator principles' of social and environmental responsibility are beginning to attach socioenvironmental conditions to their loans, reducing the risk associated with their investments as they force thousands of farmers to obey the law and adopt good land stewardship practices. Similarly, agricultural commodity traders are seeking socially and environmentally benign suppliers and are important participants in the development of international criteria for 'responsible' soy, palm oil and other commodities.[16] In one of the most dramatic illustrations of these trends, the companies that buy most of the soy produced in the Amazon recently declared a 2-year moratorium on the purchase of soy grown on recently cleared Amazon rainforest soil.[17]

Also, Amazon farmers and ranchers are voluntarily responding to market pressure. For example, landowners of Mato Grosso state support the Registry of Social Environmental Responsibility (*Cadastro de Compromisso Socioambiental*, CCS) initiative.[18] It is essentially a 'best practice' registry for agricultural properties committed to a set of environmental and social principles and practices. The landowners receive diagnostic reports of their properties and are provided with action plans that would bring them into compliance with existing regulations and with practices of sound land stewardship. There are well over 1 million hectares currently in CCS, including roughly 400,000 hectares of standing forest.

A REDD mechanism under the UNFCCC

Effective and voluntary emissions reductions of rates of tropical deforestation can and should result in substantial deeper mandatory reductions in GHG emissions for developed countries while simultaneously providing greater benefits to the atmosphere. This argument can be demonstrated by considering two scenarios:

1   Annex I countries decide to simply stabilize emissions at the first commitment period levels (repetition of Kyoto goals). No compensation for deforestation reduction would be viable in this case.
2   Annex I countries agree to substantially increase their reduction goals for the second commitment period.[19] Under this scenario, parties might authorize some quantity or proportion of the target for which Annex I countries could use avoided deforestation offsets. Post-2012 global emissions reductions targets should be based on science-based measures of what is needed to mitigate climate change and the evaluation of all feasible means of achieving reductions. Under this second scenario, tropical nations would obtain significant rewards and developed countries would be stimulated to establish higher goals than previously contemplated.

Fears over the risk of 'flooding' the market with cheap carbon from avoided deforestation are often voiced (see Michaelowa and Dutschke, Chapter 8 in this volume). Obviously some limit could be placed on allowable offsets as mentioned earlier in the discussion, but even in the absence of a cap, 'flooding' is unlikely to occur given potential growing demand for emissions reductions in developed countries, possibly including the United States.[20]

Regarding the equitable distribution of REDD benefits to society, a recent study proposed a scheme comprising three funds (Nepstad *et al.*, 2007). The first one could be a 'public forest stewardship' fund to compensate forest people such as indigenous people, rubber tappers, Brazil nut gatherers and smallholder populations who have defended forests against forest-replacing economic activities. The second fund, a 'private forest stewardship fund' would compensate those legal private landholders who retain forest on their properties. Finally, a 'government fund' could compensate government programmes and expenditures that are necessary for REDD above and beyond current budget outlays.

Conclusion

The carbon storage capability of tropical forest will influence humanity's ability to prevent dangerous alteration of the global climate system. REDD mechanisms have the potential to keep many of these forest ecosystems intact and healthy, preventing the release of vast quantities of carbon to the atmosphere. Brazil is a major emitter of GHG related to deforestation, but has begun promoting policy in favour of deforestation reduction that can be useful for the REDD debate in the context of the UNFCCC. However, there are several challenges related to implementation of a REDD mechanism in Brazil. First, there is no consensus on the options to sustain the funding mechanisms for REDD: the market (carbon credits) linked to developed countries' emissions reduction targets, incentives based on donations made by developed countries or a hybrid mechanism combining elements of both. Second, the profusion of initiatives promoted by the federal government and Brazilian Amazon states impose a barrier for establishment of a common REDD mechanism for the entire country. Finally, the technical debate around baseline, permanence and additionality issues still represent an additional obstacle for implementation of REDD mechanism in future. Nevertheless, through the capture of carbon values REDD still represents possibly the most powerful mechanism in history for conserving the biodiversity, the culture and myriad ecosystem services of these magnificent forest ecosystems.

Acknowledgements

The authors thank the Bluemoon Foundation, William and Flora Hewlett Foundation, and Packard Foundation for financial support for work related to this paper.

Notes

1   See http://unfccc.int/files/meetings/dialogue/application/pdf/wp_21_braz.pdf.
2   This drought (during El Niño years) also destroyed trees directly, without fire. In that year about 30 per cent of the Amazon forest was under fire risk with the impacts varying from state to state. In 1998 the cost of the fires related to accidental pasture fires, property losses, forest losses, carbon emissions and impacts on human health (due to respiratory problems provoked by smoke) was estimated at US$90 million to US$5 billion (0.2–9 per cent of the GDP of Brazilian Amazonia).
3   See http://www.brasil.gov.br/pac/.
4   Ecoregions are large areas of land geographically distinguished and containing an assemblage of natural communities containing species adapted to similar environmental conditions.
5   See http://www.rainforestcoalition.org/eng/.
6   See http://lba.cptec.inpe.br/lba/index.php?lg=eng.
7   See http://unfccc.int/files/methods_and_science/lulucf/application/vnd.ms-powerpoint/060830_capobianco.ppt.
8   According to the clause 1, b (iii) of the Bali Action Plan CP.13.
9   See http://www.climaedesmatamento.org.br/image/layout/icoPDFVerde.png.
10   See http://unfccc.int/files/meetings/dialogue/application/pdf/wp_21_braz.pdf.
11   In fact, clause 1, b, (v) of the Decision CP.13 approved in Bali determines the use of: 'Various approaches, including opportunities for using markets, to enhance the cost-effectiveness of, and to promote, mitigation actions, bearing in mind different circumstances of developed and developing countries'.
12   See http://money.cnn.com/2008/04/07/magazines/fortune/marriott_amazon.fortune/.
13   See www.climaedesmatamento.com.br (in Portuguese). Also http://www.socioambiental.org/banco_imagens/pdfs/Sumriodoc-fundamentos%20economicos%20desmatamento%20zero%20SUM%20EXEC.pdf (in Portuguese).
14   See http://www.eorc.jaxa.jp/ALOS/kyoto/KC-Science-Plan_v2.pdf.
15   Throughout history, people have cleared forest lands in preparation for planting crops and raising livestock, then subsequently abandoned large areas that are of marginal

suitability for agriculture (Rudel *et al.*, 2005). Of the many causes of land abandonment in the tropics, low soil fertility, high soil erodibility, steep slopes, poor drainage, excessive rain and high transport costs to markets are among the most important. In the Brazilian Amazon, for example, and since the 1970s, nearly one-third of the lands used for agriculture and cattle ranching have been abandoned (Vera Diaz *et al.*, 2008). Forest recovery on this abandoned land is low due to reduced soil fertility and disturbance produced by frequent fire events.

16 Established agricultural sectors in industrialized countries, however, sometimes see higher standards as a way of protecting their products from competition.

17 See http://www.abiove.com.br/english/ss_moratoria_us.html.

18 See http://www.whrc.org/policy/BaliReports/assets/3-Strategies-Dec-07.pdf.

19 Note that the Decision CP.13 of Conclusions adopted by the Ad Hoc Working Group on Further Commitments for Annex I Parties under the Kyoto Protocol at its resumed fourth session held in Bali, 3–11 December 2007 indicates that: 'Global emissions of greenhouse gases (GHGs) need to peak in the next 10–15 years and be reduced to very low levels, well below half of levels in 2000 by the middle of the twenty-first century in order to stabilize their concentrations in the atmosphere at the lowest levels assessed by the IPCC to date in its scenarios ... This decision also recognizes that ... Working Group III to the AR4 indicates that achieving the lowest levels assessed by the IPCC to date and its corresponding potential damage limitation would require Annex I Parties as a group to reduce emissions in a range of 25–40 per cent below 1990 levels by 2020, through means that may be available to these Parties to reach their emission reduction targets.' See UNFCCC (2007).

20 See http://www.whrc.org/policy/BaliReports/assets/GettingREDDRight.pdf.

References

Alencar, A., Nepstad, D. and Diaz, M. del C.V. (2006) 'Forest understory fire in the Brazilian Amazon in ENSO and non-ENSO years: area burned and committed carbon emissions', *Earth Interactions*, 10(6): 1–17.

Alves, D. (2002) 'An analysis of the geographical patterns of deforestation in Brazilian Amazonia in the 1991–1996 period', in C. Wood and R. Porro (eds) *Land Use and Deforestation in the Amazon*, Gainesville, FL: University Press of Florida.

Amazonas (2007) *Política Estadual sobre Mudanças Climáticas, Conservação Ambiental e Desenvolvimento Sustentável do Amazonas* (in Portuguese), Amazonas: state government [online]. Available at: http://www.amazonas.am.gov.br [accessed 20 September 2007].

Campos, M. and Nepstad, D. (2006) 'Smallholder farmers, the Amazon's new conservationists', *Conservation Biology*, 20(5): 1553–1556.

Diaz, M. del C.V., Kaufmann, R., Nepstad, D. and Schlesinger, P. (2008) 'An interdisciplinary model of soybean yield in the Amazon Basin: the climatic, edaphic, and economic determinants', *Ecological Economics*, 65(2): 420–431.

Diaz, M. del C.V. and Schwartzman, S. (2005) 'Carbon offsets and land use in the Brazilian Amazon', in P. Moutinho and S. Schwartzman (eds) *Tropical Deforestation and Climate Change*, Belém: Instituto de Pesquisa Ambiental da Amazônia (IPAM) and Washington, DC: Environmental Defense (ED).

Economist (2008) 'Paying for the forest', 9 August, London: The Economist.

Energy Information Administration (2004) *Official Statistics from the U.S. Government* [online]. Available at: http://www.eia.doe.gov/emeu/iea/carbon.html [accessed 31 July 2008].

Fearnside, P. (2001) 'Environmentalists split over Kyoto and Amazonian deforestation', *Environmental Conservation*, 28(4): 295–299.

Houghton, R.A. (2005) 'Tropical deforestation as a source of greenhouse gases', in P. Moutinho and S. Schwartzman (eds) *Tropical Deforestation and Climate Change*, Belém: Instituto de Pesquisa Ambiental da Amazônia (IPAM) and Washington, DC: Environmental Defense (ED).

INPE (2006) (in Portuguese), INPE/PRODES [online]. Available at: http://www.obt.inpe. br/prodes/ [accessed 31 July 2008].

IPCC (Intergovernmental Panel on Climate Change) (2007) *Climate Change 2007 – Mitigation of Climate Change. Working Group III contribution to the Fourth Assessment Report of the IPCC*, Cambridge: Cambridge University Press.

Kellndorfer, J., Shimada, M., Rosenqvist, A., Walker, W., Kirsch, K., Nepstad, D. *et al.* (2007) *New Eyes in the Sky: Cloud-Free Tropical Forest Monitoring for REDD with the Japanese Advanced Land Observing Satellite (ALOS)* [online]. Available at: http://www.whrc.org/policy/BaliReports/assets/Bali_ALOS.pdf [accessed 31 July 2008].

Lamy, C., Moutinho, P. and Mertens, F. (2007) *Historical Barriers and Future Perspectives on the Inclusion of Tropical Forests into International Debate on Climate Change* (in Portuguese), Brasilia: Brasília University.

Lecocq, F. and Capoor, K. (2005) *State and Trends of the Carbon Market 2006*, Washington, DC: World Bank and International Emissions Trading Association.

Lefsky, M.A., Harding, D.J., Keller, M., Cohen, W.B., Carabajal, C.C., Del Bom Espirito-Santo, F. *et al.* (2005) 'Estimates of forest canopy height and aboveground biomass using ICESat', *Geophysical Research Letters*, 32: L22S02.

Mendonça, J.C. de, Diaz, M. del C.V., Nepstad, D., da Motta, R.S., Alencar, A., Gomes, J.C. *et al.* (2004) 'The economic cost of the use of fire in the Brazilian Amazon', *Ecological Economics*, 49(1): 89–105.

Merry, F.D., Soares-Filho, B.S., Nepstad, D.C., Amacher, G. and Rodrigues H. (2008) *Amazon Logging as a Valuation Benchmark and Conservation Catalyst*, mimeo, Falmouth, MA: Woods Hole Research Center (WHRC).

MMA (Ministério do Meio Ambiente) (2007), *Relatório de Gestão 2003–2006,* Brasília: Ministry of the Environment.

Moutinho, P., Santilli, M., Schwartzman, S. and Rodrigues, L. (2005) 'Why ignore tropical deforestation? A proposal for including forest conservation in the Kyoto Protocol', *Unasylva*, 222(56): 27–30.

Moutinho, P. and Schwartzman, S. (2005) *Tropical Deforestation and Climate Change*, Belém: Instituto de Pesquisa Ambiental da Amazônia (IPAM) and Washington, DC: Environmental Defense (ED).

Nepstad, D.C., Schwartzman, S., Bamberger, B., Santilli, M., Ray, D. Schleseninger, P. *et al.* (2006a) 'Inhibition of deforestation and fire by Amazon parks and indigenous lands', *Conservation Biology*, 20(1): 65–73.

Nepstad, D.C., Soares-Filho, B., Merry, F., Moutinho, P., Rodrigues, H.O., Bowman, M. *et al.* (2007) *The Costs and Benefits of Reducing Carbon Emission from Deforestation and Forest Degradation in the Brazilian Amazon* [online]. Available at: http://www.whrc.org/policy/BaliReports/assets/WHRC_Amazon_REDD.pdf; see also http://www.whrc.org/policy/BaliReports/assets/WHRC_Amazon_REDD_supp_info.pdf; see also http://www.whrc.org/policy/BaliReports/assets/WHRC_Amazon_REDD_Addendum.pdf [accessed 31 July 2008].

Nepstad, D.C., Stickler, C.M. and Almeida, O.T. (2006b) 'Globalization of the Amazon soy and beef industries: opportunities for conservation', *Conservation Biology*, 20(6): 1595–1603.

Nepstad, D.C., Stickler, C.M, Soares-Filho, B., Brando, P.M., Merry, F. (2008) 'Ecological, economic, and climatic tipping points of an Amazon forest dieback', *Philosophical Transactions of the Royal Society B*, 363(1498): 1737–1746.

Rudel, T.K., Coomes, O.T., Moran, E., Achard, F., Angelsen, A., Xu, J. *et al.* (2005) 'Forest transitions: towards a global understanding of land use change', *Global Environmental Change*, 15(1): 23–31.

Santilli, M., Moutinho, P., Schwartzman, S., Nepstad, D., Curran, L. and Nobre, C. (2005) 'Tropical deforestation and the Kyoto Protocol: an editorial essay', *Climate Change*, 71: 267–276.

Soares-Filho, B., Nepstad, D., Curran, L., Cerqueira, G., Garcia, R., Ramos, C. *et al.* (2006) 'Modeling Amazon conservation', *Nature*, 440: 520–523.

Stern, N. (2007) *The Economics of Climate Change: The Stern Review*, Cambridge: Cambridge University Press.

Stickler, C., Coe, M., Nepstad, D., Fiske, G. and Lefebvre, P. (2007) *Readiness for REDD: A Preliminary Global Assessment of Tropical Forested Land Suitability for Agriculture* [online]. Available at: http://www.whrc.org/policy/BaliReports/assets/Bali_crop_suitability.pdf [accessed 10 June 2008].

UNFCCC (United Nations Framework Convention on Climate Change) (2007) *Decision-/CP.13 Bali Action Plan* [online]. Available at: http://unfccc.int/files/meetings/cop_13/application/pdf/cp_bali_action.pdf [accessed 15 June 2008].

Viana, V. (2006) *Amazonas Initiative for Forest Conservation and Ecosystem Services*, Nairobi: 12th Conference of Parties, United Nations Framework for Climate Change (UNFCC).

Viana, V., Cenamo, M.C. and Manfrinato, W.M. (2005) *Reducing Emissions from Deforestation in Amazonas, Brazil: A State Government's Proposal for Action*, Montreal: 11th Conference of Parties, United Nations Framework for Climate Change (UNFCC).

7 Choosing avoided deforestation baselines in the context of government failure

The case of Indonesia's plantations policy

Charles Palmer and Krystof Obidzinski

Introduction

In 1992 Indonesia signed the United Nations Framework Convention on Climate Change (UNFCCC), which it then ratified on 1 August 1994.[1] On becoming a 'Party to the Conference', Indonesia's state minister for the environment issued the country's first (and so far only) 'national communication' report, outlining how it intended to meet its climate change commitments (Government of Indonesia, 1999). In this, it was reported that the country was a net emitter of greenhouse gases (GHG), reaching 904 million tonnes CO_2 equivalent ($MtCO_2e$), in 1994. Indonesia signed the Kyoto Protocol in 1997, ratifying it in 2004.[2]

Between 1994 and 2006 Indonesia's GHG emissions rose by 233 per cent resulting in the country becoming the world's third leading emitter, behind the USA and China. A recent study commissioned by the World Bank and the UK's Department for International Development (DFID) shows how Indonesia's current position is primarily a result of its high rates of deforestation (PEACE, 2007). About 85 per cent (2563 $MtCO_2e$) of its total emissions apparently resulted from forest fires, peat burning and forest clearance. To date, Indonesia, the world's 22nd largest economy by GDP, has had little success in controlling the forest fires and deforestation that contribute to its disproportionately high GHG emissions.

Indonesia currently contains the third largest area of tropical forest after Brazil and the Democratic Republic of the Congo. The country has forest cover of around 90 million ha, including degraded areas. Its rate of deforestation increased from 1.6 per cent between 1990 and 2000, to 1.9 per cent between 2000 and 2005 (FAO, 2005). This rate is equivalent to around 1.8 million hectares of forest cover lost each year. Acknowledging its struggle to control deforestation and forest degradation, the Indonesian government appealed to rich countries to help pay for efforts in conserving its forests. In January 2007, Rachmat Witoelar, Indonesia's minister of the environment was reported as saying:

> Preserving our forest means we can't exploit it for our economic benefits. We can't build roads or mines. But we make an important contribution to the world by providing oxygen. Therefore countries like Indonesia and Brazil should be compensated by developed countries for preserving their resources. (Reuters, 2007)

Underlying this statement is an assumption about the allocation of property rights to economic development and the environment. From Indonesia's perspective, the country has a right to the economic benefits from natural resource exploitation inside its borders regardless of the costs and benefits imposed on people outside its borders. Forgoing the rights to such benefits and instead preserving Indonesia's forests may lead to the provision of environmental benefits or 'positive externalities' to the rest of the world, for example, in the form of reduced GHG emissions to the atmosphere. It is these international externality effects to which Witoelar was referring to and claiming compensation for via, for instance, a future payments scheme to reduce emissions from deforestation and forest degradation (REDD).[3] Of course, forgoing economic benefits from forest conversion may also lead to national-level positive externalities such as improved water retention and quality, although Indonesia currently has only a few schemes that attempt to internalize these (see, for example, Arifin, 2005).

Understanding the drivers underlying the key sources of GHG emissions is important when considering the implementation of REDD policy in any country. In particular, the expansion of Indonesia's plantation estate, dominated by palm oil and timber, in areas of undisturbed, natural forest is identified as the main driver underlying deforestation (PEACE, 2007). This expansion is encouraged via a variety of direct and indirect government subsidies, which lower the costs of forest conversion and increase profits. These distortionary policies are known as 'government failures' or 'policy failures' (Pearce, 1995). While it seems that current rates of deforestation and forest degradation in Indonesia may not be desirable or 'optimal' from the global perspective, the presence of government failures suggest that these rates may not be optimal from the national perspective either.

In the context of the debate on the choice of deforestation baselines to be used in any potential avoided deforestation scheme, the presence of government failures raises an important question: should international payments for avoided deforestation be used to reduce a deforestation rate that may also be suboptimal from the perspective of Indonesian society? Our chapter considers this question and contributes to the debate on the assessment of deforestation baselines and policy options to decrease deforestation in Indonesia.

We begin our chapter with detail on Indonesia's carbon stocks and emission trends and how these are related to trends in land use. This is followed by an examination of Indonesia's position with respect to international climate change policy. We describe recent trends in the plantations sectors and how government (policy) failures contribute to Indonesia's current deforestation rates. Reforms to plantations policy, including the subsidy regimes, are discussed in the following section along with their implications for economic development and climate policy. How plantations policy might impact on the choice of emissions baselines is examined in the final section.

Carbon stocks and emissions trends

In 1994 land-use changes and forestry were reported to account for almost three-quarters of Indonesia's CO_2 emissions (Government of Indonesia, 1999). Since

1994 Indonesia has become one of the three largest emitters of GHG in the world (PEACE, 2007). By 2005 annual emissions from energy, agriculture and waste together totalled 451 $MtCO_2e$, while land-use change and forestry released an estimated 2563 $MtCO_2e$ (Baumert *et al.*, 2005).[4] Thus, similar to the patterns recorded in the 1990s, forestland use changes were responsible for the majority of Indonesia's overall GHG emissions. To place these figures into context, global forestry and land-use changes accounted for up to 20 per cent of all CO_2 emissions in 2005, with Indonesia ranked first (accounting for 34 per cent of the global total).

Around 74 per cent (1897 $MtCO_2e$) of CO_2 emissions originating in the land-use change and forestry sector were caused by a combination of deforestation and land conversion (Baumert *et al.*, 2005). The remaining 26 per cent (666 $MtCO_2e$) originated from forest-related energy consumption and industrial processes. Much deforestation and land conversion was due to forest fires, although these can also be an indirect effect of forest clearance (Reinhardt *et al.*, 2007). 'Slash and burn' is a more cost-effective and faster method of forest clearance than any other and one that has been widely used by plantation companies after the removal of any valuable timber stocks. Such 'controlled burning' can, however, get quickly out of control, hence leading to the liquidation of other forest areas close by. The huge fires during the 1997/1998 El Niño season accounted for 7 per cent of all GHG emitted worldwide during those years, and about 30 per cent of all manmade CO_2 emissions globally in 1997 (World Bank, 1999).[5] Palm oil and other plantation firms were mainly responsible for these forest fires despite total bans on the use of fire for forest clearance imposed by the Indonesian government in 1997 (Barber and Schweithelm, 2000).

In particular, fires from peatland have been a major source of CO_2 emissions due to the fact that large areas of Indonesian forest are located in peat or organic soils containing substantial amounts of carbon (see Brown, 2002). About half of the world's tropical peatland are located in Indonesia covering about 21 million ha. Peatland fires apparently contributed to between 60 and 90 per cent of Indonesia's total GHG emissions during the 1997/1998 El Niño season, thus underscoring the importance of peatland forest areas for climate policy (BAPPENAS-ADB, 1999).

Indonesia's Ministry of Environment estimated the country's total potential carbon stock to be at least 25,000 $MtCO_2e$, using data on land use collected in 2000 (see PEACE, 2007). Of this, around 80 per cent was contained in standing forest. Hence, there is clearly potential for the sustained release of high levels of GHG if Indonesia's land-use patterns continue as before.

Indonesia and international climate change policy

In theory, the key ministry responsible for developing national climate policies is the Ministry of Environment. It has a number of mandates ranging from coordinating environmental policies to enforcing environmental laws and regulations. On signing the UNFCCC in 1992, it established the National Commission on Climate Change (NCCC), an advisory body that provides assistance to the government in formulating policy. Since its establishment, the NCCC has performed relatively ineffectively due to institutional and funding constraints (NEDO, 2006). The Ministry of Environment has little involvement in development programmes. It has only been able to try and engage other government agencies in incorporating 'climate-friendly' aspects into their respective policies (PEACE, 2007).

In 2001 a national strategy was developed for attracting CDM investment and for the implementation of CDM projects. Since ratifying the Kyoto Protocol in 2004, Indonesia has been eligible to participate in the CDM as a non-Annex I country. Despite the development of a CDM strategy that has been greatly influenced by numerous stakeholders, including international donors and NGOs, CDM project development has been relatively slow and uneven in contrast to other countries such as China and India. As of 2007 there were only 11 approved projects in the whole country, dominated by waste utilization and renewable energy (Ministry of Environment, 2007). One key reason for this paucity of projects is that so few forest areas being proposed were already deforested by the CDM-mandated date of 1 January 1990 (Obidzinski, 2008). This problem applies to both timber and palm oil plantation developments, although it should be noted that until recently, palm oil was not encouraged as an alternative energy source within the CDM framework (Pastowski, 2007).[6]

In early 2007 the government began lobbying the UNFCCC to consider forest conservation incentives (PEACE, 2007). Indonesia has begun prioritizing the issue of reducing GHG through reducing deforestation, as well as its need for continued and sustainable economic development. The government also proposed an alternative definition of deforestation as: the loss of forest due to human activities, including forest conversion to other uses that have lower carbon stocks and the loss of forest due to continuous degradation resulting from repeated fires and illegal logging. This definition covers a variety of 'eligible' actions that could claim compensation from targeted emissions reduction through the avoidance of forest conversion to other land uses with lower carbon stocks. It also includes actions that relate directly to problems specific to Indonesia, such as combating illegal logging and fires.

Instead of the Ministry of Environment, the Ministry of Forestry has been the key institution charged with leading the REDD debate. Along with the Ministry of Finance, it coordinated the Indonesian government's overall position for the COP-13 (13th Conference of the Parties) meeting of the UNFCCC in Bali in December 2007. In collaboration with the World Bank, and with support from DFID, Germany's *Gesellschaft für Technische Zusammenarbeit* (GTZ), and other donors, the Ministry of Forestry established the Indonesian Forest Climate Alliance (IFCA), in early 2007. The IFCA is the single most important instrument shaping Indonesia's approach to carbon sequestration issues in general and REDD in particular.[7] It launched the 'REDD Strategy for Indonesia' (REDDI) at Bali (IFCA, 2007). With support from Australia, Indonesia is hoping to be the first country to develop and host a REDD project, beginning in late 2008 (Jakarta Post, 2008).

These developments therefore suggest a readiness on the part of the government to engage with the climate change policy debate. While it is noteworthy that it recognizes the challenges in its forest sector, which would need to be incorporated into any avoided deforestation strategy, the overall objective should focus on reducing deforestation rates below some kind of credible baseline (see later). The means by which this can be achieved first require an understanding of the underlying causes of deforestation and forest degradation in Indonesia.

Indonesia's land-use trends and policies

Indonesia's current forest area is estimated at around 90 million ha. With a 28 million ha decline in forest cover observed since 1990, the annual rate of deforestation increased from 1.6 per cent between 1990 and 2000, to 1.9 per cent between 2000 and 2005 (FAO, 2005). Of this total forest loss and of importance in the context of avoided deforestation, 7.2 million ha was classified as primary forest with the annual deforestation rate increasing from 2.1 per cent between 1990 and 2000, to 2.6 per cent between 2000 and 2005. In absolute terms, the overall rate reached 1.8 million ha per year between 2000 and 2005.[8] Indonesia's lowland tropical forests, the richest in timber and biodiversity, in Sumatra, Sulawesi and Kalimantan, have been particularly prone to deforestation and degradation.

As described in the introduction to this volume, the underlying causes of deforestation and forest degradation are a combination of market and government failures. Key proximate causes in Indonesia include extensive land conversions of forest to agriculture and timber estate plantations following the removal of timber stocks via legal or illegal means (PEACE, 2007). While much agriculture is still controlled by smallholders, the commercial plantation sector, in particular the oil palm and forestry (timber) sectors have been expanding rapidly with large-scale support from the government. Since 1984, for example, the government has provided nearly half a billion dollars in direct subsidies for timber plantation development along with indirect subsidies, mainly in the form of underpriced, i.e. essentially tax-free, timber harvests (Obidzinski, 2008).[9] Direct subsidies enabled firms to undertake logging as an end in itself.[10] The rationale behind these subsidies has been the fact that timber and biofuel plantations typically only become profitable within 10 years of planting. For a number of years, these subsidy regimes along with poor governance, weak institutions and the presence of externalities have all, to some extent, contributed to deforestation and forest degradation in Indonesia (see Palmer, 2001). The following two subsections detail the current state and future plans of the plantations sectors.

The logging, timber-processing and plantation sectors

Once among the world's leaders in timber and plywood production, the country's logging and timber-processing sectors have long been in decline (Sugiharto, 2006a). The uncontrolled expansion of the timber-processing industries in the 1980s along with the subsidization of pulp and papermills in the 1990s were undertaken without ensuring a sustainable supply of timber (MFP, 2006). A lack of sufficient due diligence in private sector financing contributed to the sector's over-capitalization and created an unsustainable timber supply. Officially, 10 million ha of plantations have been established since 1990, even though a substantially larger area of natural forest has actually been cleared (World Bank, 2006). As a result, there has been a significant gap between the demand and legal supply of timber for at least 20 years.

The Ministry of Forestry reported an average supply–demand gap of up to 40 million m³ each year that was apparently met with illegally harvested logs (Sinar Harapan, 2006). Of the so-called 'legal' supply,[11] the majority of logs were harvested from natural forest concessions earmarked for conversion to agricultural and other kinds of plantation. For example, of the 23 million m³ of timber officially harvested in 2006, only 2.2 million m³ originated from natural forest concessions, far below the allocated selective logging quota of 8.1 million m³ (Bisnis Indonesia, 2006b). This reflects the declining ability of Indonesian forests to sustain commercial logging caused by decades of overexploitation (World Bank, 2006). Nevertheless, the Ministry of Forestry intends to increase the annual allowable cut over the next few years, in order to prevent the need for further restructuring of the timber processing sector (Tempo Interaktif, 2006). This will also serve as a time-buying measure to implement a plantation-based forestry programme (Obidzinski, 2008).

A plan for such a programme was released by the Ministry of Forestry in 2006 (Bisnis Indonesia, 2006a). On the back of this and given steadily rising demand for pulp and paper, planners hope that the country can either host new pulp and paper-mill investment or become a supplier of raw material for mills located elsewhere in Asia. Indonesia aims to establish nine million ha of productive timber plantations and build up to five new pulp and papermills on top of the six mills currently operational (Suara Pembaruan, 2006).[12] Annual forestry revenues are projected to rise fivefold to US$20 billion by 2016. Moreover, the government hopes to utilize the CDM in order to benefit the forestry plantation sector (IGES *et al.*, 2006).

In 2007, the government established a number of incentives to stimulate investment in the development of timber plantations, including simplified application procedures for timber plantation concession permits, extended concession times[13] and tax exemptions for plantation firms. It also plans to set up a national commission for clean development mechanism (NCCDM) and task it with streamlining application and financing procedures for CDM projects. Prospective timber plantation investors will be allowed to continue using the available natural timber stock on their plantation concessions as collateral for bank loans (Koran Tempo, 2006). Another US$1 billion in subsidies will be provided for timber plantation development through the Ministry of Forestry's Funding Body for Forest Development (Bisnis Indonesia, 2007; Suara Pembaruan, 2007). The relation between plantation development and deforestation is discussed further in the following section.

Biofuel plantations

In 2004 over 80 per cent of crude palm oil (CPO) produced globally originated from Malaysia and Indonesia, split more or less evenly between the two countries (ISTA Mielke, 2004). In Indonesia, this was equivalent to over 12 million tonnes of oil, produced from around 3.3 million ha of palm oil plantations. Another estimate puts Indonesia's current palm oil estate at 5.6 million ha (see Casson, 2007). Since the mid-1970s, both Indonesia and Malaysia have been at the forefront of a huge expansion of palm oil production. For instance, Indonesian production tripled between 1995 and 2004 (Reinhardt *et al.*, 2007).

In late 2006 Indonesia launched a policy that seeks to radically expand biofuel plantations over the coming years. To this end, the government formed the National Biofuel Development Committee (NBDC) and tasked it with attracting the necessary investment to facilitate the development of 5.2 million ha of new biofuel plantations by 2010 (Jakarta Post, 2007a). While the initial plan was to divide this land area more or less evenly among palm oil (1.5 million ha), jatropha (1.5 million ha), cassava (1.5 million ha) and sugar cane (750,000 ha) plantations, most of it is currently intended for palm oil estates (Jakarta Post, 2007, 2007d). As of July 2007 the NBDC had secured US$12.4 billion worth of foreign direct investment for 54 biofuel projects (Jakarta Post 2007a, 2007b). The government estimates that reaching its target area of productive plantations and associated infrastructure will require investment of up to US$20 billion (Kompas, 2007).[14]

Biofuel plantation development is driven by various factors. One key factor is the desire by government planners to reduce the fiscal burden of fossil fuel subsidies. Approximately 80 per cent of all fossil fuel consumed in Indonesia is subsidized. In 2006 alone, these subsidies cost the government over US$1 billion. Biofuel consumption could significantly reduce these expenditures although cost reductions would need to be set against the level of subsidies spent on biofuel developments. New plantations are also expected to generate up to 3.5 million jobs in rural areas.

Another key factor driving biofuel plantation planning is rising global demand for alternatives to carbon-based fuels, whether driven by policy based on climate change concerns or other considerations such as governments' desire for increased diversification of energy sources. For example, almost one-quarter of Indonesia's current palm oil exports are imported by the EU alone mainly for use in power generation (Webster *et al.*, 2004). The EU has set a target of 5.75 per cent share of the energy content of all gasoline and diesel fuels for the transport sector to be made up of biofuels by 2010, possibly rising to 10 per cent by 2020 (European Commission, 2006, 2007). It will not be able to meet this target with domestic production alone and gaps between domestic production and consumption are expected, at least in part, to be filled by imports of biofuels (Pastowski, 2007).[15] Indonesia is thus a likely beneficiary of this growth in biofuel consumption in Europe and elsewhere. Together with Malaysia, Indonesia will reserve 40 per cent of palm oil exports for biofuels. The Indonesian government predicts future annual earnings of US$1.3 billion from biofuel exports, with plans to build or expand 11 refineries for this purpose by 2010 (ibid.).

Similar to its plans for expanding the timber plantation sector, the government is offering a number of incentives to prospective investors in order to fast track palm oil plantation development. It plans to relax restrictions on plantation size.[16] Palm oil plantation licence holders like timber plantation licence holders will be able to use the available natural timber stock in project sites as collateral for commercial bank loans (Koran Tempo, 2006). Access to a special government fund facility of US$1 billion will be provided. Additionally, they will be able to secure interest free commercial loans, with the government providing subsidies to cover interest rate payments. Private banks in Indonesia, led by Bank Rakyat Indonesia (BRI), have already set aside US$3 billion for these loans. The government plans to spend another US$100 million per year on plantation related infrastructure to encourage more investment by reducing startup costs. Finally, biofuel licensees will also be able to benefit from project joint ventures involving foreign direct investment, for example, China's funding of US$3 billion via the China National Offshore Oil Corporation (CNOOC) for a 1.2 million ha plantation in the province of West Papua.

Reconciling land use and GHG emissions policies

Indonesian government plans to expand the palm oil and timber plantation sectors have the potential to exacerbate an already serious decline in its forest stock and associated environmental services. Indonesia's GHG emissions would in all probability continue to rise via land clearance and deforestation with important consequences for the global climate. We examine, first, the problems underlying current plantation plans and some possible, countervailing policy measures to minimize the impacts of plantation expansion on natural forest areas. Second, we examine the implications of plantations policy for climate policy.

Problems with plantation plans and countervailing measures

Much of the available information on the current state of all plantation development and its growth prospects is overly optimistic and often contradictory. Regarding timber plantations, there is relatively little, high quality information on the current extent of productive estates. Government estimates in 2005 ranged from 1.5 to 2.5 million ha. In reality, the planted area of currently effective plantations may be substantially smaller; perhaps one-third of the officially quoted numbers (World Bank, 2006). Similarly, the planted area of effective biofuel plantations is not known with any great certainty.

Regarding future growth, government estimates of the annual timber planting rate are disputed by forestry and plantation sector insiders (World Bank, 2006). They contend that not only is Indonesia far from planting 400,000 ha of plantations per year, but also that only about 60 per cent of whatever is planted survives the first year. Projections for the expansion of biofuel plantations also vary wildly with government estimates of up to 30 million ha of land required for new plantations (see Reinhardt *et al.*, 2007). These uncertainties with regards to the projected amount of land required for plantation development clearly imply a need for better data on existing plantations, for example through the application of new technologies such as the use of remote sensing data (Johns and Schlamadinger, Chapter 5 in this volume).

The government's timber plantation plan focuses almost exclusively on creating new plantations and ignores the necessary restructuring of the timber industries, for example, by reducing processing capacities. Despite government claims that the plantation timber supply will be sufficient to fulfil all timber needs in 15 to 20 years, research shows that even if the plantation expansion is implemented flawlessly, there will continue to be supply shortfalls (MFP, 2006). Moreover, while the government stresses the importance of the CDM mechanism for plantation development, it is unlikely that the majority of sites currently targeted for timber plantation development will meet CDM criteria, particularly the date (1 January 1990) by which they are supposed to have been deforested (Obidzinski, 2008).

As the plantation plans currently stand, natural forest areas are likely to continue to be cleared. The main land-use category targeted for plantations in Indonesia is known as 'conversion forest' which, in 2003, covered around 23 million ha (World Bank, 2006).[17] It is generally assumed that this land-use category includes many forest areas that are already degraded beyond recovery. However, there may be over 10 million ha within this category with good forest cover (ibid.). The establishment of new plantations, both for timber and for palm oil in cleared natural forest areas is more profitable than converting fallow land (Wakker, 2006). Both the timber plantation and palm oil industries are dominated by groups of companies that also operate in the logging and cellulose/paper manufacturing industries (Reinhardt *et al.*, 2007).

The use of natural forest as collateral for bank loans encourages inefficient, rent-seeking behaviour. In the past, profiteering from subsidized bank loans and the subsequent clear felling of the forest became an end in itself (Obidzinski, 2008). Despite the government's high profile anti-corruption campaigns, business in Indonesia's natural resource sectors is still based on client–patron relationships among rent-seeking politicians, businessmen and local government officials (see, for example, Brown, 1999; McCarthy, 2000).[18] At the time of writing, the government may only allow natural forest timber stocks to be used as collateral for plantation development up until 2009, although this is by no means certain.

In the past, forest sector financing has created inappropriate incentives, whether originating from the public or private sectors. Thus, current systems of subsidies as described in the previous section are likely to further encourage rent seeking and forest conversion. Reforms are clearly necessary.[19] In the public sector, more emphasis should instead be placed on stimulating plantation investment and development, for example, through streamlining administrative procedures. Furthermore, due diligence processes in the private sector would need to be improved in order to properly evaluate raw material supplies, plantation development prospects and the likelihood of increasing illegal logging (World Bank, 2006).

Many forest areas are fraught with legal uncertainty with conflicting land-use plans established by different levels of government. These tend to be based on differing interpretations of laws and regulations brought in since the onset of regional autonomy and the acceleration of decentralization reforms in the late 1990s. For example, local level government institutions are keen on revising land-use plans so as to access as much commercially usable forest as possible by assigning it to the conversion category (Barr *et al.*, 2006; Djadjono, 2007).[20] While intact forestland somehow needs be excluded from the category of conversion forest, this will not be enough to ensure that it remains unconverted. Indonesia has at least 50 million ha of degraded forest areas and fallow land in need of rehabilitation, which could be allocated to plantation development (World Bank, 2006). Later we discuss potential incentives for plantation development in fallow land areas.

The legal uncertainty of plantation projects is exacerbated by the unclear status of the property rights of indigenous communities inhabiting the concession areas even with the recent introduction of a government regulation (No. 6/2007) concerning new concepts of community forest rights (Obidzinski, 2008). Since an estimated 30 million ha or more of forest area is claimed by communities (World Bank, 2006), more legal changes are needed. The implementation of plantation projects is thus likely to be highly prone to conflict, given patterns of property rights conflicts between communities and commercial interests since the end of the 1990s (see Palmer and Engel, 2007). Although the government appears determined to retain full property rights over Indonesia's forest estate, the status of community property rights needs to be addressed if the planned projects are to avoid conflict.[21]

A number of laws and regulations have already been issued, which sum up to a reasonable body of policies in support of sustainable forest management in Indonesia (PEACE, 2007). Moreover, in response to the problems of forest fires and illegal logging, the government has put in place strategies to deal with these (World Bank, 2006). But current and future decrees, laws and regulations such as a prohibition on plantation development in natural forest areas provide little guarantee of changing forest conversion patterns. This is due to a number of critical issues relating to governance and the implementation and enforcement of rules, as well as a lack of transparency in the allocation of land and forest use rights (ibid.). A continued crackdown on corruption would help raise the quality of governance, in addition to continued reform of the public sector, subsidy regimes and so on. However, at least in the short to medium term, Indonesia's natural resource sectors will in all probability continue to be characterized by poor governance and corruption.

Plantation development and climate policy

First, it is clear that timber plantations are important for ensuring a sustainable supply of raw materials for Indonesia's forest industries. Second, Indonesia is also well positioned to benefit from the current biofuel boom given its established palm oil sector. But if the government's plans for plantation development are carried out then it is likely that these sectors will continue to contribute to Indonesia's current high rates of deforestation and forest degradation. Any reforms to change the way in which these sectors operate, even if only partially successful, may have implications for Indonesia's business-as-usual baseline rates of GHG emissions from deforestation and forest degradation.

How deforestation rates can change according to the presence or absence of market and government (or policy) failures is described in a simple didactic

(Figure 7.1). The horizontal axis shows the amount of forest converted to plantations, which is increasing from left to right. MB_I represents the marginal benefits of deforestation for Indonesia, showing that marginal profits decline as more land is deforested. This results from rising conversion costs as the conversion frontier is spatially extended or declining land productivity. Deforestation causes local externalities such as soil erosion. These are represented in Figure 7.1 as the marginal cost line, MC_I. Where $MB_I = MC_I$, the rate of conversion is given as the local social optimum, D_I, with local externalities captured, for example, using local taxation or land zoning. A complete failure to capture these local externalities leads to a higher rate of deforestation, where MB_I crosses the horizontal axis, i.e. where $MB_I = 0$. The line MC_W represents the global externalities from forest conversion, including climate and biodiversity damages, in addition to the local externalities. Thus, from the global perspective, the optimal deforestation rate, D_W, occurs where $MB_I = MC_W$. Global transfers to Indonesia equal to the value of these international externalities could, in theory, shift deforestation rates to this global optimum.

Government subsidies such as timber being used as collateral for bank loans or government-built roads lower deforestation costs and raise profit margins for deforesters. In Figure 7.1, these government (policy) failures are represented as a shift in marginal benefits from the line MB_I to $MB_{I,S}$. As a consequence of distortionary policies, the actual, current rate of deforestation in Indonesia is given by $D_{I,S}$, i.e. where $MB_{I,S} = MC_I$. It can easily be seen that $D_W < D_I < D_{I,S}$. Thus, if, for example, plantations are prevented from using timber as collateral then deforestation will fall from $D_{I,S}$ to D_I. What this and the removal of other distortionary policies might mean for avoided deforestation policy is discussed in the final section.

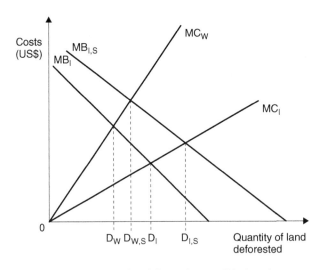

Figure 7.1 Deforestation rates, market failures (externalities) and government (policy) failures

Source: Authors, adapted from Pearce (1995)

For avoided deforestation or REDD, incentive schemes would be established both internationally, i.e. with the participation of Indonesia's national government, and within the country itself. In any international scheme, payments made to the government would be conditional on reducing deforestation rates below some agreed baseline regardless of how it designs its incentive scheme within the country. Within country, transfers could either be made directly to deforesters or indirectly, to fund systems or policy aiming to discourage deforestation, for example, for monitoring or enforcement. Direct payments to deforesters would compete with their opportunity costs. The cost (to deforesters) of reducing CO_2 emissions from deforestation can be broken down into the per ha profits foregone by maintaining forest rather than converting it and the difference in carbon storage between a conserved forest and a field or pasture (Chomitz *et al.*, 2006). Then, assuming that the deforester can be identified despite unclear property rights,[22] conditional payments could be made based on carbon prices and the amount of carbon stored in intact forest.

Indonesia's current plantations policies imply potentially high opportunity costs of reducing deforestation for deforesters. Tomich *et al.* (2005) demonstrate the implicit costs of reducing carbon emissions through forest conservation, although their Indonesian examples assume a baseline of already logged, depleted forest. Hence, these analyses may underestimate the true opportunity costs of leaving natural forest standing. Including the value of natural forest as collateral, i.e. the timber values, Grieg-Gran (Chapter 2 in this volume), shows that opportunity costs in Indonesia are high compared to those in other tropical countries. This is at least partly due to government failure and subsidies that reduce plantation business costs and increase profits.

Discussion and conclusions

This chapter has examined Indonesia's role and the importance of its forests in climate change policy. It then looked at how its plantations sectors contribute to Indonesia's current patterns of deforestation and forest degradation. A number of policy measures to remove economic distortions in the plantations sectors were discussed that could potentially reduce deforestation and forest degradation, i.e. moving from $D_{I,S}$ to D_I in Figure 7.1, irrespective of avoided deforestation incentives. This rate of deforestation, D_I, while optimal from Indonesia's perspective, may still be suboptimal from the perspective of the rest of the world due to, for example, continued GHG emissions. Yet, policies to shift the marginal benefits curve back from $MB_{I,S}$ to MB_I in Figure 7.1 may be optimal for Indonesia even in the absence of incentives to reduce GHG emissions through reductions in deforestation and forest degradation.

One key issue for avoided deforestation or REDD policy is in establishing national-level emissions baselines for monitoring progress and calculating reductions in GHG emissions. How might the optimal deforestation rate for the country, D_I in Indonesia's case, be measured in practice? A so-called 'normative reference level' could be calculated depending on the identified, key factors in a country's forest emissions behaviour (Chomitz *et al.*, 2006). Such a reference level could be, for example, based on a standardized estimate of the rate of increase in palm oil production. This would need to be adjusted for an estimate in the increase in plantation productivity and the mean forest carbon content at the forest frontier. Separate estimates could be made for logging-related emissions and the rate of abandonment of current lands. A normative reference point may reward countries already trying to reduce deforestation. With its plantations polices, this may not be the case with Indonesia at the present time. While a normative baseline may also be distorted due to past policy failure, it at least would not introduce any more perverse incentives into these sectors.

If the optimal deforestation rate for Indonesia, D_I, is chosen as an emissions baseline then this may limit its benefits from foregone economic development, i.e. from plantations as currently observed. At the time of writing, the Indonesian government's informal position in the REDD discussion is to push for a higher national emissions baseline based on historical and recent deforestation trends, i.e. closer to $D_{I,S}$ in Figure 7.1 (for more on different baseline options, see Murray, Chapter 9 in this volume). As noted by Rachmat Witoelar in our introduction, Indonesia is clearly not going to forgo the economic benefits from plantations and accept a rate nearer to D_I. Note that $D_{I,S}$ is a rate that is not only suboptimal from the global perspective but is also suboptimal from a purely national perspective. International avoided deforestation payments, supposedly designed to capture climate externalities, would thus be used to reduce emissions at a rate that is already suboptimal from Indonesia's perspective.

Deforestation rates have been trending upwards in recent decades. The government may have an incentive to allow deforestation to continue rising in order to obtain a higher target and therefore claim higher payments, particularly if instead of historical rates, baselines are estimated on the basis of business-as-usual projections. In the short run at least, it would then have little incentive to bother with policy reforms or incentives that attempt to reverse government failures, hence constraining plantation sector deforestation behaviour. The question that follows is whether, in the absence of international incentives to reduce GHG emissions from deforestation, Indonesia would have greater incentives to implement these measures in order to reach D_I compared to the situation where international incentives are present. International payments for emissions reductions in a context of no domestic policy reform would result in a move from $D_{I,S}$ to $D_{W,S}$ rather than D_W. By contrast, not paying international payments and enabling domestic policy reform would lead to D_I. The relative difference in emissions reductions from these two scenarios, (D_I to $D_{W,S}$), gives the net emissions gain of avoided deforestation payment implementation, which is likely to be smaller than the case where Indonesia implements reforms in the presence of incentives for avoided deforestation, i.e. where (D_I to D_W). Thus, in the absence of domestic policy reform but with international payments, Indonesia's deforestation rate will remain globally suboptimal.

Should Indonesia attempt to reform its plantations' subsidy regimes in the presence of international avoided deforestation payments, would there be a need to differentiate between reductions in deforestation due to international payments or those due to policy reforms? Not if these payments are made to the national government conditional on policy reforms being a part of achieving international avoided deforestation commitments. And should that be the case then at least it would show that Indonesia is committed to moving closer to D_W thus internalizing a greater level of the carbon externality than would occur at $D_{W,S}$.

Indonesia may not agree to remove distortionary policies on condition of receiving avoided deforestation or REDD payments. If, however, it still receives international payments then the distribution of these via a within-country payment for environmental services (PES) scheme may have to overcome deforesters' high opportunity costs. In this case, additional incentives may need to come into play, for example via the CDM. The use of fallow land for plantation development could yield potential savings of GHG as well as more direct economic benefits. This is more pertinent for biofuel than timber plantations.[23] Other incentives such as new sources of collateral could be used to encourage plantation development in degraded areas, for example, investment funds that invest only in projects according to ethical and/or sustainable development criteria. There may also be a role for timber certification (for plantation timber situated on degraded land) or biofuel labelling (for palm oil plantations situated on degraded land), although the international trade in palm oil for the production of biofuels is currently subject to the general WTO regulations on trade in agricultural products.[24]

The challenge for avoided deforestation policy in Indonesia would therefore be to provide incentives for reducing emissions at the national level while, at the minimum, encouraging the reversal of government failures in the plantations sectors. Moreover, Indonesia should not be discouraged from benefiting from the global demand for biofuels and plantation timber. There are early signs that at least some parts of the corporate sector in Indonesia are becoming more progressive in terms of making investments in plantations that may allow them to demonstrate sustainability and efficiency in global markets (World Bank, 2006). Some corporate actors have realized that international perceptions of Indonesia influence their ability to access lucrative foreign markets. Plantation actors should be encouraged to participate in pilot programmes to develop fallow land.

In addition to encouraging 'greener' corporate behaviour along with regulatory reform, carbon sequestration activities would need strong coordination and consultation among the national and various levels of local government and among government agencies at any given level. To prevent conflict among forest stakeholders, measures are needed that support rural communities' claims and access to land and forest resources. This could involve the strengthening of tenure institutions and instigating transparent benefit-sharing arrangements; for example, along the lines of community–company plantation forest partnerships already established in Sumatra and Kalimantan (see Nawir *et al.*, 2003).

Finally, if historical baselines are chosen for an international avoided deforestation or REDD mechanism then these could at least be reset, say every 10 years, in order to allow for the readjustment of incentives. Resetting baselines would enable such a mechanism to flexibly deal with emerging economic realities and institutional conditions including any future policy reforms in the country's plantations sectors (see Sohngen and Harris *et al.*, Chapters 4 and 10 in this volume, respectively).

Notes

1 Through an Act of Ratification No. 6/1994 (*Undang-undang tentang Pengesahan Konvensi Kerangka Kerja PBB tentang Perubahan Iklim Nomor. 6/1994*).
2 Act of Ratification No. 17/2004.
3 This can be understood in terms of the application of the 'beneficiary pays' principle. By the same token, the exploitation of natural resources can also be viewed in terms of the creation of 'negative externalities' at the international level, e.g. increasing GHG or biodiversity losses. This perspective can be understood in terms of the 'polluter pays' principle whereupon the international community could demand compensation for climate and biodiversity damages. While Indonesia itself may also suffer from climate change-induced impacts, such as more common outbreaks of disease and changing hydrological cycles (PEACE, 2007), these cannot be attributed to the GHG emission behaviour of any particular state due to the global public good nature of the climate change problem.
4 Note that the data used for the comparison of different emissions sources were collected in different years.
5 Almost 12 million ha of forest were burned resulting in costs totalling billions of US dollars (see Tacconi, 2003).
6 Thus, the number of CDM projects involving palm oil production is still small despite their potential to help improve the GHG balance. This is due to general methodological difficulties of implementing CDM projects in the transport sector (Pastowski, 2007).
7 See www.dephut.go.id/INFORMASI/LITBANG/IFCA/IFCA.htm.
8 This rate is lower than the official Ministry of Forestry's rate, of 2.8 million ha per year, highlighting uncertainties in the data (see, for example, Angelsen and Kaimowitz, 1999; Chomitz *et al.*, 2006).
9 It has been estimated that the government allowed firms to capture up to 98 per cent of the value of timber from natural forests (see Maturana, 2005).
10 The source of these subsidies was a reforestation fund that has ironically helped further deforestation in Indonesia. Further perverse incentives in the form of frequent markup schemes (where plantation developers obtain loans based on inflated cost estimates thus ensuring a profit upfront) created profits from plantation projects before they were actually implemented (Barr, 2001).
11 It is well documented that legal concessionaires have, for the most part and for many years, failed to follow Indonesian forestry regulations, for instance through overharvesting concession areas and not applying practices to prevent soil erosion (see Ross, 2001).
12 The most immediate target is to establish five million hectares of timber plantations by 2009, assuming an annual planting rate of 400,000 ha (Investor Indonesia, 2006). By 2016 the government envisages that 9 million ha of productive timber plantations will be established.
13 Valid for up to 100 years (Koran Tempo, 2006).
14 Poor governance and the weak enforcement of regulations may, however, inhibit Indonesia's ability to raise all the funding necessary to expand its palm oil refinery capacity (Reinhardt *et al.*, 2007). This suggests points of leverage for external investors in directing both palm oil and timber plantation expansion down a more sustainable path (see final section).
15 At the time of writing, palm oil biodiesel does not meet the EU's fuel standards. However, a 'planned amendment' to the fuel standard is expected, which will allow the production of palm oil biodiesel (see Reinhardt *et al.*, 2007). By 2010, the EU oil and proteinmeal industry, FEDIOL, expects that EU-wide biodiesel consumption (for fuel)

will average 12 million tonnes, made up of at least 2.5 million tones of imported palm oil (Fediol, 2006).

16 Until recently, private oil palm plantation companies in Indonesia were limited to 25,000 ha per plantation. In February 2007 this limitation was removed and the upper limit for the plantation size has been increased to 100,000 ha. In West Papua province, companies can develop up to 200,000 ha per plantation. Government-owned plantations and publicly listed companies are exempt from these limitations altogether.

17 Note that plantations are also situated in other forest areas such as so-called 'production forest' (see Anon, 2007).

18 During the development of Indonesia's forest sector, many private sector firms and trade associations benefited from political connections and rent seeking (World Bank, 2006).

19 For example, subsidies could be limited to small-scale community-based projects only (Obidzinski, 2008).

20 Local governments have the right to 'rededicate' forestland from permanent forest estate into areas for conversion into plantation zones, on proof of forest degradation (Obidzinski, 2008). However, post-rededication, local governments often allow natural forest conversion in order to enable plantation firms to generate the capital necessary for plantation investment. Thus the figure for conversion forest quoted in the text does not remain constant over time, and according to government data has increased from 21.8 to 23.2 million ha between 2000 and 2003 (Ministry of Forestry, 2007).

21 This may require supporting central government regulations and local level legislation necessary to operationalize the concepts of community forest rights, followed by accompanying regulations on community participation in plantation ventures.

22 The Indonesian government is the 'forest owner', although with weak property rights, forests can be de facto claimed by actors on the ground such as concessionaires or communities (see Engel and Palmer, 2008).

23 Palm oil as a source of energy is CO_2 neutral where it is combusted directly (Reinhardt *et al.*, 2007). Where plantation development for biofuel feedstocks involves clear cutting existing forests or disturbing the carbon pool in peat swamps, production may therefore generate higher GHG emissions than oil.

24 It would, however, be difficult to monitor any special treatment of agricultural products that are used exclusively to produce energy sources, because the decision on use is not taken until the oil is in the importing country (Pastowski, 2007). The situation is different for palm oil that has already been processed for biofuel in the growing country since its use as an energy source is the only option in this case.

References

Angelsen, A. and Kaimowitz, D. (1999) 'Rethinking the causes of deforestation: lessons from economic models', *World Bank Research Observer*, 14(1): 73–98.

Anon (2007) *Production Forests Land Use Strategies: Expanded Inception Report*, mimeo.

Arifin, B. (2005) *Institutional Constraints and Opportunities in Developing Environmental Service Markets: Lessons from Institutional Studies on RUPES in Indonesia*, Bogor: World Agroforestry Centre (ICRAF).

BAPPENAS-ADB (*Badan Perencanaan dan Pembangunan Nasional*-Asian Development Bank) (1999) *Causes, Extent, Impact and Cost of 1997–1998 Fires and Drought*, Planning for Fire Prevention and Drought Management Project, ADB TA 2999–INO, Jakarta: BAPPENAS-ADB.

Barber, C. and Schweithelm, J. (2000) *Trial by Fire: Forest Fires in Indonesia's Era of Crisis and Reform*, Washington, DC: World Resources Institute (WRI).

Barr, C. (2001) *Banking on Sustainability: Structural Adjustment and Forestry Reform in Post-Suharto Indonesia*, World Wildlife Fund, Washington, DC and Bogor: Center for International Forestry Research (CIFOR).

Barr, C., Resosudarmo, I.A.P., Dermawan, A., McCarthy, J., Moeliono, M. and Setiono, B. (eds) (2006) *Decentralization of Forest Administration in Indonesia: Implications for Forest Sustainability, Economic Development and Community Livelihoods*, Bogor: Center for International Forestry Research (CIFOR).

Baumert, K., Herzog, T. and Pershing, J. (2005) *Navigating the Numbers: Greenhouse Gas Data and International Climate Policy*, Washington, DC: World Resources Institute (WRI).

Bisnis Indonesia (2006a) *RI Berpotensi Dominasi Industri Kehutanan*, Bisnis Indonesia, 19 June, Jakarta: Bisnis Indonesia.

Bisnis Indonesia (2006b) *Industri Hutan Gagal Penuhi JPT 2006*, Bisnis Indonesia, 29 November, Jakarta: Bisnis Indonesia.

Bisnis Indonesia (2007) *Badan Pembiayaan Kehutanan Terbentuk*, Bisnis Indonesia, 12 February, Jakarta: Bisnis Indonesia.

Brown, D. (1999) *Addicted to Rent: Corporate and Spatial Distribution of Forest Resources in Indonesia; Implications for Forest Sustainability and Government Policy*, Report No. PFM/EC/99/06, Jakarta: Indonesia-UK Tropical Forest Management Programme (ITFMP).

Brown, S. (2002) *Forest and Climate Change and the Role of Forest as Carbon Sink*, Western Ecology Division, National Health and Environmental Effects Research Laboratory, United States Environmental Protection Agency (USEPA), Oregon: USEPA.

Casson, A. (2007) *Strategies to Reduce Carbon Emissions from the Oil Palm Sector in Indonesia*, revised inception report, September 2007, mimeo.

Chomitz, K., Buys, P., De Luca, G., Thomas, T. S. and Wetz-Kanounnikoff, S. (2006) *At Loggerheads? Agricultural Expansion, Poverty Reduction, and Environment in Tropical Countries*, World Bank Policy Research Report, Washington, DC: World Bank.

Djadjono, A. (2007) *Menyongsong Reforma Agraria*, AgroIndonesia, 26 December–2 January, Jakarta: AgroIndonesia.

Engel, S. and Palmer, C. (2008) 'Payments for environmental services as an alternative to logging under weak property rights: the case of Indonesia', *Ecological Economics*, 65(4): 799–809.

European Commission (2006) *Communication from the Commission: An EU Strategy for Biofuels* [online]. Available at: http://ec.europa.eu/energy/res/biomass_action_plan/doc/2006_02_08_comm_eu_strategy_en.pdf [accessed 2 July 2007].

European Commission (2007) *Biofuels for Transport* [online] Available at: http://www.euractiv.com/en/transport/biofuels-transport/article-152282 [accessed 12 October 2007].

Government of Indonesia (1999) *First National Communication on Climate Change to the United Nations Framework Convention on Climate Change (UNFCCC)*, Jakarta: Government of Indonesia.

Grieg-Gran, M. (2009) 'The costs of avoided deforestation as a climate change mitigation option', in C. Palmer and S. Engel (eds) *Avoided Deforestation: Prospects for Mitigating Climate Change*, London: Routledge.

FAO (Food and Agriculture Organization of the United Nations) (2005) *Global Forest Resources Assessment: Progress Towards Sustainable Forest Management*, Rome: FAO.

FEDIOL (European Union Oil and Proteinmeal Industry) (2006) 2010 *Vegetable Oils. Supply-Demand Projections*, Brussels: Fediol.

Harris, N., Petrova, S. and Brown, S. (2009) 'A scalable approach for setting avoided deforestation baselines', in C. Palmer and S. Engel (eds) *Avoided Deforestation: Prospects for Mitigating Climate Change*, London: Routledge.

IFCA (Indonesia Forest Climate Alliance) (2007) *Reducing Emissions from Deforestation and Forest Degradation in Indonesia (REDDI). REDD Methodology and Strategies, Summary for Policy-makers*, Jakarta: Ministry of Forestry.

IGES (Institute for Global Environmental Strategies), Ministry of the Environment Japan, Ministry of the Environment Indonesia, CER Indonesia (2006) *CDM Country Guide for Indonesia*, Tokyo: Ministry of the Environment.

Investor Indonesia (2006) *Korea Sepakat Kembangkan HTI 500 Ribu Ha*, Investor Indonesia, 3 August, Jakarta: Investor Indonesia.

ISTA Mielke (2004) *Oil World Annual 2004*, Hamburg: ISTA Mielke GmbH.

Jakarta Post (2007a) *59 Energy Firms, Institutions to Invest $12.4b in Biofuel*, 9 January, Jakarta: Jakarta Post.

Jakarta Post (2007b) *Indonesia the Focus of Massive $12.4 Billion in Biofuels Investments; Signing Ceremony in Indonesia*, 9 January, Jakarta: Jakarta Post.

Jakarta Post (2007c) *RI Moving Fast on Biofuel Development*, 10 January, Jakarta: Jakarta Post.

Jakarta Post (2007d) *Massive Biofuel Program to Go Ahead Despite International Concerns*, 6 February, Jakarta: Jakarta Post.

Jakarta Post (2008) *RI to Begin Forest Carbon Projects*, August 4 2008 [online]. Available at: http://www.thejakartapost.com/news/2008/06/17/ri-begin-forest-carbon-projects.html [accessed 4 August 2008].

Johns, T. and Schlamadinger, B. (2009) 'International policy and institutional barriers to reducing emissions from deforestation and degradation in developing countries', in C. Palmer and S. Engel (eds) *Avoided Deforestation: Prospects for Mitigating Climate Change*, London: Routledge.

Kompas (2007) *Kredit Biofuel Mengalir*, 10 January, Jakarta: Kompas.

Koran Tempo (2006) *Indonesia Gandeng Investor Korea Selatan Bangun Hutan Industri*, 2 August, Jakarta: Koran Tempo.

Maturana, J. (2005) *Economic Costs and Benefits of Allocating Forest Land for Industrial Tree Plantation Development in Indonesia*, CIFOR Working Paper 30, Bogor: Center for International Forestry Research (CIFOR).

McCarthy, J. (2000) 'The changing regime: forest property and *Reformasi* in Indonesia', *Development and Change*, 31(1): 91–129.

MFP (Multistakeholder Forestry Programme) (2006) *Timber Industry Revitalization in the 1st Quarter of the 21st Century*, Policy Brief, Jakarta: MFP.

Ministry of Environment (2007) *Komnas MPB* [online]. Available at: http://dna-cdm. menlh.go.id/id/database [accessed 7 July 2007].

Ministry of Forestry (2007) *Forestry Statistics of Indonesia 2000–2004*, Jakarta: Ministry of Forestry.

Murray, B. (2009) 'Leakage from an avoided deforestation compensation policy: concepts, empirical evidence and corrective policy options', in C. Palmer and S. Engel (eds) *Avoided Deforestation: Prospects for Mitigating Climate Change*, London: Routledge.

NEDO (New Energy and Industrial Technology Development Organization) (2006) *CDM Development in Indonesia: Enabling Policies, Institution and Programmes, Issues and Challenges*, Jakarta: NEDO.

Nawir, A., Santoso, L. and Mudhofar, I. (2003) *Towards Mutually-Beneficial Company–Community Partnerships in Timber Plantation: Lessons Learnt from Indonesia*, CIFOR Working Paper 26, Bogor: Center for International Forestry Research (CIFOR).

Obidzinski, K. (2008) 'Transition to timber plantation based forestry in Indonesia: towards a feasible new policy', mimeo, Bogor: Center for International Forestry Research (CIFOR).

Palmer, C. (2001) *The Extent and Causes of Illegal Logging: An Analysis of a Major Cause of Tropical Deforestation in Indonesia*, CSERGE Working Paper, London: Centre for Social and Economic Research on the Global Environment (CSERGE), University College London.

Palmer, C. and Engel, S. (2007) 'For better or for worse? Local impacts from the decentralization of Indonesia's forest sector', *World Development*, 35(12): 2131–2149.

Pastowski, A. (2007) 'Future demand for palm oil and politics', in *Rain Forest for Biodiesel? Ecological Effects of Using Palm Oil as a Source of Energy*, Germany: World Wildlife Fund (WWF).

PEACE (2007) *Indonesia and Climate Change: Current Status and Policies*, Jakarta: Pelangi Energi Abadi Citra Enviro (PEACE).

Pearce, D.W. (1995) 'Global environmental value and the tropical forests: demonstration and capture', in W. Adamowicz, M. Luckert, W. Phillips and W. White (eds) *Forestry, Economics, and the Environment*, Wallingford: CABI International.

Reinhardt, G., Rettenmaier, N. and Gärtner, S. (2007) 'Palm oil as a source of bioenergy', in *Rain Forest for Biodiesel? Ecological Effects of Using Palm Oil as a Source of Energy*, Germany: World Wildlife Fund (WWF).

Reuters (2007) *INTERVIEW-Indonesia Wants Countries Paid to Keep Forests*, 30 January [online]. Available at: http://www.alertnet.org/thenews/newsdesk/JAK537.htm [accessed 14 June 2007].

Ross, M. (2001) *Timber Booms and Institutional Breakdown in Southeast Asia*, Cambridge: Cambridge University Press.

Sinar Harapan (2006) *Dephut Segera Kembangkan HTI 3.6 Juta Hektar*, 28 November, Jakarta: Sinar Harapan.

Sohngen, B. (2009) 'Assessing the economic potential for reducing deforestation in developing countries', in C. Palmer and S. Engel (eds) *Avoided Deforestation: Prospects for Mitigating Climate Change*, London: Routledge.

Suara Pembaruan (2006) *2014, Kehutanan Sumbang US$ 20 Miliar*, 17 May, Jakarta: Suara Pembaruan.

Suara Pembaruan (2007) *Dephut Siapkan Rp 11 Triliun Untuk Pembangunan Hutan Masyarakat*, 8 February, Jakarta: Suara Pembaruan.

Sugiharto (2006a) *Kinerja Industri Kehutanan Makin Buruk*, AgroIndonesia, 19–25 December, Jakarta: AgroIndonesia.

Tacconi, L. (2003) *Fires in Indonesia: Causes, Costs and Policy Implications*, CIFOR Occasional Paper 38, Bogor: Center for International Forestry Research (CIFOR).

Tempo Interaktif (2006) *Jatah Tebangan Kayu Naik Untuk Penuhi Target Ekspor Rp 74 Triliun*, 22 July, Jakarta: Tempo Interaktif.

Tomich, T., Cattaneo, A., Chater, S., Geist, H., Gockowski, J., Kaimowitz, D. *et al.* (2005) 'Balancing agricultural development and environmental objectives: assessing tradeoffs in the humid tropics', in C. Palm, S. Vosti, P. Sanchez and P. Ericksen (eds) *Slash and Burn Agriculture: The Search for Alternatives*, New York: Columbia University Press.

Wakker, E. (2006) *The Kalimantan Border Oil Palm Mega-Project*, Amsterdam AIDEnvironment.

Webster, R., Rimmer, L. and Bennet, C. (2004) *Scandal, Whitewash, Cover-up: Palm Oil, the Hidden Ingredient in Thousands of Everyday Products is Driving Rainforest Destruction*, London: Friends of the Earth.

World Bank (1999) *Ensuring a Future for Indonesia's Forests*, paper presented to the Consultative Group on Indonesia, Paris, 29–30, July, Jakarta: Consultative Group on Indonesia (CGI).

World Bank (2006) *Sustaining Indonesia's Forests: Strategy for the World Bank 2006–2009*, Washington, DC: World Bank.

8 Will credits from avoided deforestation in developing countries jeopardize the balance of the carbon market?

Axel Michaelowa and Michael Dutschke

Introduction

Avoiding emissions from deforestation as a greenhouse gas (GHG) mitigation activity in the international climate policy regime has been under discussion since 1995, when the pilot phase of activities implemented jointly (AIJ) for GHG abatement projects in developing countries and countries in transition was initiated. While the Marrakech Accords did not allow credits from avoided deforestation in the clean development mechanism (CDM), the topic has resurfaced in the negotiations for climate policy regime after 2012, now under the acronym REDD (reductions of emissions from deforestation and forest degradation). We will give a short description of the negotiation history as a background for the subsequent assessment of REDD's contribution to the carbon market.

Land use, land-use change and forestry (LULUCF) as a means of climate change mitigation has had its ups and downs over the years. The UN Conference on Environment and Development in 1992 failed to agree on a forest convention and the process initiated there has been languishing ever since until the recent decision on a 'non-binding agreement' by the UN Forum on Forests. The United Nations Framework Convention on Climate Change (UNFCCC) explicitly mentions land use on various occasions. In the pilot phase of AIJ, forest climate projects had their place. The Kyoto Protocol failed to mention climate forestry in its Article 12 on the CDM, in contrast to the differentiated and at the same time integral treatment of land use in Articles 3.3 and 3.4 with regards to industrialized countries.

The GHG targets stipulated in Annex A of the Kyoto Protocol were a lot weaker than the 15 per cent reduction originally intended by the European Union. Therefore, the EU was not prepared to accept any additional mechanisms that would allow industrialized countries to shift mitigation efforts to developing countries. Moreover, environmental NGOs perceived forest climate mitigation as a 'loophole' to avoid serious mitigation action. At the second part of the Sixth Conference of the Parties (COP-6 'bis') held in Bonn in 2000, Article 3.4 on forest management in Annex I[1] countries was adopted, allowing Annex I countries to account for increases in land-based carbon stocks up to an agreed level for the first commitment period. At the same time, afforestation and reforestation (AR) were made eligible under the CDM. This is contrary to the wording of Article 12, as it only refers to emission reductions, but the choice of carbon removal from afforestation instead of reductions from avoided deforestation was a compromise with the EU that intended to minimize the inflow of GHG credits from developing countries during the first commitment period. As a side effect, LULUCF-based mitigation in developing countries was fragmented, which has been criticized since (see, e.g., Schlamadinger *et al.*, 2001). It has been widely discussed whether crediting LULUCF activities can be made compatible with GHG emission reductions from industrial activities and how different mitigation activities should be timed (Dutschke, 2007).

Avoided deforestation has received new attention in the context of post-2012 policy scenarios. Notably since COP-11 in Montreal in 2005, different approaches for 'reducing emissions from deforestation and degradation' (REDD) have been discussed. Two intergovernmental workshops in 2006 and 2007 discussed methodologies and international policies, leading to a set of four approaches with wide overlaps and some contradictions.

The Coalition for Rainforest Nations (CfRN) promoted *compensated reductions*, whereby a country voluntarily commits to emission reductions over one commitment period. In case these reductions are not achieved, no consequences will arise (i.e. a 'no-lose target'). In case the country overcomplies with its voluntary commitment, emissions below the agreed reference level would be credited ex post and could be sold to industrialized countries. Brazil proposed a voluntary *fund-based mechanism* for REDD. Its contributors would come from Annex II states.[2] Such a fund would offer a subsidy per ton of CO_2 avoided. At the time of writing, Brazil opposes any solution that would allow crediting towards Annex I emission targets (see Moutinho *et al.*, Chapter 6 in this volume, for more).

The countries of the Congo Basin form part of the CfRN. They promoted a *stabilization fund* in addition to the CfRN model. The need for this fund is explained by the specific situation of the Central African countries, where civil wars have recently ended, which is likely to increase pressure on the forests. The proposed fund would compensate for costs of sustainable forest management to achieve a stabilization of existing forest cover. India, supported by China, has taken the issue further. In opposition to compensated reductions, it proposed *compensated conservation*. However, conservation of natural forests is not the aim of the proposed mechanism. In both Asian states, there is now only a low level of natural forest cover remaining. Instead, both countries are fostering afforestation and forest management, which is what they would like to see rewarded. This claim is far beyond REDD, but it is to some extent logical, because it considers forest land use in an integrated manner and bears resemblance to the provisions of Article 3.3 and 3.4 of Kyoto for Annex I Parties.

Most parties and observers agree that early action on REDD should be rewarded. In order to secure existing forests and to avoid perverse incentives for the private and public sectors, activities carried out during the first commitment period should be taken into account in the post-2012 period, for example, through banking. In Bali, a REDD decision was achieved that covers deforestation (UNFCCC 2007c), forest management and – to certain extent – reforestation. In cross-reference to this decision, the Bali Road Map (UNFCCC 2007e) calls for:

[E]nhanced national/international action ..., including inter alia, consideration of ... (iii) Policy approaches and positive incentives on issues relating to reducing emissions from deforestation and forest degradation in developing countries; and the role of conservation, sustainable management of forests and enhancement of forest carbon stocks in developing countries.

In case sufficient funding will be provided by the parties for this loosely defined REDD, afforestation/reforestation CDM may become an 'undead' mechanism post-2012. A similar fate occurred with one of the AIJ, the without-credit mitigation pilot that was initiated by COP-1 at Berlin in 1995. AIJ projects that started before 2000 still exist but without anybody paying attention to them. Thus, conflict among the different approaches that seemed imminent before Bali may be avoided. After long discussions, even the 'nested approach' promoted by Latin American countries was accepted. It foresees bottom-up sub-national activities in parallel with national REDD endeavours. Nevertheless, actual REDD covers up a lot of diverging interests. This is the reason why the Bali decision remains mute on funding and financing modes. Until the Copenhagen COP (COP-15) in December 2009, the precise methodologies remain to be resolved. Given the amount of open questions, this is an extremely tight schedule.

It is clear from the outset that countries wishing to participate in any type of REDD mechanism will need reliable forest inventories and institutions capable of detecting forest losses and enforcing legislation. These institutional preconditions can only be financed on a grant basis. The other part of a future finance mechanism is to offer incentives for effective forest management. While parties agree that funds should be 'new and additional' to existing facilities like official development assistance (ODA), the global environment facility (GEF), adaptation or special climate fund, it is hard to conceive that long-term finance will be provided by states (see Rametsteiner et al., Chapter 3 in this volume). For private sector involvement, some kind of credit trading is inevitable. Brazil has been tough on the issue, in order not to weaken future Annex I targets. Nevertheless, if, as proposed by Brazil, Annex II states – voluntarily or not – contribute to a REDD fund, they would have to recover these expenses from their respective taxpayers. Hence, the discussion over market- or non-market- based funding for REDD comes back to the old discourse in environmental economics between a Pigou tax and a cap-and-trade approach. The latter has proved more robust at the international level, as market regulations offer more reliability for market participants than a global tax regime. Additionally, the allocation of funds through trading tends to be more cost effective than the allocation of tax revenues.[3]

Will REDD be the elephant in the carbon market's china shop?

Besides the undeniable methodological differences in comparison with industrial GHG mitigation,[4] the key argument against including REDD in the international carbon market has been the fear of a glut of cheap credits with the potential to destabilize the market. The portent of such a destabilization was the oversupplied

European allowance market that crashed at the end of its first trading period in 2007. We will look into this question for the pre-2012 as well as the 2012–2020 periods, estimating demand and supply from different sources.

Expected credit supply from REDD until 2012 and 2020

According to the World Resource Institute, only 24 developing countries had LULUCF emissions of more than 50 million tons CO_2 ($MtCO_2$) in 2000, six of which surpassed 200 $MtCO_2$ (WRI, 2007).[5] Most of the countries with high deforestation rates are characterized by high degrees of corruption. In a climate of corruption and other institutional failures, it is unlikely that REDD will pick up rapidly. Estimates of REDD potential made to date have not taken these governance aspects into account. We therefore estimate the REDD credit potential using a set of three quantitative indicators: current deforestation rate, general institutional stability and capacity and corruption intensity (see Table 8.1). For these three indicators we apply the following values. First, the baseline from which REDD is counted is assumed to be the level of deforestation in 2000 (WRI, 2007). Second, institutional stability and capacity are addressed through the Institutional Investor credit rating[6] (Institutional Investor, 2007) and the success of CDM projects in the country to date; we assume that the ability to mobilize REDD projects requires similar capacity as the one needed for CDM projects. Third, corruption intensity is assessed via the corruption perception index[7] of Transparency International (2007).

In our view, any country with an Institutional Investor credit rating of less than 20, a corruption perception index of less than 2.5 or no submitted CDM project does not have the potential to generate REDD credits before 2012 due to the need to upgrade institutions before a credible reduction of deforestation can be achieved.[8] For countries with an Institutional Investor credit rating of more than 50, a corruption perception index of more than 4 and at least one registered CDM project we assume that from 2010 could reduce their deforestation rate by 10 per cent from the baseline. Countries in between these thresholds are assumed to reduce deforestation by 5 per cent.

The critical period for REDD will be from 2012 to 2020 because with unfettered deforestation, many tropical forests will have vanished before 2020. Given that there is over a decade to implement a REDD strategy, for the time after 2012 we assume that the CDM experience does not count as much as in the short term. Thus, only countries with an Institutional Investor credit rating of less than 20 and a corruption perception index of less than 2.5 are assumed to have little potential to generate REDD credits. We assume that countries are able to improve their current corruption perception index ratings by 0.2 points within the next decade. Countries with an Institutional Investor credit rating of more than 50 and a corruption perception index of more than 4 are assumed to reduce their deforestation rate by 50 per cent from the baseline until 2020. Countries in between these thresholds would be assumed to reduce deforestation by 20 per cent. These projected reductions in rates of deforestation while arbitrarily chosen, can be considered conservative given the relatively low costs of attaining these (for cost estimates, see Sathaye *et al.*, 2006).

Table 8.1 Deforestation, governance, attractiveness for CDM and REDD potential 2012 and 2020

Country	Emissions from deforestation (MtCO₂) in 2000[a]	Institutional investor ranking (%, March 2007)[b]	Transparency international ranking (CPI 2006)[c]	CDM participation (share in registered and submitted projects 28 June 2007 in %)[d]	REDD potential by 2012 (MtCO₂)	REDD potential 2012–2020 (MtCO₂)
Angola	18	27.2	2.2	0/0	0	0
Argentina	55	40.2	2.9	1.3/0.6	15	56
Belize	21	25.1	3.5	0/0	0	32
Benin	36	26.0	2.5	0/0	0	56
Bolivia	84	28.1	2.7	0.3/0.5	20	96
Botswana	20	65.4	5.6	0/0	0	80
Brazil	1372	58.2	3.3	14.4/9.6	345	1640
Cambodia	56	22.1	2.1	0.1/0.1	0	0
Cameroon	77	22.9	2.3	0/0	0	120
Chile	15	76.4	7.3	2.4/1.3	5	48
Colombia	106	53.7	3.9	0.8/0.7	25	384
Congo	10	19.0	2.2	0/0	0	0
Congo, DR	317	12.7	2.0	0/0	0	0
Costa Rica	10	52.0	4.1	0.6/0.3	5	8
Côte d'Ivoire	91	14.8	2.1	0/0.1	0	0
Ecuador	59	33.1	2.3	1.3/0.7	0	96
Ghana	28	34.2	3.3	0/0	0	48
Guatemala	57	41.5	2.6	0.7/0.7	15	88
Guinea	10	16.1	1.9	0/0	0	0
Guyana	35	28.5	2.5	0/0	0	56
Honduras	18	33.6	2.5	1.4/0.6	5	24
Indonesia	2563	47.0	2.4	1.3/1.3	5	4104
Kenya	12	27.7	2.2	0/0.1	0	0
Laos	24	23.8	2.6	0.1/0	5	32
Liberia	39	8.8	n.a.	0/0	0	0

Madagascar	60	20.1	3.1	0/0	0	96
Malawi	27	20.5	2.7	0/0	0	40
Malaysia	699	71.2	5.0	2.2/2.8	350	2240
Mexico	97	68.4	3.3	12.0/4.7	25	120
Myanmar	425	12.5	1.9	0/0	0	0
Nepal	123	21.8	2.5	0.3/0.1	30	144
Nicaragua	54	21.1	2.6	0.4/0	15	56
Nigeria	195	34.2	2.2	0.1/0.1	0	0
Pakistan	33	37.5	2.2	0.1/0.1	0	0
Panama	47	53.4	3.1	0.6/0.2	10	56
Papua New Guinea	146	35.6	2.4	0.1/0	0	232
Paraguay	21	30.7	2.6	0/0	0	32
Peru	187	53.9	3.3	0.7/0.6	45	224
Philippines	95	48.0	2.5	1.4/1.8	25	112
Sierra Leone	13	11.6	2.2	0/0	0	0
Sri Lanka	30	32.7	3.1	0.5/0.3	5	40
Sudan	30	14.1	2.0	0/0	0	0
Tanzania	15	27.9	2.9	0.1/0	5	16
Thailand	48	63.7	3.6	0.3/2.5	10	64
Uganda	39	26.9	2.7	0.1/0.1	10	48
Venezuela	144	45.3	2.3	0/0	0	224
Zambia	235	24.3	2.6	0/0	0	376
Zimbabwe	47	8.5	2.4	0/0	0	0
Total	**7944**				**970**	**11,088**

Sources:

a WRI (2006)

b Institutional Investor (2007)

c Transparency International (2007)

d UNFCCC (2007c)

Under these assumptions, a total supply of 1 billion REDD credits (where one credit is equal to one ton of CO_2 emissions avoided) would be generated until 2012 and 11 billion until 2020 at costs that are much lower than current prices for certified emission reductions (CERs) from CDM projects.

Expected carbon market demand by 2012

Model-based forecasting of the carbon markets is a challenge that has not yet been resolved in a convincing manner. Several key parameters such as the coverage and stringency of emission commitments and the possibility to import emissions credits from abroad are political and thus lend themselves only to a scenario analysis. Other parameters such as abatement costs of different technologies, for example, renewable energy and energy efficiency equipment, and fuel prices are dependent on the overall development of the economy and technological progress. They can be modelled but past experience with the performance of such forecasts is mixed at best. No carbon market information service managed to forecast the surplus of EU allowances that materialized in 2005, despite the very short forecasting period. Regarding long-term model-based forecasts, the experience of the Club of Rome 'limits of growth' study in the 1970s is probably the most telling example.

The main driver for global carbon markets is the political willingness to set and enforce mandatory greenhouse gas emissions commitments. Until 2012 the commitments have been specified by the Kyoto Protocol. However, the carbon market will be influenced by decision making on the post-2012 climate policy regime, which is likely to be finalized in 2009. If the Bali timetable is adhered to, it will have a huge impact on the carbon market for both the pre- and post-2012 periods.

Industrialized countries have had a prolonged period of economic growth and there are some signs that this is about to end. If developed economies enter a period of sluggish economic growth, caused, for example, by the current crisis in the financial markets and assuming that sluggish growth would not lead to a substantial decline in energy prices, then the 2005 GHG emissions level could be representative for the commitment period 2008–2012. The latest greenhouse gas inventory data for 2005 for Annex B countries having ratified the Kyoto Protocol (UNFCCC, 2007b), multiplied by five to cover the entire commitment period, show the following surplus/shortfall positions for Kyoto parties (see Figure 8.1).

Figure 8.1 shows that the aggregated, non-LULUCF demand from the countries participating in Kyoto with a shortfall would reach 3.4 billion tCO_2 equivalent ($GtCO_2e$) for the commitment period. If the EU would use the surplus of the accession countries, the remaining demand would reach only 2 Gt. Total oversupply, commonly called 'hot air', from Russia and Ukraine would reach 7.9 Gt, much more than total demand. Russia and Ukraine, both of which successfully negotiated extremely lenient targets for the first commitment period, could theoretically dominate the carbon market and drive down prices at their will. So far, however, they have been sitting on their surplus without any indication of seriously contemplating large sales.

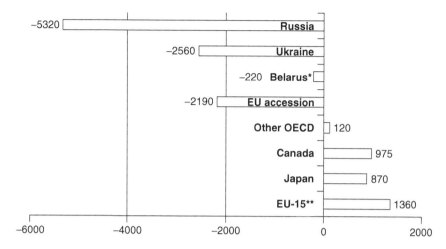

Figure 8.1 Projected surplus (−) and shortfall (+) of Kyoto Annex B parties in 2008–12 ($MtCO_2e$) for a 'sluggish growth' scenario

Source: UNFCCC (2007a)

* Belarus can only sell its surplus if an amendment on its accession to Annex B of the Kyoto Protocol is entering into force, which is unlikely.
** EU-15 is composed of Austria, Belgium, Denmark, Finland, France, Germany, Greece, Ireland, Italy, Luxembourg, the Netherlands, Portugal, Spain, Sweden and the United Kingdom.

A continuation of the current buoyant growth of industrialized countries would entail upward pressure on greenhouse gas emissions. We use projections for the year 2010 for the EU from the European Environment Agency (EEA, 2006). For Canada and Japan, we use the projection for 2010 provided to UNFCCC (Canada, 2006; UNFCCC, 2007d). For Australia, we use the high 'with measures' projection of the Australian Greenhouse Office (AGO, 2008). For Russia, Ukraine and the small OECD countries, we linearly extrapolate from their 2000–2005 UNFCCC inventory emissions trend. The 2010 projection is again multiplied by five to cover the commitment period[9] and the result is shown in Figure 8.2.

Under this scenario and assuming that at the resultant carbon prices no substantial domestic abatement takes place, the aggregated demand from the countries with a shortfall would reach 3.8 $GtCO_2e$ for the commitment period. If the EU uses the surplus of the accession countries, the remaining demand would reach 2.2 Gt. Total supply from Russia and Ukraine would still reach 6.6 Gt, over 50 per cent more than the demand. Theoretically, the price on the international carbon market would have to be zero. But this is not the case. What are the reasons?

So far, actual non-LULUCF demand on the Kyoto markets has focused on CDM and almost completely ignored the (over-)supply of Russia and Ukraine. This is maybe due to the perceived political risks of transactions with the Russian and Ukrainian governments where a deal closed today may not be honoured at the

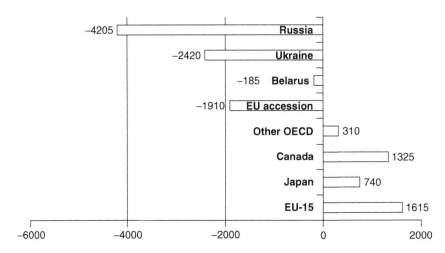

Figure 8.2 Projected surplus (−) and shortfall (+) of Kyoto Annex B parties in 2008–12 (MtCO$_2$e) for a 'buoyant economies' scenario

Sources: Australian Greenhouse Office (2008); author estimates; Canada (2006); EEA (2006); UNFCCC (2007a)

agreed time of delivery. In 2007, about 1 billion certified emission reductions (CERs)[10] were sold; total CER trades since 2003 reach almost 2 billion (Point Carbon, 2008). CDM projects registered by end of 2007 project the generation of 1.2 billion CERs by 2012 whereas submitted projects forecast another 1.3 billion. While it is likely that up to one-third of submitted projects will not be registered and that registered projects will generate only about 85 per cent of projected CERs, the steady inflow of new projects at a rate of over 100 per month makes it likely that total CER supply will reach more than 2.5 billion by end 2012. Varying the inflow and success rates of CDM projects, Michaelowa (2007b) estimates CER supply to be in a range of 1.9 to 4.4 billion, with business-as-usual reaching 3.1 billion. ERU[11] supply from joint implementation projects does not play a role as ERUs are deducted from the overall emissions budget of the host country, reducing the surplus accordingly.

Carbon market balance by 2012 under 'business-as-usual'

Estimating carbon market demand in the middle ground between 'sluggish growth' and 'buoyant economies' and business-as-usual CER supply gives the result shown in Figure 8.3. We assume that cohesion countries of the EU-15, Japan and Canada are willing to buy 'hot air' under 'green investment schemes',[12] while the other OECD countries only use CERs. The EU-15 would probably prefer buying from accession countries, while 'hot air' from Ukraine would be preferred to 'hot air' from Russia due to the higher political credibility of the former compared to the latter.

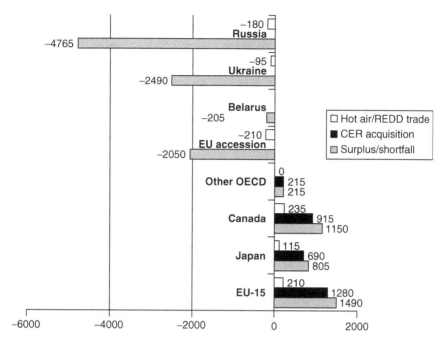

Figure 8.3 Projected surplus (–), shortfall (+) and emission trades of Kyoto Annex B parties in 2008–12 (MtCO$_2$e)

Source: Author estimates

Under such a scenario, demand for REDD credits would be limited and compete with 'hot air'. Most probably, REDD credits would be banked for post-2012, a strategy that has formally been endorsed by the Russian government. Total surplus of 'hot air' and REDD credits would reach 10 billion.

Expected carbon market demand by 2020

Given ongoing negotiations regarding post-2012 climate policy, one can only make rough assumptions about the stringency of emissions targets and the countries covered by these. We will use the negotiation proposals currently on the table as the upper bound for stringency as it is unlikely that the agreement would get more stringent: –30 per cent for the EU and other OECD compared to 1990 levels. Furthermore, we assume that Australia, Belarus, Japan, Russia, Ukraine and the USA will agree to –10 per cent from 2012 levels, whereas the new OECD members Chile, Israel, Mexico and South Korea[13] would take up –5 per cent. There would be a 7-year commitment period from 2013 to the end of 2019. The demand situation, rounded to the nearest 100 million tonnes, is shown in Figure 8.4.

Total demand under this scenario would be 18.8 GtCO$_2$e while banked volumes would sum up to 8.6 Gt. The net shortfall would thus reach 10.2 Gt. It is unlikely

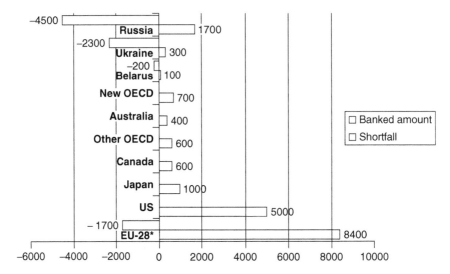

Figure 8.4 Projected shortfall (+) and banked volumes of parties with emission targets in 2012–19 (MtCO₂e)

Source: Author estimates

* EU-28 includes all current EU member states (2008).

that in the short period of 7 years, substantial emission reductions could be mobilized in industrialized countries at costs that are lower than market prices. How then could this gap be closed?

Currently registered and submitted CDM projects estimate 0.4 billion annual reduction credits once all projects are operational. Under high demand as presented in this scenario, it is likely that supply could triple until 2020. Assuming a linear growth from 0.4 billion CERs in 2013 to 1.2 billion CERs in 2019,[14] CDM could thus generate 5.5 billion credits. According to our estimate in section 2.1, banked and newly generated REDD credits would supply 12 billion t, leading to an oversupply of 7 billion t. This result shows that even under a scenario of stringent commitments REDD could jeopardize the supply–demand balance of the carbon market unless the availability of REDD leads to a further strengthening of emissions commitments.

REDD: the saviour of the long-term carbon market?

Long-term estimates of CO₂ emissions from deforestation by the different modelling studies used for IPCC assessment reports are compiled in Sathaye *et al.* (2006). For market prices of US$5.5/tCO₂, they calculate a cumulative REDD volume of 72 Gt until 2050. As their estimates do not take into account governance aspects, we think that they may be on the high side. We thus apply our governance-related approach to estimate post-2012 REDD supply.

In the time perspective of more than a decade, it can be hoped that most countries shown in Table 8.1 will reach and go beyond the thresholds to enable a more effective fight against deforestation. We therefore assume that even those countries with a current corruption perception index rating of above 2 and a current Institutional Investor credit rating above 15 will improve these values to a level where REDD becomes institutionally feasible and reach 20 per cent reduction of deforestation. As an improvement in the trend would also apply to countries with higher index values, those with an Institutional Investor credit rating of more than 40 and a corruption perception index of more than 3 would achieve a reduction of their deforestation rate by 50 per cent. Countries in between these thresholds would be assumed to reduce deforestation by 20 per cent. Countries that had reached a 50 per cent reduction by 2020 would by now have been able to completely stop deforestation within their borders. The results are shown in Table 8.2.

These numbers are at the upper bound of the range given by the IPCC 4th Assessment Report (IPCC, 2007) of between 290 and 1,098 $MtCO_2$ per year during the period 2020 to 2050. Until 2100, annual reductions are expected to soar to an average of 3290–3733 $MtCO_2$. Generating demand sufficient to cover these volumes would require a rapid strengthening of emissions commitments and an expansion of the set of countries covered by those commitments.

Not all these expected emission reductions should generate GHG emission credits. This is due to the additionality principle underlying the international GHG market. Projects or programmes aimed at reducing emissions should only generate emissions credits if they would not have happened in a business-as-usual situation. This situation then defines the baseline for calculating emission reductions. Experience from the CDM shows that the baseline scenario can be based on a historical emissions level if it can be shown that barriers exist that would prevent a change from the historical emissions level. In the case of REDD, this situation would be equal to a baseline deforestation rate in a recent period. For countries like Brazil and Indonesia, where institutional and political barriers to a reduction in deforestation can be shown (see Moutinho *et al.*; Palmer and Obidzinski, Chapters 6 and 7 in this volume, respectively), such an approach should be applied.[15] The situation becomes more complex if, as in the case of the Congo Basin countries,

Table 8.2 Post-2020 credit supply

Country group	Reduction in deforestation (%)	Emissions from deforestation in 2000 (MtCO₂)	Annual REDD potential after 2020 (MtCO₂)
Botswana, Chile, Malaysia	100	734	363
Brazil, Costa Rica, Mexico, Panama, Peru, Thailand	50	1761	528
Angola, Cambodia, Kenya, Nigeria, Pakistan	20	314	63
Total			**954**

Source: Author estimates

deforestation rates are expected to increase. Therefore, these countries are promoting some kind of voluntary 'growth cap'. It will obviously be extremely difficult to estimate how deforestation would increase in a business-as-usual situation.

An approach to estimate baseline deforestation rates could be based on the results of Rudel *et al.* (2005) who determine a U-shape for the share of forest in total land use in a country over time. Most of today's industrialized countries have experienced deforestation in the past but in most cases deforestation did stop well above zero forest share. Rudel *et al.* explain this in a threefold manner:

1   With increasing scarcity the remaining resources are better managed and reforestation becomes profitable.
2   At a certain point, forest remnants are so remote that transport costs become prohibitive.
3   Moreover, in the process of industrialization, the workforce concentrates in the industrial centres and wages for logging become less attractive.

Empirical evidence of 20 cases over 200 years suggests that the average turning point in forest cover occurs at an increasing share of forest in total land use. Similar results are found in Sathaye *et al.* (2006) who analyze a secular long-term decline in deforestation rates. In Africa, they expect the increase in deforestation to peak in 2020, in the rest of Asia in 2010, while in Central and South America, deforestation rates have already peaked. Emission reductions from deforestation can therefore be expected to be permanent if overall they flatten the forest loss curve (Dutschke, 2007). In this case, a temporary delay of deforestation will result in a higher forest remnant by the time the deforestation pressure is released. The turning point for carbon content is later than the one for the forest cover, because usually carbon content is lower in growing and managed forests. After the forest carbon content turning point, the deforestation baseline becomes zero. For instance, for the Costa Rican case, it might be argued that the turning point has already passed, so that emission reductions might not be considered additional any longer. Sooner or later during this century, in most tropical countries this turning point will be reached. From this moment on, the composition of forestry mitigation options will change and afforestation, reforestation and forest management will be the main forestry mitigation options. Deforestation will belong to the past and its avoidance should no longer create new credits. By way of contrast, baselines must not directly follow the erratic short-term variations in deforestation trends; there is a need to provide reliable economic incentives for sustainable land use alternatives.

Having national baselines as a starting point for (voluntary) target setting, is a novel feature in international climate change policy. However, the instruments for these are in place. For national Annex I communications, there is an international review process. In the same manner, non-Annex I REDD baselines could be determined by the tropical countries themselves and reviewed by the international expert review teams. The approach, whether trend based, modelled or a benchmark would be defended by these parties taking into account their own national circumstances. Only then would the country REDD targets be negotiated.

In the preceding discussion, we are describing the ideal case that REDD can really have an impact in reducing worldwide GHG emissions. This is most likely to occur with stabilization at a temperature increase below 2°C, which could be reached below a GHG concentration of 450 ppm. We assume that any steeper temperature increases will lead indirectly to human-induced carbon losses in forests, the so-called 'forest die-off' from degradation and deforestation. In that case, REDD may not be available in the more distant future. This is because at a certain yet unknown point of global temperature increase, in some regions non-managed forests will die and change into savannahs. Consequently, these forests will be transformed from a carbon sink into a source thus increasing atmospheric GHG loads even more. On a global scale, these die-off losses will likely be compensated by increased vegetation cover in the subarctic and boreal forests. For the REDD market, however, this situation may lead to a liability crisis. Permanence of REDD credits can only be granted as long as the UNFCCC's ultimate objective of climate stabilization at safe temperature levels is maintained.

Market manipulation through REDD?

In the discussions about integrating REDD into the carbon market, concerns have been voiced that there could be a deliberate distortion of the market. From a theoretical standpoint, several possibilities of market distortion exist:

- The rules for crediting of REDD are less demanding than those for other types of mitigation activity.
- The credit prices do not reflect their true production costs. This would be the case if external costs are not accounted for. Also future monitoring, verification and self-insurance costs could be neglected, meaning that permanence is not ensured.
- Credit sellers intentionally distort the market by selling credits below production costs. This would require that sales are essentially coordinated by a cartel of governments.

All three possibilities are relevant in the REDD debate. The market needs uniformity and transparency. Baseline determination, monitoring and accounting need to be standardized. These methodological concerns have to be solved before any market can start. In the current CDM setup, performance has been poor in terms of there being fewer credits generated than expected. As shown in Table 8.1, Brazil and Indonesia are responsible for 50 per cent of deforestation in developing countries.[16] There is an undeniable risk that these countries would be able to manipulate the market. Given that REDD could dominate the market between 2012 and 2020, this is an issue that requires careful design of the REDD crediting system.

After 2020, all depends on the stringency of emission commitments and the calculation of baselines for REDD, taking into account the additionality principle. There is a risk that with stabilization occurring above 2°C, forests, even under the best societal conditions, may not be able to contribute to mitigation, because global warming may severely damage existing forests, leading to important feedback effects. As a consequence, REDD credits can contribute most in the mitigation scenario of highest stringency. Not all emission reductions from deforestation will be politically and economically additional, so that a significant part of the reductions achieved may not enter the market in the form of credits. Obviously, governance of the REDD process is key. The CDM executive board is a good precedent for a body governing the market for project activities. At the national level, strong international governance is still missing. The fear that REDD credits may flood the market for emission allowances merely reflects the overall lack of stability in Kyoto markets. Once a clear internationally binding emissions trajectory towards 2050 is defined and monitored, any mitigation options will be welcome.

Clearly, a totally separate REDD target for industrialized parties is unlikely to create a liquid market. Integrating emission reduction credits from REDD into the global greenhouse gas emissions market will harness all market power for the stabilization of worldwide forest cover. In order to establish the needed scarcity for a market, the following conditions need to be fulfilled:

1   There needs to be sufficient demand, best achieved by a long-term climate stabilization target that can be priced in by the market participants.
2   REDD countries need to build up human and technical capacities to assess and monitor forest carbon stocks and their variation.
3   Seller liability for reductions achieved needs to be clarified, so as to create a fungible asset.
4   Supply needs to be limited by:
     •   setting realistic baselines
     •   certifying in a way that measurement uncertainties and erratic variations are factored out.
5   An upfront funding mechanism is needed for pre-financing REDD activities.

Opening the emissions market for REDD credits will leave the choices of timing and allocation to the market participants. The result might be that for some years higher cost industrial emission reductions are disregarded, because it is more profitable to take advantage of REDD, as long as these mitigation options are still available at low prices. Also, the market may not find the optimal solution to socioeconomic and biodiversity concerns.

In case the international community intends to direct the choice of mitigation options, and for countries, where one or more of the conditions just examined are not fulfilled, full market integration can be reduced. This could be done in the form either of price or of quantity control. Both will ultimately lead to a form of devaluation of REDD credits.

Conclusions

Emission markets are an important instrument for mitigating GHG effects, but they have no value in themselves so long as whole sectors of the economy remain outside the reach of climate policy. Moreover, markets only work if there is scarcity – a lesson learned in the first phase of the EU emissions trading scheme. Avoided deforestation (REDD) can be an important instrument to integrate countries into the international carbon market that so far have been sidelined in the CDM process. However, REDD credits have the potential to cause imbalances between supply and demand in the carbon market, especially if the international climate policy regime is not substantially strengthened after 2012. But politically the availability of REDD could lead to more stringent emissions commitments for industrialized countries.

Under the assumption that the governance problems that plague most countries with high deforestation rates will not vanish easily, total REDD credits are likely to remain below 1 $GtCO_2$ before 2012 while they could reach 11 $GtCO_2$ from 2013 until 2020. After 2020, only a qualitative analysis is feasible given the impossibility to project quality of governance in key REDD host countries. The key challenge to enable REDD to play an important role without destabilizing the global carbon market will be to give clear, long-term market signals through ambitious quantitative emission targets for a growing group of countries. Such targets should in turn be based on a long-term GHG concentration stabilization commitment.

Notes

1 Annex I to the UNFCCC lists the countries that were members of the Organization for Economic Cooperation and Development (OECD) in 1992 plus selected states of the former Soviet Union, which bear a higher share of historical responsibility for the accumulation of greenhouse gases in the atmosphere.
2 Annex II of the UNFCCC lists country parties that were OECD members in 1992.
3 This can be clearly shown by comparing the experiences of the CDM, where resources have quickly been channelled in thousands of cheap abatement options such as industrial gases, with the climate change window of the global environment facility where two-thirds of the achieved reductions projects was concentrated in three projects (see GEF, 2005, p. 34; UNFCCC, 2007a). Moreover, the portfolio suffered 'from lack of targets; unrealistic estimates, especially for replication; unavailable data; and inconsistencies in estimates' (GEF, 2005, p. 38).
4 These have led to a lengthy debate about defining the baseline for avoided deforestation (see, for example, Brown *et al.*, 2006; Chomitz *et al.*, 2006; Dutschke *et al.*, 2006; see also Johns and Schlamadinger, Chapter 5 in this volume).
5 There are huge differences between assessments of emissions from deforestation given by WRI (2007), FAO (2005) and UNFCCC (2007e) (see Wilkie, 2006). We use WRI figures because they are the most widely available of the three datasets.
6 The Institutional Investor ranking list shows the creditworthiness of countries on a scale of 0 (worst) to 100 (best). Updated every 6 months, it is based on the opinion of international finance specialists and bankers.
7 The corruption perception index is compiled by the NGO Transparency International. It ranks countries on a scale of 0 (worst) to 10 (best).
8 The thresholds for the indices have been selected in a way that only countries with bad governance and low economic performance fall below these. Those countries are generally unable to attract substantial foreign investment.
9 2010 is in the middle of the commitment period and thus representative for the whole period, if one does a linear approximation.
10 The units traded from the clean development mechanism (CDM).

11 Emission reduction units, the units traded from joint implementation (JI) between industrialized country parties.
12 A green investment scheme is an agreement where a country sells 'hot air' and invests the sales revenues in projects that directly or indirectly reduce greenhouse gas emissions. This is generally seen to make buying 'hot air' palatable to policymakers and has been pursued by Japan, the Netherlands and the World Bank.
13 Emissions estimates for those countries from Michaelowa (2007a).
14 If the CDM mobilizes projects in industrial and domestic energy efficiency, which so far has been sidelined, supply could easily reach volumes of up to 2 billion CERs per year (see Bakker *et al.*, 2007).
15 Our model based on 2000 deforestation emissions is simplistic, because there may be stochastic errors in the deforestation rate for one year, due to weather phenomena like El Niño or market peaks for agricultural goods. For approaches to baseline estimation see Harris *et al.*, Chapter 10 in this volume.
16 The values for Brazil vary from 0.7 to 2.7 billion ton CO_2 per year and those for Indonesia from 0.2 to 2.5 billion ton CO_2 (FAO, 2005; UNFCCC, 2007e; WRI, 2007).

References

AGO (Australian Greenhouse Office) (2008) *Tracking to the Kyoto Target. Australia's Greenhouse Emissions Trends 1990 to 2008–2012*, Canberra: Department of Climate Change, Australian Government.

Bakker, S., Arvanitakis, A., Bole, T., van de Brugg, E., Doets, C. and Gilbert, A. (2007) *Carbon Credit Supply Potential beyond 2012*, Petten: Energy Research Centre of the Netherlands (ECN).

Brown, S., Hall, M., Andrasko, K., Ruiz, F., Marzoli, W., Guerrero, G. *et al.* (2006) 'Baselines for land-use change in the tropics: application to avoided deforestation projects', *Mitigation and Adaptation Strategies for Global Change*, 12(6): 1001–1026.

Canada (2006) *Canada's Fourth National Report on Climate Change. Actions to Meet Commitments Under the United Nations Framework Convention on Climate Change*, Ottawa: Environment Canada, Government of Canada.

Chomitz, K.M., Buys, P., De Luca, G., Thomas, T.S. and Wertz-Kanounnikoff, S. (2006) *At Loggerheads? Agricultural Expansion, Poverty Reduction and Environment in the Tropical Forests*, World Bank Policy Research Report, Development Research Group, Washington, DC: World Bank.

Dutschke, M. (2007) 'CDM forestry and the ultimate objective of the climate convention', *Mitigation and Adaptation Strategies for Global Change*, 12(2): 275–302.

Dutschke, M., Butzengeiger, S. and Michaelowa, A. (2006) 'A spatial approach to baseline and leakage in CDM forest carbon sinks projects', *Climate Policy*, 5(5): 517–530.

EEA (European Environment Agency) (2006) *Greenhouse Gas Emission Trends and Projections in Europe 2006*, EEA Report, 9, Copenhagen: European Environment Agency.

FAO (Food and Agriculture Organization of the United Nations) (2005) *Global Forest Resources Assessment Progress towards Sustainable Forest Management*, Rome: FAO.

GEF (Global Environment Facility) (2005) 'Progressing towards environmental results', in *Third overall performance study of the GEF*, Washington, DC: GEF.

Institutional Investor (2007) *Country Credit Ratings*, March issue, 120–121. Institutional Investor Inc.

IPCC (2007), 'Climate change 2007: mitigation', *Contribution of Working Group III to the Fourth Assessment Report of the Intergovernmental*, Cambridge: Cambridge University Press.

Johns, T. and Schlamadinger, B. (2009) 'International policy and institutional barriers to reducing emissions from deforestation and degradation in developing countries as a climate change mitigation strategy', in C. Palmer and S. Engel (eds) *Avoided Deforestation: Prospects for Mitigating Climate Change*, London: Routledge.

Michaelowa, A. (2007a) 'Graduation and deepening', in J. Aldy and R. Stavins (eds) *Architectures for Agreement*, Cambridge: Cambridge University Press.

Michaelowa, A. (2007b) *How many CERs will the CDM produce by 2012?*, Discussion paper CDM-2, Oxford: Climate Strategies.

Moutinho, P., Cenamo, M.C. and Moreira, P.F. (2009) 'Reducing carbon emissions by slowing deforestation: REDD initiatives in Brazil', in C. Palmer and S. Engel (eds) *Avoided Deforestation: Prospects for Mitigating Climate Change*, London: Routledge.

Palmer, C. and Obidzinski, K. (2009) 'Choosing avoided deforestation baselines in the context of government failure: the case of Indonesia's plantations policy', in C. Palmer and S. Engel (eds) *Avoided Deforestation: Prospects for Mitigating Climate Change*, London: Routledge.

Point Carbon (2008) *Carbon 2008*, Oslo: Point Carbon.

Rametsteiner, E., Obersteiner, M., Kindermann, G. and Sohngen, B. (2009) 'Economics of avoiding deforestation', in C. Palmer and S. Engel (eds) *Avoided Deforestation: Prospects for Mitigating Climate Change*, London: Routledge.

Rudel, T., Coomes, O., Moran, E., Achard, F., Angelsen, A., Xu, J. *et al.* (2005) 'Forest transitions: towards a global understanding of land use change', *Global Environmental Change*, 15(1): 23–31.

Sathaye, J., Makundi, W., Dale, L., Chan, P. and Andrasko, K. (2006) 'GHG mitigation potential, costs and benefits in global forests: a dynamic partial equilibrium approach', *Energy Journal*, 27: 127–163.

Schlamadinger, B., Obersteiner, M., Michaelowa, A., Grubb, M., Azar, C., Yamagata, Y. *et al.* (2001) 'Capping the cost of compliance with the Kyoto Protocol and recycling revenues into land-use projects', *The Scientific World*, 1: 271–280.

Transparency International (2007) *Corruption Perception Index* [online]. Available at: http://www.transparency.org/policy_research/surveys_indices/cpi [accessed 9 July 2007].

UNFCCC (United Nations Framework Convention on Climate Change) (2007a) *CDM Website* [online]. Available at: http:/cdm.unfccc.int [accessed 9 July 2007].

UNFCCC (United Nations Framework Convention on Climate Change) (2007b) *GHG Emission Profiles for Annex I Parties* [online]. Available at: http://unfccc.int/ghg_emissions_data/items/3954.php [accessed 9 July 2007].

UNFCCC (United Nations Framework Convention on Climate Change) (2007c) *Decision-/CP.13 Bali Action Plan. Advance Unedited Version*, Bonn: UNFCCC.

UNFCCC (United Nations Framework Convention on Climate Change) (2007d) *Report of the Centralized In-Depth Review of the Fourth National Communication of Japan*, FCCC/IDR.4/JPN, Bonn: UNFCCC.

UNFCCC (United Nations Framework Convention on Climate Change) (2007e) *Decision -/CP.13; Reducing Emissions from Deforestation in Developing Countries: Approaches to Stimulate Action. Advance Unedited Version*, Bonn: UNFCCC.

Wilkie, M. (2006) 'Avoided deforestation: poor information and data, and what to do about it', presentation at FAO COP-12 Side Event, 11 November 2006, Nairobi [online]. Available at: http://regserver.unfccc.int/seors/file_storage/7ienj725qk87tsr.pdf [accessed 9 July 2007].

WRI (World Resources Institute) (2007) *CAIT Database*, Washington, DC: WRI.

Part III

Insights for effective and efficient avoided deforestation policy

9 Leakage from avoided deforestation compensation policy

Concepts, empirical evidence and corrective policy options

Brian C. Murray

Introduction

The accumulation of greenhouse gases (GHG) in the atmosphere is inextricably linked to activities on the ground via the global carbon cycle. Activities in land use, land-use change and forestry (LULUCF) remove carbon dioxide (CO_2) from the atmosphere by sequestering carbon in trees, other vegetation and soils, but can also increase GHG concentrations through the release of carbon stored in forested ecosystems via deforestation. The main ways in which forestry can mitigate GHG and thereby reduce the threat of climate change can be classified as follows:

1 *Afforestation and reforestation (AR)*: building new terrestrial carbon stocks by establishing trees on non-forest land through afforestation or reforestation.
2 *Forest management (FM)*: enhancing existing forest carbon stocks through changes in management practices.
3 *Avoided deforestation (AD)*: reducing the incidence and emissions from the conversion of forest cover to less carbon-intensive land cover.

Some also include reduced emissions from forest degradation in this list of LULUCF mitigation activities.[1] The collective term for this activity is reduced emissions from deforestation and degradation (REDD), which is the focus of this volume.

This is not the first time that the international community has considered ways in which to compensate parties for REDD activities. The first such approach was during the design stages of the Kyoto Protocol, the component of the UNFCCC that imposes binding emission commitments for Annex I countries. Those commitments can be met in part by the development of GHG ('carbon') offset projects producing emission reductions or sequestration of carbon from uncapped sources (countries or sectors). Under a project-based system, emission reduction activities are undertaken by entities that are not otherwise required to cut their emissions. These projects involve purposeful action to reduce net emissions below some level. The amount of the reduction can then be used to offset emissions from capped sources. Compensation is usually paid to the project developer when the emission offset they create can be used as a compliance mechanism by the capped entity, thereby allowing them to forego their own emission reduction while meeting the overall emissions cap. In the case of LULUCF, emissions and carbon storage are likely to remain outside of any national caps, due to their dispersed nature.

Under the Kyoto Protocol, project-level participation by non-Annex I countries occurs primarily through the clean development mechanism (CDM).[2] The purpose of the CDM is to allow participation of developing countries in climate mitigation on a voluntary, incentive-based (rather than penal) foundation, while creating economic and sustainable development opportunities for developing countries and low cost mitigation options for Annex I countries facing GHG caps. CDM projects can occur in most emitting sectors, but in the LULUCF sector, activities are currently limited to afforestation and reforestation.

After much deliberation, avoided deforestation was not included as a CDM activity in the first phase of the Kyoto Protocol. The exclusion of avoided deforestation from the CDM can be attributable in significant part to the notion that emission reductions from avoided deforestation will be difficult or impossible to measure, monitor and demonstrate that they are real reductions (see Johns and Schlamadinger, Chapter 5 in this volume).

Regardless of whether the compensated reduction of deforestation emissions is tied to a global carbon market – but perhaps emphatically if it is – it is important to ensure that compensation is paid for real emission reductions only. The first order of business in determining 'real' reductions is that they should be measured, monitored and verified using scientifically valid methods and data of an appropriately high quality (Brown *et al.*, 2007; DeFries *et al.*, 2006; Olander *et al.*, 2008). But the focus of this chapter is on the accounting dimensions of the problem rather than on measurement and monitoring, although the two are clearly related.

The core of the real reductions issue is that while a project accounting system can be set up to adequately track emissions for the project area for a given period of time, it may not capture factors that are out of a project's direct control, even though they affect the project's net GHG benefits. To demonstrate that emission reductions are real, a project's emission reductions receiving credit or payments within the system should have the following characteristics:

- *Additionality*: emissions are below what they otherwise would be without the policy.
- *Permanence*: deforestation emissions are reduced for good and not simply shifted to another period.
- *Absence of leakage*: emissions are not simply shifted to another location or sector where they remain uncontrolled or uncounted.

The concepts of additionality, permanence and leakage have been cornerstone concerns for project-based GHG mitigation policy almost since its inception, particularly in the LULUCF sector (IPCC, 2000; Murray *et al.*, 2007). These issues have been dealt with adequately in some sectors, as project-based methodologies have been tested, approved and implemented in the field across several different sectors and regions. However, the CDM has had very limited success in the LULUCF sector, with only one of the nearly 800 approved projects being an LULUCF afforestation project (CDM Statistics, 2007). Meanwhile, deforestation continues to mount in developing countries, as efforts to reverse it cannot overcome the various economic and institutional factors driving the trend. Given the exclusion of deforestation from the CDM and the failure of the CDM to substantially enhance forest carbon sequestration, it is no surprise that new approaches are now being considered to provide substantial incentives for REDD as part of the international climate policy framework.

Current proposals for including avoided deforestation emissions in international climate policy regimes, including the proposals now being considered in the UN Framework Convention on Climate Change (UNFCCC) have focused on national-level approaches in part to combat the leakage problems found in the project-based approaches. Nonetheless, leakage risks still persist with a policy that will likely only have partial international coverage and they should be addressed in developing avoided deforestation compensation policies. Policy development is moving ahead with the somewhat vague notion that leakage is problematic and needs to be addressed, but with a less than complete picture of why it occurs, how big a problem it might be, and what can be done to minimize its impact on the success of the policy. The purpose of this chapter is to shed some light on these issues.

The chapter continues with a discussion of leakage concepts and their economic roots. This is followed by a synthesis of the empirical evidence to date from studies that have directly or indirectly estimated leakage magnitude for avoided deforestation policies. A discussion of how policies can reduce leakage opportunities and deal with the leakage that remains in the system follows.

Leakage concepts

In the context of GHG controls, leakage occurs when efforts to control emissions in one place cause emissions to shift to another place that is not subject to the policy. The potential for leakage arises when rules, regulations and incentives for action affect only part of the potential participants. A REDD programme is likely to be limited in coverage. In particular, most policy proposals are being targeted exclusively at tropical forest nations that have not signed up to binding GHG reduction targets under the Kyoto Protocol. The REDD policy is likely to be voluntary, meaning countries can opt out and not be subject to compensation and the terms thereof. If a country does not opt into the programme, it cannot receive compensation for reducing deforestation. But it will also not be penalized for any deforestation that occurs. In that case, they have neither positive nor negative incentives to reduce deforestation.

Under the circumstances just described, leakage can occur when forests are protected in Country A via a REDD compensated reductions programme, but the activity that placed pressure on the forest (e.g., land clearing for agriculture) and the corresponding emissions gets shifted to Country B, which is not covered by the

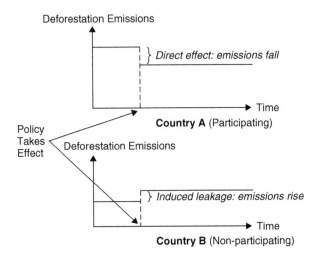

Figure 9.1 Leakage between countries

Source: Author

Note: Leakage occurs when actions taken in one country (Country A) to cut emissions cause a shift in activity and emissions to another country (Country B) not covered by the policy.

programme (see Figure 9.1). Suppose Country A worked hard to develop, implement and enforce policies and market institutions that reduce deforestation by 1 million hectares per year and reduce emissions by 100 million tons of CO_2 ($MtCO_2$). But if the deforestation that would have occurred in Country A (e.g., to supply global timber or agricultural markets) is shifted elsewhere (e.g., 0.4 million ha of deforestation, generating 40 $MtCO_2$ emissions) this can clearly undermine the success of the compensated reduction policy and undermine its integrity if it is not properly accounted for.

Economic foundations of leakage

The primary drivers of leakage are economic. LULUCF activities have special characteristics that not only make leakage an important factor to consider, but that also make it complicated to estimate. First, society places demands on the goods and services produced by land, but the amount of land available to produce them is fixed. Land-use economics studies have clearly shown that policy-targeted changes on land use in one place are quite likely to cause a reallocation of land use, i.e. a shift between forest and agricultural land, on the rest of the landscape unless specifically and effectively prohibited by the policy (e.g., Wear and Murray, 2004; Wu, 2000). Second, agriculture and forest commodities produced on land are likely to be traded in markets that operate at local, regional, national or global scales. Therefore, market forces may translate changes in the supply of commodities in one part of the landscape into changes in the demand for and supply of commodities in other, distant locations. Markets tend to expand the spatial impact of seemingly localized actions. Third, there is a complex dynamic adjustment pattern associated with the management of different types of land and in particular with respect to forestry. Trees store different levels of carbon at different ages in their lifecycles. Any adjustments in prices resulting from carbon policies today have a time path of impacts on forest inventories. To the extent that society values carbon sequestration that occurs in the present, more than that which occurs in the future, all else equal (i.e. it discounts future carbon benefits relative to current carbon benefits), the measurement of leakage can become complicated.

Leakage from tropical deforestation depends on the factors underlying deforestation in the first place and the extent to which those factors are mobile. Agricultural expansion is the most significant determinant of deforestation across the tropics (Barbier, 2001). Reducing this activity in one country might shift expansion to another country, particularly if land clearing was for the purposes of cash crop production for global commodity markets. But if subsistence agriculture or local market production is the driver of a country's deforestation, reducing deforestation there may not cause much international leakage unless it heightens reliance on cash crops produced abroad.

Other significant drivers of deforestation include logging for timber resources and fuelwood (Bashaasha *et al.*, 2001; Köhlin and Parks, 2001), road building and human settlement (Cropper *et al.*, 2001), each of which has different spatial and market feedback implications for leakage. Reducing logging in one location often just shifts it either to another location within the country (Wear and Murray, 2004) or to other countries (Gan and McCarl, 2007), and thus leakage potential can be high if no counteracting provisions are put in place (Murray *et al.*, 2004; Sohngen and Brown, 2004).

Leakage need not be produced by a corresponding increase in deforestation elsewhere. It can be produced by other forms of land-use change or management. For instance, if deforestation avoided in Country A reduces agricultural output there and increases production in Country B, this may be met by clearing of grasslands or increased intensification of agricultural inputs in Country B, neither of which involves deforestation, but both of which have GHG effects that can contribute to leakage.

Figure 9.2 gives a simple depiction of market phenomena producing leakage. Assume that 'Country A' represents all countries adopting the avoided deforestation policy and 'Country B' reflects all those that do not. Avoided deforestation in Country A leads to the contraction of commodity supply (e.g., timber or agricultural good produced via deforestation in Country A), which is depicted by the inward shift in Country A's supply function from S^A_0 to S^A_1 in (a) of Figure 9.2. Countries A and B together make up the world market depicted in (c). The contraction of world supply through Country A's actions is depicted by the shift in world supply from S^W_0 to S^W_1. Given world demand represented by D^W, the global price of the commodity rises, which induces a supply response from Country B, going from Q^B_0 to Q^B_1 in (b). This supply response, and corresponding GHG emissions,

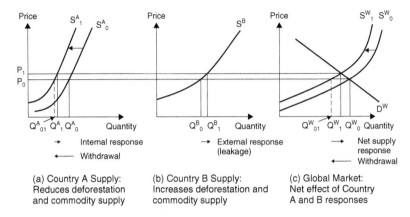

Figure 9.2 Market phenomena causing leakage

Source: Author

comprise the external leakage induced by Country A's actions. There can also be some internal response in Country A (Q^A_{01} to Q^A_1), which is the increase in supply from Country A's (contracted) supply function in response to the rise in the world price, but this response and any associated emissions should be captured with a national accounting system and therefore does not constitute leakage (in a project-based system, this intra-national response would be unaccounted for and, hence, would constitute leakage).[3] Only the response in terms of associated emissions from non-participating countries produces leakage, since these remain unaccounted for in the system.

How important is leakage empirically?

The previous section creates the case that leakage is relevant in concept, but how quantitatively important is it likely to be in the policy setting of interest? In contrast to biophysical phenomena in land-use change, there are no special sensors that detect leakage. Leakage is not directly observable. Rather, it is a market phenomenon that must be estimated using economic data and models.

The magnitude of leakage is typically expressed in proportional or percentage terms for the relationship in Equation 9.1 shows:

$$Leakage = \frac{GHG\ emissions\ shifted\ elsewhere}{GHG\ emissions\ directly\ reduced\ by\ the\ policy} \tag{9.1}$$

So if a policy achieves 1 million tons of reduction in Country A but induces 200,000 tons of emissions in other countries, leakage is 20 per cent.

Estimating leakage values in real market settings requires some analytical device to characterize market behaviour and responses. Ideally, this would come through the use of sophisticated economic models of the relevant markets and regions. That approach has been used in some applications and the results of those studies are highlighted later. However, in cases where no studies have been conducted or models are, perhaps, not readily available, a general analytical approach building on the shifting supply and demand functions of Figure 9.2 can be employed to develop a rough estimate of leakage potential.[4] This is the approach outlined in the next section.

Analytical approach: parameterized supply and demand shift

Figure 9.2 illustrates the shifting in market output that creates leakage, but as Equation 9.1 shows, leakage is denominated in emission units, not timber or agricultural output units. Murray *et al.* (2004) integrate parameters for the partial equilibrium market shifts implied in Figure 9.2 with the corresponding GHG effects to develop a more mathematically explicit variant on Equation 9.1. Leakage, *L*, is defined as:

$$L = \frac{100 \cdot e \cdot C_B}{[e - E \cdot (1 + \Phi_A)] \cdot C_A} \tag{9.2}$$

where e and E represents the elasticities of supply and demand, respectively, in the commodity markets of interest,[5] C_B reflects the emissions caused by an increase in output (e.g., harvests) in countries not subject to the compensated reductions policy, measured in tons of emissions per year, C_A reflects the emissions avoided by reducing output in the countries subject to the policies, and Φ_A is the ratio of the supply removed from the market by Country A's action divided by the quantity supplied by the rest of the world. If Country A is just a small supplier in world markets or if Country A's policy produces just a small shift in world markets, the value of Φ_A is close to zero. As Country A becomes a larger share of global output, Φ_A approaches infinity.

Murray *et al.* (2004) provide an example of the following parameter values: unitary elasticities of supply ($e = 1.0$) and demand ($E = -1.0$), equal carbon sequestration rates per unit by country ($C_A = C_B$), and the ratio of market output produced by policy participants relative to non-participants is somewhat modest ($\Phi_A = 0.10$). The leakage estimate in this case is $L = 47$ per cent; in other words, about half of the emission reduction benefits in participating countries are countered by emissions diverted to non-participating countries.

Comparative static analysis can show that leakage is amplified under the following conditions:

- relatively inelastic demand (low absolute value for E)
- carbon losses per unit of output are greater in the uncovered countries (C_B) than in the covered countries (C_A)
- covered countries have a small share of the world market (lower values of Φ_A).

Inelastic demand implies that the market will be inclined to seek supplies from any sources that will supply it rather than simply cut consumption or switch to other commodities in response to the price rise. This exacerbates the market forces that lead to leakage. Murray *et al.* (2004) provide an example with timber as the commodity driving deforestation. Their analysis shows that leakage can diminish if the timber potentially supplied from Country B is a poor demand substitute for the timber preserved in Country A. In this case, the market is less likely to move toward Country B supplies when Country A product is removed from the market. This does not completely eliminate leakage tendencies, as there could be substitution away from, say, tropical hardwoods to other materials that have potentially higher GHG emissions in their production. If these products are supplied through manufacturing processes not subject to a GHG cap, then intersectoral leakage can occur. A more general equilibrium analysis would be required to capture all secondary sources of leakage, although such models capable of capturing all economic and GHG flows, along with the nuances of deforestation and carbon dynamics do not exist at this time.

When leakage causes supply shifts to countries that incur relatively high emissions per unit of product produced, this too enhances leakage. Alternatively, if carbon-rich forests protected in one place shift timber harvesting to locations managed sustainably with little net loss of carbon over time, then this can greatly diminish leakage.

Finally, when the avoided deforestation actions of the covered countries have a collectively small impact in the global market, the supply contraction is easily replaced by increased supply elsewhere, thereby creating leakage. This is often a misunderstood point. Some would argue that leakage is inconsequential when only a small part of the market is affected. That is because small market disruptions have virtually no effect on market prices. With no market price change, the argument goes, how can leakage occur? The critical point here is that the reason that no market price effects occur is that the rest of the market can easily fill the supply gap produced by reduction of Country A's supply, when that supply is a small share of the world market. In other words, it is the realization of leakage that fills the supply gap and reduces pressure on the market price. On the other side of the spectrum, leakage dissipates the larger the share of the world market that is covered by avoided deforestation policies. The policy implication, discussed further later, is that including all of the world's deforesters or potential deforesters in a REDD policy can greatly diminish leakage and improve policy effectiveness. In the limit, if all countries are covered by the policy, leakage is zero as all emissions are accounted for.[6]

The preceding example, although helpful for providing basic conceptual and empirical insight into how leakage works its way through a single commodity market, is only a partial equilibrium view focusing on traded commodities and on only one commodity. In reality, leakage might still occur in cases when traded commodity production may not be directly affected (e.g., in subsistence settings, where subsistence activity shifts elsewhere). Moreover, even in a market setting, changes in land use often affect the production of multiple commodities in multiple regions. The next section provides an extension into these more complicated cases.

Integrated modelling

The preceding example provides a fairly straightforward way to benchmark leakage potential given parameter values for supply and demand, carbon emission rates and market shares for a single commodity market. But, in reality, there may be multiple markets affected simultaneously by an avoided deforestation compensation

Table 9.1 Published leakage estimates from avoided deforestation or forest preservation setaside (stop logging) policies

Region	Policy action	Modeling approach	Estimated leakage magnitude (%)	Source
Product volume displacement estimates				
Temperate, Pacific Northwest US	Stop logging public lands	Ex post partial equilibrium econometric model of US timber market	Within region: 43 National: 58 Continental: 84	Wear and Murray, 2004
Global	Reduce forest output at national and regional level	Ex ante global computable general equilibrium model	45–92	Gan and McCarl, 2007
Carbon emissions displacement estimates				
Temperate/ US regional	Avoid deforestation and logging setasides on private lands (regional policies in isolation)	Ex ante integrated model of US forest and agricultural sectors	Avoided deforestation Northeast: 41–43 Pacific NW: 8–9 Other regions: 0–92 Logging setaside Pacific NW: 16 South: 64	Murray *et al.*, 2004
Tropics/Bolivia	Logging setasides in national park	Ex ante partial equilibrium model of Bolivian timber market	2–38	Sohngen and Brown, 2004

Source: Authors adapted from Sathaye and Andrasko (2007)

system, especially forest and agriculture, but possibly other sectors as well (e.g., energy). This requires a more complex modelling framework, one that simultaneously solves for multiple markets and integrates carbon accounting with the simulated changes in market outcome. Relatively few studies to date have used these approaches to estimate leakage from avoided deforestation. Those that have are summarized in Table 9.1, along with studies of the closely related phenomena of forest preservation policies to set aside forest areas from logging.

The studies are divided between those that track the displacement of forest products as a result of restrictions in one location – the type of market behaviour referenced in Figure 9.2 – and those that track the emissions displacement associated with this product movement. The latter are the ultimate measure of interest because of their unit of measure, but the former studies provide a glimpse of the empirical magnitude involved in the economic forces underlying leakage.

Wear and Murray's (2004) econometric study of timber harvesting restrictions on US federal lands in the Pacific Northwest starting in the late 1980s is unique in that it is the only study that estimated displacement effects after the fact (ex post) using observed market data from the period of interest rather than predict displacement or leakage before the fact (ex ante) using predictive simulation. Their study estimates that about 43 per cent of the foregone harvests on public lands in the Pacific Northwest were shifted to private lands within the region, another 15 per cent shifted to other regions in the USA, and another 26 per cent to harvests in Canada, thereby providing strong empirical evidence that efforts to stem logging in one place do tend to shift harvests elsewhere. But as discussed already, and demonstrated later, the emissions leakage effect may not be as strong as the product leakage if harvests are shifted to less carbon-rich regions than the Pacific Northwest.

Gan and McCarl (2007) examine displacement potential internationally, simulating the effect of unilateral supply reductions by one country or multilateral reductions by regional groups of countries on the global distribution of forest product supply. This is the only study that gives an estimate of international leakage potential, although, as mentioned, the displacement is a measure in product flow not emissions. The displacement potential they find is quite large. Countries acting unilaterally will generally find a majority of their reduced production shifted to other countries. Only Canada had leakage effects of less than 50 per cent. When combined in regional coalitions, total displacement drops as expected, but not as dramatically as one might expect. The authors conclude it would take much larger international coalitions, rather than regional ones to substantially dampen leakage effects, as discussed in the previous section.

Studies showing emissions leakages are confined to the USA (Murray *et al.*, 2004) and Bolivia (Sohngen and Brown, 2004). The US study simulates emissions leakage from logging setaside and avoided deforestation policies using the FASOM (forest and agricultural sector optimization model) model (Adams *et al.*, 1996). The Murray *et al.* study looks at policies that would be implemented unilaterally by regions within the USA to examine how leakage fundamentals might vary by region. Such a regional policy, if implemented, would likely exacerbate leakage as shifts occur within the country. But actual policy implementation would likely not be confined to individual regions, but would be national or international in coverage. So the leakage estimates from the Murray *et al.* study might be seen as high end estimates relative to a national or international programme. That said, the regional estimates range from quite low (near zero) to extremely high (over 90 per cent). Sohngen and Brown's study of the Noel Kempff Mercado National Park in Bolivia estimates the effects of a logging ban and how this might shift harvests and emissions within Bolivia. They find leakage estimates somewhat on the lower end of the range by other studies (less than 40 per cent) and they also find that leakage in the short run is tied to capital constraints.

Policies to address leakage in an avoided deforestation compensation policy

The previous sections suggest that leakage is a real and present concern for the success of policies to combat deforestation and associated greenhouse gas emissions. While leakage results from natural economic forces that are difficult to restrain, the international system in which compensation for avoided deforestation emissions operates can be modified to reduce it and address it as a problem. Specific options are discussed in the following.

Establish national baselines that encourage international participation

Leakage is one of the concerns that kept avoided deforestation out of the project-based CDM, but policy options now being proposed address some of these concerns by proposing national accounting rather than project-level accounting. This helps matters considerably, as the evidence discussed in the previous section suggests within-country leakage from project-based approaches can be a real problem. Yet there is still international leakage to contend with as emissions shift from participating countries with complete accounting of emissions to non-participating countries that remain outside of the system. Therein the focus must be on international engagement to address these concerns.

The Berlin Mandate, signed by the UNFCCC in 1995 stipulates that countries will have 'common but differentiated' responsibilities in achieving climate goals. Right now, this means that emission reduction commitments are held by the developed countries that have ratified the Kyoto Protocol. Developing country participation is limited to voluntary measure such as hosting CDM projects. So developing country participation in an avoided deforestation compensation programme would be, to all intents and purposes, on a voluntary basis. To increase participation, countries would need to expect that the benefits exceed the costs. For REDD compensation policies, this may boil down to the issue of the size of the baseline they are granted. Baselines determine the level of emissions below which a country can receive credits for their reductions (see Figure 9.3).

The following sections discuss several approaches for developing national baselines that have been submitted for consideration in UNFCCC deliberations (UNFCCC, 2007).

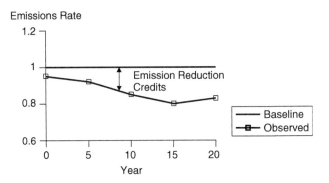

Figure 9.3 Observed vs. baseline emissions

Source: Author

Note: Credits are generally assigned for emissions that fall below a baseline level. This creates incentives for countries to seek a high baseline.

Historical reference period emissions: national

This is the approach carrying most weight at this time. It sets a country's deforestation emissions baseline equal to its emissions observed or estimated during a historical reference period (e.g., a 5- or 10-year period before implementation of the programme). Setting a future baseline emissions rate equal to the rate from a recent historical reference period is straightforward and has precedent for national GHG accounting. However, this takes a very static view of the conditions affecting deforestation that may not apply in many cases. The deforestation path is often not a linear process, depending on a number of factors including a country's position along its development path, shifts in commodity markets affecting a country's land use and the size of the remaining forests subject to clearing. The past, even recent, may not be the best predictor of the future.

Historical reference period emissions: global or pan-tropical

For the purposes of encouraging international participation, the biggest problem with the national historic reference period emissions approach is that countries with historically low emissions rates will have low baselines and little incentive to participate . If the opportunity for generating sizeable credits is taken off the table, the country may opt not to participate in the compensation system and become a potential haven for leakage. One proposal to address this problem is to set a global or pan-tropical deforestation baseline as a point of reference for all countries in the system. This has been proposed as one means for differentiating between countries with high versus low deforestation rates relative to the global average. This effectively would adjust upward the national baselines for countries with lower than average historic deforestation as an incentive for maintaining these low deforestation rates

(Mollicone *et al.*, 2007; Santilli *et al.*, 2005). The problem is that such an approach could create 'hot air' reductions – credit for no action from countries that have had their baselines inflated to the global/pan-tropical average. Also, if countries with historically above average emissions are required to use average emissions rates for their baseline, this will require steeper cuts by them to generate credits than if they used their own historic baseline, a situation that could undercut their incentive to participate. In short, using a highly aggregated global or pan-tropical average for all countries and applying it as a baseline for each country may improve incentives for some countries, but it will reduce incentives for others and is likely an inefficient way to engage fuller participation.

Business-as-usual (BAU) projection

The previous two baseline approaches suggest a balancing act between creating incentives for both historically low and historically high emitters without giving windfall credits to either. One way towards this would be to let the baselines reflect more than just recent historical emissions and incorporate moving trends and factors expected to influence future emissions. This is sometimes called a projection or 'business-as-usual' (BAU) baseline and is contrasted with an historic reference period (Figure 9.4). Countries with historically low rates of emissions might have their baseline adjusted upwards above the historic reference rate if conditions with higher deforestation pressure are expected to emerge.[7] This would be more likely to

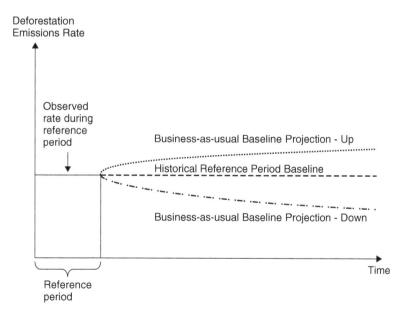

Figure 9.4 Business-as-usual vs. historic reference period baselines

Source: Author

engage the involvement of those countries. But the same principles also apply to countries with historically high deforestation with opposite consequences. If the factors that have pressured deforestation historically are expected to decline or if the country has been heavily deforested to date and cannot be expected to yield as much deforestation in the future, then its historic emission baseline could be adjusted downward to avoid overcrediting.

The BAU projection can be developed using formal models incorporating the economics of land use, commodity markets, trade and related biophysical processes or less formal (e.g., Delphi) methods using expert opinion forecasts of deforestation; or some combination of the two. Along these lines, Chomitz *et al*. (2006) recommend the use of a *normalized* baseline, which is based on standardized projections of agricultural land clearing, changes in productivity and carbon content of forests on the agriculture land-clearing margin for the country in question. This moves beyond the simple acceptance of past rates as indicative of the future and avoids creating perverse incentives for a country to ramp up deforestation emissions to artificially inflate their baseline and future credit-generating potential (see Palmer and Obidzinski, Chapter 7 in this volume, for a discussion of baseline choice for Indonesia).

Fixed baseline with negotiated targets

Ultimately, the choice between the simpler but possibly flawed, historical reference period baseline and the more rigorous but complex BAU projection method could boil down to a political decision about whether the value of improved information in the last method justifies the additional complexity, uncertainty and cost. One option is to keep with the simpler approach, tie the baseline directly to the historic reference period emissions and then negotiate future targets based on national circumstances. For example, one country's observed emissions rate for the period 2000–2005 might be 50 million tons per year, but they might receive future credits only for emissions below 40 million tons. Another country might have a historic rate of 2 million tons per year, but receive credits for emissions below 3 million tons, and so on. This has precedent in the Kyoto Protocol, where all countries have an emissions baseline set at the 1990 level, but each has differentiated targets for emissions during the first commitment period. For instance, the EU-15 countries must collectively reduce emissions 8 per cent below 1990 levels, while Iceland is allowed to increase emissions to 10 per cent over and above its 1990 level.[8] Presumably, these negotiated targets reflect the differentiated abilities of each country to meet or exceed its 1990 levels and similar logic could be applied to the historic deforestation emissions baseline.

To summarize, leakage is minimized when more countries participate in the compensation system. At this point, REDD participation is expected to be voluntary at the national level. Whether countries opt in could depend on rules for setting the national reference emissions baseline. A balance must be struck between making these rules flexible enough to allow countries with high deforestation potential to participate and ensuring that the rules do not allow for baseline inflation and over crediting of reductions.

Core participation requirement

One way to induce fuller participation would be to make the fungibility of REDD credits in the global carbon market contingent on some threshold participation of countries. Such a core participation requirement (Murray and Olander, 2008) could work so that once a core level of participation of REDD source countries is met (e.g., countries representing a significant majority of global REDD emissions), REDD credits would exchange freely with other emission sources in the global market. Until the participation threshold is met, the credits would have to trade at a discount to regular allowances to account for leakage potential of a more limited coverage system. There is precedent for such a threshold requirement in the original architecture of the Kyoto Protocol, which did not take effect until 55 per cent of global emissions were covered.

Decouple REDD compensation from GHG target compliance

Alternative proposals have been advanced, most prominently by Brazil (UNFCCC, 2007), that would similarly compensate non-Annex I countries for reducing their emissions from deforestation, but would not tie these reductions to Annex I country commitments or a global GHG market (see also Moutinho *et al.*, Chapter 6 in this volume). In other words, REDD compensation would not be part of an international GHG offset market. The reasoning advanced by Brazil's proposal is that any emission reductions from deforestation ought to be supplemental to emission reductions in Annex I countries, rather than as an offset to them. There are also concerns in some corners that tying REDD compensation to the international GHG market might crowd out demand for existing and yet to be developed CDM projects (Prior *et al.*, 2007; see also Michaelowa and Dutschke, Chapter 8 in this volume).

Separating REDD compensation from international commitments directly reduces the problem of leakage undermining the environmental integrity of an international offset system simply by prohibiting the use of REDD credits as an offset mechanism. Therefore, this avoids the risk that an Annex I country increases their emissions by 10 million tons by purchasing 10 million REDD credits, only to realize that generating the REDD credits in participating countries has shifted some leaked emissions to non-participating countries, with the result that the overall 'offset' transaction increased, rather than neutralized, emissions. Complete decoupling is certainly a clean way to deal with the environmental integrity problem of leakage, although by no means the only one. For instance, REDD credits could be bought and sold at a discount to reflect the leakage potential. This discount could be based on econometric modelling estimates of leakage such as those referenced in this chapter. For instance, if leakage is estimated at 40 per cent, then a 40 per cent discount could be applied to a REDD credit to account for the shortfall potential. To employ this approach, however, more empirical work in this area is needed to make these estimates more robust.

Decoupling REDD compensation from the international carbon market, however, could greatly reduce the scale of funds available to avoided deforestation efforts. The demand for REDD credits in an international carbon market could be in the tens of billions of dollars (Olander and Murray, 2007). It is unclear what type of funding a decoupled approach would be able to generate for avoided deforestation issues through the normal channels of official development assistance, NGO funding and the like, but previous history suggests it would be difficult to match the numbers referenced earlier for the carbon market (see Rametsteiner *et al.*, Chapter 3 in this volume).

Although decoupling funds for REDD compensation from the carbon market might address the integrity risks from leakage it will not necessarily eliminate leakage. As long as compensation is targeted for (or adopted by) a subset of the relevant countries, leakage is possible and it will undermine the effectiveness of the compensation programme by producing less emissions reduction than what is paid for. So decoupling can best be viewed as a leakage management strategy, but not a leakage *elimination* strategy. Leakage potential cannot be eliminated, as long as countries are free to opt in and out of a REDD system, but it can in principle be measured and accounted for to better assess the effects of global efforts to reduce deforestation and corresponding emissions.

Expand scope of policy beyond deforestation

As discussed earlier, one key hindrance to voluntary adoption of REDD compensation is that countries with low deforestation rates have little scope for credits and little incentive to participate. As shown in Table 9.2, this may limit interest to a relatively small number of countries with high deforestation rates. Many countries, however, are on the other end of the spectrum, experiencing little deforestation and in many cases having reforested large areas of land in recent years (see Table 9.3).

Given that none of the countries with high reforestation rates in Table 9.3 is also a high deforestation country in Table 9.2, a compensation system targeted at deforestation produces no incentive to maintain or expand the carbon stocks accumulating in the high reforestation countries or in countries with a relatively stable forest

Table 9.2 Non-Annex 1 countries with the highest deforestation rates between 2000 and 2005

Country	Deforestation rate (ha/yr)
Brazil	3,103,000
Indonesia	1,871,000
Sudan	589,000
Myanmar	466,000
Zambia	445,000
United Republic of Tanzania	412,000
Nigeria	410,000
Democratic Republic of the Congo	319,000
Zimbabwe	313,000
Venezuela (Bolivarian Republic of)	288,000

Source: FAO (2005); FAO Forest Resource Assessment (2005)

Table 9.3 Reforestation rates, 2000–2005: top 10 countries

Country	Reforestation rate 2000–2005 (ha/yr)
China[a]	4,058,000
Vietnam	241,000
Chile	57,000
Cuba	56,000
India	29,000
Rwanda	27,000
Algeria[a]	27,000
Côte d'Ivoire	15,000
Costa Rica	3000
Egypt[a]	2000

Source: FAO (2005); FAO Forest Resource Assessment (2005)

Note
a Less than half of the country is considered tropical.

base. This not only creates leakage risks of the type described throughout this chapter, it could leave off the table a range of opportunities to expand carbon stocks through market-based incentives. One way to address this problem would be to expand compensated activities beyond deforestation to include potentially all sources of forest carbon stock changes at the national level. This would minimize leakage within the forest sector of participating countries by capturing forest degradation and management as well as deforestation. Moreover, it could greatly expand the number of countries interested in participating. Measurement and monitoring issues should be tractable, as methods exist at the international level through the IPCC Good Practices Guidelines (IPCC, 2003) in order to undertake national-level forest carbon accounting. There may be concerns, however, that including all forest carbon stock changes could encourage the conversion of native ecosystems to non-native forest plantations, possibly undermining biodiversity and water resource provision (Jackson *et al.*, 2005). However, these concerns can be addressed via agreed on protocols (IPCC, 2000). This broader, sector-based view of covering forest carbon in a post-Kyoto UNFCCC process was discussed at the Bali Conference of Parties in December 2007 and is still under further consideration.

One final point to make on the option of including afforestation and reforestation (AR) activities in the compensation system is that these activities are already covered under the CDM. However, as referenced earlier, AR projects have been virtually non-existent under the CDM to date because of inherent difficulties in project-level implementation. There are reasons to expect that at least some of these issues (e.g., dealing with permanence, additionality and leakage) can be better handled at a national level with more complete monitoring and accounting systems in place.

Conclusions

This chapter has focused on the importance of recognizing, estimating and where possible ameliorating the risks of leakage from REDD compensation policies that are likely to be applied to a subset of countries with deforestation potential. Key summary points include:

- *Fundamentally, leakage arises from economic processes.* Leakage occurs when protective action in one place shifts problems to another. When taking action to reduce deforestation in one country or a subset of countries that in turn reduces the supply of certain globally traded commodities, the market will seek out suppliers unbound by those same constraints. This is natural and hard to confine.
- *From a policy standpoint, leakage is an accounting problem.* The fact that markets shift deforestation activity and emissions from place to place is not, in and of itself, a problem so long as all emission sources are governed by the same rules. Rather, it is the fact that deforestation emissions may be reduced in a country receiving compensation to offset emissions from a regulated country only to see emissions shifted to a country that is neither regulated nor subject to national-level accounting of deforestation emissions. This means that emission reductions will appear larger on paper than they are in reality, thereby undercutting the climate and other environmental goals of the programme.
- *The empirical evidence to date suggests leakage from avoided deforestation policies could be substantial if not addressed in policy design.* Unfortunately, the empirical evidence on leakage effects of avoided deforestation and forest conservation policies is somewhat thin and is not customized to address the specific compensation policies now at hand; nevertheless, the evidence suggests that leakage potential could be large and should be taken seriously by those charged with developing policy options.
- *One way to take leakage seriously is to impose discounts that reduce the number of REDD credits issued to account for the leakage in the system.* This will require more robust estimates of leakage than currently exist and should be re-evaluated over time as the policy evolves and leakage conditions change. This form of discounting also reduces compensation and the incentive to participate, which could undermine efforts to expand programme scope and combat leakage that way, as referenced in the next two points.
- *One way to reduce leakage potential through policy design is to expand the scope of policy coverage as wide as feasible.* The more at-risk forests that are covered by REDD compensation and accounting, the smaller the opportunity for leakage to undermine the system. Scope expansion could involve covering more countries or more activities.
- *Scope expansion has its challenges.* Expanding the number of countries involved in a voluntary system involves the delicate balancing act of enhancing incentives for their participation through, among other things, generous baselines making credits easier to generate and maintaining the environmental integrity of the system by not crediting 'hot air' ('would happen anyway') credits. Expanding the scope of activities covered beyond deforestation can both help lure countries with low baseline deforestation rates into the system

and ensure that deforestation emissions are not reduced at the expense of carbon losses elsewhere in the forest sector (e.g., degradation, reduced management, foregone afforestation and reforestation). However, covering all forest carbon in an international compensation system raises some concerns about spurring land-use changes that could undermine other environmental objectives such as biodiversity and water provision.

So leakage is a problem, potentially serious, and may not be so easy to solve. Yet the economic and environmental opportunities for using either markets or other sources of funds to reduce deforestation and its emissions may be too important to simply dismiss because of leakage concerns. Leakage should be taken seriously, addressed by policy design, entered into the accounting where possible and be closely monitored over time. It certainly warrants mentioning that REDD policy is not the only GHG policy situation in which leakage arises. All GHG policies now and for the foreseeable future face the same problem, due to incomplete coverage across countries and sectors. Leakage makes the job of reducing global GHG mitigation harder, but does not make it any less important. Once the problem of GHG concentrations and climate risks are accepted, the policy objective should be to cover as many sources over as long a time as possible, with as much flexibility as prudence allows. Until all sources are covered, we will have to live with the difficulties of incomplete coverage, design policies accordingly and adjust them in the future if the problem persists.

Notes

1 The Food and Agricultural Organization (FAO) defines forest degradation as 'changes within the forest class (from closed to open forest), which negatively affect the stand or site and, in particular, that lower the biological productivity capacity and diversity' (FAO, 2000).

2 Projects may also take place in uncapped sectors in Annex I countries under the joint implementation (JI) provisions of the Kyoto Protocol, but given the primary incidence of deforestation in developing countries, the clean development mechanism (CDM) is the relevant focus here.

3 Leakage involves unaccounted emissions only. If a country reports all of its deforestation emissions, then all internal responses to deforestation are included and this internal response does not contribute to leakage.

4 Note that Figure 9.2 depicts a partial equilibrium view, focusing on activity shifting within the forest and land-use sectors only and ignoring possible feedback effects in other sectors (e.g., demand for substitute goods of steel and cement) and factor markets such as labour and capital. These secondary effects are assumed to be small relative to the direct impacts in the forest sector.

5 Elasticity of supply (e) represents the relative responsiveness of suppliers to a change in price and roughly captures the steepness of the slope of the supply function in Figure 9.2. The value is generally positive. If $e = 0.5$, this means that a 10 per cent increase in price would induce a 5 per cent increase in quantity supplied from the market. Elasticity of demand (E) gives the relative responsiveness of demanders to a change in price. The value is generally negative, indicating that an increase in price leads to a decrease in quantity demanded. For example, $E = -0.3$, means a 10 per cent increase in price causes a 3 per cent reduction in the quantity demanded. Because E is negative, the leakage term is positive.

Values of e and E that are greater than 1.0 in absolute value are termed 'elastic' while absolute values less than 1.0 indicate inelastic responses.

6 As more countries enter the programme, the market participation ratio parameter (Φ_A) from Equation 9.2 approaches infinity and leakage approaches zero. In the limit (full participation), leakage is eliminated.

7 These adjustments could be made using formal land-use economic modelling tools or informally negotiated by parties using logical arguments and descriptive statistics.

8 National targets for Kyoto Protocol first commitment found at the IPCC website (http://unfccc.int/kyoto_protocol/background/items/3145.php [accessed 8 August 2008]).

References

Adams, D.M., Alig, R.J., Callaway, J.M., McCarl, B.A. and Winnett, S.M. (1996) *The Forest and Agricultural Sector Optimization Model (FASOM): Model Structure and Policy Applications*, Research Paper PNW-RP-495, Portland, OR: U.S. Department of Agriculture, Forest Service, Pacific Northwest Research Station.

Barbier, E.B. (2001) 'The economics of tropical deforestation and land use: an introduction to the special issue', *Land Economics*, 77(2): 155–171.

Bashaasha, B., Kraybill, D.S. and Southgate, D.D. (2001) 'Land use impacts of agricultural intensification and fuelwood taxation in Uganda', *Land Economics*, 77(2): 241–249.

Brown, S., Hall, M., Andrasko, K., Ruiz, F., Marzoli, W., Guerrero, G. *et al.* (2007) 'Baselines for land-use change in the tropics: application to avoided deforestation projects', *Mitigation and Adaptation Strategies for Global Change*, 12(6): 1001–1026.

CDM (Clean Development Mechanism) Statistics (2007) [online]. Available at: http://cdm.unfccc.int/Statistics/index.html [accessed 19 September 2007].

Chomitz, K., Buys, P., De Luca, G., Thomas, T.S. and Wertz-Kanounnikoff, S. (2006) *At Loggerheads? Agricultural Expansion, Poverty Reduction, and Environment in the Tropical Forests*, World Bank Policy Research Report, Development Research Group, Washington, DC: World Bank.

Cropper, M., Puri, J. and Griffiths, C. (2001) 'Predicting the location of deforestation: the role of roads and protected areas in north Thailand', *Land Economics*, 77(2): 172–186.

DeFries, R.S., Achard, F., Brown, S., Herold, M., Murdiyarso, D., Schlamadinger, B. *et al.* (2006) *Reducing Greenhouse Gas Emissions from Deforestation in Developing Countries: Considerations for Monitoring and Measuring*, Report of the Global Terrestrial Observing System (GTOS) number 46, Rome: GTOS, and Global Observation of Forest and Land Cover Dynamics (GOFC-GOLD) report 26, Alberta, Canada: GOFC-GOLD.

FAO (Food and Agriculture Organization of the United Nations) (2000) *Global Forest Resources Assessment 2000 – Main Report*, FAO Forestry Paper 140, Rome: FAO.

FAO (Food and Agriculture Organization of the United Nations) (2005) *Global Forest Resources Assessment 2005 – Main Report*, FAO Forestry Paper 147, Rome: FAO.

Gan, J. and McCarl, B.A. (2007) 'Measuring transnational leakage of forest conservation', *Ecological Economics*, 64(2): 423–432.

IPCC (Intergovernmental Panel on Climate Change) (2000) *Special Report on Land Use, Land Use Change, and Forestry*, Geneva: Cambridge University Press.

IPCC (Intergovernmental Panel on Climate Change) (2003) *Good Practice Guidance for Land Use, Land-Use Change and Forestry* [online]. Available at: http://www.ipccnggip.iges.or.jp/public/gpglulucf/gpglulucf.htm [accessed 17 September 2007].

Jackson, R.B., Jobbágy, E.G., Avissar, R., Roy, S.B., Barrett, D.J., Cook, C.W. *et al.* (2005) 'Trading water for carbon with biological carbon sequestration', *Science*, 310(5756): 1944–947.

Johns, T. and Schlamadinger, B. (2009) 'International policy and institutional barriers to reducing emissions from deforestation and degradation in developing countries', in C. Palmer and S. Engel (eds) *Avoided Deforestation: Prospects for Mitigating Climate Change*, London: Routledge.

Köhlin, G. and Parks, P.J. (2001) 'Spatial variability and disincentives to harvest: deforestation and fuelwood collection in South Asia', *Land Economics*, 77(2): 206–218.

Michaelowa, A. and Dutschke, M. (2009) 'Will credits from avoided deforestation in developing countries jeopardize the balance of the carbon market?', in C. Palmer and S. Engel (eds) *Avoided Deforestation: Prospects for Mitigating Climate Change*, London: Routledge.

Mollicone, D., Achard, F., Federici, S., Eva, H.D., Grassi, G., Belward, A. *et al.* (2007) 'An incentive mechanism for reducing emissions from conversion of intact and non-intact forests', *Climatic Change*, 83(4): 477–493.

Moutinho, P., Cenamo, M.C. and Moreira, P.F. (2009) 'Reducing carbon emissions by slowing deforestation: REDD initiatives in Brazil', in C. Palmer and S. Engel (eds) *Avoided Deforestation: Prospects for Mitigating Climate Change*, London: Routledge.

Murray, B.C., McCarl, B.A. and Lee, H. (2004) 'Estimating leakage from forest carbon sequestration programmes', *Land Economics*, 80(1): 109–124.

Murray, B.C. and Olander, L.P. (2008) *A Core Participation Requirement for Creation of a REDD Market*, Short Policy Brief, Nicholas Institute for Environmental Policy Solutions, Duke University [online]. Available at: http://www.nicholas.duke.edu/institute/pb-redd.pdf [accessed 8 August 2008].

Murray, B.C., Sohngen, B.L. and Ross, M.T. (2007) 'Economic consequences of consideration of permanence, leakage and additionality for soil carbon sequestration projects', *Climatic Change*, 80(1–2): 127–143.

Olander, L.P., Gibbs, H.K., Steininger, M., Swenson, J.J. and Murray, B.C. (2008) 'Reference scenarios for deforestation and forest degradation in support of REDD: a review of data and methods', *Environmental Research Letters*, 3: 025011.

Olander, L.P. and Murray, B.C. (2007) *A New Opportunity to Help Mitigate Climate Change, Save Forests, and Reach Development Goals*, Nicholas Institute for Environmental Policy Solutions, Duke University [online]. Available at: http://www.nicholas.duke.edu/institute/ [accessed 8 August 2008].

Palmer, C. and Obidzinski, K. (2009) 'Choosing avoided deforestation baselines in the context of government failure: the case of Indonesia's plantations policy', in C. Palmer and S. Engel (eds) *Avoided Deforestation: Prospects for Mitigating Climate Change*, London: Routledge.

Prior, S., O'Sullivan, R. and Streck, C. (2007) *A Carbon Stock Approach to Creating a Positive Incentive to Reduce Emissions from Deforestation and Forest Degradation*, Joint Submission to the UNFCCC Secretariat on reducing emissions from deforestation in developing countries. Centre for International Sustainable Development Law and Global Public Policy Institute (23 Feb, 2007) [online]. Available at: http://www.climatefocus.com/downloads/CISDL_and_GPPI_UNFCCC_Submission-Carbon_Stock_Approach.pdf [Accessed 20 September 2007].

Rametsteiner, E., Obersteiner, M., Kindermann, G. and Sohngen, B. (2009) 'Economics of avoiding deforestation', in C. Palmer and S. Engel (eds) *Avoided Deforestation: Prospects for Mitigating Climate Change*, London: Routledge.

Santilli, M., Moutinho, P., Schwartzman, S., Nepstad, D., Curran, L. and Nobre, C. (2005) 'Tropical deforestation and the Kyoto Protocol', *Climatic Change*, 71(3): 267–276.

Sathaye, J. and Andrasko, K. (2007) 'Special issue on estimation of baselines and leakage in carbon mitigation forestry projects', *Mitigation and Adaptation Strategies for Global Change*, 12(6): 963–970.

Sohngen, B. and Brown, S. (2004) 'Measuring leakage from carbon projects in open economies: a stop timber harvesting project in Bolivia as a case study', *Canadian Journal of Forest Research*, 34(4): 829–839.

UNFCCC (United Nations Framework Convention on Climate Change) (2007) *Views on the Range of Topics and Other Relevant Information Relating to Reducing Emissions from Deforestation in Developing Countries: Submissions from Parties*, UN Framework Convention on Climate Change, Subsidiary Body for Scientific and Technical Advice (SBSTA). Item 5 of the provisional agenda: Reducing emissions from deforestation in developing countries, SBSTA Meeting May, Submitted, 2 Mar, 2007, Bonn [online]. Available at: http://unfccc.int/methods_and_science/lulucf/items/3896.php [accessed 8 August 2008].

Wear, D.N. and Murray, B.C. (2004) 'Federal timber restrictions, interregional spillovers, and the impact on U.S. softwood markets', *Journal of Environmental Economics and Management*, 47(2): 307–330.

Wu, J. (2000) 'Slippage effects of the conservation reserve programs', *American Journal of Agricultural Economics*, 82(4): 979–992.

10 A scalable approach for setting avoided deforestation baselines

Nancy L. Harris, Silvia Petrova and Sandra Brown

Introduction

On a global scale, land use, land-use change and forestry (LULUCF) activities historically have been, and are currently, net sources of carbon dioxide to the atmosphere. During the 1990s carbon dioxide (CO_2) emissions to the atmosphere caused by changes in land use were estimated to be 1.6 billion tons C/yr (GtC/yr; Bolin and Sukumar, 2000), with tropical deforestation and degradation responsible for most of this source. Activities that reduce deforestation rates offer significant potential for mitigating greenhouse gas (GHG) emissions, thereby reducing the potential impacts of climate change. Through management, humans have the potential to change the direction and magnitude of the flux of carbon dioxide between the land and atmosphere while at the same time providing multiple co-benefits to meet environmental and socioeconomic goals of sustainable development.

Afforestation and reforestation projects are generally accepted as projects that can generate tradable greenhouse gas (GHG) emission reductions (e.g., under the clean development mechanism of the Kyoto Protocol). Forest conservation projects, by way of contrast, have faced obstacles to acceptance due to the difficulty in determining key elements of the project cycle – in particular, methods for determining the *baseline*, or *reference case*, scenario (see Johns and Schlamadinger, Chapter 5 in this volume). However, without inclusion of projects that are designed to avoid deforestation, a large opportunity is lost (Niles *et al.*, 2002). Ongoing discussions under the United Nations Framework Convention on Climate Change (UNFCCC) are now considering reductions in emissions from deforestation and degradation (REDD) in developing countries. As a potential, additional LULUCF activity to be allowed post-2012, REDD has generated substantial policy debate among countries worldwide. The outcome of these negotiations will have important implications with regards to the extent of tropical developing country participation in future international agreements to mitigate climate change. The development of a standardized baseline approach for avoided deforestation activities is therefore a key step towards the adoption of any future REDD mechanism.

A baseline scenario has two major components: the projected land use or land cover change and the corresponding carbon stocks in live and dead vegetation and soil. Of the two components needed for baseline development, the projections of land-use change are the more difficult to address analytically (OECD/IEA, 2003). This is because many difficult-to-predict socioeconomic and environmental factors affect the way people use land. Furthermore, once REDD activities are implemented the baseline rate and pattern of land-use change can no longer be monitored.

Unfortunately, there are currently no standard practices for developing avoided deforestation baselines at the project, regional or national scale. For many of the existing pilot forestry-based carbon projects, estimates of changes in land use and associated baselines have been determined on a project-by-project basis using simple logical arguments that assumed continuation of observed past trends for the project area or region because agreed on methods did not exist. If this project-by-project approach continues into the future, investment costs are likely to remain high and the lack of transparency will lead to the perception of subjective and highly uncertain LULUCF baselines.

What is needed is a standardized, scalable baseline approach to estimate carbon emissions from deforestation that is accurate, transparent, credible and conservative. The purpose of this chapter is to outline such an approach. In a previous study (Brown *et al.*, 2007), three different models of land-use change were compared and applied to six geographic regions. First, we summarize and compare the modelling options used for projecting baselines. We then present in more detail a spatial modelling approach, known as 'GEOMOD', which can be used to develop consistent baselines at the project, regional and/or national scale. This is followed by a description of the steps necessary for developing a reference case scenario and an application of this methodology to a case study of East Kalimantan province in Indonesia.

Options for modelling deforestation baselines

In previous work, Brown *et al.* (2007) compared three competing methodological approaches to setting deforestation baselines that ranged from models that used readily available non-spatial data for relatively large geographical areas (e.g., millions of hectares) to models that required more intensive data collection but could operate in smaller geographic areas. The three models compared were the forest area change (FAC) analytical model (FAO, 1993; Sciotti, 1991; revised by Sciotti, 2000), the land-use carbon sequestration (LUCS) simulation model (Faeth *et al.*, 1994) and the geographical modelling (GEOMOD) regression model (Dale, 1994; Hall *et al.*, 1995; Pontius *et al.*, 2001).

The FAC model was produced initially for the Food and Agriculture Organization (FAO) Forest Resources Assessment Project, implemented during 1990–1994 (FAO, 1993; Sciotti, 1991; revised by Sciotti, 2000). It was developed to overcome the lack of multi-temporal information on forest cover in tropical countries. The goal was to develop a generalized modelling approach that could produce the required forest area change information for all countries. This approach was developed on the basis of multi-date observations for a limited number of countries, in combination with another set of correlated variables for which data were available for all countries. In building this model, it was assumed that the overall pattern of deforestation would be described by a logistic curve of two key variables, with different parameters for different ecological zones within a country. The model uses historical data on forest cover and associated population density to develop two key variables, generally expressed at a sub-national level: the dependent variable – ratio of non-forest area to total area – and the independent variable – population density. Then, using projections of human population growth for the area in question, the model simulates the change in forest cover over time.

The LUCS model was developed to estimate land-use change in rural areas that depend largely on low productivity agriculture for subsistence and fuel wood for energy (Faeth *et al.*, 1994). The model assumes that land-use change is driven primarily by changes in population and land management so that as population grows, more land is required to supply food, livelihoods and, in some cases, fuelwood. While demand for food and income grows, the land's ability to meet that demand may increase or decrease depending on changes in productivity and other factors. The key parameters used in this model are: the rate of population growth and the year it is expected to stabilize; the initial area of principal land uses (agricultural and forested); and the amount of agricultural land required as a function of population, agricultural land required per person, fraction of food imported and agricultural land required for export production. The main driving force after model initialization is the predicted population change in the modelled area.

The GEOMOD model was developed to replicate spatially explicit land-use change in Costa Rica and was subsequently applied in Southeast Asia and Africa to estimate carbon releases from tropical deforestation over time (Dale, 1994; Hall *et al.*, 1995; Pontius *et al.*, 2001). It uses spatially distributed data to simulate changes from one land cover category to another in a geographical information system (GIS) (Hall *et al.*, 2000; Hall *et al.*, 2006; IDRISI Project, 2003). GEOMOD is a module in the IDRISI Kilimanjaro software package (IDRISI Project, 2003). There are two components to this model: the rate and location of land-use change. Rates of land-use change are extrapolated from historical rates that are based on interpreted satellite imagery for two or more points in time for the study area. The location of land-use change is simulated using numerous spatial data layers of biophysical and socioeconomic factors (e.g., elevation, slope, soils, distance from rivers, roads and already established settlements, etc.) to explain a pattern of deforestation. The model is calibrated by assigning weights to map cells based on the importance of each of these driving factors, singly and in combination.

A comparison of the three modelling approaches, including advantages and disadvantages of each approach, is shown in Table 10.1.

Models were evaluated against a set of five criteria and 13 indicators (Brown, 2003) to determine which model was feasible and practical to use for establishing a deforestation baseline. The five criteria (with corresponding indicators in parentheses) were:

1 *transparency* (ease of comprehension, replicability)
2 *accuracy and precision* (model calibration, validation and uncertainty in databases)
3 *applicability* (ability to deal with multiple scales and multiple land uses)

Table 10.1 Comparison of three different land-use change models used to project future rates of deforestation

Model	Advantages	Disadvantages	Spatial scale of data inputs	Model drivers
Forest area change (FAC)	Minimal data requirements Potentially reduced costs Applicable to large regions	Lack of spatial resolution Only two variables used (simplistic) Cannot be used at small geographic scales if key variables are not available	Sub-national (political units)	Population density
Land use carbon sequestration (LUCS)	Applicable to many scales Applicable to many different land-use change activities	Lack of spatial resolution Model code and structure not readily understandable by the operator Assumptions needed for many poorly known parameters	Sub-national (political units)	Rate of population growth Year of population stabilization Initial area of principal land uses Amount of agricultural land required
Geographical modelling (GEOMOD)	Spatial resolution at any scale Can analyze deforestation or degradation provided imagery is available to 'see' it Kappa-for-location statistic allows evaluation of model performance (see later)	Large data requirements Experimentation needed with large number of variables to identify those providing the most explanatory power for predicting deforestation Potentially high cost of data acquisition and analysis	Any scale for which satellite imagery can be acquired	Spatial data for biophysical and socioeconomic factors

Source: Brown et al. (2007)

4   *compatibility* with international standards (i.e., standard definitions of forest)
5   *cost effectiveness* (intensity and availability of data needs, time to simulate models, knowledge and skills needed to run the models).

For each indicator, a score (from 1 denoting the lowest to 5 for the highest) was assigned, then averaged for each criterion and summed for all criteria for a maximum score of 25 points. The overall evaluation gave the GEOMOD model the highest score (22.6) with little difference in scores between the FAC (18.6) and LUCS (17.5) models. The score for each criterion for the three models is listed in the Appendix at the end of this chapter (Table 10A.1). For some criteria, the order of the evaluation was different from the overall trend, for example:

- *Transparency*: the GEOMOD and FAC models scored the highest and LUCS scored the lowest. The last's model code and structures are not as readily understandable to the operator compared to GEOMOD and FAC.
- *Accuracy and precision*: the databases needed for all three models tend to have a high degree of uncertainty associated with them, because they depend on interpretation of remote sensing imagery (GEOMOD), on national statistics (FAC and LUCS) or on assumptions for many parameters that are poorly known (LUCS). None of the models considered deals directly with spatial autocorrelation.
- *Applicability*: the GEOMOD and LUCS models were the most applicable for modelling land-use change, as they can be applied to any scale and to many changes in land uses; the FAC model was built to simulate only deforestation at sub-national political units with population growth as a single driver.
- *Compatibility with international requirements*: the FAC model is compatible with international requirements because it has been officially used and accepted by the FAO to estimate deforestation for the years 1990 and 1995 for all developing countries. It was developed using a clear and internationally accepted definition of 'forest'.
- *Cost effectiveness*: the FAC model scored the highest on cost-effectiveness indicators, whereas the other two models require more data, time and effort to simulate.

This chapter explains the GEOMOD model in further detail due to its high overall ranking in the evaluation.

The GEOMOD model

The actual threat of unsanctioned deforestation or degradation in any given country or region may be high in some places while it is practically zero in others, depending on several biophysical and socioeconomic factors that affect the way people use land. Whereas all models compared in Brown *et al.* (2007) estimate the *rate* of deforestation, GEOMOD is the only one of the three developed specifically to project *where* deforestation is likely to occur in the future as well. In GEOMOD, rates of land-use change are extrapolated from historical rates based on interpreted satellite imagery for two or more points in time for the study area. The GEOMOD model can be used to simulate any type of land-use change (including forest loss or gain and degradation), as long as empirical spatial data (remote sensing products, etc.) exist for the particular area of interest. The location of land-use change is simulated using numerous spatial data layers of biophysical and socioeconomic factors to explain the pattern of deforestation. An advantage of the GEOMOD approach is its capability to operate at any scale for which data are available. Because it operates on map grids, the model can give deforestation estimates for any pixel or geographic scale requested within the analytic domain.

The IDRISI software program also has an internal validation procedure – the Kappa-for-location index – that measures the model's improvement over what a random selection would achieve (Pontius, 2000, 2002). Therefore, GEOMOD quantifies some of what has been termed 'counterfactual uncertainty' (Kerr, 2001; Moura-Costa, 2001) inherent in all models used to estimate the business-as-usual baseline. The Kappa-for-location statistic represents a standardized procedure for assessing some of the aspects of this 'counterfactual uncertainty' because it quantifies model performance compared to random allocation of change. Like other models, however, it must still make projections based on assumptions with associated uncertainties. The difference between GEOMOD and other models is that GEOMOD tests the validity of the assumptions.

Methods for explaining the empirical pattern of land-use change

Spatially explicit models can project the location and pattern of estimated deforestation over time (Dale *et al.*, 2003). Spatial data on biophysical and socioeconomic factors such as those given in Table 10.2 can be used to create heuristically and/or empirically derived *factor maps* that can potentially explain the pattern of land-use change across a landscape. Heuristically derived factor maps are created on the assumption that deforestation decreases with increasing distance from features (roads, rivers, cities, etc.). With the heuristic decision rule, actual distances from features are used to determine suitability for change from forest to non-forest. Empirically derived factor maps are created using prior knowledge. Distance maps are reclassified into categorical 'bins' of set distances and the value assigned to each 'bin' is calculated based on the proportion of deforested area in the first reference year for which data are available (Time 1).

After factor maps are created from all major factors that potentially affect the spatial pattern of land-use change, they are used singly and in combination in GEOMOD to produce *suitability for change* (SFC) maps. Each SFC map represents a different weighted-average combination of spatial drivers and is used with the quantity of non-forest pixels in Time 1 to simulate the location of non-forest area in Time 2. The model's ability to simulate change from forest to non-forest using a specific SFC map is validated through the Kappa-for-location statistic; the SFC map that yields the best Kappa-for-location statistic in the Time 2 simulation is called the *potential land-use change* (PLUC) map and can be used to develop the baseline scenario.

Table 10.2 Types of variable that could potentially explain the spatial distribution of forest and non-forest lands in a given region

Type of spatial data/variable	Examples
Infrastructure	Distance to centres of government/commerce
	Distance to towns and communities
	Distance to roads (primary, secondary, all)
	Political district
Biophysical	Elevation
	Slope
	Aspect
	Watershed
	Precipitation
	Temperature
	Distance to major rivers/navigable water
	Presence of wetlands
	Soil type
Biological	Vegetation type
	Ecozone
Human disturbance	Distance to logging camps
	Distance to forest edge
	Distance to previously cultivated areas
	Distance to previously deforested land
Socionomic/demographic	Land tenure
	Density of land-based economic sector of population
	Percentage of marginalized population
Historical/cultural	Distance to archaeological sites

Source: Brown *et al.* (2007)

Even though a large initial list of explanatory factors can be included in the spatial modelling, the factors that provide the best fit in validation are generally reduced to a few key ones, based on the vast literature on the typical drivers of deforestation throughout the tropics (Brown *et al.*, 2007; Geist and Lambin, 2002). Targeting a few key factors per activity type per region could offer potential for streamlining and standardizing the PLUC map on which the baseline scenario is developed, thereby reducing data requirements and costs of baseline development. For example, Brown *et al.* (2007) found that distance to roads was included in the final set of factors in five out of six regions studied. The types of spatial variable that could potentially explain the spatial distribution of forest and non-forest lands in a given region are shown in Table 10.2. Missing from this list are non-spatial factors that may influence deforestation. If the study area overlaps political, sociocultural or biophysical boundaries, the area can be stratified and GEOMOD can be run separately for each subregion so that these differences are captured. While GEOMOD does not explicitly include non-spatial economic factors such as agricultural commodity prices, these factors could theoretically be incorporated into the rate portion of the analysis. Although the simplest way to estimate deforestation rates used in GEOMOD is from remote sensing imagery, other methods could also be employed if, for example, relationships between agricultural commodity prices or construction of new roads and the rate of deforestation are developed.

Determining deforestation threat

For an avoided deforestation project or programme to produce credible carbon benefits, the baseline needs to demonstrate that the area was under real threat of deforestation in the near future. An analysis of deforestation threat using spatial models is suitable for this task.

The PLUC map described in the previous section indicates each map cell's likelihood for future deforestation; the cells with the highest values on the PLUC map are most likely to be deforested while the cells with the lowest values are least likely to be deforested. The GEOMOD model simulates the distribution of potential future deforestation by selecting the highest value cells on the PLUC map in descending order up to the amount of area projected to be lost to deforestation over a specified time period. These mapped cells with varying potentiality of deforestation essentially provide the estimated timing (or order) and location of deforestation differentially across a landscape over the period of projection. Thus, they also provide a spatially resolved estimate of each map cell's relative departure with respect to a baseline or reference case scenario. Lands assigned a low probability of deforestation on the PLUC map would presumably have relatively low departure from the baseline scenario over time, i.e. the REDD scenario would be more or less equivalent to the baseline scenario because these lands were not under immediate deforestation threat. Lands with high probability of conversion would have higher departure from the baseline, provided that REDD activities were effective at preventing forest conversion.

An additional advantage of using PLUC maps is that other development criteria could be overlain on the map to help select areas that meet multiple goals. For example, maps of ranges of threatened or endangered species, poverty indicators or critical watersheds could be overlain on the PLUC maps. The intersection of other development goals with the highest threat for deforestation could then be used at the planning stage to identify areas where different ecosystem services are maximized and areas where these services overlap (see also Engel *et al.*, Chapter 12 in this volume).

Baseline timeframe

The temporal dimension for estimating avoided deforestation baselines is a significant analytic and policy issue. How far into the future can (and should) the baseline be projected? Rates and patterns of land-use change are subject to biophysical factors that regulate human use of the land that change marginally over time, but socioeconomic and political factors are more dynamic and less predictable through time. Thus, the farther business-as-usual baseline scenarios are projected into the future, the less reliable they are likely to be.

We suggest that a 10-year period is a reasonable timeframe for projecting baselines forward, for two reasons. First, historical data are often collected over the decadal timeframe (e.g., population data) and may indicate future projections over the same time period given the dynamics of development and growth in most countries. Second, from a policy perspective, a decade is two Kyoto commitment periods (of 5 years), and roughly two political election cycles (averaging 4–6 years generally, varying by political system).

We propose a project timeframe for land-use changes and associated carbon benefits equal to the proposed project length, which is currently set at 20–60 years under the guidelines developed for the CDM. A baseline timeframe could, however, be 'locked in' only for the first 10-year period and then reviewed and adjusted throughout the project duration as required. Any revisions to a baseline are likely to affect the carbon credits ascribed to the project in the subsequent time period because the projected rate of deforestation could change. New conservation activities implemented during the second 10-year period would, of course, use the revised baseline.

A baseline methodology for carbon projects

So far, the focus of this chapter has been on developing the land-use change component of the baseline. However, the baseline for carbon projects and programs need to project future carbon emissions or removals, not future land-use change. To achieve this, projections of the rate of land-use change over a given time period are combined with carbon stock data. The benefit of using spatially explicit models to project where the land-use change will occur is that the locations in which corresponding carbon stocks must be measured or estimated are provided simultaneously. This is particularly advantageous in areas where forest types vary across a country, region or project area; the 'location' aspect tells us which forest type is being cleared.

In this section, we propose a standardized methodology to advance the development of credible baselines for avoided deforestation projects and programmes. The methodology is applicable at the project level, but as negotiations continue for including national-level accounting schemes for REDD in developing countries, it should be noted that the approach is scalable to the regional and national levels as well. To demonstrate the feasibility of this approach at a 'national' level (i.e. for a large geographic region), we summarize in the next section the results from a GEO-MOD analysis applied to the province of East Kalimantan in Indonesia.

Step 1: develop historical rates of land-use change and deforestation estimates

Task 1

Determine the analytic domain and obtain historical data:

*   Delineate the approximate geographic domain of the spatial analysis. For national level baselines, the domain should be defined as the country's political boundaries. For projects, the domain should be about five to seven times

the area of large projects (on the order of several hundred thousand hectares) or regions or 20 to 40 times the area of smaller projects (on the order of tens of thousands of hectares; Brown *et al.*, 2007), although the recommended magnitude and thresholds will vary with regional conditions.

- Obtain historic data on land use and socioeconomic characteristics for the past 10 years or so, ideally including at least 2 (more than 2 is preferable if available) recent remote sensing imagery datasets at least 5 years apart.

Task 2

Analyze and identify potential major factors that influence deforestation:

- Analyze satellite imagery to produce maps of land use/land cover. Using experience as well as local knowledge, analyze candidate baseline factors to find the three or four key factors that best describe patterns of historic land-use change. Weight these drivers according to their importance in the Time 1 or calibration period and select those that produce the best simulation map compared to a Time 2 validation map (see 'Methods for explaining the empirical pattern of land-use change' on page 178).
- The only legitimate factor maps for GEOMOD are those that would have been available in the Time 1 map year. For example, we cannot use roads in 2005 as a legitimate factor map for predicting deforestation over the period 2000–2005. If necessary, GEOMOD can be run for different time periods so that, for example, roads can be brought in as a factor when needed. However, the relationship between deforestation rate and roads would need to be known.

Step 2: generate a baseline projection for deforestation

Task 3

Use the key drivers identified in Task 2 to project potential land-use change (PLUC):

- Use all factor maps identified in Task 2 in various combinations to derive 'suitability for change' (SFC) maps, each of which reflects a unique combination and weighting scheme of factor maps.
- Predict the spatial pattern of deforestation in GEOMOD over the reference period between Time 1 and Time 2 using each SFC map. The goodness of fit of each simulation is based on both the per cent of cells simulated correctly and the Kappa-for-location index (Pontius, 2000).
- Use the three to four key drivers of land-use change that generate the highest Kappa-for-location statistic to generate a PLUC map or a map of areas projected to have high to low risk for deforestation. For easy visualization, the PLUC map can be divided into quartiles, from high risk to low risk.

Task 4

Project rates of deforestation into the future:

- A 10-year baseline projection for estimation of project GHG emissions and crediting purposes is suggested because baseline projections beyond a 10-year period are unlikely to be realistic. As noted previously, this is due to the fact that rates of land-use change are subject to many factors that are difficult to predict over the long term. Also, this is a common time period over which national data censuses are undertaken.
- To calculate rates, it would make sense to employ change detection of satellite imagery because such images would already be on hand as part of the database for the PLUC map. Other information could be used at this stage of the analysis to modify the past rates to either increase or decrease the projected rate, such as known development actions (e.g., paving a road) that could increase population density and hence increase deforestation in the region.

Task 5

Combine the PLUC map with projected rates of deforestation and carbon stock estimates and make baseline projections:

- Estimate the carbon stocks in the forests being cleared from measurements in the potential project area or from a well-designed national carbon inventory programme. If data are not available, literature values may be used depending on the status of project/programme development. If it is only a feasibility study, then literature data or limited field studies would suffice, but if the project or programme is beyond a feasibility stage, more detailed measurements and analyses of the carbon stocks would be needed.
- Combine the rate and location of projected forest loss over the 10-year period with carbon stock data to produce the deforestation baseline. If a potential avoided deforestation project is at an implementation stage, the GEOMOD model could be used to simulate where the land is likely to change in the project area using the rate data and subsequently to match these with the corresponding carbon stock data.
- For reporting estimated GHG benefits, a project could submit its baseline driver assumptions to a GHG registry for review. Some form of certification of these assumptions, the baseline they produce and hence the estimated project GHG benefits would need to be issued.
- Reporting at the national level is still under negotiation as part of a REDD mechanism. However, at a national scale, it would be useful to perform a GEO-MOD analysis upfront to guide policymakers on decisions about which areas within a country or sub-national region are most important to protect for maximum REDD impact (i.e. areas of overlap between high deforestation threat and high carbon stocks).

Step 3: at an agreed interval (e.g., 10 or more years), review and re-assess the baseline

Where a 10-year baseline might be considered to be too short and given an interest in longer term projects or programs, it could be envisaged that the spatial PLUC map and estimates of rates of land-use change would need to be re-evaluated on a 10-year cycle. This would allow for the rates and changes in spatial drivers (e.g., new roads, new communities, new protected areas, etc.) to be incorporated into the derivation of the new PLUC map and for adjustments in the estimation of the rate of land-use change and carbon stocks.

The steps and tasks outlined in the preceding section clearly represent a fairly substantial modelling and analytical effort that begs the question of how such effort could be supported. We propose that such an effort could be supported by traditional overseas development assistance and performed by relevant agencies within a country after a period of training, particularly if other land-use changes were also modelled and analyzed. Not only would such analyses provide regional or national baselines for GHG mitigation activities and position countries to participate in the nascent carbon market, but they may, in addition, provide information to assist in the identification of other carbon sequestration opportunities. The approach outlined here could also help a country to identify its future, potential GHG emission liabilities and provide an opportunity for the country to plan alternative development pathways.

Application at the national scale: East Kalimantan, Indonesia

If a country is to plan where to make REDD interventions to maximize the net reductions of GHG and their return on investments, it is important to determine the likelihood that a given area will be deforested and be able to estimate the carbon benefits that REDD activities could potentially produce. We applied the baseline approach outlined in earlier to the province of East Kalimantan, Indonesia to demonstrate the feasibility of our approach for a 'national-level' analysis (see Petrova *et al.*, 2007).

Step 1: develop historical rates of land-use change and deforestation estimates

Task 1

Determine the analytic domain and obtain historical data:

*   Historical data were obtained from the Ministry of Forestry in Indonesia in the form of two land cover maps of 1997 and 2003.
*   The geographic domain of the spatial analysis is the province of East

Kalimantan, Indonesia. The temporal and spatial (250 m pixel size) resolution for the analysis was constrained by the availability of land cover maps.

Task 2

Analyze and identify potential major factors that influence deforestation:

- Six factor maps were created using the heuristic decision rule: distance from already deforested land, cities, sawmills, rivers, roads and allocated land.
- Five factor maps were created using the empirical decision rule: distance from cities, sawmills, rivers, roads and slope.
- These factor maps were combined in different combinations to derive 102 different 'suitability for change' (SFC) maps (automatically done in the GEO-MOD module of the IDRISI Kilimanjaro software package), each reflecting a unique factor map combination and weighting scheme.

Step 2: generate a baseline projection for deforestation

Task 3

Use key factors identified in Task 2 to project potential land-use change (PLUC):

- A Kappa-for-location statistic was generated for each of the 102 SFC maps. The Kappa-for-location statistic is a measure of the 'goodness of fit' between the actual land-use change that occurred (as determined from the Time 1 and Time 2 reference land cover maps) and the simulated land-use change that was predicted using each SFC map.
- The SFC map that yielded the best Kappa-for-location statistic (0.63, with 0 indicating an essentially random prediction and 1 indicating a perfect simulation) used the heuristic driver combination of: (1) distance from already deforested land; (2) distance from sawmills; and (3) elevation. This SFC map (now referred to as a PLUC map) was used to assess the future deforestation threat (Figure 10.1).

Task 4

Project rates and locations of deforestation into the future based on the PLUC map:

- The projected baseline rate of deforestation (1.34 per cent yr^{-1}) was calculated based on the change in forest cover between 1997 and 2003 land cover maps. No additional information was available to indicate any reason to modify the past deforestation rate going into the future 10-year period.
- The location of deforestation from 2003–2013 (Figure 10.2) was modelled based on the PLUC map developed in Task 3.

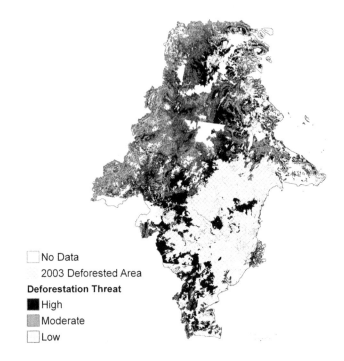

Figure 10.1 Map of deforestation threat for East Kalimantan, Indonesia

Source: Petrova *et al.* (2007)

Task 5

Combine the PLUC map with projected rates of deforestation and carbon stock estimates and make baseline projections:

*   A carbon stock map (Brown *et al.*, 1993) was used to estimate stocks in East Kalimantan, which varied from 39 to 170 kilotons C/ha across the study area. The change in forest area during the simulation period was combined with forest carbon stock estimates to produce estimates of potential baseline CO_2 emissions of 135 megatons C (MtC), or 500 megatons CO_2 equivalent ($MtCO_2e$), over a 10-year period (i.e., 50 $MtCO_2e$ per year).

Step 3: at an agreed interval (e.g., 10 or more years), review and re-assess the baseline

This step was not completed for this analysis. However, areas of high carbon stocks and high deforestation threat were identified that would be important to protect if carbon benefits are to be maximized in the region (Figure 10.3).

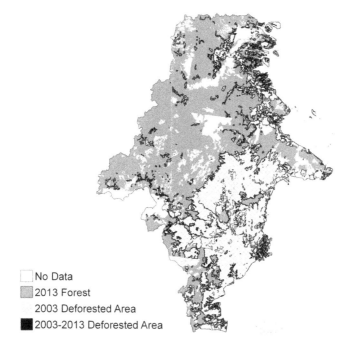

No Data
2013 Forest
2003 Deforested Area
2003-2013 Deforested Area

Figure 10.2 Simulated deforestation in East Kalimantan, Indonesia between 2003 and 2013

Source: Petrova *et al.* (2007)

Conclusion

Of the three models analyzed at the beginning of this chapter, the GEOMOD model offers the best approach for setting a quantitative baseline prediction of CO_2 emissions for avoided deforestation and other land-use change activities. Because it produces baseline estimates that are spatially represented, the GEOMOD approach is also useful for identifying where in a region or a country it makes sense to focus resources on interventions to reduce emissions. Weaknesses of GEOMOD include the large size of input databases required, the somewhat high cost of implementation with respect to capacity, resources and datasets available in many countries, applicability only for unplanned land-use change and the limitation of explanatory factors of deforestation to those that can be spatially represented. However, GEOMOD is superior to other models of land-use change that are currently available because it uses empirical information to predict not only the rate (how much), but also the location of future deforestation (where) based on a potential suite of drivers and factors that reflect regional and/or national circumstances. The GEOMOD model operates at any spatial scale, so it can be applied to small sub-national regions all the way up to national-scale analyses.

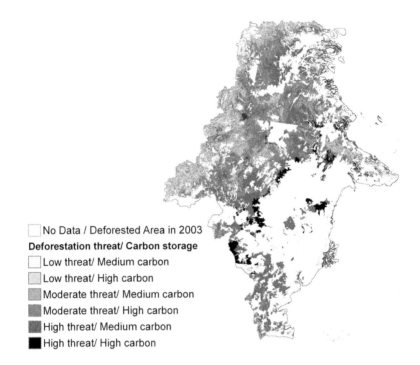

Figure 10.3 Map of East Kalimantan, Indonesia, showing forested areas with high carbon stocks under high deforestation threat that would be important to protect if carbon benefits from avoided deforestation are to be maximized in the region

Source: Petrova *et al.* (2007)

We have applied the GEOMOD approach to a real-world scenario by analyzing deforestation trends in East Kalimantan, Indonesia, and shown how such an analysis could be carried out and what information would be needed to do the analysis. The GEOMOD model can also be used as a planning tool for focusing REDD intervention activities on key regions within a country that make sense to protect in terms of high deforestation threat, high carbon stocks and, potentially, other environmental and socioeconomic benefits. For example, maps of potential carbon emissions (maps of deforestation threat combined with estimates of carbon stocks) can be overlain with other spatial databases such as range maps of endangered species, critical watersheds, poverty indices, social infrastructure-poor areas (e.g., lack of employment opportunities and educational or health facilities) to assist in locating areas that maximize multiple benefits.

APPENDIX

Table 10A.1 Criteria and indicators for evaluating the three models considered and the scoring of the models against these criteria

Criteria	Model FAC	LUCS	GEOMOD
1 Transparency	**4.5**	**3.5**	**5**
Understandable	4	3	5
Replicable	5	4	5
2 Accuracy and precision	**3.3**	**3**	**4.3**
Empirically calibrated	5	3	5
Validation and internal checks	2	3	5
Certainty of databases	3	3	3
3 Applicability	**1.5**	**4.5**	**4.5**
Simulate multiple land-use changes	1	5	4
Simulate at multiple scales	2	4	5
4 Compatible with international requirements	**5**	**3**	**5**
5 Cost efficiency[a]	**4.8**	**3.5**	**3.8**
Intensity of data needs	5	3	4
Availability of data	5	3	4
Time needed for data acquisition	5	3	3
Special technological needs	5	5	4
Knowledge needed to use model	4	3	5
Time to apply and simulate model	5	4	3
Total score	**18.6**	**17.5**	**22.6**

Source: Brown *et al.* 2003

Notes
a Most of the indicators under this criterion are scored high if the cost-efficiency indicator is low; for example if data needs are not intense then the score is high or if time needed to acquire data is long then the score is low, etc.

References

Bolin, B. and Sukumar, R. (2000) 'Global perspective in land use, land use change, and forestry', in R.T. Watson, I.R. Noble, B. Bolin, N.H. Ravindranath, D.J. Verardo and D.J. Dokken (eds) *Special Report of the IPCC*, Cambridge: Cambridge University Press.

Brown, S. (2003) *Finalizing Avoided Deforestation Project Baselines*, final report to the U.S. Agency for International Development, Contract No. 523-C-00-02-00032-00 [online]. Available at: http://www.winrock.org/ecosystems/files/Deforestation-baselines-Report-ENG.pdf [accessed 8 August 2008].

Brown, S., Hall, M., Andrasko, K., Ruiz, F., Marzoli, W., Guerrero, G. *et al.* (2007) 'Baselines for land-use change in the tropics: application to avoided deforestation projects', *Mitigation and Adaptation Strategies for Climate Change*, 12(6): 1001–1026.

Brown, S., Iverson, L.R., Prasad, A. and Dawning, L. (1993) 'Geographical distribution of carbon in biomass and soils of tropical Asian forests', *Geocarto International*, 4: 45–59.

Dale, V.H. (ed.) (1994) *Effects of Land Use Change on Atmospheric CO_2 Concentrations. South and Southeast Asia as a Case History*, New York: Springer Verlag.

Dale, V.H., Brown, S., Calderon, M.O., Montoya, S. and Martinez, R.E. (2003) 'Estimating baseline carbon emissions for the Eastern Panama Canal watershed', *Mitigation and Adaptation Strategies for Global Change*, 8(4): 323–348.

Engel, S., Wünscher, T. and Wunder, S. (2009) 'Increasing the efficiency of forest conservation: the case of payments for environmental services in Costa Rica', in C. Palmer and S. Engel (eds) *Avoided Deforestation: Prospects for Mitigating Climate Change*, London: Routledge.

Faeth, P., Cort, C. and Livernash, R. (1994) *Evaluating the Carbon Sequestration Benefits of Forestry Projects in Developing Countries*, Washington, DC: World Resource Institute (WRI).

FAO (Food and Agriculture Organization of the United Nations) (1993) *Forest Resources Assessment 1990 – Tropical Countries*, Forestry Papers 112, Rome: FAO.

Geist, H.J. and Lambin, E.F. (2002) 'Proximate causes and underlying driving forces of tropical deforestation', *BioScience*, 52(2): 143–149.

Hall, C.A.S., Tian, H., Qi, Y., Pontius, G., Cornell, J. and Uhlig, J. (1995) 'Modeling spatial and temporal patterns of tropical land use change', *Journal of Biogeography*, 22(4/5): 753–757.

Hall, M.H.P., Dushku, A. and Brown, S. (2006) 'Methods for examining scale issues in projecting land-use change in the tropics and their application to developing a deforestation baseline for the region of the Noel Kempff Mercado climate action project, Bolivia', in G. LeClerc and C. Hall (eds) *Making Development Work: A New Role for Science*, Albuquerque: University of New Mexico Press.

Hall, M.H.P., Hall, C.A.S. and Taylor, M.R. (2000) 'Geographical modeling: the synthesis of GIS and simulation modeling', in C.A.S. Hall (ed.) *Quantifying sustainable development: the future of tropical economies*, San Diego: Academic Press.

IDRISI Project (2003) *Kilimanjaro Edition*, Clark Labs, Worcester: Clark University [online]. Available at: http://www.clarklabs.org [accessed 8 August 2008].

Johns, T. and Schlamadinger, B. (2009) 'International policy and institutional barriers to reducing emissions from deforestation and degradation in developing countries as a climate change mitigation strategy', in C. Palmer and S. Engel (eds) *Avoided Deforestation: Prospects for Mitigating Climate Change*, London: Routledge.

Kerr, S. (2001) 'Seeing the forest and saving the trees: tropical land use change and global climate policy', in R. Sedjo and M. Toman (eds) *Can Carbon Sinks be Operational? Resources for the Future Workshop Proceedings*, 30 April 2001 [online]. Available at: http://www.rff.org/Documents/RFF-DP-01-26.pdf [accessed 4 April 2008].

Moura-Costa, P. (2001) 'Elements of a certification system for forestry-based greenhouse gas mitigation projects', in R. Sedjo and M. Toman (eds) *Can Carbon Sinks be Operational? Resources for the Future Workshop Proceedings*, 30 April 2001 [online]. Available at: http://www.rff.org/Documents/RFF-DP-01-26.pdf [accessed 1 April 2008].

Niles, J.O., Brown, S., Pretty, J., Ball, A. and Fay, J. (2002) 'Potential carbon mitigation and income in developing countries from changes in use and management of agricultural and forest lands', *Philosophical Transactions of the Royal Society A*, 360(1797): 1621–1639.

OECD/IEA (Organization for Economic Cooperation and Development/International Energy Agency) (2003) *Forestry projects: lessons learned and implications for CDM modalities*, OECD/IEA Information Paper, Paris: OECD.

Petrova, S., Stolle, F. and Brown, S. (2007) *Carbon and Co-Benefits from Sustainable Land-Use Management. Deliverable 22: Quantification of Carbon Benefits in Conservation Project Activities Through Spatial Modeling: East Kalimantan, Indonesia as a Case Study*, Winrock International, Report submitted to USAID. Cooperative Agreement No.

EEM-A-00-03-00006-00 [online]. Available at: http://www.winrock.org/ecosystems/ files/Deliverable_22-GEOMOD_modeling-Indonesia_2-2007.pdf [accessed 8 August 2008].

Pontius, R.G. Jr. (2000) 'Quantification error versus location error in comparison of categorical maps', *Photogrammetric Engineering & Remote Sensing*, 66(8): 1011–1016.

Pontius, R.G. Jr. (2002) 'Statistical methods to partition effects of quantity and location during comparison of categorical maps at multiple resolutions', *Photogrammatic and Remote Sensing*, 63(10): 1041–1049.

Pontius, R.G. Jr., Cornell, J. and Hall, C. (2001) 'Modeling the spatial pattern of land-use change with GEOMOD: application and validation for Costa Rica', *Agriculture, Ecosystems and Environment*, 85(1): 191–203.

Sciotti, R. (1991) *Estimating and Projecting Forest Area at Global and Local Level: A Step Forward*, FAO FRA-1990 project report, Rome: Food and Agriculture Organization of the United Nations (FAO).

Sciotti R. (2000) 'Demographic and ecological factors in FAO tropical deforestation modeling', in M. Palo and H. Vanhanen (eds) *World Forests from Deforestation to Transition*, Dordrecht: Kluwer Academic Publishing.

11 Human choices and policies' impacts on ecosystem services

Improving evaluations of payment and park effects on conservation and carbon

Alexander Pfaff and Juan Robalino

Introduction

Conservation policies are receiving increased attention in light of the potential, under new climate change policies, for rewarding avoided deforestation. Deforestation could be avoided in many ways, from alterations of development policies through many forms of conservation, for example, the creation of protected areas. In particular, the potential of payments for environmental services has received significant attention of late (see Chomitz et al., 1999; Echavarria et al., 2004; Frank and Muller, 2003; Miranda et al., 2003; Rojas and Aylward, 2003; Rosales, 2003; Smith, 1995; Szentandrasi et al., 1995; Tikka, 2003) and it is a focus of this volume and chapter.

Neither payments nor more common conservation policies such as forest reserves are typically subjected to rigorous impact evaluation. Ferraro and Pattanayak (2006) call for the empirical evaluation of conservation actions, while noting that forest impact is complicated to measure because 'avoided deforestation' involves a constructed counterfactual – an estimate of the deforestation that would have occurred had the forest not received policy protection. Andam et al. (2008) is the first evaluation of protected area impact, as far as we are aware, to construct such an estimate in light of the non-random distribution of protection that can easily arise from the choices that determine policy location and programme enrolment. Generally, for evaluation, it is crucial to understand the effects of both agencies' and landowners' choices.

Correct evaluation of policy impact is crucial for avoided deforestation. Consider the impacts on the environment. With incorrect evaluation, credits for avoided deforestation can be given for policy that does not avoid deforestation. If so, a buying entity's rise in emissions after buying the credit will actually be increasing total greenhouse gas emissions. And, on the other side of the errors possible due to imperfect evaluation, if we do not credit all those who have, in fact, avoided deforestation, the incentive to generate further avoidance falls. In the likely setting of learning by doing, i.e. global trial and error, if the impacts of all reasonable early efforts to avoid deforestation cannot be distinguished then the costs of deforestation that is actually avoided will be much higher than expected; also, recall, emissions could increase.

This chapter conveys why human choices complicate correct evaluations of impacts. Unobservable land choices, choices affecting policy location and interactions among choices complicate both ex post impact evaluation and ex ante policy planning. Based on application of proper methods to Costa Rica, we then suggest how these hurdles can best be addressed.

We provide examples of: how a best practice deforestation baseline rightly conveys the constraints on the impact the pioneering Costa Rican eco-payments programme could have; why it may be critical to have different baselines for different locations to correctly infer the impacts of Costa Rican protected areas; and how choices by conservation agencies and landowners can determine the bias within heretofore typical approaches to impact evaluation.

Finally, focusing on ecosystem services payments in particular, we discuss the effect of scale of the policy. International payments for carbon based on national baselines may face a lower 'baseline hurdle' than that facing a domestic agency making payments to landowners, since baseline errors at site level cancel out if baselines are right on average. However, when nations act to earn global payments, the domestic issues reappear. Having seen how common these issues are, we suggest their implications for conservation planning in the final section.

Choice-based hurdles for impact evaluation

Unobservable choices: the need to guess at the baseline without any policy

Any number of public or environmental economics textbooks convey the general idea that conservation policies could help to achieve the socially efficient amount of conservation. Should the benefits of conservation accrue to society as a whole, and not just to those who make costly choices to provide habitat, then private choices may provide too little habitat.

There are many ways in which public actions might increase habitat. Altering planned development policy is one, such as moving a planned road to a more benign location (perhaps with global funding of incremental costs). If we were sure of what the less benign road would have caused in terms of degradation, we could confidently estimate the impact of this policy-altering project by comparing the observed actual degradation to what would have occurred.

Yet the baseline estimate of the less benign impacts would likely be imperfect. In that same light, consider the taxation of deforestation. It may well reduce clearing but how would we know? We observe how much deforestation occurs with the tax. But how much clearing would have occurred without a tax? We will never observe that by making the calculation of the impact of tax a challenge. A comparison with similar but taxless locations could help.

The same ideas apply to protected areas. If we are sure they would have been cleared without protection, then we know how much clearing protection avoids. Yet if protection is implemented we will never, in fact, be sure what would have happened without protection. Thus, again, for doing impact evaluation we are limited to comparing the outcomes in places with implemented policies to those in places without. This can lead to errors in evaluation.

For ecosystem services payments the same reasoning applies. Payments go to land that starts and stays in forest. If we knew it would be cleared without payments, then we could know payment impact. But we do not know what would have occurred without the policy. Thus, most programmes will pay anybody who enrols with forested land and maintains forest. However, that opens the door to paying people who were not going to clear forest anyway.

Such payments that do not make a difference arise due to missing information. We do not know the baseline, 'no policy' choices for places that are paid. If we did, we could write contracts to pay only when land use changed relative to a baseline, for example, land that was going to be cleared otherwise stayed in forest. That would guarantee that the policy has impact. Our discussion of Figure 11.1 shows how to get that information completely wrong.

Figure 11.1, which depicts landowners' choice of land use in order to maximize returns, provides a useful framework for communicating constraints both on payments' impacts and on impact estimation. Land is ordered, along the horizontal axis, according to relative profitability of clearing (clearing profit minus forest profit), with clearing profit more favoured to the right. When relative clearing profit is positive, the land will be deforested; with no payments, the forest remains within $[0, x^N]$ while the rest of the forest, i.e. to the right of x^N, will be cleared.

If environmental services payments of P per forested unit compete with non-forest land uses, landowners sign up for payments in $[0, x^P]$. A crucial point is that not all who sign up would modify their behaviour as a result of the payment. Those within the interval $[0, x^N]$ do not clear their forest even without payments. In contrast, the parcels in the interval $[x^N, x^P]$ would be deforested in the absence of payments but would be kept in forest if P is being paid.

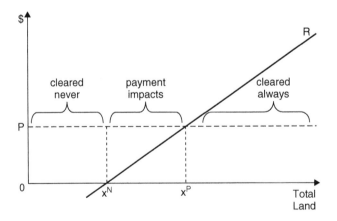

Figure 11.1 Baselines are what people would have chosen without the policy

Source: Authors

Thus, the impact of a programme of such payments impact depends critically on the fraction of total enrolled land coming from the interval $[x^N, x^P]$, a fraction we denote by α. If α equals 1, i.e. only land from $[x^N, x^P]$ is enrolled, then all payments prevent deforestation. But if α equals 0, i.e. only land from $[0, x^N]$ is enrolled, then the payments have no impact.

We emphasize that if all of those would benefit (within $[0, x^P]$) in fact apply,[1] which parcels are enrolled affects not only impact but also the accuracy of simple impact estimates. If $\alpha = 1$, i.e. targeting is 'good' in that all of $[x^N, x^P]$ but none of $[0, x^N]$ is enrolled, then forest locations outside the programme are $[0, x^N]$. Those are not similar to the enrolled parcels. None will be cleared, although all of the enrolled would have been. If we estimate what would have happened on enrolled parcels using the non-enrolled parcels, we get the baseline completely wrong. We would estimate zero impact from payments when, in fact, each payment mattered.

Relevant human choices: agencies, landowners and bias

In the preceding example, not only was a baseline based on non-enrolled parcels wrong, it was wrong in a particular way and that bias resulted from the agency's excellent targeting. If the agency is well informed and able to exclude applicants, it can enrol only the applicants who would have cleared without a payment. As noted, that is good for true payment impact.

However, when as analysts we are estimating impact after the fact, we do not observe the 'no policy' choices in locations with payments. We are constrained to compare the lack of clearing in enrolled places with the clearing in non-enrolled places. If the agency chose in a very sensible but clearly non-random way who to enrol, such a comparison yields an impact estimate that is biased. With excellent agency targeting, the estimate will be too low (as in the example, it could be zero). With poor agency targeting, the estimate will instead be too high. Landowner choices can bias estimates too. If the agency uses first-come-first-served basis, i.e. does not target, which landowners might get into the programme? It could be that those who are sure they will lose money in agriculture would be most likely to apply. In the extreme, if only parcels that would not have been cleared anyway are enrolled, then the actual impact of payments is zero. Any non-zero impact estimate is in fact an overestimate of the true impact.

Generally if the parcels treated by a policy (whether those receiving payments or those in protected areas or those near new roads) is not a random subset of all parcels, then policy impact estimates may be biased. As we have seen, this bias could be in either direction. What determines the bias is the net impact, on non-random enrolment, of all the actors' choices. Put another way, we are constrained to compare policy locations only with no policy locations but choices by agencies and landowners can imply that these are not similar groups. The method for better impact estimation we now demonstrate tries to create similar subsets.

Spatial and temporal choice interactions: various spillovers

Spatial interactions

Human choice also implies that policy can have impacts on locations without policies. One implication is that in comparing policy with no policy locations to estimate impacts, we need to be careful not to include the no policy locations onto which policy impacts spillover. Even if avoiding that estimation pitfall, however, we may want to consider such 'spillovers'. For instance, in cost–benefit analysis of a policy, likely all of its impacts should be included.

For example, when a new protected area is created, those who were using or planning to clear the forest for private reasons may relocate themselves and/or their planned activities to nearby forest areas that would not otherwise have been cleared. Thus no policy locations, i.e. parcels outside of the protected area, are cleared more. The total net reduction of clearing due to the protected area is lower than one would think if looking only within the boundaries of the protected area. This idea is referred to as 'leakage' in various parts of this volume (see Murray, Chapter 9 in this volume).

Further, recall that we will estimate the impact within the protected area's boundaries by comparing deforestation there with outcomes outside. If the latter includes locations near the protected area that are cleared because of the spatial spillover then these will bias the estimate of protection's impact upwards. Protection appears to have a greater deforestation-retarding influence within its own boundaries because it raises clearing nearby.[2] This could happen for payments, for example, a landowner can accept payments for a forested parcel and instead clear others.

Such a bias can also go in the other direction. A policy could lower deforestation rates in no policy locations. It is claimed, for instance, that payments to some parcels may create awareness of the value of nature and/or the fact that one can receive payments. Alternatively, private or public choices to conserve forest could lead neighbours to band together to do the same. Pointing in that same direction, in terms of bias, a choice to clear and to produce could lead neighbours to produce (see, for instance, Robalino and Pfaff, 2008 for related empirical analyses).

Temporal interactions

Human response to a policy may also occur over time for any given location in space. Above we note that policy in location A can affect contemporaneous behaviours at location B or many such locations. Here we note that the policy could also affect behaviours in location A in the periods before or after the policy is implemented. This, too, is a form of policy spillover.

An example is pre-emptive clearing of species habitat based on expected public action. For instance, when the US Environmental Protection Agency (EPA) moves a species upwards in the hierarchy of protection under the Endangered Species Act, owners of land where that species resides may well revise upwards their expectations of restrictions on their land-use choices. In response, they may reduce that species' habitat on their land immediately in order to extract their private value from that land before potential public action takes place (see related discussion and empirical analysis in, e.g., Ferraro et al., 2007; List et al., 2006). Then a policy action that was aiming to conserve habitat has instead hastened its degradation.

Private land-use choice in expectation of policy is also observed in forest frontiers. If a new road plan is announced, or even simply leaked, private land speculators acquire land in its path to realize gains. An example that in a way blends these other examples concerns a canal announced in the state of Ceará in northeast Brazil that was intended to create new options for allocating scarce freshwater. Not only did private landowners purchase land in the path, ahead of the canal's arrival, but their investments also increased the total demand for water.[3]

Not surprisingly, policy can also change behaviour after the policy is implemented. For instance, a road's arrival will often lead to follow-on investments, including new roads.[4] Thus, for instance, if a conservation policy succeeds in relocating a new road around a forest, its impact in reducing deforestation may be much greater over time than is observed early on.

Choice-adjusted impact estimation

Matching analysis

What is 'similar'?

As noted, we are unable to observe the 'without-policy' outcomes for policy locations. Thus, we estimate policy impact by comparing the outcomes in untreated, i.e. without policy, locations with outcomes in locations that are treated (are protected or receive payments). Matching is an effort to compare treated locations with the most 'similar' untreated parcels (see, for example, Rosenbaum and Rubin, 1983; Rubin, 1980). However, what is 'similarity'?

To highlight the importance of this definition, we consider two matching estimators. The first is a nearest neighbour propensity score-matching estimator (Hill et al., 2003; Rosenbaum and Rubin, 1983), using a fixed number of matched observations per treated observation. Such estimators define similarity based on the estimated probabilities of being treated, which are generated by a first-stage regression that attempts to explain which locations are treated using observed characteristics of locations (such as slope, soil quality, distance to markets).

Another approach is nearest neighbour covariate matching using an inverse weighting matrix to account for the difference in the scale of the covariates (Abadie and Imbens, 2006a). Again one might employ a fixed number of best matches per treated observation. Covariate matching estimators define similarity without a first-stage regression but rather using the simple distances, in the space of the matching covariates, between the treated and matched. Thus, for any treated location, say, a parcel in a protected area, we search for the four parcels outside protected areas whose observed characteristics (such as slope, soil quality, distance to markets) are most similar to the observed characteristics of the treated location in question.

These two approaches define similarity quite differently and, as a result, will compare the treated locations to different subsets of the untreated locations, although in both cases that subset of the untreated is made up of those similar to the treated. The computation of standard errors, to indicate when differences are statistically significant, also differs across these and other approaches to matching (see Abadie and Imbens, 2006b).[5]

Whichever of these approaches is chosen, the commonality is the basic method. Thus, the chosen number of most similar untreated points for each treated location is identified and then the outcomes for those untreated points are compared to the outcomes for the treated. For instance, if average deforestation in protected areas is zero, then the average deforestation in the matched untreated locations can be used as the estimate of the impact of protection. If the treatment is, in fact, non-randomly allocated over space, this matched impact estimate often will differ from the typical impact estimate based on all of the untreated locations. With the matched subset of untreated locations in hand, another option is to run a regression using only those untreated plus the treated locations including data on the observed characteristics.

Match quality

The point of matching is to use a subset of the untreated, i.e. no policy, parcels which are more like the treated parcels than is the entire set of untreated locations. The extent to which using a subset improves similarity needs to be checked and demonstrated. The typical first approach for doing so is a balancing test, in which the means of the characteristics of the matched subset of untreated parcels are tested for significant difference from the means for the treated parcels. One may check whether the full set of untreated parcels is different from the treated and then check whether the matched untreated locations more closely approximate the treated. Even if closer, however, the goal is for the matched points to be indistinguishable.

Yet even if a balancing test is passed after all the matching choices described earlier, matching controls solely for the impacts of the group differences in all the *observable* factors. On recognizing this, many analysts ask whether, and if so, why, typical regression analysis for all the available observations is inferior to matching analyses in this policy setting. For comparison, consider the matching regression with observed covariates but using just treated locations plus the matched untreated observations instead of typical use of all observations – those are very similar regressions differing in terms of which untreated points are included.

To the extent that the observed characteristics of locations (slope, soil, others) are not in fact similar in the treated and untreated groups, any regression using all of the observations applies the information at hand to control for the impact of the differences in characteristics. However, when group characteristics differ, the burden on the specification is considerable.[6] If the specification of the regression is not correct, the control for characteristics is wrong.

Matching is intended precisely to reduce that burden by comparing 'apples to apples' or using untreated and treated locations with similar characteristics. Yet this problem will plague matching, too, when match quality is not good. That can motivate the use of a subset of the treated observations, too, in particular dropping all of the treated points with poor matches.

Crump et al. (2006) address a lack of covariate overlap between untreated and treated, noting that many common estimators become sensitive to the choice of specification (much as Cochran noted and following related prior work including Heckman et al., 1997, 1998). Crump et al. (2006) characterize optimal subsamples for which treatment effects can be estimated most precisely. In the following, we do not use optimal subsamples but do emphasize this by examining robustness to dropping high probability of treatment treated observations for which we do not find good untreated matches (Cochran and Rubin, 1973).

Application I: Costa Rican ecopayments

Unobserved choices: low deforestation baseline

We do not observe what would have happened without payments in parcels receiving payments. However, as in Sánchez et al. (2007), we can estimate this by looking at locations not receiving payments. From Figure 11.1, this is not sensible if either all land that would not be cleared without payments or all land that would be cleared without payments is included in the programme. However, the Costa Rican PSA programme was quite small so both are unlikely.

Anecdotally (de Camino-Velozo et al., 2000; Hartshorn et al., 2005), starting in 1997 Law 7575 on forestry greatly slowed clearing. Consistent with this observation, simple measures of forest find that during the first 3 years of the PSA payment programme (which started in 1997) the annual deforestation rate outside the programme areas was 0.21 per cent, i.e. one-fifth of 1 per cent. Thus, very little of the land enrolled in PSA was actually being protected from deforestation. That may reflect significant impacts of all previous conservation policies (1997 law, protection, ecotourism and more). If other policies more or less put a halt to forest clearing, then there may not have been very much deforestation for payments to prevent.

Landowner choices: lower deforestation impact

We believe that the 1997–2000 payments were not strongly targeted by the relevant agency (see also Engel et al., Chapter 12 in this volume). Thus, agency choice may not be a major issue during this time period. However, landowner choices seem likely to matter, since the PSA programme was voluntary. That is, parcels were volunteered by their owners. While this is not necessarily the dominant story, there is good reason to believe that owners may have frequently volunteered for the forest-maintenance payments those parcels which were the poorest for agriculture, perhaps so poor that they would never have been cleared anyway.

Pfaff et al. (2007a) directly examine this possibility, a general issue for such payments and relevant for countries without Costa Rica's low deforestation baseline. First, a pixel-level regression generates the predicted probabilities of 1997–2000 deforestation. Then we examine whether enrolment leans towards areas of higher or lower deforestation. Without question the bias, if any, is towards lower pressure. That is, the land that is less likely than average to be cleared without payments is over-represented in enrolment for payments. That suggests that even the low deforestation national baseline will overestimate the PSA policy's impact.

Pfaff et al. (2007b) go beyond this bounding argument by applying matching analysis (as described previously). We compare the treated (or payment) parcels with untreated (or no payment) parcels, which, per their observable characteristics (such as slope of the land, distance from urban markets and from roads) are most similar to the treated. This will avoid or ameliorate errors in policy-versus-no-policy comparisons such as discussed earlier. In this fashion, for example, using the propensity score-matching approach, we estimate the 1997–2000 Costa Rican eco-payment impact at 0.08 per cent or less than one-tenth of 1 per cent rate of deforestation per year prevented, i.e. impact well below the average of 0.21 per cent for all untreated areas.

Robalino et al. (2007) then examine payments after 2000 given that, by all accounts, the programme increased targeting after 2000. Yet our understanding is that targeting was not of land more likely to have been cleared without payments but instead land whose conservation would most matter ecologically or, more generally, in terms of ecosystem services provision. The baseline for this period is essentially unchanged from the very low 1997–2000 clearing, although net clearing was even lower during 2000–2005 and, in fact, was negative. However, there was more deforestation (even if it was outweighed on net by reforestation). This implies more potential for deforestation prevention by payments. Preliminary results suggest in addition that post-2000 payments were not as biased towards low pressure areas. Between the shifts in baseline trends and in the allocation of payments over space, we find that 0.5 per cent, of deforestation per year, was prevented. This is still a relatively low rate but it conveys that changes in policy design and trends can affect impact.

Application II: Costa Rican protected areas

Unobserved choices: temporal shifts affect the baseline

For the same country, of course, the facts about the 1997–2000 baseline will still apply. However, protected areas raise the issue of shifts over time in forest baselines because within Costa Rica, most of the protected areas were created well before the ecopayments had begun.

Andam et al. (2008) considers the impacts of protection from the 1960s onward and find that significant amounts of deforestation were prevented (although much less than usually assumed – more later). That is not surprising neither does it contradict the ecopayments result because the deforestation rate in Costa Rica used to be much higher than it was after 1997 and thus any effective protection (i.e., zero deforestation in protected areas, which is true in Costa Rica if not in all other countries) certainly could be expected to have had an impact.

Comparing this with Pfaff et al. (2007c) emphasizes the importance of understanding the default or baseline rate of land clearing that an effective policy prevents. Pfaff et al. (2007c) examine forest impacts for the period 1986–1997. They, too, find some significant impact but its magnitude is lower than in Andam et al. (2008) as deforestation had already started to slow. More importantly, Pfaff et al. (2007c) find quite significant variation in the baseline over space within this time period. Thus, the baseline deforestation rate and, as a result, the conservation impact of protection is shown to vary with the distance to San José, the distance to a road and slope.

Agency targeting choices: lower deforestation impact

Whereas ecopayment policy gave a role to landowners' choices, the location of areas designated for protection did not. Agencies literally locate reserves. That need not bias the set of locations but one can imagine motivations such that it would. An agency might target locations that were going to be cleared, to maximize one kind of impact. Or an agency might want protection to last for centuries and to avoid political pressure about taking private lands (an issue which arose in Costa Rica) and might then look for low value, uncontested lands.

While differing in average impact found, due to the shifts in baselines over time, both Andam et al. (2008) and Pfaff et al. (2007c) find strong statistical evidence that protection is not on a random set of locations but rather on locations less likely to be cleared than the average parcel. Thus, estimating impact by looking at all non-protected locations will overestimate impacts of protection. The Andam et al. (2008) and Pfaff et al. (2007c) estimates of the clearing prevented by protection are under half of what one finds if ignoring the non-random location of protection by comparing deforestation under protection to that on all the unprotected land.

Spatial choice interactions

Both baseline (unobserved no policy choices) and selection (landowner and agency choices) issues that affect additionality, as discussed earlier, must be considered in estimating correctly the impact of a policy in its intended location and time period. That is not true of spatial and/or temporal interactions or leakage in space or time that result from the policy.

That such leakage is outside of the initial space-and-time focus explains in part why often it is omitted from cost–benefit analyses though it represents relevant costs and benefits. For protected areas, in considering the total net policy impact one natural question is whether completely preventing land clearing within a protected area influenced the land uses outside.

In examining whether land around a protected area was deforested more or less than in the case of no protection, baseline issues apply. We do not observe deforestation next to protection in the case of no protection. We can only compare next-to-protection with not-near-protection parcels. Yet next-to-protection parcels may not be a random set. Still they might be compared with a subset of not-next-to-protection lands. Robalino et al. (2008) examines this empirically for Costa Rica, finding preliminary evidence of some deforestation spillovers, i.e. that rates of deforestation in some areas next to protection are higher than if there was no protection.

Does scale reduce choice-based hurdles?

International 'REDD' payments

Consider the payments for avoided deforestation being considered as part of global climate change strategy. In principle, those payments could be made, as in current domestic programmes, directly to individual landowners. However, since the transactions costs of doing so could be prohibitive, instead a country could serve as the 'owner'. Thus a country could contract with other countries to receive payments if it captured more carbon, or if it emitted less carbon, than in an agreed baseline. Payments could then be distributed domestically.

Conceptually, baseline issues still apply. If a policy exists, then the world will never observe what land use would have occurred in the country without the payments incentives. Thus one asserts at a national level how much deforestation would have occurred without a policy. This has its challenges. Assertions will be too high for some countries but lower for others. However, working at the national level allows the many errors one could make at the parcel scale to cancel out. Being right on average across parcels works for any given country, in the sense of credits for reduced carbon emissions being valid (not 'hot air'). While hurdles remain conceptually, the magnitude of the baseline problem may be reduced at larger scale.

Further, spatial interaction may be greatly reduced. While Sohngen and Brown (2004) show that linkages can occur through global markets – if timber is not cut and not put on the market from one country, the global price response could induce more cutting in other sites – local leakage would not be an evaluation issue at the country scale. If a conservation policy in a given country does cause local leakage, then that is taken into account in calculating global payments to the country, as it reduces the amount of additional (i.e. above baseline) forest.

Domestic problems redux

Still selection issues can arise in an international payments scheme, analogous to landowner choices in the Costa Rican payments programme. Following the logic of Montero (1999) and its application to deforestation in Kerr (2007), we must realize that the decision to participate in a global payments policy may depend on the error in a country's assigned baseline. If it was assumed that more forest would be present without payments than the country believes is correct, it can simply refuse to join as the cost of earning payments by having a forest level above the baseline would be simply too costly. If the assumed forest level is erroneously low, a country will rapidly join. This process means the world overpays for impact. Even if baselines were right on average for all the countries, they would be biased towards assuming too little forest for those that will join. Thus as in our earlier payments example, some countries will pay some others for unchanged behaviours (or 'hot air').

At least as important is a domestic perspective on earning global payments. As noted, international payments are earned if national outcomes (forest area, carbon) are above agreed baselines. Assuming the baseline is correct, i.e. that the baseline is indeed what would occur without policy, the national agency that will receive global payments need to do something to translate that global incentive into domestic behaviours. Additional domestic ecopayments and protection are likely candidates for doing so. That brings us back to the inefficiencies in implementation of such policies shown earlier, due to a lack of baseline knowledge at parcel level. That can greatly increase the domestic transfers required to earn the global payments.

Discussion

Microeconomic theory supports the idea that conservation policy may improve social efficiency should conservation's benefits accrue to society, i.e. not just to those who provide it at a cost. Thus a basic theory of private choices that affect others suggests that policies like public forest reserves or ecosystem services payments could have impacts that are beneficial.

However, whether such conservation policies actually have those impacts in reality is another question entirely and is not usually asked. To answer it, we do not observe what would have happened had the policy not been implemented. Further, using observations of locations without policy to guess at this may provide the wrong impact estimates because the human choices that drive the location of policies often imply their locations are non-random.

These issues create challenges for ex post estimates of policy impact. However, as we demonstrated in two applications to Costa Rica (ecopayments and protected areas), there are sensible methods for 'human choice adjusting' the empirical estimation of policy impacts.

These issues with ex post impact estimation also complicate ex ante policy planning: policymakers must guess the future of each candidate parcel without policy being applied; policy location may be driven by influential actors with various goals; policies in one place may affect outcomes in other. The only difference for planning is that one is choosing where to locate a policy, which adds prediction (in place of hindsight) to all of our earlier challenges.

What can be done? A focus on forest parcels under greater clearing pressure could in principle raise impact. First, if an ecopayments programme remains oversubscribed, in selecting parcels to admit an agency can focus on those more likely to be deforested in the absence of payments. That would essentially be a form of targeting of high clearing threat. There may be countervailing arguments like land price but threat should at least be considered (see Engel et al. and Alix-Garcia et al., Chapters 12 and 13 in this volume, respectively). Putting it another way, to provide a given level of eco-services more costly land could, in fact, lower policy cost.

As noted in the discussion of the Costa Rican payments programme after 2000, targeting may be on dimensions of environmental service, i.e. not explicitly concerning threat. Those may not be correlated with threat. More threat targeting could raise gains for a given budget.

Programme design could also permit higher payments to areas under higher threat due to higher returns. One payment five times as high as current payments could yield a positive impact on one parcel even if current payments to five parcels yield nothing. Such adjustments would require an agency to have information about rents. Such information will be imperfect but it may be sufficient (again, see Engel et al and Alix-Garcia et al., Chapters 12 and 13 in this volume, respectively).

Such adjustments could change not only efficiency but also the distributional effects. For a fixed budget, having high payments means concentrating payments on fewer people, for example, providing nothing to four of any five people who would have enrolled in the current regime but five times as much as currently paid for the fifth person. Such a shift could, in principle, help to alleviate poverty if that one person is relatively poor. Targeting higher rent land, however, may mean that the person receiving payments has relatively high profits and is more likely to have relatively high wealth. Combining the targeting of the higher rents with fewer but higher payments can shift a programme away from any redistributive policy objective.

Acknowledgements

For financial support we thank the Tinker Foundation, Inc.; NSF's MMIA (National Science Foundation, Methods and Models for Integrated Assessment); NCEAS (NSF's National Center for Ecological Analysis and Synthesis); SSHRC (Social Science and Humanities Research Council of Canada); CERC/Earth Institute at Columbia University, FAO (U.N. Food and Agriculture Organization); IAI (Inter-American Institute for Global Change Research); LACEEP (Latin American and Caribbean Environmental Economics Program); and EfD (Environment for Development initiative).

Notes

1 Note that, in reality, not all of the landowners who would like to enrol (because they are in $[0, x^p]$) will in fact apply for the programme. Some landowners may not know about the programme or may face high application costs. Further, not all those who apply are guaranteed to be enrolled, if the programme lacks sufficient funds.

2 See Robalino (2007), which also discusses spillovers to the wages of those who work on land in the area.

3 Personal communication, Renzo Taddei, from field interviews with both landowners and agency officials.

4 See, for example, Pfaff, October 2006, LBA Brasilia conference presentation on evolving Amazon road networks.
5 For example, Abadie and Imbens (2006b) show that the common practice of bootstrapping standard errors is invalid with non-smooth, nearest neighbour estimators such as the propensity score-matching estimator with a fixed number of matches (versus with smoothly declining weights to less well-matched untreated locations).
6 Consider, for instance, the following claim from Cochran, in Rubin (1984):

> Unless the regression equation holds in the region in which observations are lacking, covariance will not remove all the bias, and in practice may remove only a small part or it. Secondly, even if the regression is valid in the no man's land, the standard errors of the adjusted means become large, because the standard error formula in a covariance analysis takes account of the fact that extrapolation is being employed. Consequently the adjusted differences may become insignificant merely because the adjusted comparisons are of low precision. When the groups differ widely in x, these differences imply that the interpretation of an adjusted analysis is speculative rather than soundly based.

References

Abadie, A. and Imbens, G.W. (2006a) 'Large sample properties of matching estimators for average treatment effects', *Econometrica*, 74(1): 235–267.

Abadie, A. and Imbens, G.W. (2006b) *On the Failure of the Bootstrap for Matching Estimators*, NBER Technical Working Paper 325 [online]. Available at: http://www.nber.org/papers/t0325.pdf [accessed 11 August 2008].

Alix-Garcia, J., de Janvry, A. and Sadoulet, E. (2009) 'The role of risk in targeting payments for environmental services', in C. Palmer and S. Engel (eds) *Avoided Deforestation: Prospects for Mitigating Climate Change*, London: Routledge.

Andam, K., Ferraro, P., Pfaff, A., Robalino, J. and Sánchez-Azofeifa, G.A. (2008) 'Measuring the effectiveness of protected area networks in reducing deforestation: a rigorous impact evaluation approach', *Proceedings of the National Academy of Sciences* (accepted).

Chomitz, K., Brenes, E. and Constantino, L. (1999) 'Financing environmental services: the Costa Rican experience and its implications', *The Science of the Total Environment*, 240(1): 157–169.

Cochran, W. and Rubin, D. (1973) 'Controlling bias in observational studies: a review', *Sankhya*, Series A 35: 417–446.

Crump, R.K., Hotz, V.J., Imbens, G.W. and Mitnik, O.A. (2006) 'Moving the goalposts: addressing limited overlap in estimation of average treatment effects by changing the estimand', mimeo, Department of Economics, University of California Berkeley.

de Camino-Velozo, R. and World Bank (2000) *Costa Rica: Forest Strategy and the Evolution of Land Use*, Washington, DC: World Bank.

Echavarria, M., Vogel, M.J., Alban, M. and Meneses, F. (2004) *The Impacts of Payments for Watershed Services in Ecuador: Emerging Lessons from Pimampiro and Cuenca*, London: International Institute for Environment and Development (IIED).

Engel, S., Wünscher, T. and Wunder, S. (2009) 'Increasing the efficiency of forest conservation: the case of payments for environmental services in Costa Rica', in C. Palmer and S. Engel (eds) *Avoided Deforestation: Prospects for Mitigating Climate Change*, London: Routledge.

Ferraro, P.J., McIntosh, C. and Ospina, M. (2007) 'The effectiveness of the US endangered species act: an econometric analysis using matching methods', *Journal of Environmental Economics and Management*, 54(3): 245–261.

Ferraro, P.J. and Pattanayak, S.K. (2006) 'Money for nothing? A call for empirical evaluation of biodiversity conservation investments', *PLoS Biology*, 4(4): e105.

Frank, G. and Muller, F. (2003) 'Voluntary approaches in protection of forests in Australia', *Environmental Science and Policy*, 6(3): 261–269.

Hartshorn, G., Ferraro, P.J., Spergel, B. and Sills, E. (2005) *Evaluation of the World Bank – GEF Ecomarkets Project in Costa Rica*, Report of the Blue Ribbon Evaluation Panel [online]. Available at: http://www2.gsu.edu/~wwwcec/docs/doc%20updates/NCSU_Blue_Ribbon_Panel_Final.pdf [accessed 23 June 2008].

Heckman, J.J., Ichimura, H. and Todd, P. (1997) 'Matching as an econometric evaluation estimator: evidence from evaluating a job training program', *Review of Economic Studies*, 64(4): 605–654.

Heckman, J.J., Ichimura, H. and Todd, P. (1998) 'Matching as an econometric evaluation estimator', *Review of Economic Studies*, 65(2): 261–294.

Hill, J., Waldfogel, J. and Brooks-Gunn, J. (2003) 'Sustained effects of high participation in an early intervention for low-birth-weight premature infants', *Developmental Psychology*, 39(4): 730–744.

Kerr, S. (2007) *China Workshop Presentation on Effects of Selection with Errors*, mimeo.

List, J., Margolis, M. and Osgood, D. (2006) *Is the Endangered Species Act Endangering Species?*, Working Paper 12777, Cambridge, MA: National Bureau of Economic Research (NBER).

Miranda, M., Porras, I.T. and Moreno, M.L. (2003) *The Social Impacts of Payments for Environmental Services in Costa Rica : a Quantitative Field Survey and Analysis of the Virilla Watershed*, London: Environmental Economics Program, International Institute for Environment and Development (IIED).

Montero, J.P. (1999) 'Voluntary compliance with market-based environmental policy: evidence from the U.S. acid rain program', *Journal of Political Economy*, 107(5): 998.

Murray, B. (2009) 'Leakage from an avoided deforestation compensation policy: concepts, empirical evidence and corrective policy options', in C. Palmer and S. Engel (eds) *Avoided Deforestation: Prospects for Mitigating Climate Change*, London: Routledge.

Pfaff, A., Robalino, J. and Sánchez, A. (2007a) *Into the REDD?*, mimeo, Duke University.

Pfaff, A., Robalino, J. and Sánchez, A. (2007b) *Payments for Environmental Services: Empirical Analysis for Costa Rica*, Duke Sanford Working Paper SAN08-05, Durham, NC: Terry Sanford Institute of Public Policy, Duke University.

Pfaff, A., Robalino, J., Sánchez, A., Andam, K. and Ferraro, P. (2007c) *Location Affects Protection: Observable Characteristics Drive Park Impacts in Costa Rica*, Duke Sanford Working Paper SAN08-06, Durham, NC: Terry Sanford Institute of Public Policy, Duke University.

Robalino, J. (2007) 'Land conservation policies and income distribution: who bears the burden of our environmental efforts?', *Environment and Development Economics*, 12(4): 521–533.

Robalino, J. and Pfaff, A. (2008) *Contagious Development: Neighbor Interactions in Deforestation*, mimeo, Centro Agronómico Tropical de Investigación y Enseñanza (CATIE).

Robalino, J., Pfaff, A., Sánchez, A., Alpizar, F., Leon, C. and Rodriguez, C.M. (2007). *Deforestation Impacts of Environmental Services Payments: Costa Rica's PSA Program 2000–2005*, EfD (Environment for Development) Discussion Paper 08–24, Gothenburg: University of Gothenburg and Washington, DC: Resources for the Future (RFF).

Robalino, J., Pfaff, A., Sánchez, A. and Villalobos, L. (2008) *Protected Area Spillovers: Leakage from Protection in Costa Rica 1986–1997*, mimeo, Centro Agronómico Tropical de Investigación y Enseñanza (CATIE).

Rojas, M. and Aylward, B. (2003) *What Are We Learning from Experiences with Markets for Environmental Services in Costa Rica? A Review and Critique of the Literature*, London: International Institute for Environment and Development (IIED).

Rosales, R.M.P. (2003) *Developing Pro-Poor Markets for Environmental Services in the Philippines*, London: International Institute for Environment and Development (IIED).

Rosenbaum, P.R. and Rubin, D.B. (1983), 'The central role of the propensity score in observational studies for causal effects', *Biometrika*, 70(1): 41–55.

Rubin, D.B. (1980) 'Bias reduction using Mahalanobis-metric matching', *Biometrics*, 36(2): 293–298.

Rubin, D.B. (1984) 'William G. Cochran's contributions to the design, analysis, and evaluation of observational studies', in D. Rubin (ed.) *Matched Sampling for Causal Effects*, Cambridge: Cambridge University Press.

Sánchez-Azofeifa, A., Pfaff, A., Robalino, J. and Boomhower, J. (2007) 'Costa Rican payment for environmental services program: intention, implementation and impact', *Conservation Biology*, 21(5): 1165.

Smith, R.B.W. (1995) 'The conservation reserve program as a least-cost land retirement mechanism', *American Journal of Agricultural Economics*, 77(1): 93–105.

Sohngen, B. and Brown, S. (2004) 'Measuring leakage from carbon projects in open economies: a stop timber harvesting project in Bolivia as a case study', *Canadian Journal of Forest Resources*, 34: 829–839.

Szentandrasi, S., Polasky, S., Berrens, R. and Leonard, J. (1995) 'Conserving biological diversity and the conservation reserve program', *Growth and Change*, 26(3): 383–404.

Tikka, P. (2003) 'Conservation contracts in habitat protection in southern Finland', *Environmental Science and Policy*, 6(3): 271–278.

12 Increasing the efficiency of forest conservation

The case of payments for environmental services in Costa Rica

Stefanie Engel, Tobias Wünscher and Sven Wunder

Introduction

Payments for avoided deforestation, whether made to nation states, regions or local land users, can be seen as an international type of payment for environmental services (PES). Wunder (2005) defines PES as a voluntary transaction, where a well-defined environmental service (ES) (or a land use likely to secure that service) is being 'bought' by a (minimum one) ES buyer from a (minimum one) ES provider, if and only if the ES provider secures ES provision (conditionality).

This chapter links PES to reducing CO_2 emissions from deforestation and degradation (REDD) and discusses on the basis of a specific empirical example how the efficiency of PES can be increased through improved targeting. In terms of REDD policy, relevant efficiency questions include how to select the areas with the highest carbon content, the lowest conservation cost, the highest threat of clearing and possibly the greatest synergies with other environmental services provided by the same landscape (side-objectives). These questions are relevant at various levels of REDD policy design.

First, if REDD is to be achieved through the establishment of an international fund, like the Forest Carbon Partnership Facility (FCPF), limited funds require a procedure for deciding which countries, regions or projects are selected for REDD funding. Second, arguably any country or region participating successfully in REDD will also need to provide some local-level incentives for avoiding deforestation. PES is a highly relevant approach in this context. Yet, in establishing a national or regional PES scheme, similar questions arise on how land parcels are selected for programme inclusion and about the size and allocation of conservation payments. Finally, increasing the efficiency of current forest conservation spending (whether in the form of PES or other approaches)[1] can be seen as an important complement to a strategy of raising additional funds for reducing CO_2 emissions through avoided deforestation. By increasing the efficiency of existing programmes, funds can be freed up for additional programmes or for inclusion of additional sites in a given programme ('achieving more bang for the buck'). Moreover, demonstrating efficiency can be important in attracting new funding sources, particularly from the private sector.

Later we discuss the issues, potentials and challenges of improved PES targeting, focusing on three targeting criteria: environmental services (ES) provided, threat of ES loss in the absence of PES ('additionality') and costs of ES provision. In addition to drawing on previous approaches from the literature, we adapt results from Wünscher et al. (2006, 2008), where a spatial targeting tool was developed for the Nicoya Peninsula in Costa Rica. Other issues in PES design not considered here include poverty impacts (e.g., Engel and Palmer, 2008; Pagiola et al., 2005; Zbinden and Lee, 2005), leakage (e.g., Murray et al., 2002; Sohngen and Brown, 2004), dealing with weak property rights (Engel and Palmer, 2008), and whether to pay local communities or individuals (Rojahn and Engel, 2007).

The remainder of this chapter first highlights the basic idea of PES. It then continues to emphasize the importance of PES targeting and identifies the major challenges involved. Using examples from the literature, we then illustrate to what extent improved targeting can increase the efficiency of forest conservation spending. The challenges with regard to the implementation of improved targeting are discussed in the subsequent section. The chapter closes with our conclusions.[2]

Basic ideas of PES and the example of Costa Rica

PES is increasingly used as a direct instrument in conservation. Wunder et al. (2008) provide an overview of a number of government- and private sector-financed PES schemes functioning across the world. National programmes exist, for instance, in Mexico (see Alix-Garcia et al., Chapter 13 in this volume) and the United States (e.g., Claassen et al., 2008). The idea lies in translating external values of the environment into real financial incentives at the local level. PES is based on the 'beneficiary-pays' rather than the 'polluter-pays' principle, thus providing an alternative income source to local (often poor) landowners. Moreover, as various services may be provided jointly with the adoption of a single specific land use (e.g., forest conservation), payments for one specific 'umbrella' service (e.g., carbon stock conservation) can sometimes enhance the provision of other services (e.g., biodiversity conservation and hydrological services) as 'by-products'. With a growing demand for carbon mitigation and the chance to be integrated into a post-2012 carbon market, REDD has particular potential to act as an umbrella service.

One of the most well-known schemes, the Costa Rican national PES scheme (*Pagos por Servicios Ambientales* or PSA), is illustrative (Figure 12.1). In this scheme, the implementing agency, FONAFIFO,[3] bundles funding from various sources. While most funds are drawn primarily from the Costa Rican public through a national fuel tax, other sources include international donors and some private firms, for example, ones interested in improving or maintaining high water quality as an input to production. Payments are made by FONAFIFO to landowners in return for the latter adopting specific land-use practices. Forest conservation accounts for more than 90 per cent of current payments, i.e. the Costa Rican scheme is essentially a PES scheme for avoided deforestation and forest degradation. The remaining 10 per cent of current payments are made for the establishment of timber plantations, renovation of natural forests through land retirement and agroforestry. The programme explicitly recognizes four categories of environmental service: carbon mitigation, biodiversity conservation, hydrological services and scenic

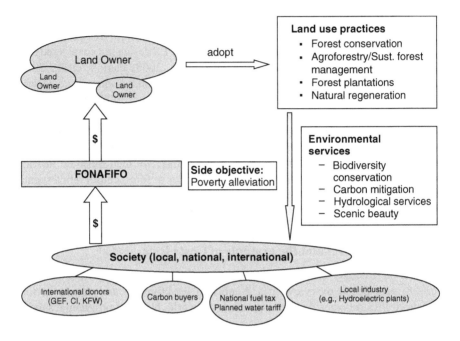

Figure 12.1 The Costa Rican PSA scheme

Source: Engel et al. (2007)

beauty. Poverty alleviation is a further side-objective of the programme (see Pagiola, 2008, for further details on the Costa Rican PSA programme).

Targeting: relevance and challenges

The Costa Rican example also highlights the relevance of PES targeting. By the end of 2004, 230,000 ha were under contract in the Costa Rican PSA programme. The number of applications far exceeded the available budget, with more than 800,000 ha of applications pending at the same time. Only sites from defined priority areas are eligible for programme entry, although exceptions are made. No differentiation of applicant sites is made within priority areas according to expected benefit delivery, and priority areas are coarsely defined: they cover nearly three-fifths (29,872 km²) of the national territory (51,101 km²) (own calculation based on data from ITCR, 2004).

Site enrolment into the programme is made on a continuous first-come-first-served basis. Payments are fixed as a flat rate for each land use (for example, US$64/ha/year since 2006 for forest conservation). Wünscher et al. (2008) developed a spatial targeting tool to demonstrate that the amount of environmental services achieved with a given conservation budget could be substantially enhanced through improved targeting. We considered three specific targeting criteria: benefits, threat levels and participation costs.

First, targeting could be based on the level of actual ES delivered from any given site. In the case of REDD policy, the main ES to consider would be carbon storage. Countries establishing a PES scheme to achieve REDD commitments may consider bundling REDD funding with other sources of funding aimed at different ES, as in the Costa Rican case. Biodiversity considerations are also often voiced in discussions on the setup of an international fund for REDD, such as the FCPF.

In practice, this poses the challenge of dealing with potential tradeoffs between multiple service provision objectives, choosing among or combining multiple indicators available even for single objectives and considering spatial interactions. For example, there may be significant synergies between the goals of achieving biodiversity protection and of preserving carbon stocks in standing forests, as both depend crucially on the preservation of existing habitat, avoiding its conversion or degradation; yet areas providing the highest carbon benefits are not necessarily also the most biodiversity-rich areas. Approaches that have been used in the literature to deal with multiple objectives and/or indicators include using a weighted sum of standardized indices (Pagiola et al., 2004) or applying a distance function (Ferraro, 2004). In Wünscher et al. (2008), we use the former approach, applying a z-value normalization[4] and equal weights both within and across objectives to compute a total ES score. In the case of REDD, we would include the carbon content of different vegetation types in the ES score vector (see Wünscher et al., 2008, for further details on data and indicators used).

A second targeting criterion to be considered is the spatially variable level of threat. Sites may have high ES scores, but may be at low or no threat to be deforested. This refers to the issue of additionality, discussed particularly in Chapters 10 (Harris et al.) and 11 (Pfaff and Robalino) in this volume. The additionality of Costa Rica's PSA programme has been highly debated (e.g., Pfaff et al., 2007; Sills et al., 2006). For example, Pfaff et al. (2007) find very low impact of the PSA scheme on deforestation. Considering threat in targeting poses the challenge of estimating spatially explicit baseline scenarios of deforestation. We know that spatial factors such as road building or other infrastructural investments have a powerful impact on deforestation, while remote areas due to the excessive transport costs remain under passive protection. Paying for the latter type of areas provides no additionality of service provision. Brown et al. (undated) lists three conceptual approaches to address this: analytical models (e.g., simple logistic curve based on population density), simulation (programming) models and regression models (see Harris et al., Chapter 10 in this volume, for a detailed discussion of baseline modelling). In Wünscher et al. (2008), we used the results and data from a spatially explicit regression model of Pfaff and Sanchez-Azofeifa (2004) in order to compute site-specific rates of expected deforestation in the absence of PES.

Finally, countries, regions and land users differ in their costs of ES provision. ES provision costs include opportunity costs (the difference in income between the most profitable land use and the one contracted under the PES scheme), direct conservation cost (e.g., firebreaks, fencing) and transaction costs (e.g., obtaining legal title, information gathering). Flat and fairly low per hectare payments, as in the Costa Rican PSA scheme, give high production rents to landowners with low to zero ES provision costs, while those with high provision costs are unlikely to participate in the scheme. When the opportunity costs of conservation within a target area are highly disparate, large cost inefficiencies can arise from a flat-rate payment approach. If a site has a high ES score and threat of deforestation, it may be worth paying more for its inclusion in the programme, while sites with low participation costs would likely still participate at lower payment levels. This implies that the amount of total ES achieved with a given budget could be increased by differentiating payments on the basis of participation costs, considering these costs as a third targeting criterion. However, estimating site-specific costs, particularly opportunity costs, can be challenging. Landowners may act strategically in reporting costs and a number of difficult-to-measure factors may influence individual opportunity costs or the minimum payment required to compensate for given costs (e.g., risk considerations, cultural preferences or distrust towards the service buyers).

The main approaches for estimating opportunity costs have included using land values, computing farm budgets or inferring values on the basis of farm and household data. Moreover, inverse auctions could be applied to elicit landowners' minimum willingness to accept for including a site in the programme, as for example in the US Conservation Reserve Programme and the Australian Bush Tender scheme (see Ferraro, 2008, for a discussion of auction design). In Wünscher et al. (2008), we used survey data to estimate ES provision costs, as will be described in the following section.

Improving the efficiency of PES through improved targeting

Wünscher et al. (2008) conducted a random sample of 107 forest owners in Nicoya Peninsula to compute site-specific per hectare estimates of returns from pasture, and used the spatially explicit data to compute the potential efficiency gains from improved targeting. Specifically, we developed a targeting tool that combines all three of the targeting criteria just listed to maximize ES additionality (defined as the total ES score multiplied by the expected probability of deforestation) with a given budget, while allowing for flexible payments equalling site-specific participation costs. The results were compared to a baseline scenario, in which sites are selected purely on the basis of whether they lie within the predefined priority areas and where payments are held fixed at a level of US$40/ha[5] (this baseline also sets the budget limit for the improved targeting scenario).

Given a fixed budget of US$30,028, we find that the total ES score and ES additionality both nearly doubled through improved targeting (from 52,148 to 98,259 and from 1969 to 4033, respectively). Similar results were found by Alix-Garcia et al. (2005; also Chapter 13 in this volume) for the Mexican PES scheme and by Ferraro (2003) for an easement programme for Lake Skaneateles in the USA. The former found a fourfold increase in efficiency through improved targeting while the latter shows that the non-consideration of benefit/cost information reduced environmental benefits obtained by more than 50 per cent. We also ran additional scenarios allowing for the consideration of only some of the targeting criteria. We found that most of the potential for efficiency gain in the Costa Rican context comes from flexible payments being customized to highly variable participation costs. However, in other countries with either higher average deforestation risks than in Costa Rica or marked spatial differences in site-specific service provision, these other factors could come to dominate the overall efficiency outcomes and boost the efficiency gains from targeting to levels that are much higher than in the Costa Rican case.

Challenges in implementing improved targeting

Implementing improved targeting is not without challenges. In addition to the aforementioned scientific challenges, administrative challenges include the fact that an application of our improved targeting tool would require simultaneous decisions on all applications after a deadline, rather than as now, continuously as applications are filed. Perhaps most importantly, targeting is likely to face political challenges, especially as it may be perceived as inequitable, thus diminishing popular (and voters') support, while channelling public scheme payments to selected recipients only. In particular, landowners may resist differential payments once homogenous payments have already been introduced, as these may be seen as arbitrary discrimination. Thus, transparency of the selection process is key. Inverse auctions where landowners pose bids of their minimum willingness to accept for being included in the scheme may be able to overcome this problem. However, if landowners are poor, and buyers are much better off, as is arguably the case in many REDD scenarios, it may be seen as unethical to squeeze service providers for the last cent of rent, in favour of maximizing returns to the service buyers. Contrariwise, implementing bodies may have latent side-objectives of their own (e.g., PSA may be seen as compensation for strict environmental legislation rather than for achieving additional environmental benefits). Finally, gross environmental efficiency gains need to be compared to the incremental transaction costs of targeting. In our study, we estimated these costs for Costa Rica to amount to approximately 0.27 per cent of the total PSA budget, thus being negligible with respect to the potential efficiency gains.

Conclusions

PES is an increasingly widespread instrument both for financing and implementing conservation. It is also a very relevant instrument in the context of REDD. The Costa Rican PSA scheme is often considered a leading model in this regard, but is currently being criticized for not being sufficiently efficient in achieving additional environmental benefits. With 90 per cent of the scheme's payments allocated to forest conservation, it is also a highly relevant example for the discussion of REDD. We find that improved targeting could substantially increase the efficiency of the programme, in the sense that total environmental services achieved with a given budget were found to nearly double when environmental benefits, threat and participation costs are jointly considered in site selection. This finding confirms similar results of studies conducted on PES in Mexico and the USA.

Moreover, efficiency should be considered more generally when upscaling PES (e.g., in form of a global fund of the FCPF type) or the selection among potential conservation projects. Nevertheless, targeting involves incremental implementation costs and may face scientific, administrative and, in particular, political challenges. Approaches for overcoming these challenges include:

- development of simple targeting tools
- improving data availability
- implementing targeting from the very start of a programme
- using inverse auctions to elicit individual participation costs.

There are thus several lessons to be learnt also for the design of nascent REDD mechanisms. Spatial variation in the service provided (carbon content) typically occurs across areas with respect to biophysical factors (regional differences in tree height and growth density) and the history of anthropogenic interventions (logging, burning, clearing or secondary regrowth), which in large forested regions such as the Amazon can lead to significant differences (Saatchi et al., 2007). Threat levels and opportunity costs may vary even more in space, thus introducing real dangers of paying for 'hot air' (protection of de facto unthreatened forest) and, conversely, offering insufficient payments to those with real intentions and motivation for forest clearing. REDD mechanisms should thus use local payments that are flexible in space, based on spatially explicit threat baselines and opportunity cost calculations.

Notes

1 The choice between direct policy instruments like PES and more indirect instruments (e.g., integrated conservation and development projects) is an efficiency issue in itself (see, for example, Ferraro, 2001; Ferraro and Kiss, 2002; Ferraro and Simpson, 2002; Swart et al., 2003). In general, this choice should be based on a careful analysis of the sources of market failure for a specific situation (Engel et al., 2008). In this chapter, we focus on the particular instrument of PES and on the issue of efficient instrument design. Nevertheless, similar considerations apply to conservation spending more generally.
2 This chapter is based on Engel et al. (2007).
3 *Fondo Nacional de Financiamiento Forestal.*
4 The z-normalization yields comparable scores with a mean equal to zero and standard deviation and variance equal to one.
5 The Costa Rican PSA programme used to pay US$40/ha/year before it was raised to US$64/ha/year in 2006.

References

Alix-Garcia, J., de Janvry, A. and Sadoulet, E. (2005) *The Role of Risk in Targeting Payments for Environmental Services* [online]. Available at: http://ssrn.com/abstract=836144 [accessed 12 August 2007].

Alix-Garcia, J., de Janvry, A. and Sadoulet, E. (2009) 'The role of risk in targeting payments for environmental services', in C. Palmer and S. Engel (eds) *Avoided Deforestation: Prospects for Mitigating Climate Change*, London: Routledge.

Brown, S., Hall, M., Andrasko, K., Ruiz, F., Marzoli, W., Guerrero, G. et al. (undated) *Baselines for Land-Use Change in the Tropics: Application to Avoided Deforestation Projects* [online]. Available at: http://ies.lbl.gov/iespubs/61456.pdf [accessed 10 April 2008].

Claassen, R., Cattaneo, A. and Johansson, R. (2008) 'Cost-effective design of agri-environmental payment programs: U.S. experience in theory and practice', *Ecological Economics*, 65(4): 737–752.

Engel, S., Pagiola, S. and Wunder, S. (2008) 'Designing payments for environmental services in theory and practice – an overview of the issues', *Ecological Economics*, 65(4): 663–674.

Engel, S. and Palmer, C. (2008) 'Payments for environmental services as an alternative to logging under weak property rights: the case of Indonesia', *Ecological Economics*, 65(4): 799–809.

Engel, S., Wünscher, T. and Wunder, S. (2007) 'Increasing the efficiency of conservation spending', in C.B. Schmitt, T. Pistorius and G. Winkel (eds) *A Global Network of Forest Protected Areas under the CBD: Opportunities and Challenges.* Proceedings of an international expert workshop held in Freiburg, Germany, 9–11 May 2007, *Freiburg Schriften zur Forst- und Umweltpolitik*, 16, Remagen: Kessel.

Ferraro, P. (2001) 'Global habitat protection: limitations of development interventions and a role for conservation performance payments', *Conservation Biology*, 15(4): 990–1000.

Ferraro, P. (2003) 'Conservation contracting in heterogenous landscapes: an application to watershed protection with threshold constraints', *Agricultural and Resource Economics Review*, 32(1): 53–64.

Ferraro, P. (2004) 'Targeting conservation investments in heterogenous landscapes: a distance function approach and application to watershed management', *American Journal of Agricultural Economics*, 86(4): 905–918.

Ferraro, P. (2008) 'Asymmetric information and contract design for payments for environmental services', *Ecological Economics*, 65(4): 810–821.

Ferraro, P. and Kiss, A. (2002) 'Direct payments to conserve biodiversity', *Science*, 298(5599): 1718–1719.

Ferraro, P. and Simpson, D. (2002) 'The cost-effectiveness of conservation payments', *Land Economics*, 78(3): 339–353.

ITCR (Instituto Tecnológico de Costa Rica) (2004) *Atlas Digital de Costa Rica*, Cartago: Escuela de Ingeniería Forestal.

Murray, B.C., McCarl, B.A. and Lee H. (2002) *Estimating Leakage from Forest Carbon Sequestration Programs*, Working Paper 02_06, Durham, NC: RTI (Research Triangle Institute) International.

Pagiola, S. (2008) 'Payments for environmental services in Costa Rica', *Ecological Economics*, 65(4): 712–724.

Pagiola, S., Agostini, P., Gobbi, J., de Haan, C., Ibrahim, M., Murqueitio, E. et al. (2004) *Paying for Biodiversity Conservation Services in Agricultural Landscapes*, Environment Department Paper 96, Environmental Economics Series, The World Bank Environment Department, Washington, DC: World Bank.

Pagiola, S., Arcenas, A. and Platais, G. (2005) 'Can payments for environmental services help reduce poverty? An exploration of the issues and the evidence to date from Latin America', *World Development*, 33(2): 237–253.

Pfaff, A., Robalino, J.A. and Sanchez-Azofeifa, G.A. (2007) *Payments for Environmental Services: Empirical Analysis for Costa Rica* [online]. Available at: http://www.apec.umn.edu/documents/AlexPfaffEnvirSem07.pdf [accessed 12 August 2008].

Pfaff, A. and Sanchez-Azofeifa, G.A. (2004) 'Deforestation pressure and biological reserve planning: a conceptual approach and an illustrative application for Costa Rica', *Resource and Energy Economics*, 26: 237–254.

Rojahn, A. and Engel, S. (2007) *Direct Payments for Biodiversity Conservation, Watershed Protection and Carbon Sequestration: Contract Theory and Empirical Evidence*, mimeo, Chair of Environmental Policy and Economics, ETH Zurich.

Saatchi, S.S., Houghton, R.A., dos Santos Alvala, R.C., Soares, J.V. and Yu, Y. (2007) 'Distribution of aboveground live biomass in the Amazon Basin', *Global Change Biology*, 13(4): 816–837.

Sills, E., Arriagada, R., Pattanayak, S., Ferraro, F., Carrasco, L., Ortiz, E. et al. (2006) *Impact of the PSA Program on Land Use*, paper presented at the Workshop on Costa Rica's Experience with Payments for Environmental Services, San José, 25–26 September 2006.

Sohngen, B. and Brown, S. (2004) 'Measuring leakage from carbon projects in open economies: a stop timber harvesting project in Bolivia as a case study', *Canadian Journal of Forest Research*, 34: 829–839.

Swart, J.A.A., Ferraro, P.J. and Kiss, A. (2003) 'Will direct payments help biodiversity?', *Science*, 299(5615): 1981–1982.

Wunder, S. (2005) *Payments for Environmental Services: Some Nuts and Bolts*, CIFOR Occasional Paper 42, Bogor: Center for International Forestry Research (CIFOR).

Wunder, S., Engel, S. and Pagiola, S. (2008) 'Taking stock: lessons learnt for the design of payments for environmental services programs', *Ecological Economics*, 65(4): 834–852.

Wünscher, T., Engel, S. and Wunder, S. (2006) 'Payments for environmental services in Costa Rica: increasing efficiency through spatial differentiation', *Quarterly Journal of International Agriculture*, 45(4): 319–337.

Wünscher, T., Engel, S. and Wunder, S. (2008) 'Spatial targeting of payments for environmental services: a tool for boosting conservation benefits', *Ecological Economics*, 65(4): 822–833.

Zbinden, S. and Lee, D.R. (2005), 'Paying for environmental services: an analysis of participation in Costa Rica's PSA program', *World Development*, 33(2): 255–272.

13 Role of risk in targeting payments for environmental services

Jennifer Alix-Garcia, Alain de Janvry and Elisabeth Sadoulet

Introduction

Programmes of payments for environmental services (PES)[1] are becoming an increasingly popular way of creating, conserving and restoring natural resources throughout the world. Mayrand and Paquin (2004) inventoried more than 300 such schemes. In recent years, PES programmes have increasingly been implemented in developing countries, with one of the earliest efforts occurring in Costa Rica in 1997 and pilot programmes mushrooming throughout Latin America and Asia (World Bank, 2005). Payments for the conservation of standing forests are among the most numerous of such programmes.

The targeting strategy in these programmes has typically been to pay a flat fee per hectare of standing forest, where the forest owners whose forests fall in specific geographical regions voluntarily enrol hectares but where there is a limit on the number of allowable hectares. Examples of this type of targeting can be found in Ecuador (Echavarría, 2002) and in Costa Rica and Mexico (Zbinden and Lee, 2005; Wünscher et al., 2008), among others. China's 'Grain for Green' also implements flat payment strategies, although they pay for conservation activities such as reforestation rather than standing forests (Uchida et al., 2005). The appeal of this sort of strategy clearly lies in its transparency, ease of implementation and impression of fairness. Unfortunately, it is highly unlikely that one could find a situation in which such a scheme would maximize the environmental benefits accrued per dollar spent. Given limited budgets for conservation, the search for an efficient, readily implementable targeting scheme is imperative. In this chapter, we use the case of Mexico to illustrate the efficiency gain in including the risk of deforestation in the targeting criteria for payments for environmental amenities provided by standing forest.

There is a growing literature on cost effective targeting of conservation programmes, much of it inspired by the US Conservation Reserve Program (Babcock et al., 1996, 1997). The main preoccupation of much of the current research is with the proper way to measure environmental amenities. Daily et al. (2000) discuss the general requirements for sound valuation of environmental services, recognizing the importance of uncertainty in the ecosystem relationships underlying such techniques. Several economists have proposed biodiversity metrics, including the total species measure of Ando et al. (1998), Ferraro's (2004) distance function approach and Weitzman's (1998) expected genetic diversity ranking. Ferraro (2003) compares the impacts of several different index measurements for water quality benefits and finds that all of them are highly correlated. For carbon services, markets exist to establish at least lower bound prices. The actual contribution of specific tracts of land, be they forest, agricultural land or restored ecosystems, is more highly debated. It requires models that take into account sequestration capacity of various ecosystems, as well as release of carbon as waste or from soils. Newell and Stavins (2000), as well as Stavins (1999) have examined the costs of carbon sequestration by forests, finding considerably lower benefit to cost ratios for avoiding deforestation rather that promoting afforestation and a thorough review of the literature can be found in Richards and Stokes (2004).

Our contribution to this discussion is to point out that regardless of the choice of amenity measure, it is a waste of money to pay for amenities that are at no risk of being lost. Mexico provides an excellent opportunity for studying payments for services provided by forests, in large part because it is in the early stages of implementing a nationwide PES programme for standing forest. The programme objective is to preserve forest in overexploited watersheds in order to help address the increasingly pressing problem of water scarcity in Mexico. Since the implementation of this programme in 2002, the government has also established a parallel programme to pay for the preservation of forests providing biodiversity and carbon sequestration services. The conclusions of this chapter apply equally to all PES programmes that depend on preservation of existing ecosystems. This presents the problem of potentially paying for activities that individuals would have undertaken even in the absence of payments, a challenge that is perhaps not unique to PES programmes.

Presently, 80 per cent of Mexico's forests are located in *ejidos*. These communities, which were created by the post-revolution land reform, hold their forestry and grazing lands in common property. Their large share of national forest holdings makes them an essential place in which to begin addressing the deforestation problem. Using data obtained from a 2002 *ejido* survey, we compare the following three targeting strategies for payment based on the analysis conducted in Alix-Garcia et al. (2008):

1   *Flat payment per hectare, H*: a flat payment over all forested hectares with a cap on the number of hectares per enrolee. This scheme is used as a reference as it is similar to that currently observed in many existing PES programmes.
2   *Risk-weighted flexible payments, R*: a payment for all hectares at risk of deforestation at the level of income potentially generated by the deforested land, without a budget constraint or a cap.
3   *Benefit-maximizing payments, B*: a payment that maximizes the expected environmental benefits per dollar paid using an index of environmental value and is equal to the potential income generated by hectare at risk, for a given budget and without a cap.

The main result of these simulations is that, while the benchmark scheme, H, is very egalitarian, it is highly inefficient in terms of environmental benefits per dollar spent. The risk-weighted flexible payments scheme, R, generates more than three times the environmental benefits at the same cost as the flat payments programme, H. Simulation of the expected benefit-maximizing programme, B, increases efficiency over the flat payments programme, H, by approximately a factor of four. The intuition behind the result is simple: paying everyone to preserve their forest may achieve the goal of income redistribution, but at a high cost – much of the payments will go to forests which would remain standing even in the absence of incentive schemes.

A targeting strategy based on previous deforestation behaviour has the potential to change an individual's propensity to cut down forest – if one *ejido* observes that another received payments as a result of cutting down trees, they may decide to engage in this activity themselves in order to receive future payments. In order to illustrate how to avoid such strategic behaviour on the part of recipients, we conduct a final simulation which uses the predicted rather than actual risk to implement the benefit-maximizing programme B. Here, we find that there are errors in targeting, but that efficiency is still much greater than in a flat payments programme.

Since policymaking is often concerned about the tradeoffs between efficiency and equity, we analyze the distributional impacts of the first and the last schemes that we consider. The results show that the budget from the flat payments programme, H, is more equitably distributed among *ejidos* of different size and poverty classes, while the benefit-maximizing programme, B, allocates more funds to larger and poorer communities. Programme B, however, gives smaller payments to poor *ejidos* on a per capita basis, while flat payments per capita are equal for the poor and non-poor.

The chapter proceeds as follows. We begin by discussing the context surrounding PES programmes. Then we describe the theoretical considerations behind the different targeting strategies under consideration, which leads us to the empirical strategy. The following sections describe the data to be used for the simulations and the results. Some practical considerations for the implementation of our most efficient strategy are discussed before the final section and conclusion of the chapter.

Alternative payment schemes: theoretical considerations

There are many possible ways of designing an environmental payment scheme. Any variation in design will change the kind of environmental services obtained and the identity of the people who receive payments. Conceptually, there are lower and upper bounds on the 'prices' that one can pay per hectare in a PES programme: the opportunity cost of the land and the value of the environmental services provided by the land, respectively. In this section, we discuss some principles that apply regardless of the programme design chosen.

Basic principles

Two essential criteria for the establishment of a PES programme are targeting and payment magnitude. In theory, these should be jointly defined to maximize environmental benefits for a given budget. The optimal scheme, therefore, depends on how the recipients make their deforestation decisions. Each *ejido* has an optimal deforestation level, which depends on the size of its forest, the income it might earn from cutting it down and the characteristics of the *ejido* itself. This deforestation level generates benefits for the *ejido*, both monetary and non-monetary. The *ejido* will accept a contract not to deforest only if the payment offer exceeds the deforestation benefits.

Ideally, one would like to know the monetary value equivalent to the total benefits in terms of 'utility' (a measure of well-being) that *ejidos* derive from the remaining standing forest, as well as the utility from the income that they earn from hectares of land that they deforest. Standing forest benefits include use of the forest for recreation, hunting, collection of firewood and other potential forest goods. The foregone income from deforestation includes the value of alternative agricultural or pastoral activities and the utility cost also measures any pleasure individuals might have derived from undertaking the productive activities. The optimal deforestation rate for the community is therefore a function of the size of the initial standing forest, the potential income per hectare of the forest and community characteristics. In the absence of an accurate valuation of foregone income and benefits from standing forest, one can use the foregone income as a lower bound of the acceptability of the scheme to the *ejido*, which amounts to ignoring both the non-pecuniary gains from changing productive activities as well as the benefits of the remaining standing forest.

We assume that *ejidos* accept the payment and agree not to deforest if the payment is at least as high as the foregone income of converting the land into pasture/crops and reject the contract if the offered payment is below this amount. The question that follows is: should one pay the minimum value necessary to preserve the environmental benefits, i.e. the potential income of the land, or the entire value of the good being purchased, i.e. the environmental benefit? In reality, this is a question of property rights. In both cases, payments can only be socially justified if the benefits offered by the land are greater than or equal to the value of the land in alternative activities.

Note that the optimal contract only pays for the hectares that would otherwise be deforested, which varies with the deforestation rate. In actuality, one frequently observes a flat payment per hectare of currently standing forest with a cap, or limit on the number of hectares enrolled in the programme. In many places, this payment varies with forest quality to reflect variation in benefits, but the point here is that it does not depend on the deforestation rate. An argument in favour of this flat payment is the simplicity of implementation and the impression of fairness that it gives, as it does not take into account deforestation behaviour.

Regardless of the choice of targeting scheme, the contract must be made over the entire area of the *ejido*. Neglecting this consideration could lead to 'leakage' or 'slippage' (a term coined by Wu, 2000), that is, if a contract is incomplete, then deforestation may simply be transferred from a contracted to an uncontracted area of forest. Hence, typically, the contract should specify a payment against no deforestation on all of the hectares that have a level of foregone income (or opportunity cost) below their environmental benefits.

Proposed simulations

In this section, we specify the alternative payment schemes that are simulated. Building from the theoretical considerations established in Alix-Garcia et al. (2008), we have selected three payment schemes:

1   A flat payment over all hectares with a cap, with the objective of simulating a scheme similar to those observed in most current schemes [*H*].
2   A payment for all hectares at risk of deforestation at their opportunity cost [*R*] without a budget constraint. The total budget of this programme provides the constraint for [*H*], where payments are set at a rate that gives the same aggregate budget as *R*.
3   A targeted payment that maximizes environmental benefits per dollar paid using an index of environmental benefits (as opposed to actual benefits in dollar terms) and a payment at opportunity cost for each hectare at risk, for a given budget (here arbitrarily set at two-thirds of the budget of the first scheme to illustrate how the budget constraint could be optimally dealt with) [*B*].

Flat payment, H

We assume a flat payment per hectare, up to a maximum number of hectares, as is the case in the current programme in Mexico and as one also observes in Costa Rica. The total payment to an *ejido* is thus the rate per hectare multiplied by either the sum of all forest hectares or by the maximum allowable hectares, whichever is smaller. All *ejidos* are offered a contract, but an *ejido* will only accept the contract and thus participate in the scheme if the opportunity cost of the area it would otherwise deforest is less than the offer. In order to facilitate comparison of the schemes, the rate is established at the level that equalizes the total budget to the budget of the scheme *R*, which pays the opportunity cost for each hectare of land at risk of deforestation and will be detailed in the next section.

Rental of hectares at risk, R

We allow for heterogeneity of environmental benefits within *ejidos*, meaning that each hectare of forest is characterized by an environmental benefit associated with that type of forest. Ideally, one would prefer an actual monetary value for the environmental benefits offered by a given piece of land. In reality, however, this is quite difficult to establish, as markets are missing for many of these services and, when they do exist, as in the case of carbon, it is unclear whether they reflect the true value of the good. For the purpose of our simulations, we establish an index value that allows for the ranking of each hectare of forest by its relative environmental value, for example, tons of CO_2 sequestered per hectare. Note that this does not allow us to exclude lands with a true environmental value that is less than the potential income generated by the deforested land.

It is important to clarify that this type of payment scheme should vary over time. To see why this is the case, consider the following logic: if an *ejido* wishes to deforest 10 hectares per year, the first year of the programme they need to be paid for 10 hectares of potential deforestation. The second year, they need to be paid for the 10 hectares that they wanted to convert in the previous year, plus the 10 that they intended to convert in the second year. The logic continues in subsequent years. If the programme is to prevent deforestation over time, it should thus 'rent' an increasing share of the forest. Payments based on the income-generating potential, assuming that the environmental benefits of all hectares exceed this number would be the sum over all the hectares to be deforested multiplied by the income they would have generated. Because we are paying exactly compensating participants for their lost income, *ejidos* are assumed to accept the contract.[2] The participating *ejidos* are only those that would otherwise deforest. Note that the contract is for no deforestation on the total initial *ejido* area with income potential below environmental benefits.

In the rest of the analysis, since we are only concerned with comparing programmes, we will only consider the first year of payment. Assuming that all communities have a fixed deforestation rate or that any changes in the rate occur equally for all communities, calculating programme outcomes for the first year will give us the same relative results for payment schemes that depend on deforestation risk.

Note that by restricting ourselves to the first year of payments we are showing the flat payment scheme in the best possible light. That is to say, since the flat payments do not change over time unlike the opportunity cost, the first year gives the maximum number of communities that will accept the payments at any given time.

Benefit-maximizing programme, B

If the total payments to communities exceed the available budget, the optimal scheme consists of ranking the *ejidos* by a decreasing ratio of benefits over potential income and paying the potential income of the hectares at risk of deforestation to those with the highest ratio until the budget is exhausted.

Description of the data

In the summer of 2002 Mexico's National Ecology Institute (INE), together with the Iberoamericana University, the Center for Economic Education and Research (CIDE), the University of California at Berkeley and the World Bank, conducted a survey of Mexican *ejidos*. The purpose of the survey was to understand the deforestation process in these communities in order to inform the design of a PES programme[3] that the Mexican government was interested in introducing. The survey randomly sampled 407 *ejidos* larger than 100 hectares located in the forested

Table 13.1 Distribution of forest ejido universe by region

Region	Total number of ejidos	Percentage of population	Number of sampled ejidos	Percentage of sample
Central	2488	32.4	122	29.6
Gulf	795	10.4	37	9.5
North	1499	19.5	99	24.2
Peninsula	745	9.7	39	10.0
South	2152	28.0	110	26.8
Total	**7679**	**100**	**407**	**100**

Source: Instituto Nacional de Ecología, Mexico

regions of the country. The total amount of *ejidos* with forest over 100 hectares is 7679. The total amount of forest covered by our sample is 2,106,592 hectares of primary and secondary forest. Table 13.1 shows the distribution of communities across regions.

The sample included *ejidos* in all states with the exception of Baja California, Coahuila, Guanajuato, Zacatecas, Morelos and Aguascalientes. In order to measure forest cover and its change over time, we use the Forest Inventories for 1994 and 2000, which were constructed by visual interpretation from satellite images with pixels of 30 metres at a scale of 1:250,000 (Velázquez et al., 2002). In addition, we obtained slope measurements from digital elevation models with 100-metre pixels from the Mexican government.

Overall, 86 per cent of the *ejidos* in our sample currently have primary forest. The area of primary forests is largely related to *ejido* size, which varies considerably across *ejidos*. Total *ejido* area ranges from 180 to 170,143 hectares in our sample. The average percentage of a given *ejido* in primary forest is 34.7 per cent. On a per capita basis, the distribution of forest is quite skewed. Though the average number of hectares per capita is 37, the median is 6.5 and the Gini coefficient[4] 0.83. This suggests that any payment programme disbursed on a per hectare basis will be similarly unequal in its distribution across communities and individual members.

The deforestation rate over the total forest in our sample is 1.2 per cent per year from 1994 to 2000, which is comparable to what Torres-Rojo and Flores-Xolocotzi (2001) term the 'conservative estimate' of 1.3 per cent per year. In our sample, the average *ejido* deforested about 1.3 per cent per year over the period 1994–2000. Sixty-one per cent of the *ejidos* in the sample deforested over the study period, where deforestation is defined as the change from primary or secondary forest to agriculture or pasture. Among those who deforest, the average rate of forest loss is 2.1 per cent per year.

Empirical results

Calculation of the cost

In order to measure the opportunity cost of forested land, we use the rainfed land rental rates reported in the 2002 *ejido* survey. Because *ejido* land cannot actually be

Table 13.2 Prediction of rainfed land rental rate as US$ per hectare of land per year

Variable	Coefficient	T-statistic
Average distance from village to forest (km)	−48.9	1.7
Average distance (km) squared	2.1	1.5
Average altitude of forest (m)	−0.13	1.3
Average slope of forest	10.8	1.1
Distance · slope	−0.45	0.53
Distance · altitude	0.02	1.3
Total size in 1000 ha	1.2	3.7
State level maize yield per ha	68.5	2.2
Yield · slope	−4.3	1.5
Yield · altitude	−0.02	1.3
Distance to nearest town (km)	−0.17	0.88
Constant	237.5	1.5
Observations	91	
R-squared	0.23	

Source: Authors

rented, the numbers reported were the farmers' assessment of the land rental rate for a piece of land *similar to the one* that had been deforested. These rates were observed for those *ejidos* that experienced deforestation and refer to areas from which forest had been removed between 1994 and 2000. We consider this rate to be a fair estimate of the opportunity cost of the land that is most likely to be deforested, although it is unlikely to be as accurate for the more remote areas of the *ejido*. Since this rate was not reported for some *ejidos*, we use as a measure of the opportunity cost the value of the rental rate predicted by the regression equation in Table 13.2. The average rental rate per hectare is US$103 US (standard deviation: US$70) and the Gini coefficient of the per hectare rate is 0.37.

Calculation of the environmental benefits index

Ideally, environmental benefits should be expressed in monetary terms. This requires use of a valuation technique for services with missing markets. In the case of carbon, one could use existing market prices as a lower bound estimate, although one would still need to understand how standing forest translates into carbon values. For services where markets do not exist, such as hydrological benefits, values remain highly debated, with estimates ranging from US$20/ha (Chomitz et al., 1999) to US$188 (Hernández et al., 2003).[5] Hesitant to enter into this valuation debate, we have instead established an environmental index based on both the scale of payments for the existing PES scheme in Mexico and the country's environmental priorities. The details of this calculation can be found in Alix-Garcia et al. (2008). Table 13.3 describes the values that we use for ranking the environmental benefits provided by different types of forest in different locations. The average benefits per hectare are 30.6 points (standard deviation 5.3) and the Gini coefficient is 0.11.

Table 13.3 Environmental index

Characteristic	Points per hectare
Cloud forest	
Primary	40
Secondary	30
Other types of forest	
Primary	30
Secondary	20
Added to each hectare of above:	
Overexploited watershed	5
Within $\frac{1}{2}$ mile of a river	
Primary	20
Secondary	10

Source: Authors

Payments and participation

To compare the payment schemes, we begin by assuming perfect foresight in predicting deforestation by using the observed deforestation rate between 1993 and 2000. We will relax this assumption later in the chapter by using a predictive equation for deforestation in discussing implementation of the optimal scheme. We simulate the three schemes as if they were put into place in 1994 with observation of the results one year later. The results are reported in Tables 13.4 and 13.5. The flat payment (H) ended up being US$5 per hectare with the opportunity costs budget as a constraint. This level is actually considerably lower than the rates used in the actual programme in Mexico, which vary between US$40 and US$60 per hectare. In the risk-weighted payment programme, R, all the deforesting *ejidos* (61 per cent of the sample) are paid in 1994, although the payments are quite unequally distributed,

Table 13.4 Summary of payments and participants in different programmes

	Payment rule		
	Flat payment with a cap at 2000 ha	Opportunity cost for forest at risk	Opportunity cost for forest at risk with highest environmental benefit per US$ paid
	H	R	B
Percentage of ejidos enrolled	87	61	57
Average payment per participating ejido (US$)	7341	10,202	7418
Median payment per participating ejido (US$)	7234	1744	1586
Gini coefficient of payments over participants	0.32	0.81	0.77

Source: Authors

Table 13.5 Costs and benefits of different payment programmes

	Payment rule		
	Flat payment	Opportunity cost for forest at risk	Opportunity cost for forest at risk with highest environmental benefit per opportunity cost
	H	R	B
Total hectares enrolled	1,022,133	1,836,535	1,534,405
Hectares at risk enrolled	6732	22,667	19,225
Environmental benefits	216,378	682,643	606,729
Total budget (US$)	2,598,870	2,550,596	1,713,509
Efficiency (environmental benefits/opportunity cost)	0.08	0.27	0.35

Source: Authors

with a Gini coefficient of 0.81. In the flat payments programme H, the participation rate is much higher, at 87 per cent, due to the fact that many *ejidos* without deforestation participate, although some deforesters with an opportunity cost higher than the flat payment offer do not. The distribution of these payments is much more equitable, with a Gini coefficient of 0.32. In the optimal constrained programme, B, where we use two-thirds of the budget of the first programme, 57 per cent of *ejidos* participate, and the Gini coefficient is 0.77, indicating a high inequality of payment distribution.

Table 13.5 highlights the tradeoffs that exist between the inequality of the programmes R and B and their efficiencies. The total number of hectares deforested in the sample between 1994 and 2000 is 22,667, which is the amount enrolled in the opportunity cost programme. Despite its higher participation, the flat payments programme enrols less than one-third of the total hectares at risk of deforestation, 6732 hectares. Moreover, the amount of environmental benefits per dollar spent (or 'efficiency level'), at 0.08, is also less than one-third of that of the opportunity costs programme. This is due to the fact that it enrols many *ejidos* that do not have positive deforestation. The optimal distribution of the constrained budget, programme B, shown in column three, results in the enrolment of 19,225 hectares, which is nearly all those at risk and an efficiency level of 0.35, four times higher than that of the flat payments scheme.

Table 13.6 illustrates another measure of efficiency – the dollar amount paid for each hectare at risk of deforestation. This number was calculated only for those *ejidos* with positive deforestation and corresponds to the overall payment divided by the number of hectares deforested. Note that this is extremely large for the flat payment scheme H (despite the fact that those with zero deforestation cannot be included) at US$7610 per hectare and smallest for the optimal strategy, which pays US$86 per hectare, on average. This very high number for the flat payments results from the fact that a very high price is paid for hectares that have a very low risk of

Table 13.6 Payments per hectare at risk of deforestation

	Payment rule		
	Flat payment	Opportunity cost for forest at risk	Opportunity cost for forest at risk with highest environmental benefit per opportunity cost
	H	R	B
Mean payment per hectare at risk (US$)	7610	96	86
Minimum payment per hectare at risk (US$)	34	5	5
Maximum payment per hectare at risk (US$)	654,222	331	275

Source: Authors

deforestation. This is effectively a form of leakage of programme funds to non-critical forests, i.e. reflecting a lack of additionality in provision of forest environmental services.

Who gets the payments?

In this section, we examine the distribution of both the flat payments programme, H, and programme B over different structural and social characteristics of participants. Table 13.7 shows the distribution of the flat payments programme, H, and the more efficient payments B over size and poverty classes. In the case of the payments by poverty class, we consider per capita receipts rather than total payments. This is calculated under the simplifying assumption that payments at the community level will be shared equally among members. Participation in programme H is much higher in all area classes, while it increases across classes in the programme B. This is due to the fact that the number of hectares deforested in larger communities is higher. Efficiency, which is relatively constant across distance classes in programme B, is increasing with area in the flat payments programme because as the properties get larger, the flat payments programme is more likely to enrol hectares at risk of deforestation. There is an interesting result with regards to equity. Although participation in both programmes is higher for the poor than it is for the non-poor, it is relatively greater in B – 63 versus 50 per cent – than it is in H – 89 versus 85 per cent. In addition, the optimal programme allocates a greater share of the budget to the poor – 61 as opposed to 54 per cent. At an individual level, however, we find that payments per capita to the poor, US$51, are much lower than to the non-poor, who receive US$135 per capita. This is likely the result of the smaller endowments of environmentally valuable resources (as measured by the benefits index) among poorer and indigenous *ejidos*, which are also likely to have more members among whom to divide the payments.

Table 13.7 Distribution of payments from schemes H and B over ejido size and poverty classes

Area and distance classes	Participation rate (%)		Average payment per community (US$)		Efficiency		Percentage of overall budget	
	H	B	H	B	H	B	H	B
Area								
1st quartile	97	43	3216	1006	0.04	0.39	11	2
2nd quartile	91	50	6748	3371	0.04	0.29	23	10
3rd quartile	88	67	9698	4054	0.08	0.35	33	16
4th quartile	74	71	11,300	17,325	0.14	0.36	32	72
Poverty								
Non-poor	85	50	120	135	0.06	0.30	46	39
Poor	89	63	120	51	0.10	0.39	54	61

Source: Authors

Note
The thresholds for the area quartiles are 1240, 2270 and 5160 hectares. The distance threshold is 27 kilometres. The threshold level for the poor is 53% of the population predicted to receive oportunidades.

Implementation with predicted deforestation rate, I

In order to implement payment schemes that take deforestation risk into account, it is necessary to use the predicted rather than the actual deforestation rate. Using the actual rate to predict hectares at risk would induce strategic behaviour on the part of *ejidos* – that is to say, an *ejido* that did not deforest might see that its neighbour received payments to stop its deforestation and then decide to engage in the same behaviour in order to receive a payment. This section focuses on the application of two different predictions of the deforestation rate to the most efficient programme. Whatever prediction is chosen, it must be based *exclusively* on determinants that are truly exogenous to the behaviour of the *ejido* (so that the scheme does not reward bad behaviour), i.e., physical endowments of the *ejido* (area of different types of land, maybe on a per capita basis) and structural characteristics such as distance, population, ethnicity, etc. We assume a uniform deforestation rate per *ejido* (i.e. all forest types have the same deforestation rate) and perform the estimation on the observed sample of *ejidos*.

Armed with this analysis, we simulate the most efficient scheme based on the predicted deforestation rate as follows: we first rank *ejidos* by decreasing ratio of environmental benefits over opportunity cost (which is independent of the deforestation rate), as before. We then pay the predicted deforestation multiplied by the expected opportunity cost per hectare starting with those with the highest benefits per dollar until the budget is exhausted.

A specific *ejido* will accept the scheme if the payment compares favourably to the income it might have generated on deforested land. Since the predicted deforestation rate will necessarily equal the average deforestation rate for all *ejidos* with the same characteristics,[6] *ejidos* with higher actual deforestation rates than this average will not accept the contract. Conversely, all *ejidos* with predicted rates lower than the average are compensated for their 'good' behaviour by being paid a larger amount than they need to be paid. For example, suppose that the average deforestation rate for 1000 hectare *ejidos* with an average altitude of 700 metres is 200 hectares. All *ejidos* with these two characteristics will be predicted to have a deforestation rate of 200 hectares per year. Some of them will, of course, actually want to deforest 150 hectares and others 220. The compensation scheme, however offers the same payment to all of these – 200 multiplied by the potential foregone income. The *ejido* that has an actual deforestation rate of 220 hectares would reject this offer, while the *ejido* with an actual deforestation rate of 150 hectares will happily accept it. The programme can offer a slightly higher payment by adding a small amount to all the predicted deforestation rates. By proposing a slightly higher payment, the programme faces a tradeoff in paying more than necessary for many *ejidos* but attracting more of them into the scheme. It follows that the optimal value for the payment level, that is, the correct amount by which to increase each payment is determined by balancing out this tradeoff.

Two prediction equations

We present in Table 13.8 two different prediction equations for deforestation. The first is a parsimonious specification, containing only easily observable, mostly

Table 13.8 Prediction equations for deforestation

Variable	Parsimonious specification	Full specification
Total area of the ejido in hectares	0.01 (0.91)	0.01 (1.22)
Hectares of forest in 1994	0.09 (3.58)**	0.09 (3.58)**
Forest squared	$3 \cdot 10^{-6}$ (2.95)*	$-3 \cdot 10^{-6}$ (2.98)**
Forest cubed	$3 \cdot 10^{-11}$ (2.41)*	$3 \cdot 10^{-11}$ (2.95)*
Percentage of total area in forest, 1994	−20.1 (2.50)	−18.5 (2.25)
Average distance to forested area	−3.4 (0.29)	−9.9 (0.83)
Average slope of forested area	6.9 (0.75)	−8.6 (0.93)
Average altitude of forested area in metres	−0.09 (1.45)	−0.12 (1.89)
Average distance · average slope	−1.2 (1.36)	−1.1 (1.20)
Average distance · average altitude	0.01 (1.91)	0.02 (1.91)
Ejido practises forestry	84.7 (1.16)	94.8 (1.17)
Number of ejidatarios in 1990		−0.31 (1.06)
Gini coefficient of private parcels		−1.06 (2.82)*
Membership ratio · forestry ejido		−39.70 (0.44)
Ratio of members to total population in ejido		−4.75 (3.04)**
Gini coefficient of private parcels		−206.9 (1.53)
Predicted proportion of population receiving progresa	−144.2 (0.40)	
Constant	145.34 (1.21)	704.84 (2.70)**
Observations	395	395
Adjusted R-squared	0.38	0.42

Source: Authors

Notes
Robust t-statistics in parentheses.
* significant at 5% level.
** significant at 1% level.

physical variables, while the second includes a range of variables associated with deforestation behaviour in common property communities (see Alix-Garcia et al., 2005). The former represents a technique suitable for application in policy settings. The intention of presenting both options is to see how much targeting precision is lost in omitting variables representing community behaviour.

The first estimation includes total *ejido* area, forest area, forest squared and forest cubed, the average distance to, slope and altitude of the forested area of the *ejido*, interactions of these terms, the number of *ejido* members in 1990 and a dummy for whether or not the *ejido* practises forestry. The fact that community members cannot easily manipulate these variables helps avoid the problem of strategic behaviour – where *ejidos* change their actions or characteristics in order to receive payments. Among these variables, the largest impacts on deforestation are through the size of the forest in 1994, the average slope of the forested area and whether or not the *ejido* practises forestry. The second specification includes, in addition to the physical variables, some characteristics that might influence group behaviour, such as the number of people per household with secondary education, the average size of individual parcels, the Gini coefficient of the distribution of private parcels, the ratio of members to total population in the *ejido*[7] and the predicted proportion of the population receiving *oportunidades* – an educational subsidy programme distributed to the poor. The largest impacts come from the Gini coefficient and the predicted proportion of the population receiving *oportunidades*. The second specification shows a small gain in the regression adjusted R-squared over the parsimonious specification – from 0.38 to 0.42. This suggests that the second specification has superior predictive power over the first, although this difference is not appreciably large. In general, however, an R-squared of 0.38 is quite respectable for such a cross-sectional estimation.

Since there is not much gain from the expansion of the variable set in (2), with only a small change in R-squared, Table 13.9 shows the payments calculated using only the parsimonious (1) specification. The efficiency level is considerably lower than that of the most efficient programme using the actual deforestation rates, at 0.35, but is still twice as efficient as the flat payments' 0.08. As in the actual

Table 13.9 Summary of payments and participants in predicted deforestation programme

Payment rule	Specification
Percentage of participating ejidos	50
Average payment per participating ejido	US$8744
Median payment per participating ejido	US$2058
Gini coefficient of payments over participants	0.77
Total hectares enrolled	1,197,210
Hectares at risk enrolled	7822
Environmental benefits	265,691
Total budget	US$1,757,652
Efficiency (environmental benefits/opportunity cost)	0.15
Payment level (μ)	0.009

Source: Authors

Table 13.10 Errors in payment distribution result from predictions

Characteristics	Did not receive payments but should have (Type I)	Received payments and should have	Received payments and should not have (Type II)
Number	121	109	92
Tot Actual size in hectares	5106	10,872	2647
Hectares of forest, 1993	4029	9567	1678
Average deforestation rate	0.031	0.010	0
Predicted deforestation rate	0.014	0.014	0.016
Predicted proportion of progresa recipients	0.52	0.54	0.53
Average environmental benefits per hectare	30.2	34	66
Average opportunity cost per hectare	US$105	US$66	US$72

Source: Authors

programme, the Gini coefficient of payments for the predicted programme is considerably higher than that of the flat payments programme, which has a value of 0.32.

This leads us to the question of where the misallocation of payments occurs. Table 13.10 shows the characteristics of communities with payments in different error categories. The type II error comes entirely from deforestation rates that are estimated to be positive for *ejidos* that, in reality, had no deforestation. These communities also have very high benefits and low opportunity costs, which means they ranked quite high on the benefits to cost scale. Communities with type I error have very high deforestation rates (and were under-predicted). In addition, their opportunity costs are large relative to the benefits that their land provides.

In sum, the more worrying type I error comes from *ejidos* with very high opportunity costs and very high rates of deforestation. These are also communities with somewhat low environmental benefits per hectare. In avoiding the strategic behaviour associated with using observed deforestation rates, we end up with a lower level of environmental benefits per dollar spent, although this is still nearly twice as high as the efficiency level generated by using a flat payments programme.

Conclusion

The most important contribution of this chapter is to point out that including risk into the targeting of environmental services programmes can greatly increase their efficiency. We illustrate this point by comparing a flat payment scheme to a scheme that takes into account the risk of deforestation. We simulate three programmes: a flat payment scheme, a payment of potential income for each hectare of forest at risk of deforestation and, in order to illustrate the optimal manner of dealing with a budget constraint, a programme that distributes payments according to the highest benefit/cost ratio and pays the opportunity cost for each hectare of forest at risk of deforestation. Comparing these approaches, we find that the most egalitarian approach is to pay a flat rate per hectare per year but to cap the number of allowable hectares. This is also the least efficient strategy in terms of environmental benefit per dollar spent. The highest efficiency comes from maximizing environmental benefits per dollar spent. The driving force behind these results is the lack of additionality inherent in ignoring deforestation risk in the targeting process – in a programme that gives the same payment for any hectare of forest very high prices are paid to conserve hectares of forest that were at no risk of being lost in the first place.

When we consider the distribution of payments of the flat and efficient programmes according to characteristics of recipient communities, we find that in the case of the efficient programme, larger *ejidos* receive the lion's share of the budget, although they are not always the most efficient in providing environmental services. We also find poor *ejidos* have higher participation rates, receive a larger proportion of the budget and provide higher benefits per dollar spent that non-poor *ejidos*. In the optimal programme, payments per member to the poor and indigenous are much lower than to their counterparts, reflecting the fact that non-poor and non-indigenous *ejidos* possess more environmentally valuable resources per capita as measured by the environmental benefits index. In the more egalitarian flat scheme, the budget is distributed relatively equally across size and poverty classes and payments to the poor and non-poor are equal.

Finally, we also address one of the important factors in implementing a scheme which accounts for deforestation risk. In order to avoid strategic behaviour, one must use predicted deforestation using variables that cannot be manipulated. We show that there is little advantage in venturing beyond easily observable variables in order to make this prediction. There is an efficiency loss in using the prediction as opposed to the actual rate of forest loss, but a programme using the predicted deforestation rate is still twice as efficient as a flat payment programme.

The basic lesson here is a simple one: if one wishes to design a PES programme to avoid deforestation, the most efficient way to do so is to pay for hectares of forest that are at risk of being lost. Any other strategy will result in payments to individuals for continuing behaviours that they would have engaged in even in the absence of such monies. This basic principle can be applied to payments for any environmental resource generated by standing forest, including carbon sequestration, biodiversity, landscape amenities and water services. In fact, the principle can be applied to a variety of non-environmental policies as well, including any sort of payment to induce behavioural change in a population. In the context of avoided deforestation, this concept accomplishes exactly the goal – to preserve the most trees possible given limited financial resources.

Notes

1 Such programmes are also known as programmes of payments for environmental amenities, conservation payments, ecosystem services and environmental service payments.

2 In reality, the decision of the *ejido* may be more complex, e.g., in considering risk aversion, mistrust towards the government, transaction costs, etc. See Engel et al., Chapter 12 in this volume.

3 This programme was effectively introduced in 2003.

4 The Gini coefficient is a measure of inequality that varies between zero and one, with perfect equality indicated by zero and perfect inequality by 1.

5 Still other studies suggest that a mixture of pasture and forest cover generates even higher hydrological benefits than contiguous forest (see Aylward and Tognetti, 2002).

6 This is a mechanical result of ordinary least squares, the statistical technique used to predict the deforestation rate based on observable characteristics.

7 Note that the number of *ejido* members was determined at the time of the founding of each *ejido*, with rights to membership legally passed on to only one family member. Although some *ejidos* conducted a one-time expansion of membership with the 1992 land reform, most *ejido* villages house a number of individuals who do not hold *ejidal* rights.

References

Alix-Garcia, J., de Janvry, A. and Sadoulet, E. (2005) 'A tale of two communities: explaining deforestation in Mexico', *World Development*, 33(2): 219–235.

Alix-Garcia, J., de Janvry, A. and Sadoulet, E. (2008) 'The role of deforestation risk and calibrated compensation in designing payments for environmental services', *Environment and Development Economics*, 13(3): 375–394.

Ando, A., Camm, J., Polasky, S. and Solow, A. (1998) 'Species distributions, land values, and efficient conservation', *Science*, 279(5359): 2126–2128.

Aylward, B. and Tognetti, S. (2002) *Valuation of Hydrological Externalities of Land Use Change: Lake Arenal Case Study, Costa Rica*, Land-Water Linkages in Rural Watersheds, Case Study Series, Rome: Food and Agriculture Organization (FAO).

Babcock, B.A., Lakshminarayan, P.G., Wu, J. and Zilberman, D. (1996) 'The economics of a public fund for environmental amenities: a study of CRP contracts', *American Journal of Agricultural Economics*, 78(4): 961–971.

Babcock, B.A., Lakshminarayan, P.G., Wu, J. and Zilberman, D. (1997) 'Targeting tools for the purchase of environmental amenities', *Land Economics*, 73(3): 325–339.

Chomitz, K., Brenes, E. and Constantino, L. (1999) 'Financing environmental services: the Costa Rican experience and its implications', *The Science of the Total Environment*, 240(1): 157–169.

Daily, G., Söderqvist, T., Aniyar, S., Arrow, K., Dasgupta, P., Ehrlich, P. et al. (2000) 'The value of nature and the nature of value', *Science*, 289(5478): 395–396.

Echavarría, M. (2002) 'Financing watershed conservation: the FONAG Water Fund in Quito, Ecuador', in S. Pagiola, J. Bishop and N. Landell-Mills (eds) *Selling Forest Environmental Services: Market-based Mechanisms for Conservation and Development*, London: Earthscan Publications.

Engel, S., Wünscher, T. and Wunder, S. (2009) 'Increasing the efficiency of conservation spending: the case of payments for environmental services in Costa Rica', in C. Palmer and S. Engel (eds) *Avoided Deforestation: Prospects for Mitigating Climate Change*, London: Routledge.

Ferraro, P.J. (2003) 'Conservation contracting in heterogeneous landscapes: an application to watershed protection with threshold constraints', *Agricultural and Resource Economics Review*, 32(1): 53–64.

Ferraro, P.J. (2004) 'Targeting conservation payments in heterogeneous landscapes: a distance function approach and application to watershed management', *American Journal of Agricultural Economics*, 86(4): 905–918.

Hernández, O., Cobos, C., Ortiz, A. and Méndez, J.C. (2003) *Valoración Económica del Servicio Ambiental de Regulación Hídrica del Lado Sur de la Reserva de la Biosfera Sierra de las Minas, Guatemala*, paper prepared for Foro Regional sobre Sistemas de Pago por Servicios Ambientales, Aréquipa.

Mayrand, K. and Paquin, M. (2004) *Payments for Environmental Services: A Survey and Assessment of Current Schemes*, Unisfera International Center (for the Commission for Environmental Cooperation of North America) [online]. Available at: http://www.cec.org/files/PDF/ECONOMY/PES-Unisfera_en.pdf [accessed 12 August 2008].

Newell, R. and Stavins, R. (2000) 'Climate change and forest sinks: factors affecting the costs of carbon sequestration', *Journal of Environmental Economics and Management*, 40(3): 211–235.

Richards, K. and Stokes, C. (2004) 'A review of carbon sequestration studies: a dozen years of research', *Climate Change*, 63(1–2): 1–48.

Stavins, R. (1999) 'The costs of carbon sequestration: a revealed preference approach', *American Economic Review*, 89(4): 999–1004.

Torres-Rojo, J.M. and Flores-Xolocotzi, R. (2001) 'Deforestation and land use change in Mexico', *Journal of Sustainable Forestry*, 12(1/2): 171–191.

Uchida, E., Xu, J. and Rozelle, S. (2005) 'Grain for green: cost-effectiveness and sustainability of China's conservation set-aside program', *Land Economics*, 81(2): 247–264.

Velázquez, A., Mas, J. and Palacio, J. (2002) *Análisis del cambio de uso del suelo Convenio INE-IGg (UNAM) Oficio de autorización de inversión* 312.A.-00215, Enero: Instituto de Geografía, UNAM (in Spanish).

Weitzman, M.L. (1998) 'The Noah's ark problem', *Econometrica*, 66(6): 1279–1298.

World Bank (2005) *Current World Bank Work on Payments for Ecological Services* [online]. Available at: http://lnweb18.worldbank.org/ESSD/envext.nsf/44ByDocName/PaymentsforEcologicalServicesCurrentProjects [accessed 4 July 2007].

Wu, J. (2000) 'Slippage effects of the conservation reserve program', *American Journal of Agricultural Economics*, 82(4): 979–992.

Wünscher, T., Engel, S. and Wunder, S. (2008) 'Spatial targeting of payments for environmental services: a tool for boosting conservation benefits', *Ecological Economics*, 65(4): 822–833.

Zbinden, S. and Lee, D. (2005) 'Paying for environmental services: an analysis of participation in Costa Rica's PSA program', *World Development*, 33(2): 255–272.

14 Prospects for mitigating climate change through avoided deforestation

Conclusions and outlook

Stefanie Engel and Charles Palmer

Introduction

The chapters presented in this volume, *Avoided Deforestation: Prospects for Mitigating Climate Change*, highlight the importance of avoided deforestation as part of a global strategy to mitigate the build-up of anthropogenic GHG emissions into the earth's atmosphere. Not only is deforestation the second largest single source of greenhouse gas (GHG) emissions, accounting for up to one-fifth of global emissions, but it also makes up more than one-third of developing countries' emissions. Incorporating deforestation could provide an opening for the active participation of developing countries in emission reduction efforts under an international climate change regime (Dutschke and Wolf, 2007).

Since this book was initiated in early 2007, progress has been made at the international level: in December 2007, the Bali Conference of Parties (COP) agreed to create a mechanism for 'reducing emissions from deforestation and degradation' (REDD)[1] in the post-2012 regime (UNFCCC, 2007). It was decided that more precise rules and modalities are to be developed by COP-15, which is to take place in Copenhagen, in December 2009. This is a tight schedule and many open questions remain as to how to set up and credibly implement a REDD mechanism. Despite some progress being made with regards to scientific issues at COP-14 in Poznan, held in December 2008, specific policy solutions are yet to be devised. It is our hope that this book, in focusing on the economics and policy aspects of REDD, can make a contribution to improving our understanding of the relevant issues and assist in moving towards more concrete policy proposals. This, we hope, will occur via a transfer of knowledge from the scientific to the policy communities, and vice versa.

The volume is divided into three parts. The first focuses on the cost effectiveness of avoided deforestation as a strategy to mitigate climate change, while the second examines the barriers to the adoption of such a strategy, primarily those related to policy and institutions. The final part looks at policy design, with a focus on overcoming additionality and leakage constraints and maximizing the efficiency and effectiveness of potential avoided deforestation schemes. The main findings of all three sections are summarized and discussed in what follows, with some further issues for discussion presented at the end. It should be noted upfront, however, that providing a full review of related literature is beyond the scope of this volume.[2]

Excellent studies are constantly adding to the existing body of knowledge relevant for REDD policy design. We conclude by addressing some of the key, remaining open questions along with suggestions for future research.

Cost effectiveness of avoiding deforestation

The three chapters in Part I employ different approaches to estimate the costs of avoiding deforestation. To derive the cost estimates, different assumptions have been made and the numbers themselves are evaluated in different, comparative ways. In general, because avoiding deforestation involves a change in land use, opportunity costs (i.e., the costs of foregone net benefits from the next best alternative activity) tend to constitute the most important source of costs. Building on background research carried out for the Stern Review (Stern, 2007), *Maryanne Grieg-Gran* examines the cost effectiveness of avoided deforestation as a mitigation option using empirical data for eight tropical countries. Her estimates of average opportunity costs per tonne of CO_2 avoided range from US\$1.2 to 6.7, depending on the scenario under consideration. This chapter also highlights the spatial variation in cost estimates across countries. While perhaps 'cheap' in say parts of Africa, avoided deforestation may turn out to be less cost effective in Indonesia, depending on land use. Additionally, Grieg-Gran incorporates administration costs into her estimates. These particular transactions costs range from US\$0.1 to US\$0.2 per tonne of CO_2. Average cost estimates overall compare favourably with most other mitigation options, although higher transactions costs could potentially account for a substantial proportion of the total cost per tonne of CO_2 avoided through reducing deforestation.[3]

Combating deforestation will, of course, still require substantial funds. *Ewald Rametsteiner, Michael Obersteiner, Georg Kindermann* and *Brent Sohngen* develop a global land-use model, which indicates that a 50 per cent reduction of carbon emissions from deforestation over the next 20 years would require financial resources of some US\$33 billion per year. This is a figure that easily exceeds all current annual overseas development assistance (ODA) spending on forestry. Given that ODA alone would fall short of funding requirements, a combination of funding sources and policy mechanisms would be required for reducing emissions from avoiding deforestation (RED or 'avoided deforestation') or REDD (forest degradation included). Carbon trading, now active in various forms all over the world, could be one potential component of funding. Using a global timber market model, *Brent Sohngen*'s analysis in the following chapter confirms the conclusion that carbon credits for reductions in deforestation may be cheap in comparison to other options both in forestry, for example, afforestation, and in the energy market. In a related study (see Tavoni *et al.*, 2007), Sohngen found that reductions in deforestation can achieve levels of annual sequestration similar to those achieved with carbon capture and storage but earlier and at lower prices. The results presented in Part I are not only consistent with other studies[4] but also highlight the need to include avoided deforestation or REDD as a mitigation option in global climate change models. Currently, these models often ignore this option.

Policy and institutional barriers

Opening Part II, *Tracy Johns* and *Bernhard Schlamadinger*'s chapter nicely reviews the main policy, institutional and methodological barriers that prevented the inclusion of REDD strategies in the Kyoto Protocol and the progress that has been made since to overcome these. It seems that the most contentious issue relates to the financing of REDD activities. The challenge is to provide adequate, consistent, long-term funding of REDD activities, while also providing real and additional climate benefit. Developing countries have been arguing strongly that financial assistance for REDD should not be drawn from existing development-funding streams.

Current proposals mostly fall into one of three categories: (i) trading REDD credits in the carbon market (similar to CDM afforestation/reforestation credits); (ii) a voluntary, fund-based approach not linked to the carbon market; and (iii) indirect market approaches, drawing proceeds from the market but without a direct link to market credits. Hybrid approaches appear promising, in that they could capture the larger financing potential of the market while benefiting from advantages of a fund, such as allowing for equity and biodiversity considerations in targeting. Alternative or complementary funding could be obtained through a tax on Kyoto mechanisms and/or on emissions from international air and maritime transport or through an obligatory contribution by Annex I countries to a revolving compliance fund (Dutschke and Wolf, 2007). Another issue is whether a REDD mechanism should follow a CDM-type project-based approach, a national approach or a 'nested' approach. A strong argument for a national approach relates to the issue of 'leakage', i.e. the possibility that REDD in one area may be at least partially offset by increases in deforestation and degradation elsewhere. While international leakage can still occur under a national approach, it could be addressed in different and separate ways compared to the leakage that might occur at the sub-national project scale (see following section).

Significant progress has been made in identifying and analysing the large range of drivers of deforestation at varying spatial scales (Chomitz *et al.*, 2006). It is clear that any feasible REDD mechanism needs to be built on an understanding of these drivers and be flexible enough to support solutions tailored to specific local and regional conditions. A limited capability to monitor deforestation and estimate forest-based emissions has long been another barrier to the inclusion of REDD in an international climate regime. Recent advances in the field of remote sensing in combination with appropriate ground truthing provide a solid basis, as described both in Johns and Schlamadinger and the following chapter by *Paulo Moutinho, Mariano Cenamo* and *Paula Moreira*. The remaining uncertainties can be treated by taking lower bound estimates of the quantity of emissions reduced. Yet improvement in access to data and training in new technologies is still required. The degree to which forest degradation and forest regrowth are to be considered as activities included in a REDD mechanism is another crucial issue still to be resolved. While there are good reasons to include both activities, the difficulty and increased cost involved in emission monitoring and estimation poses a real challenge. Baseline setting, i.e. the estimation of rates of change in, say, deforestation rates or emissions levels in the absence of policies to change these, is another highly political issue, which is discussed in further detail later.

Institutional barriers, while they have not been the centre of negotiations thus far, have now increasingly become a focus of attention and discussion, as countries, NGOs, and financing institutions grapple with the so-called 'readiness process'. This is supposed to ascertain what it will take for a country to be ready to participate in an international REDD mechanism (Dutschke, 2008). Institutional barriers include, for example, appropriate land tenure and forest protection law; adequate capacity for monitoring and enforcement; and effective engagement of civil society, including forest-dependent and indigenous communities.

The chapter by Moutinho and his co-authors along with that by *Charles Palmer* and *Krystof Obidzinski* discuss some of the issues just raised as they relate to the two main contributors of CO_2 emissions from forestry and land-use changes in the world: Brazil and Indonesia, respectively. In addition to illustrating some of the country-specific policy and institutional challenges in more detail, these chapters highlight the fact that REDD requires a coordination between different levels of governance of the implementing country (from local to national) as well as across different sectors of the economy. Both chapters present interesting ongoing policy reforms and initiatives that would go hand in hand with an international mechanism.

Moreover, both chapters make the important point that pressures on forests, whether in the absence or presence of an effective REDD mechanism, are likely to increase over time. As can be readily seen throughout this volume, increases in agricultural product prices such as biofuels, exchange rates effects and road construction may all enhance pressure on forests, yet are often ignored in baseline estimation. In Indonesia, the situation is particularly dramatic as growing demand for timber products and biofuels have driven Indonesian government plans for a massive expansion of these sectors. This expansion is supported through substantial government subsidies including the use of timber stands as collateral in plantation development. These have the effect of reducing deforesters' costs with implications for the estimation of deforestation baselines. The chapter by Palmer and Obidzinski draws attention to the potential that the prospect of an international REDD mechanism may induce perverse incentives, by slowing the reforms necessary to correct government failures, in order to achieve higher baselines. This may, however, be more of an issue with the adoption of a business-as-usual baseline projection rather than one drawn from a historical reference period. In Brazil, land speculation and 'land grabs' by prospective landowners and driven by agricultural commodities' and livestock prices, have long dominated deforestation behaviour at the Amazon frontier. Property rights claims underlying such behaviour raises similar baseline issues as in Indonesia but may also present opportunities in the context of a REDD payment regime, as discussed further later under 'Some further thoughts'.

Finally in Part II, the chapter by *Axel Michaelowa* and *Michael Dutschke* picks up on one of the major concerns related to including REDD credits in the carbon market: the fear that the potentially large supply of carbon credits from reducing emissions through avoiding deforestation could upset the balance of the market. The authors estimate and project expected credit supply and market demand scenarios for carbon until 2020. Their supply analysis incorporates governance problems plaguing most countries with high deforestation rates, while demand is determined by the relative stringency of the climate policy regime. They find that, due to governance problems in many tropical countries, the credit supply from REDD would pick up slowly during the initial years of programme implementation. Nevertheless, any integration of credits from reducing emissions through avoiding deforestation into the carbon market should be accompanied by long-term target setting.

Insights for effective and efficient REDD policy

Part III of the volume presents some recent studies that demonstrate specific insights for effective and efficient REDD policy. While this selection is by no means complete, it addresses the issues of leakage estimation, baseline setting, dealing with tradeoffs in objectives and increasing the efficiency of current mechanisms compensating for avoided deforestation.

Brian Murray's chapter focuses on the importance of recognizing, estimating and where possible ameliorating the risks of leakage from compensation policies that are likely to be applied to a subset of countries with deforestation potential. It provides a very useful review of different approaches that can be used to estimate leakage empirically and of the relatively small number of studies that have attempted to do so to date. The results of these studies suggest that international leakage from avoided deforestation policies could be substantial if not addressed in policy design. One way to reduce leakage is to expand the scope of policy coverage as wide as feasible. Scope expansion could involve covering more countries or more activities.

However, an important point made by Murray is that expanding the number of countries involved in a voluntary system involves the balancing act of enhancing incentives for their participation through, among other things, generous baselines against the need to maintain the environmental integrity of the system by not crediting 'hot air'. Expanding the scope beyond deforestation may both help lure countries with low baseline deforestation rates into the system and ensures that deforestation emissions are not reduced at the expense of carbon losses elsewhere in the forest sector. Covering all forest carbon in an international compensation system, however, raises some concerns about spurring land-use changes that could potentially undermine other environmental objectives such as biodiversity and water provision unless addressed via agreed on protocols, for example, discouraging the conversion of native ecosystems to plantations.

As mentioned earlier, one crucial issue for any REDD mechanism is the setting of the hypothetical baseline (or business-as-usual projection) against which REDD progress is measured. A baseline for forest conservation has two main components: the projected land-use change and the corresponding carbon stocks in applicable pools in vegetation and soil. For the latter, there are now standard values recommended by the Intergovernmental Panel on Climate Change (IPCC) for different vegetation types that can be used (Dutschke and Wolf, 2007). The most commonly discussed method for baseline estimation is the use of some sort of national historical reference period of emissions from deforestation. Alternative, more sophisticated approaches have been proposed, as described in the chapters by both Johns and Schlamadinger, and Murray. These include more or less sophisticated projections of past trends into the future or a normative baseline.

Nancy Harris, *Silvia Petrova* and *Sandra Brown* emphasize the need for a standardized, scalable baseline approach that is accurate, transparent, credible and conservative. They briefly review three specific models for baseline estimation applied elsewhere and evaluate how they differ in terms of transparency, accuracy and precision, applicability at various scales, compatibility with international requirements and cost effectiveness in terms of data, time and expertise needed for application. They then describe in detail a spatial modelling approach that ranked highest in their evaluation. The so-called GEOMOD approach is interesting because it can be used to estimate a deforestation baseline at the project, regional or national scale and to predict the spatial location of deforestation. One weakness of the approach is that estimated overall rates of deforestation are based purely on historic rates, while driving factors are used to predict location only. Such weakness, however, needs to be considered in light of the overriding need for setting the most objective, transparent and comparable REDD standards possible at the international level.

The following chapter by *Alexander Pfaff* and *Juan Robalino* further demonstrates the importance of correct baseline estimations. They explained how impact evaluation and policy planning are complicated by several factors: the inability to observe how land choices would have differed without a policy; the fact that policy location may be affected by private and public choices; and the spatial and temporal interactions among land-use choices. Using empirical examples from Costa Rican policies, specifically the widely cited payments for environmental services (PES) policy and Costa Rican parks and protected areas, the authors convey how impact analysis could address these hurdles. Pfaff and Robalino's results also show that forest conservation policies that appeared to have been very successful at first sight may have added much less in the way of conservation benefits once the appropriate baselines are considered. In other words, once policy impacts were evaluated in a thorough manner, conservation policy resulted in much lower levels of 'additionality' than was originally expected. These results have two important implications for REDD. First, they cast doubt on very simplistic baseline approaches, for example, those based on simple historic deforestation data. Second, they highlight the need for more efficiency in conservation spending. The latter issue is picked up in the next two chapters.

Finding ways to increase the efficiency of forest conservation spending, whether at the international, national or sub-national level, is important for several reasons. First, the actual cost of REDD will depend on how efficiently available funding is used, which depends, in turn, on the design of a future REDD mechanism. If REDD is to be achieved through the establishment of some type of international fund like the Amazon Fund,[5] the fact that financial sources are limited requires a procedure for deciding which countries, regions or projects are selected for REDD funding. Moreover, increasing the efficiency of current forest conservation spending can be seen as an important complement to a strategy of raising additional funds for reducing carbon emissions through avoided deforestation. As argued by *Stefanie Engel, Tobias Wünscher* and *Sven Wunder* in their chapter on funds' targeting in Costa Rica's PES scheme, demonstrating efficiency can be important in attracting new funding sources, particularly from the private sector. By increasing the efficiency of existing programmes, funds can be freed up for additional programmes or for inclusion of additional sites in a given programme ('achieving more bang for the buck').

Both increasing cost effectiveness of funding and dealing with institutional or policy-related barriers on the ground requires a careful consideration of policy choice and policy design. There are a variety of policies that could be applied to avoided deforestation from so-called 'command and control' instruments such as state-protected areas to ones based on a market mechanism (see Gupta *et al.*, 2007). Policy choice may depend on a number of factors including the source(s) of market failure and in the particular case of deforestation, the identification and level of understanding of the drivers and agents of deforestation (Engel *et al.*, 2008).

PES, the focus of both Engel and her co-authors, and the chapter by *Jennifer Alix-Garcia, Alain de Janvry* and *Elisabeth Sadoulet*, is an increasingly used instrument both for financing and implementing forest conservation and thus has potential in application to payments for REDD. The relevance of PES to the REDD debate is demonstrated by cost studies such as the chapters in Part I, which tend to assume that some type of PES will be put in place to compensate landowners (or land users) for the profits foregone by avoiding deforestation. The defining characteristic of PES lies in its conditionality (Wunder, 2005): payments are made by an environmental service buyer conditional on the environmental services provided by an environmental service seller. Such 'beneficiary-pays' positive incentives have not only been shown to be relatively more cost effective compared to more indirect conservation approaches (see Ferraro and Kiss, 2002) but may also be politically more acceptable than instruments such as taxes on forest products or land clearance.[6]

The Costa Rican national PES scheme is often considered a pioneer and leading model of PES. Payments there are made largely for avoided deforestation, although as shown by Pfaff and Robalino, these have not had the impact on deforestation rates claimed by the scheme's proponents. In establishing a national or regional PES scheme, questions arise on how land parcels are selected for programme inclusion and about the size and allocation of conservation payments. Voluntary PES projects within a country could lead to the leakage of emissions to non-enrolled parcels. While national accounting may capture this, there will still be efficiency issues, which could be at least partially dealt with through improved payments targeting. The chapter by Engel *et al.* shows that the amount of environmental services achieved with a given budget for a region in Costa Rica could be nearly doubled through improved targeting in site selection. In particular, they develop a tool for selecting among applicant sites on the basis of three criteria: the amount of environmental services provided by the site; the probability that these services would be lost in the absence of PES (additionality); and the cost to land owners of providing the services. The following chapter by Alix-Garcia and her co-authors finds similar efficiency gains when targeting is considered for the national PES scheme in Mexico.

The chapters by Engel *et al.* and Alix-Garcia *et al.* both deal with issues related to national-level schemes.[7] The lessons drawn from these chapters can also, to some extent, be applied to international-level mechanisms. The CDM is an example of an international PES scheme. One of the main declared objectives of the World Bank's prototype Forest Carbon Partnership Facility (FCPF) is to test a system of performance-based incentive payments for REDD services. There is considerable spatial variation in the carbon content of forests. Moreover, a fund-type REDD mechanism may also want to consider additional environmental services like biodiversity conservation, or equity arguments, all of which can in principle be integrated as targeting criteria for PES, as demonstrated by Engel *et al.* Threat levels and opportunity costs may vary even more in space. Some of the methods presented in other chapters of this volume could be applied here; for example, the estimation of location-specific deforestation baselines à la Harris *et al.* The chapters by Engel *et al.* and Alix-Garcia *et al.* also discuss scientific, administrative and political challenges of targeting and how these may be overcome. Such challenges may be even greater at the international level. Efficiency gains need to be weighed against political feasibility and increases in implementation costs.

Some further thoughts

In this section, we present some further thoughts relating to the role of REDD in climate change mitigation, permanence in REDD carbon benefits, the importance of incentives, avoiding 'hot air' credits and governance and readiness.

Role of REDD in global climate change mitigation

There are several reasons why the inclusion of REDD, or at least RED, in an international climate regime should be considered as part of a portfolio of mitigation options (Stern, 2007) alongside an agreement containing stringent curbs in global GHG emissions.

First, as demonstrated by Michaelowa and Dutschke, modest emissions reduction targets imply that, in the mid-term, a glut of REDD credits may lead to low carbon prices that remain low. Cheap prices for combating climate change while intuitively a good thing for climate policy (see Chomitz *et al.*, 2006) may dampen incentives for more long-term investments in other mitigation options such as improving energy efficiency (Kremen *et al.*, 2000; Schneider, 1998). This may have serious implications for long-run climate policy objectives, although technological change needs to be complemented with public investment in research and development as well as price incentives. For the worst predicted effects of climate change to be overcome, sharp curbs of perhaps up to 70–80 per cent of current global emissions may be required (IPPC, 2007).[8] In 2008, cuts of 50 per cent were agreed, in principle, by the Group of Eight (G8) at its annual meeting, which are expected to be achieved by 2050 (G8, 2008). Since deforestation accounts for around one-fifth of current emissions, it is obvious that incentives will also be necessary to ensure emissions reductions in other sectors, particularly energy production, transport, and industry, in order to realize ambitious global targets (IPPC, 2007). A glut of REDD credits could potentially send out price signals that would not be sufficient to push producers and consumers towards a low carbon economy over the coming decades. Contrariwise, today's cheap REDD potential may decrease with every year that it is not taken advantage of while the reduction of energy-related emissions could become more accessible over time with technological advancement. It is possible, however, that uncertainty about the supply of REDD credits, particularly in the early years of scheme implementation, might make it difficult to tune the supply–demand balance in a CDM or allowance-type approach.

Second, in the event of considerable global warming occurring, there is a risk that forests, even if conserved by society, may be severely damaged by climate change, which could trigger a chain reaction of forest die-off and carbon release that would be difficult to stop (see Nepstad *et al.*, 2008). Thus, an important point made by Chomitz *et al.* (2006) and emphasized by Michaelowa and Dutschke (this volume) is that REDD credits can contribute most in a climate change mitigation scenario of high stringency.

Third, the inclusion of REDD as a low cost mitigation option may be needed in order to provide incentives to bring more emitters into a collective climate agreement post-2012. Given the relative cost effectiveness of REDD as compared to other mitigation options, including REDD (or at least RED) in a global strategy to combat climate change could increase the likelihood of both getting industrialized countries to agree to stricter targets (if REDD credits can be used to meet these targets) and getting developing countries on board as well. In this sense, the large potential magnitude of REDD credits may be seen as a hope rather than a concern (Chomitz *et al.*, 2006). For example, developing countries inspired by the Brazilian government's initiative (Moutinho *et al.*, this volume) are keen to see industrialized countries reduce rather than simply offset their emissions elsewhere. While some major emitters such as those in the EU might agree with this position, others such as the USA and Japan may like to see a larger role for emission offsets than is presently allowed under Kyoto. A compromise between the extreme 'domestic reductions' and 'offsetting' positions may be the best hope of getting not just as many countries as possible to agree on a single climate regime but also one that commits the parties to stringent emissions reductions.

Permanence in REDD carbon benefits

An issue that was only marginally addressed in this volume and that is closely related to the previous point is that of permanence, i.e. whether emissions from deforestation and degradation are reduced for good and not simply shifted to another period (Murray, this volume). A lack of permanence can, in principle, be viewed as a form of 'temporal leakage', similar to spatial leakage discussed earlier. As forest systems interact with climate and hydrological systems, unforeseen changes may occur including feedback effects and forest 'die-back'. Moreover, local deforestation may vary with market conditions, leading to unexpected outcomes. For example, biofuel policies may increase the demand for arable soils, thereby increasing emissions from deforestation. The approach of temporary crediting applied under the CDM could also be an option for REDD. However, the flipside is that the market value of a temporary emission allowance can be very low, as it depends on price expectations for the subsequent commitment period. Countries might thus prefer to take over liability for longer periods, while insurance could help reduce the risk of non-permanence in emissions reductions. The former point implies the need for institutions that would be able to hold countries to their long-term commitments.

Most current proposals include a carryover of commitments to the subsequent commitment period in case deforestation has increased beyond the agreed on level, combined with some obligatory banking of some share of the credits (Dutschke and Wolf, 2007). Averaging emission reductions over longer commitment periods, for example, of 10 years, would also help to deal with difficulties in predictability (ibid.). Within countries, incentive mechanisms like PES could be more directly linked to market prices. Even if a significant portion of REDD turns out to be non-permanent in the longer run, REDD may still serve an important role in bridging the time to a less CO_2-intensive global economy (Lecocq and Chomitz, 2001).[9] The idea of 'carbon rental' may also get around the problem of locking in certain land uses in perpetuity, which has been perceived by some countries as an infringement of sovereignty over their natural resources (Laurance, 2007). Moreover, the idea of perpetuity is simply not feasible in many developing countries given unstable political and economic conditions, all of which implies that, at most, REDD can create temporary carbon credits in these countries.

Importance of incentives

Many of the chapters in this volume have stressed the importance of incentives. It is important to acknowledge that at the local level deforestation is usually a profitable activity. To some degree this also holds at the country level as halting deforestation can imply foregone economic development. Yet policy failures are also widespread at that level, resulting in above optimal deforestation rates even from the national perspective. A PES-type mechanism appears promising both at the international and the within-country level. Particularly, making incentives conditional on actual REDD performance is an essential part of avoiding 'hot air'. Paying nations contingently on their REDD performance also opens up options to leverage policy reforms (CIFOR, 2008). At the local level, bundling REDD with other environmental services such as biodiversity conservation or hydrological services may help raise additional funds for avoiding deforestation. Again, whether a national

PES scheme is the best approach for individual countries in achieving compliance with national REDD commitments will depend on the underlying sources of deforestation and on the governance system in place. For example, where deforestation is driven by credit market imperfections or perverse incentives in other sectors, it would be preferable to address these issues directly (Engel *et al.*, 2008). PES is likely to work best in a situation of secure property rights to forest lands and requires some basic quality of governance. This also holds, however, for other types of conservation policy.

Avoiding 'hot air' credits

The issues of additionality, permanence and leakage have been cornerstone concerns for project-based GHG mitigation policy (Murray, this volume). The fear is that REDD could become a feel-good market, achieving insignificant real emissions reduction (CIFOR, 2008). Indeed, recent empirical evidence on the lack of additionality of existing forest conservation policies, some of which has been presented in this volume, reinforces the need for solid baseline assessment. As Harris *et al.* (this volume) put it, the development of an accepted, standardized baseline approach for avoided deforestation activities is therefore a key step towards the adoption of any future REDD mechanism. Such an approach also needs to balance the gains from more accurate baseline estimates against the associated costs. One major challenge in this regard is to agree on a method that could effectively incentivize emissions reductions in high deforestation countries, while still supporting the maintenance of forests that may be under more threat of deforestation or degradation in the future (Johns and Schlamadinger, this volume). Potential REDD mechanisms that can minimize hot air at the international level should be given serious consideration (e.g. see Strassburg *et al.*, 2008).

Another important point made by Murray (this volume) is the potential tradeoff between increasing additionality and decreasing leakage: the less stringent baselines are set, the greater the incentive for a large number of countries to participate in a REDD mechanism that will help control international leakage. There is also some urgency in agreeing on baselines. The chapter by Palmer and Obidzinski clearly demonstrates the potential for perverse behaviour, with the adoption of a business-as-usual baseline approach leading to increased deforestation and reduced incentives for policy reform. A related issue, and one that may partly help to address this challenges, is the optimal length of baseline projection. For example, Harris *et al.* (this volume) propose a project length of 20–60 years, but with baselines 'locked in' for 10 years only (see also Sohngen, this volume).

Governance and readiness

Participating in an international REDD mechanism and setting up an effective and efficient local incentive system (whether through PES or other measures), is only possible if basic institutional prerequisites are satisfied. These include, for example, a system of secure and well-defined property rights over forest lands, the capacity to quantify forest inventories and assess future land-use trends and related carbon flows, a functioning legal system, the capacity to monitor and enforce existing rules and regulations and the political will to establish new institutions for forest conservation.

The FCPF explicitly aims to help countries build up the necessary capacity for participating in a REDD mechanism. About a third of the FCPF funding is earmarked to a so-called 'readiness fund', which would:

1   help interested developing countries to arrive at a credible estimate of their national forest carbon stocks and sources of forest emissions
2   assist in defining their reference scenario based on past emission rates for future emissions estimates
3   offer technical assistance in calculating opportunity costs of possible REDD interventions
4   help design an adapted REDD strategy that takes into account country priorities and constraints (World Bank Carbon Finance Unit, 2008).

Such an approach appears promising to facilitate participation of least developed countries in a future REDD mechanism. Another approach is the establishment of bilateral forest partnerships between an Annex I Party and a developing country (Dutschke and Wolf, 2007).

While capacity building is necessary, it should be acknowledged that improvements in governance take time. In the meantime, prospective landowners, whether local communities, government agencies or firms, are likely to continue to claim de facto (and sometimes de jure) property rights in remote and poorly governed forest areas. Could such speculative behaviour, typically made in anticipation of earning future rents from the land, also occur in the context of a local REDD payments mechanism? And if so, does it matter? We would expect similar rent-seeking behaviour, although with a system of conditional payments, the 'new' forest owners would have incentives not to convert forest. They may even be expected to proactively protect it. REDD payments could then potentially have a positive impact on the environment, particularly where there are weak, endogenous property rights (Engel and Palmer, 2008). Adding carbon values to landowners' value of the standing forest may increase their ability to protect their de facto property rights against intrusion. Although this would to some extent deal with the open access problem of forests, there could be distributional problems if richer actors colonize forest areas at the expense of poorer ones. A nationally administered, carefully targeted payments scheme could be one way around this problem (see Hall, 2008; see also Moutinho *et al.*, this volume).

Concluding remarks

There appears to be a strong case for including REDD in a global climate change mitigation strategy post-Kyoto. Significant progress has been made in addressing previous concerns to such an inclusion. It is now time to synthesize approaches and develop an integrated REDD mechanism. The success of REDD will depend on the ability to show that it can be done. The establishment of the FCPF as a prototype for REDD measures as well as other current pilot activities has an important role to play in this regard. In doing so, it will be crucial that these initiatives incorporate the lessons from recent studies highlighting the complexities and weaknesses of existing forest conservation policies. Upscaling policies such as PES without improving on scheme additionality and cost-effectiveness could undermine the success of a performance-based incentive payment system for REDD services and raise costs of REDD beyond expectations.

In focusing on REDD as a potential strategy for mitigating climate change, this volume has neglected some key elements of the climate change policy debate. First, adaptation strategies have been ignored. It is clear that neither adaptation nor mitigation alone will avoid climate change impacts (IPPC, 2007) and that forests play a crucial role in adaptation as well. Second, while potential mechanisms for including REDD in an international climate framework have been considered, the practical and legal arguments, for example, of whether to include REDD in an extension to the Kyoto Protocol or to create an entirely new Protocol altogether were not (see Forner *et al.*, 2006; Gupta *et al.*, 2007). Related to this, the international political economy of REDD inclusion was only briefly touched upon when discussing the possible preferences of different nation states and the political tradeoffs being made at the international level in fora such as the UN and G8. For example, recent US legislation considers a potentially important role for REDD and other international forest carbon offsets in domestic climate policy.[10]

REDD should, however, be viewed through a prism of scarcity and tradeoffs between competing uses for the world's resources. With the world's population forecast to reach 7 to 11 billion by 2050 (United Nations, 2004), the global demand for energy and food will continue to rise in the coming decades. Ultimately, decisions over the allocation of natural resources will probably be political ones. At the very least, allocations based on economic criteria will be substantially affected by political forces. In this context, the introduction of REDD, or at the minimum, RED, should be seen as an opportunity to reverse deforestation trends and capture forest carbon values but only as one, perhaps particularly cost-effective way of mitigating climate change. For it to work, it must remain competitive with other land uses. Other mitigation options also require further opportunities for development and implementation; avoided deforestation should not be allowed to stunt investment in other mitigation technologies and economic sectors.

Notes

1 As noted in the introduction to this volume, we distinguish REDD from RED or 'avoided deforestation' through the additional consideration of forest degradation for the former.
2 For example, a recent overview of the issues can be seen in Dutschke and Wolf (2007). A discussion of avoided deforestation in the context of climate change and deforestation can be seen in the relevant chapters of Stern (2007) and Chomitz *et al.* (2006), respectively. Policy-related issues alongside the legal and technical considerations of avoided deforestation are covered by Moutinho and Schwartzman (2005). See also Murdiyarso

and Herawati (2005) for chapters relating to livelihood issues, in addition to those focusing on the CDM and carbon sequestration from a bioscience perspective. International policy issues and how REDD might fit into climate policy from a practical perspective are covered by Streck *et al.* (2008).

3 Note, however, that the price of avoided deforestation as a mitigation option will be determined by the marginal cost and not the average cost. We expect there to be differences between the two depending on the shape of the marginal cost curve.

4 Existing studies are too numerous to list here. For a good overview, see Richards and Stokes (2004).

5 The Amazon Fund was launched by the Brazilian government in July 2008 with an initial donation of US$100 million from the Norwegian government (Economist, 2008). See http://www.amazonfund.org/.

6 A recent comparison of 15 PES or 'PES-like' systems around the world favourably reviews their conservation outcomes and efficiency, thus providing a number of possible models for REDD (see Wunder *et al.*, 2008). Nonetheless, PES, despite being a focus in this volume, is not a panacea for dealing with all environmental problems (see Engel *et al.*, 2008).

7 Alternatively, and instead of making direct payments to potential deforesters (assuming that they can be identified in the first place), any transfers received by a particular country say from an international fund like the FCPF could simply be invested in systems that discourage deforestation behaviour, e.g., for monitoring and enforcement.

8 In order to stabilize the CO_2 concentration in the atmosphere at around 400–450 ppm (IPPC, 2007).

9 A time delay in emissions reduced by abatement measures could result in permanent climate benefits if the cumulative atmospheric concentrations of GHG are lower at any future point in time (Ebeling and Yasué, 2008).

10 The Lieberman-Warner Climate Security Act of 2008: http://www.epa.gov/climate-change/downloads/s2191_EPA_Analysis.pdf.

References

Chomitz, K.M., Buys, P., De Luca, G., Thomas, T.S. and Wertz-Kanounnikoff, S. (2006) *At Loggerheads? Agricultural Expansion, Poverty Reduction and Environment in the Tropical Forests*, World Bank Policy Research Report, Development Research Group, Washington, DC: World Bank.

CIFOR (2008) *CIFOR's Sven Wunder Discusses How REDD Can Learn From PES* [online]. Available at: http://www.cifor.cgiar.org/Highlights/redd_interview.htm [accessed 30 July 2008].

Dutschke, M. (2008) *Simply REDD? Konzeptionen, Modelle, Vorschläge zur Emissionsverringerung aus Entwaldung und Walddegradierung*, paper presented at the Workshop *Wald und Klima*, GTZ Eschborn, Germany, 12 February 2008.

Dutschke, M. and Wolf, R. (2007) *Reducing Emissions from Deforestation in Developing Countries. The Way Forward*, Climate Protection Programme, Federal Ministry for Cooperation and Development (GTZ), Eschborn, Germany: GTZ.

Ebeling, J. and Yasué, M. (2008) 'Generating carbon finance through avoided deforestation and its potential to create climatic, conservation and human development benefits', *Philosophical Transactions of the Royal Society B*, 363: 1917–1924.

Economist (2008) *Paying for the Forest*, 9 August, London: The Economist.

Engel, S., Pagiola, S. and Wunder, S. (2008) 'Designing payments for environmental services in theory and practice – an overview of the issues', *Ecological Economics*, 65(4): 663–674.

Engel, S. and Palmer, C. (2008) 'Payments for environmental services as an alternative to logging under weak property rights: the case of Indonesia', *Ecological Economics*, 65(4): 799–809.

Ferraro, P.J. and Kiss, A. (2002) 'Direct payments to conserve biodiversity', *Science*, 298(5599): 1718–1719.

Forner, C., Blaser, J., Jotzo, F. and Robledo, C. (2006) 'Keeping the forest for the climate's sake: avoiding deforestation in developing countries under the UNFCCC', *Climate Change*, 6(3): 275–294.

G8 (Group of Eight) (2008) *Summary of the Hokkaido Toyako Summit* [online]. Available at: http://www.g8summit.go.jp/eng/news/summary.html [accessed 3 August 2008].

Gupta, S., Tirpak, D.A., Burger, N., Gupta, J., Hoehne, N., Boncheva, A.I. *et al.* (2007) 'Policies, instruments and co-operative arrangements', in B. Metz, O.R. Davidson, P.R. Bosch, R. Dave and L.A. Meyer (eds) *Climate Change 2007: Mitigation. Contribution of Working Group III to the Fourth Assessment Report of the Intergovernmental Panel on Climate Change*, Cambridge and New York: Cambridge University Press.

Hall, A. (2008) 'Better RED than dead: paying the people for environmental services in Amazonia', *Philosophical Transactions of the Royal Society B*, 363: 1925–1932.

IPCC (2007) *Climate Change 2007: Synthesis Report Summary for Policymakers*, Intergovernmental Panel on Climate Change. Fourth Assessment Report. Cambridge and New York: Cambridge University Press.

Kremen, C., Niles, J., Dalton, M., Daily, G., Ehrlich, P., Fay, J. *et al.* (2000) 'Economic incentives for rain forest conservation across scales', *Science*, 288(5472): 1828–1832.

Laurance, W. (2007) 'A new initiative to use carbon trading for tropical forest conservation', *Biotropica*, 39(1): 20–24.

Lecocq, F. and Chomitz, K. (2001) *Optimal Use of Carbon Sequestration in a Global Climate Change Strategy: Is There a Wooden Bridge to a Clean Energy Future?*, Washington, DC: World Bank.

Moutinho, P. and Schwartzman, S. (eds) (2005) *Tropical Deforestation and Climate Change*, Belém: Amazon Institute for Environmental Research (IPAM) and Washington, DC: Environmental Defense.

Murdiyarso, D. and Herawati, H. (eds) (2005) *Carbon Forestry: Who will Benefit? Proceedings of Workshop on Carbon Sequestration and Sustainable Livelihoods*, Bogor: Center for International Forestry Research (CIFOR).

Nepstad, D., Stickler, C., Soares-Filho, B. and Merry, F. (2008) 'Interactions among Amazon land use, forests and climate: prospects for a near-term forest tipping point', *Philosophical Transactions of the Royal Society B*, 363: 1937–1946.

Richards, K., and Stokes, C. (2004) 'A review of forest carbon sequestration cost studies: a dozen years of research', *Climatic Change*, 63(1–2): 1–48.

Schneider, S. (1998) 'Kyoto Protocol: the unfinished agenda. An editorial essay', *Climatic Change*, 39(1): 1–21.

Stern, N. (2007) *The Economics of Climate Change: The Stern Review*, Cambridge: Cambridge University Press.

Strassburg, B., Turner, K., Fisher, B., Schaeffer, R. and Lovett, A. (2008) *An Empirically-Derived Mechanism of Combined Incentives to Reduce Emissions from Deforestation*, CSERGE Working Paper ECM 08–01, Norwich: Centre for Social and Economic Research on the Global Environment (CSERGE), University of East Anglia.

Streck, C., O'Sullivan, R., Janson-Smith, T. and Tarasofsky, R. (eds) (2008) *Climate Change and Forests Emerging Policy and Market Opportunities*, Washington, DC: Brookings Institution Press.

Tavoni, M., Sohngen, B. and Bosetti, V. (2007) 'Forestry and the carbon market response to stabilize climate', *Energy Policy*, 35(11): 5346–5353.

UNFCCC (United Nations Framework Convention on Climate Change) (2007) *Decision-/CP.13 Bali Action Plan* [online]. Available at: http://unfccc.int/files/meetings/cop_13/application/pdf/cp_bali_action.pdf [accessed 15 June 2008].

United Nations (2004) 'World population in 2300', *Proceedings of the United Nations Expert Meeting on World Population in 2300*, New York: United Nations.

World Bank Carbon Finance Unit (2008) *About Forest Carbon Partnership Facility (FCPF)*, Washington, DC: World Bank [online]. Available at: http://carbonfinance.org/Router.cfm?Page=FCPF&ft=About [accessed 20 July 2008].

Wunder, S. (2005) *Payments for Environmental Services: Some Nuts and Bolts*, CIFOR Occasional Paper 42, Bogor: Center for International Forestry Research (CIFOR).

Wunder, S., Engel. S. and Pagiola, S. (2008) 'Taking stock: a comparative analysis of payments for environmental services programs in developed and developing countries', *Ecological Economics*, 65(4): 834–852.

Index